ETHNICITY AND SUB-NATIONALISM IN NIGERIA

Ethnicity and Sub-Nationalism in Nigeria

Movement for a Mid-West State

MICHAEL VICKERS

WORLDVIEW PUBLISHING
OXFORD

PUBLISHED BY

WORLDVIEW PUBLISHING

P.O. BOX 595 OXFORD OX2 6YH

ISBN 1-872142-43-5 Hardback
ISBN 1-872142-44-3 Paperback

British Library Cataloguing-in-Publication Data Record
for this Book is available from the British Library

Printed in the United Kingdom

For Victor Inyangudor—keen researcher,
loyal friend and helper during difficult
times—wherever he may be.

FOREWORD

By Eghosa E. Osaghae*

This new book by Michael Vickers presents a master narrative of the struggle by minorities for a Mid-West State, which was one of the defining issues of the de-colonisation period in Nigeria. For the latter reason, the book is more than a story of the Mid-West State Movement; it captures the mood and trajectories of the momentous Nationalist era in Nigeria as these related to the ethnic majorities-minorities cleavage and the Mid-West issue.

In a definitive way, the book analyses Nigerian politics from the perspective of minorities, an approach which enables refreshingly different conclusions from the hackneyed ones drawn from studies set within the perspective of the majority groups which are by far in the majority. The greatest strength of the book, however, lies in the skilful manner in which Professor Vickers relates the Mid-West Movement to major and contending conceptual and theoretical perspectives in the fields of ethnic and minority politics, nationalism and federalism.

The broad analytical contextualisation makes the history told in the book, old as it is, timeless and contemporary. The location of the Mid-West Movement within broader analytical contexts recommends the book to students of ethnic nationalism who have in it the rare benefit of a success case of ethnic minority nationalism from Africa. This is more so that the Movement involved several competing minority groups whose elites warred more than they worked together.

* A leading authority on 'Ethnicity and Politics' in modern Africa, Professor Osaghae is the author of *Structural Adjustment and Ethnicity in Nigeria*, and *The Crippled Giant: Nigeria Since Independence*, recently published by Hurst & Co. (London); and has edited *The Federal Character and Federalism in Nigeria*; *Democratic Transition in Nigeria*; and *Between State and Civil Society in Africa*.

Indeed, the value of the study at this time when most countries in Africa are proving increasingly unable to cope with ethnic demands for internal political autonomy cannot be over-emphasised.

The Mid-West case shows that recourse to violent and extra-parliamentary tactics by ethnic movements is not inevitable for actualising ethnic demands. The process of politics itself, as it facilitates negotiation, mutual exchanges, coalition building and healthy opposition, provides a necessary condition for 'peaceful settlement'. Professor Vickers convincingly shows that thorough-going federalism such as Nigeria practiced at the time greatly enhances the potential of politics for peaceful settlement in divided multi-ethnic states—and especially those bedevilled by complex minority problems.

Eghosa Osagae
University of Ibadan
Nigeria

PREFACE

We live today in what might be termed the "Era of Militant Ethnicity". In "old" world and "new"; in states which are transparently "artificial", as well as those which are not, there has been an explosion of ethnic demands. Indeed in several instances—the former states of Yugoslavia, Czecho-slovakia and the Soviet Union, to name but three which come most readily to mind—we have seen dramatically swift conversion of "ethnic demands" into "ethnic attainments", albeit not without grave social, economic, political and human costs.

Forty years ago when the Mid-West Movement in Nigeria was seeking to advance its autonomy claim, the dominant ethic was very different. Then it was the "Era of the Nation-State"—so-called. Minority ethnic claimants found themselves not only up against the fully-marshalled force of newly self-governing and Independent states, but also against the International Community—both Eastern and Western Bloc countries rallying to bring formidable support to new "assimilationist" regimes. In this climate of dis-approbation—all too often expressed in blatant suppressive terms—claimant elements able to *pursue* their goals, let alone *achieve* them, were few indeed.

The Mid-West Movement was that rare exception—an ethnic minority movement which managed to secure *both*.

How this was done is something which likely will be of far greater interest to students and observers of the 1990's "ethnic phenomenon" than it was to their counterparts in the 1950's and 1960's. What was then studiously ignored or judiciously evaded in the interests of protecting and promoting the fragile stability and unity of newly-emergent African States—and equally in protecting the considerable material, ideological, strategic and monumental "applied scholastic" (particularly American) investments of the Great Powers—can now be brought forward for close examination. There are lessons—conceptual, structural and instrumental—to be   learned. And these are many.

Apart from what it is that this study may in general suggest regarding the structure and process of ethnic dynamics in the larger context of the modern state, its principal aim should be stressed. And this is to provide what it is hoped may be seen as a useful exploration and account of what, after all, was a most important and significant event in the political and constitutional history of Nigeria. The Mid-West Movement was the sole ethnic claimant to secure its object by negotiated settlement during the years of the first Republic, rather than by subsequent Military or administrative *fiat*—the basis for creating the additional *32 states* which have since followed!

This study owes much—as noted in the text—to the dominant pioneering work on ethnicity and minorities in the Nigerian and broader African contexts, of Victor Olorunsola, P.L. Van den Berghe, E.E. Osaghae, Ogbanu Okpu, Onigu Otite and J.I. Tseayo, amongst others. It is to be hoped the present work not only will extend the substantive base and indeed use of the "ethno-political" approach here deployed, but also encourage the new generation of "students of ethnicity" both to pursue studies which will further add to the still-all-too-sparse holdings of basic historical and cultural data, and to assess critically and further refine applied concepts and theoretical constructs which at this stage remain rudimentary—see particularly Chapter 16, below.

If there is any general re-assurance this study provides, it is that whether under Civil Political, or Military rule, grass-roots cultural and political realities remain largely constant. In the midst of today's strife, angst and turmoil of this stricken African giant (Nigeria), these are realities it is well to recognise and remember. Furthermore, for those of us who have been severely critical of the "Westminster Model" in its application and operation in the Nigerian, as well as in broader Colonial and African contexts, this study may cause us to pause, at least briefly, and reflect.

It was the existence of this inherited system, complete with all its acknowledged structural mal-adaptations and deficiencies, which permitted relatively open *pursuit* of a major sub-nationalist objective. At the same time, it ensured a measure of *restraint* in the response of the majority (or controll-ing/governing) Authorities challenged. It provided a medium which—contrary to the violence and extra-constitutional activity which seem the normal accompaniments of such initiatives today—afforded opportunity for arbitration, brokerage and compromise. It is a reminder that there has been—and indeed given appropriate adaptation could still be—an easier path. Resolution of differences between controlling majorities and claimant minorities in Africa and elsewhere need not lead to horrific human consequences, to social dis-location, economic bankruptcy and political breakdown—and not just of the relevant assimilationist, often authoritarian states concerned, but *entire regions*. There are *alternatives*.

This study indicates the great range of optional strategies, tactics and measures available, and in varying combinations—from carefully applied patronage and co-option, to optimum institutional provision of full-blown autonomy. *What is needed is the political will, steady nerve and discipline, first prudently to select, and then apply them; and hence to test their efficacy and utility in operation.* South Africa is a "new" state which is fast approaching a critical "ethnic moment". Will the Authorities have the needed accommodatory provisions tested and to hand when the full force of the Zulu challenge comes? They cannot afford to fail!

And now for debts of gratitude. There are many people over many years who have had a hand in this study. It was Ken Post, now of the Institute of Social Studies, at the Hague, who suggested the topic and provided early guidance. Arnold Hughes, of the Centre of West African Studies, University of Birmingham, provided much-valued oversight and encouragement. In Nigeria, America and here in Britain there were many who assisted my researches. Foremost amongst these were: Philip Mason, Director of the now-defunct Institute of Race Relations, and Joe Wormald, of the Foreign and Commonwealth Office Library, both in London; Beverley Gray (now of the Library of Congress, Washington) and Doris Calvin, Librarians in charge of the *Africana Collection* at Boston University in America; in Nigeria, Mr. Justice Chief S.O. Ighodaro provided access to a vast range of political party and Constitutional Review Conference papers; and Ken Post made available his equally vast (microfilmed) collection of the "Adelabu Papers". To all of these persons—and the many not mentioned (see also *Listing of Interviews—Nigerians and Non-Nigerians*, p.397, below)—I extend my thanks.

Finally, special commendations go to Pam Daly, who persevered mightily with my *Olivetti-Underwood*, in the days before word processors were in standard use; to Pat Smith, whose editorial eye—and pen—were put to good and valuable use; and to

Nick Raven, who performed computerised magic to create the *Maps* (I, II, and III) for the book.

It is only left for me to say that while gratefully acknowledging all the above assistance I have received, nevertheless the responsibility for what has been written, its accuracy in fact—and plausibility in theory and interpretation—is mine alone.

Michael Vickers
London, England,
September 2000

CONTENTS

PART I   BACKGROUND AND EARLY PROSPECTS

PART II   RECKONING WITH REALITY

PART III   AN UNCERTAIN PATH TO AUTONOMY

PART IV   CONCLUSIONS

LIST OF ILLUSTRATIONS

MAPS

TABLES

FIGURE

LIST OF ABBREVIATIONS

ARCHIVE REFERENCES

ADELP	—Adelabu Papers (from Microfilm collection)
BAS	—Boston University African Studies Library, Boston, Massachusetts
BCA	—Benin City Archives, Council Hall, Benin City, Nigeria.
CRO	—Commonwealth Relations Office Library, Downing Street, London.
IFEA	—University of Ife Africana Library, Ile-Ife Nigeria
IGH	—Ighodaro Papers (personal collection), Benin City, Nigeria
INA	—Ibadan National Archives, Ibadan, Nigeria
IRL	—Institute of Race Relations Library, London
OXCRC	—Oxford Colonial Records Collection, Oxford University
UIA	—University of Ibadan Africana Library, Ibadan

INTERVIEW NOTEBOOK REFERENCES

Int I	— Interview Notebook Number I
Int II	— " " " II
Int III	— " " " III
Int IV	— " " " IV
Int IVa	— " " " IVa
Int V	— " " " V
Int VI	— " " " VI
Int VII	— " " " VII

POLITICAL PARTIES

AG	—Action Group
BDPP	—Benin-Delta Peoples' Party
BTPA	—Benin Taxpayers' Association
NCNC	—National Council of Nigeria and the Cameroons (later, National Convention of Nigerian Citizens)
NEPU	—Northern Elements Progressive Union
NPC	—Northern Peoples' Congress
RBC	—Reformed Benin Community
UMBC	—United Middle Belt Congress
WIPM	—Western Ibo Peoples' Movement

NIGERIAN NEWSPAPERS

Champion	—*Mid-West Champion*
Citizen	—*Nigerian Citizen*
Defender	—*Southern Nigeria Defender*
Star	—*Nigerian Star*
Pilot	—*West African Pilot*
Tribune	—*Nigerian Tribune*

CHAPTER 1

INTRODUCTORY

In the early 1960's, an observant American writing about the contemporary African political scene, noted that "Self-Determination in the age of de-colonisation... has a relatively uncomplicated application... where the relations between the colonial subjects and their alien masters are the sole or principal issue involved".[1] He went on to observe, however, that:

> "The going gets rougher when the issue no longer significantly concerns the colonial or ex-colonial power, but centres on the relation between the local peoples themselves. The exercise of the right to Self-Determination has been asserted with a triumphant and all-embracing flourish: is it still an applicable and on-going right when the quarrel with the foreigners is ended and the newly freed peoples fall out among themselves?"[2]

Even at this early stage (1964) in the post-Independence period, the reply to Emerson's rhetorical question had been clearly and forcefully given: the controlling (or governing) majorities in Africa's new states were not hesitant about making clear that, so far as they individually were concerned, "National Self-Determination", was a once-for-all exercise; that once national independence had been achieved, there could be no legitimate subsequent exercise of this right by sub-national minority elements. The fate of Katanga; the provisions of the *1960 United Nations Declaration on the Granting of Independence to Colonial Countries and Peoples*;[3] the statements of African leaders in the forums of the Organisation of African Unity (OAU)[4] and indeed within the context of their own governmental and legislative bodies;[5] each and all of these positions made clear the determination of new ruling majorities to "tighten the ring" round their territorial holdings, and thus to contain and where necessary suppress minority elements in the espoused interests of enhancing the "sacred" goal of so-called National Unity. Thus, for aspirant minorities, whose expectations had been raised high by the pre-Independence promises of

Nationalist leaders, the post Colonial Years soon faded into what Emerson has aptly termed, the era of "Self-Determination Denied".

During these post-Independence years Africa's "nation-locked" minorities were being brought to an increasingly forceful awareness that "National Unity was not such an innocent concept";[6] that Self-Determination was a "once for all exercise" and that autonomy was not to be a right to be extended to clamouring sub-national elements. However, in the midst of these evolving realities, the Mid-West State Movement in Nigeria secured a most singular achievement. In July 1963, Mid-West protagonists, following a Referendum in the Benin and Delta Provinces of Western Nigeria, won the right to create a separate and autonomous Mid-West Region within the over-arching governmental framework of the Federation of Nigeria.

The Mid-West Movement was to become the sole minority movement in Nigeria to attain its autonomy objective during the post-Independence period of civil political rule. Moreover, in the larger context of African minority protest its achievement represented an enviable attainment, and one which in most other new state contexts was rapidly and relentlessly fading from view as National ruling authorities sought to "tighten the grip" on their newly-bequested sovereign domains. In an era characterised by the militant opposition of Africa's governing authorities to minority autonomy aspirations in any form —an era, which modern "devolutionary theorists" are quick to point out, continues to grow in strength to the present day[7]— Mid-West protagonists had managed the decidedly remarkable achievement of not just approaching, but actually attaining their goal.

What, then, were the particular circumstances which permitted the Mid-West Movement to achieve its objective? And perhaps most intriguingly, what caused Nigeria's governing authorities to adopt a course which was diametrically opposed to the position already firmly consolidated by emergent national regimes in the broader pan-African context? Indeed, in any general sense, what was the extra-ordinary combination of forces and circumstances which permitted the success of the Mid-West movement? These, it would seem, are a few of the more obvious questions which the Mid-West experience serves to raise.

NIGERIA AND ITS ETHNIC MINORITIES

The country's governing authorities have always been uneasily aware of the so-called "minorities problem" in Nigeria. Yet from the earliest years of Britain's colonial administration it was quite obvious that the massive monolithic blocs of the Northern and Southern Protectorates constituted the preferred territorial foundations for government.

In 1911, E. D. Morel in his "Unauthorised scheme of amalgamation" had proposed bringing to an end the "awkward and unwieldy" Protectorate system by splitting Nigeria into four provinces.[8] Morel maintained that the existing system of administration within the protectorates should be retained, but that a Central Province (now known as the Middle Belt) to include the peoples of the lower North in Kabba, Ilorin and Borgu should be created. The East, should be expanded northwards to the Benue River, while the West should be allowed to remain intact. Morel's scheme, however, went no further than an official memo. In 1912 Charles Temple, then Senior Resident in Northern Nigeria, went a step further than Morel. He proposed that Nigeria be divided up into seven provinces; three of these, he contended, should be carved from the North.[9] Temple's proposal, however, like Morel's was given little or no consideration. Lord Lugard was bent on pursuing his own design for amalgamation, and was not about to consider any such radical schemes which might, in his view, threaten this objective.

When one views Nigeria's constitutional development in hind-sight, it appears that after the unification of North and South under a central administration in 1914, there was no turning back. The basic form for Nigeria's political structure had been moulded; the shape of politics leading up to Independence and beyond had been cast. The opportunity to create a structure which might have served to provide the national polity with greater range and flexibility had been available. Lugard, however, choosing the "Indirect Rule" system he knew best, implemented his unwieldy plan for unification. In 1939 the division of Southern Nigeria into separate Administrations for the East and West Provinces suggested that the British Authorities might be considering some variant of structural autonomy. However, it was soon apparent that this devolution of the existing structure had really only one major purpose — to simplify administration for the colonial authorities.

Of the long-run political effect of this 1939 undertaking we are, of course, all too aware. This tri-partite division of Nigeria set firmly the foundations from which the controlling majority group in each group of provinces was, in due course, to launch governmental and political initiatives. The affected "Region-locked" ethnic minorities—the Middle Belt peoples in the North, the COR (Calabar-Ogoja-Rivers) peoples in the East, and the Mid-West peoples in the West—increasingly regarded these initiatives as discriminatory and exploitative. It was in the context of these developments that Nigeria's "minorities problem" was to take on a new and rising prominence in the years that were to follow.

From the early and mid-1940's, Nigeria's leading Nationalists, Dr. Nnamdi Azikiwe and Chief (then Mr.) Obafemi Awolowo, aware of the glaring anomaly of a "monolithic" tri-partite division in a multi-ethnic territory, suggested possible solutions to gradually awakening minority elements. In 1943, Azikiwe published his *Political Blueprint for Nigeria*. In this work he maintained that Nigeria should comprise eight "protectorates" with boundaries following roughly ethnic lines.[10] Chief Awolowo, in 1947, following the initiative earlier advanced by Azikiwe, took the argument for ethnic "protectorates" a good deal further. Contending that the existing three Regions had been created simply to suit administrative convenience, he maintained that any "true and effective" governmental system in Nigeria would require the adjustment of boundaries so that "each group, however small," should receive "the same treatment as any other group, however large. Opportunity must be afforded to each group to evolve its own peculiar political institutions".[11] In order to give expression to this fundamental multi-ethnic character of Nigeria, Awolowo asserted that since each group should be autonomous in regard to its internal affairs, then, each should have its own House of Assembly.

Finally, in 1948, the new states issue was formally launched into the forums of constitutional debate and practical political consideration when the First Annual (Kaduna) Convention of the NCNC, voted to adopt what was to become popularly known as the NCNC *Freedom Charter*. This document originated from one of the principal proposals of a memorandum on constitutional reform submitted earlier in that year to the British Colonial Secretary. It set out requirements which NCNC Nationalists contended must be fulfilled if all Nigerian ethnic elements were to have confidence in any future national government. The provision to which all aspirant minority elements gave particular attention was that prescribing "the Commonwealth of Nigeria and Cameroons... shall be organised into states on a National and linguistic basis".[12]

In this provision, minority protagonists discerned support in principle for the autonomy claims they soon would make. They saw the NCNC as the political party which would act to ensure that these claims might be fulfilled at the earliest moment.

In August 1948, the rising expectations of minority elements were further buoyed by a sudden and dramatic announcement by the new Governor of Nigeria, Sir John MacPherson. In a special address before the Legislative Council, Sir John, the man who had been brought in to replace the out-going Governor, Sir Arthur Richards, rather startled Nigerians, Nationalists and minorities activists alike, when he made the following announcement:

> "The progress already made [under the Richards Constitution]... has been, in my considered view, so rapid and so sound that I suggest that we might consider together what changes should be made, and whether they should be made earlier than intended".[13]

This was, to say the least, a curious statement by Sir John. Certainly, neither Nigerian Nationalists nor the British were under any illusions about the "success" of the 1946 Richards Constitution. If anything, developments under the provisions of this constitution during the past two years had been retrogressive rather than progressive. Setting aside Sir John's rhetoric on "rapid and sound progress", the significant revelation in his statement, so far as Nigerian Nationalists and minorities representatives were concerned, was that they very soon might be afforded the opportunity of setting forward provisions which they felt should be included in any revised constitutional arrangement.

At the next session of the Legislative Council, a Select Committee proposal made it clear that this opportunity for Nigerian participants might now be within reach. This Select Committee proposed:

> "...that a series of conferences be held, first at village and divisional level, and then at provincial level, when the various Provincial Conferences would make recommendations to be considered by Regional Conferences. ...The views of the four [including the Cameroons] Regional Conferences were then to be considered by a Drafting Committee, ...then a General Conference, and the resolution of this Conference would then be debated in the Regional Houses and by the Legislative Council before being submitted to the Governor and the Secretary of State for the Colonies".[14]

With the acceptance of this proposal by the Legislative Council, developments began which would theoretically involve in the constitutional revisions "every Nigerian from the most illiterate peasant",[15] to articulate Nationalist champions like the NCNC leader Azikiwe.

These swift and dramatic developments during 1948, had a very considerable meaning and significance for Nigeria's minority sections and their respective leaders. The *Freedom Charter* contained fundamental and committed support for the principle of political autonomy for minority ethnic sections. The decision of the Legislative Council that a comprehensive process of consultation should be started to secure the best grounds on which to effect alterations to the existing (Richards) Constitution, meant that Nigeria's minorities, in league with their NCNC "champions," would have an excellent opportunity to gain recognition for, and perhaps even secure fulfilment of, their respective autonomy demands.

EMERGENT MID-WEST POLITICAL DEMANDS

In the Mid-West provinces, the *Oba* of Benin and his pro-Mid-West Bini colleagues were not slow to exploit these favourable conditions in the political environment. Following up on the lead given by Azikiwe and the *Freedom Charter*, an indigenous Bini political/cultural organisation, the Reformed Benin Community, (RBC), at its August 1948 inaugural meeting made clear that it was fully behind the ideals of political and cultural autonomy to which the *Freedom Charter* gave support. The RBC, under the guidance of Chief H. Omo-Osagie, a 55 year-old recently retired Lagos civil servant,[16] had been founded mainly for the purpose of bringing opposition pressure to bear on the Benin Taxpayers Association, (BTPA) —the local party which was at this time dominant in Benin Divisional local government— and on its leader, Omo-Osagie's arch rival, Gaius Obaseki.[17] None the less, it affirmed its commitment to broader Mid-West objectives. Indeed in a statement of RBC goals, it was held that the principal aim of the party would be to encourage "the development and unification of the various groups of societies into which our ancestors divided the Benin Kingdom for administrative purposes". Outlining further objectives, the RBC Constitution stated that:

> "The Community [RBC] will combat vigorously all such tendencies as would jeopardise the unifying process and shall pursue this great principle with utmost consistency, as its chief policy. ...The Community will interest itself in all affairs which make for the political, economic and cultural progress of Benin natives".[18]

In elaborating on the RBC's principal aims, the *Oba* of Benin, who was Chairman of this inaugural meeting, asserted that one of the most important tasks to which the RBC should address itself was that of resolving Edo identity. "The wrong impression that there are several Edo nations or tribes", he declared, "must be removed".[19] Going on to infuse the assembly with Mid-West State sentiments, the *Oba* stressed that the issues with which the RBC should be concerned ranged far wider than Benin Division. Indeed, with an eye to what he felt would be undoubted future opportunities for advancing the Mid-West cause, the *Oba* contended that the RBC could serve a most vital function.

"I believe there is none in this assembly, who likes Benin land to lag behind. ...In the scheme of things, all Benins should strive for a place for the state or principality of Benin in the new Nigeria. ...The Hausas, the Yorubas, the Ibos and other states are on the move. ...We must not be deprived of our identity, custom, tradition, language and culture, nor must we allow ourselves to be lulled into a false sense of security".

Following the lines of the *Freedom Charter*, the *Oba* asserted that he believed Nigeria should be made up of more states "with greater autonomy than at present — each with its own Governor".[20] At the least, he continued, there must be a fourth Region, to be known as the Central or South-Western State. "An independent United States of Nigeria brought about by Federation, not fusion, will be glorious, prosperous, peaceful, strong and original". In his concluding comments the *Oba* urged RBC members to take the initiative in forming a larger cultural society or Federal Union of which Edo, Urhobo, Itsekiri, Ishan, Ora, Ivbiosakon and Sobe peoples would be principal member unions.[21]

STUDY APPROACHES AND PERSPECTIVES

It was in these statements by the RBC and the *Oba* of Benin, that the embryonic Mid-West State Movement had its origins. The seed, had been sown; soon it was to develop roots. In the study which follows, an attempt will be made to provide a detailed narrative account of the evolution and development of the Mid-West Movement from its beginnings in these heady days of great political expectations in 1948, through to the final attainment of an autonomous Mid-West State within the Federation of Nigeria in 1963.

Much time and attention will be devoted to outlining and examining the structures, leadership and methods through which Mid-West protagonists sought to advance their cause, as well as to the formidable internal and external problems with which they had to cope. It is hoped, however, that the present study may achieve rather more than this primary substantive aim. Lengthy, closely documented case-studies such as this one are hardly of any broader significance if they do not raise certain central issues and questions of more general import and relevance.[22]

Certainly, the policies and behaviour of Nigeria's then-governing authorities and National party elements will be examined and evaluated from a rather different perspective.[23] Indeed, to a very considerable extent, this study of the Mid-West Movement is at the same time a study of Nigerian political parties at close range, over an extended period (the better part of 15 years), and in relation to an issue which each in its own way considered vital to its interests. This being so, we may hope to secure a rather more informed understanding of the policies and behaviour of the NCNC, Action Group and NPC, and not solely in relation to the Mid-West and minorities issues, but in a more general sense as well. By the same token we may also be enabled to gain a greater insight into, and understanding of the British role during this final period of "disengagement" during the 1950's.

Altogether then, it may be contended that this study of "micro politics" or "cultural sub-nationalism"[24]—to use the currently fashionable terminology—will serve to provide the student of Nigerian politics with a detailed narrative account of the Mid-West Movement itself, and it may give him a fresh, somewhat different and perhaps useful interpretation of this most vital and dynamic period in Nigerian political and constitutional history—bearing in mind that this interpretation derives mainly from the Mid-West viewpoint. Furthermore, in a rather more speculative context outside the framework of Nigerian politics *per se*, it may not be too far-fetched to suggest that for the student of African politics so inclined, this study may serve to generate certain tentative and general suppositions on the nature and conduct of minority, or "micro", politics. Certainly, if today's aspirant African minorities are not to follow the paths to devastation blazed by the Biafrans and the Katangese, to give just two such instances, then it is possible that they may stand to learn much from the Mid-West struggle, a struggle which was not only essentially non-violent, but in the end, successful.

Turning briefly to sources, the data upon which this study is based come from a variety of primary and some secondary sources. In addition to public (and a variety of unpublished and private) documents, interviews with a number of leading Mid-West protagonists along with other Nigerian politicians[25] were of particular value. The breadth and detail of this information has permitted a fairly closely detailed development of the essentially narrative-historical thrust of this study. And while this has necessarily entailed an emphasis which violates the more orthodox analytical and conceptual approaches to the contemporary modes of political study, it is hoped this approach may not be without advantage. The topic of the study is broad in nature; it covers a lengthy period; and as it is concerned mainly with issues of political process, its focus is essentially upon matters of instrumentality.

In methodological terms, the evolutionary and historical approach affords an effective means of revealing, and in certain instances highlighting, these instrumental issues. It should be added that recent criticisms of "development theory", its heuristic claims[26] and "Western /European" value-orientation,[27] has given rise to a measure of support for a return to the more pedestrian "configurative" or "idiographic" study.[28] Such studies, it is maintained, are needed to build impoverished substantive data bases requisite to the modification, re-construction, perhaps total refutation of existing theoretical and conceptual orthodoxy. Insofar as theories of integration, "nation-building", and "political development" may give increasing consideration to the facts of ethnic heterogeneity in new African states, it is perhaps not too much to hope that the present study may serve to enhance and extend the data base upon which such "revisionist" theory may ultimately be constructed.

Before moving on into the substantive body of this study, it should be pointed out that the material in the chapters which follow has been divided into three parts. **Part I** is devoted to describing the relevant ethno-historical features of the Mid-West peoples, and to relating the early efforts advanced by Mid-West leaders as they sought to put the Mid-West Movement, so to speak, on its feet. In **Part II** it will be shown how Mid-West protagonists, starting to learn from already bitter experiences, and facing continuing pressure from a variety of opposition elements, commenced to extend the reach and impact of the Mid-West issue by making increasing formal and informal use of party and governmental structures. In the final section of Part II particular attention is given to describing and assessing the initiatives advanced by Mid-West protagonists before the *Minorities Commission,* [29] and then to accounting for the demise of this Movement challenge which was regarded—and, indeed, as it turned out so to be—as the last chance for Mid-West protagonists to secure a separate state before the advent of National Independence in 1960. **Part III** goes on finally to detail the swift-moving, frequently ominous events which were to lead down a most uncertain path towards the eventual creation of the Mid-West State.

References

1. Rupert Emerson, *Self-Determination Re-Visited in the Age of De-Colonisation,* Occasional Papers in International Affairs, No. 9, December 1964 (Cambridge: Harvard University Press, 1964), p. 25.

2. *Ibid.*

3. See *United Nations,* Resolution 1514 (XV); particularly Section 6 of the *Declaration.*

4. See *Proceedings of the Summit Conference of Independent African States,* (Addis Ababa, 1963), Vol.II.

5. Such expressions were, of course, common. But one of the most forthright is to be found in the 1961 address of President Houphouet-Boigny to the Abidjan Assembly. In reply to Sanwi (ethnic) dissidents, he warned that "all those who would question the unity of the country" should recognise that they would have to "cope with our Constitution and laws, ...which will severely punish any attempt to question the unity of our country". (Quoted in Aristide Zolberg, *One-Party Government in the Ivory Coast*, Princeton: University Press, 1964), p. 292).

6. Immanuel Wallerstein, *Africa: The Politics of Unity,* (New York: Random House, 1967), p.67.

7. See particularly, P. Van den Berghe, *The Ethnic Dimension*, (New York: Elsevier Press, 1981); and Dov Ronen, *The Quest for Self-Determination,* (New Haven, Yale University Press, 1979).

8. See, E.D. Morel, *Nigeria: Its Peoples and Its Problems*, (London: Smith, Elder, 1911), pp. 201-205.

9. See, Margery Perham, *Lugard: The Years of Authority, 1898-1945,* Vol. II, (London: Collins, 1960), pp.414 and 478-79.

10. See, Nnamdi Azikiwe, *Political Blueprint for Nigeria,* (Lagos: Africa Book Company, 1943).

11. Obafemi Awolowo, *Path to Nigerian Freedom*, (London: Faber, 1947), p.54.

12. Quoted in James Coleman, *Nigeria: Background to Nationalism*, (Los Angeles: University of California Press, 1958), p.390.

13. Quoted in Coleman, *ibid.*, p.311.

14. *Ibid.*

15. *Ibid.*

16. Chief H. Omo-Osagie, who was to become the Mid-West's most powerful politician —alongside the eminent Chief Festus Okotie-Eboh whom Omo-Osagie regarded as his "political god-son" — was at this time (1948) only starting his political career. Born in 1896, he was the son of an *Ezomo* (Warrior Chief) in the Bini hierarchy. Indeed, his father was said to be one of Benin's wealthiest sons, owning four villages and thousands of serving men. At the age of 50, after serving 26 years as a clerk in the medical Department of the British Administration at Lagos, he returned to Benin City in 1945. It was at this time he set out in earnest on his political career. (For biographical details, see F. A. Imoukhede, *Chief Omo-Osagie*, (Benin City: M.O.I., n.d.)).

17. Hon. Gaius Obaseki was perhaps the most wealthy and influential politician in Benin at this time (1947-50). Obaseki was the son of Agho, the *Iyase* of Benin who had proven so valuable an instrument of British interests during the inter-regnum following the banishment of *Oba* Ovonramwen in 1897. As such, Obaseki inherited the esteem and trust in which the British held his father. Until his retirement in 1945, Obaseki served as Interpreter to the Resident, Benin City. He was active also in business and politics. While managing and extending the properties bequeathed to him by his father, and serving also as a Member (representing Agricultural Interests) on the Governor's Council at Ibadan, Obaseki rose to prominence in Benin Divisional politics in the early 1940's. By 1948, Obaseki had succeeded in entrenching himself and the party he led, the Benin Taxpayer's Association (BTPA), as the virtually unassailable governing element in Benin Division. Obaseki was also believed to be head of the *Reformed Ogboni Fraternity* (ROF), a ritual body modelled on the Masonic Order and drawing on modified practices taken from the Yoruba earth cult of *Ogboni*. Many BTPA members, and all those holding office in Obaseki's Administration were believed to be ROF members or adherents of *Ogboni*-ism. (See *Papers Relating to the Reformed Ogboni Fraternity, 1948*, Ben.Prof. BP/2647,(INA). For the ROF, see also Geoffrey Parrinder, *Religion in an African City*, (London: Oxford University Press, 1953) pp. 178-84).

18. *Constitution of the Reformed Benin Community*, in BP/2647, (INA)

19. *Ibid.*

20. *Ibid.*

21. See, "The *Oba*'s Message", in *Circular*, dated 20 October, 1948, in file BP/2647, (INA).

22. Aristide Zolberg notes that the conduct of sub-national studies of the kind being undertaken here, can "afford us greater understanding of the development of political groups and cleavages, of their relations to the non-political environment, and hence in general of the characteristic structures and processes which constitute the legacy which the new African states inherited". (Quoted from Zolberg, *Creating Political Order: The Party States of West Africa*, (Chicago: Rand-McNally, 1966), p.152).

23. The classic works on Nigerian politics operate out of what might be termed a "majority" ethnic and political context. Such works include J.S. Coleman's, *Nigeria: Background to Nationalism*, op. cit.; R.L. Sklar's, *Nigerian Political Parties*, (Princeton: University Press, 1963); H.L. Bretton's, *Power and Stability in Nigeria*, (New York: Praeger, 1962); C. S. Whittaker's, *The Politics of Tradition, Continuity and Change in Northern Nigeria*, (Princeton: University Press, 1970). By the mid-1970's, however, political studies operating out of a "minority" context started to appear. See, for instance, Ugbana Okpu, *Ethnic Minority Problems in Nigerian Politics*, (Uppsala: Almquist and Wiksell International, 1977); J. Dofny and A. Akiwowo, (eds.), *National and Ethnic Movements*. (London: Sage, 1980); Alvin Magid, *Man in the Middle: Leadership and Conflict in a Nigerian Society*, (Manchester: University Press, 1976); J.I. Tseayo, *Conflict and Incorporation in Nigeria: Integration of the Tiv*, (Zaria: Gaskiya Corporation,1975); Onigu Otite, *Autonomy and Dependence: The Urhobo Kingdom of Okpe in Modern Nigeria*, (London: Hurst, 1973). See also chapters by Magid, Martin Dent and others in Robert Melson and Howard Wolpe (eds.) *Nigeria: Modernisation and the Politics of Communalism*, (East Lansing: Michigan State University Press, 1971); and Martin Dent, "A Minority Party: The United Middle Belt Congress", in J. P. Mackintosh, *Nigerian Government and Politics,* (London: Allen and Unwin, 1966).

24. See particularly, Victor A. Olorunsula (ed.), *The Politics of Cultural Sub-Nationalism in Africa*, (New York: Anchor Books,1972).

25. Two politicians not interviewed were Dr. Azikiwe and Chief Awolowo. Despite numerous efforts by correspondence, and in person while conducting field-work in Nigeria, neither meetings nor written response was secured.

26. See particularly, Stephanie Neuman, *Small States and Segmented Societies,* (New York: Praeger, 1976), Chapter 1.

27. Claude Ake, in his, *Social Science as Imperialism: The Theory of Political Development*, (Ibadan: University Press, 1979), *passim,* carries out a comprehensive and ferocious assault on "Western

assumptions" and conscious and sub-conscious "European value bias" in the bulk of social science development studies.

28. See Neuman, *op. cit.*, pp. 19-21.

29. Following completion of the (1957) London Conference on the Nigerian Constitution, the Secretary of State for the Colonies appointed a Commission (which became known as the "Minorities Commission") to "enquire into the fears of minorities and the means of allaying them". See, *Cmnd. 505*, (London: H.M.S.O., 1958).

PART I

BACKGROUND
AND EARLY PROSPECTS

CHAPTER 2

THE MID-WEST SETTING

As the *Oba* of Benin and his Bini associates prepared to set out on their quest for a separate state, they had a well-defined vision of the future developments which they wished to see for the Mid-West provinces.[1] Indeed, there were clearly strong geographic and economic grounds on which to base their claim.

In geographical terms, it seemed that the Mid-West provinces were well situated. Bounded on the East by the River Niger, on the West by the Rivers Osse, Ogbesse and Siluko dividing the Mid-West provinces from the Yoruba provinces of Owo, Ondo and Okitipupa, and enclosed on the South-West by a coast-line which opened through its maze of creeks on to the Atlantic Ocean, the Mid-West area constituted a coherent, separable and integral geographical unit.[2]

Economically, the peoples of the Mid-West area could provide for themselves quite adequately. The Mid-West provinces were leading producers of major food-stuffs for domestic consumption. By 1954-55, the Benin and Delta Provinces took the lead in the production of food staples, including yams, cassavas, sheep and goats, over all the other provinces in the West.[3] As for export commodities, the Mid-West provinces supplied almost all rubber, timber, plywood and veneers, along with a sizeable share of the Region's two major export commodities, palm oil and palm kernels.

The Mid-West controlled one of Nigeria's major sea-ports at Warri, and conditions were promising for the development of at least one additional deep-water port in the creek area near Burutu in Delta Province. This raised considerably Mid-West prospects of becoming a major supplier of vital export and import facilities for both the Western and Northern Regions, its port facilities providing a natural and economical outlet to the sea. Furthermore, in terms of the labour and manpower required to exploit the advantages afforded by these material and physical resources, the Mid West provinces seemed well set. With a population of approximately one quarter of the West Region and occupying an area of about one-third of the total area of the West,[4] the Mid-West provinces were, in addition, fortunate to possess a greater percentage of men and women capable of active economic work than did the provinces of the Yoruba West.[5]

This, however, seemed to be about as far as any rationale of Mid-West unity, based on major substantive considerations, could go. The *Oba* in his speech at the 1948 RBC inaugural conference had declared that there "Must be a fourth Region to be known as the Central or South-west State".[6] He had then gone on to state that the RBC should serve as the vanguard entrusted with the task of integrating "Urhobo, Itsekiri, Ishan, Ora, Sobe," and other Mid-West peoples into a "larger cultural society" for the purpose of promoting this aim. These were laudable sentiments for the *Oba* to express before this gathering. The question, however, was: how could such pan-ethnic unity be achieved.

The fact was that the Mid-West peoples possessed a heritage which suggested that the attainment of political unity in the modern era would be no easy task. It was true, as will be shown later in this chapter, that each of the separate ethnic elements within the Mid-West provinces had historical, and in most instances contemporary links with Benin. Common myths of origin, claims of Bini paternity, patterns of migration and settlement, the existence of shared rituals, traditions and institutions, together with the more tangible links created by the pursuit of trade and commercial interests, had obviously fostered amongst intra-Mid-West ethnic elements some measure of historical unity and common purpose. This was based on the central role and historical dominance of the *Oba* and the Bini. It was, however, another matter whether these links would serve as an effective base upon which to appeal for pan-Mid-West unity in the mid-twentieth century.

THE KINGDOM OF BENIN

Both Edo mythology and recorded history attest to the greatness of Benin. According to Edo mythology, the first *Oba* of Benin, the son of Osanobua (the High God) was sovereign over his senior brothers who settled in Yorubaland. They had "to come to him and barter their possessions in return for a place to settle".[7] When it has come to situations of conflict and competition between

MAP I

POLITICAL MAP OF THE MID-WEST (1948)

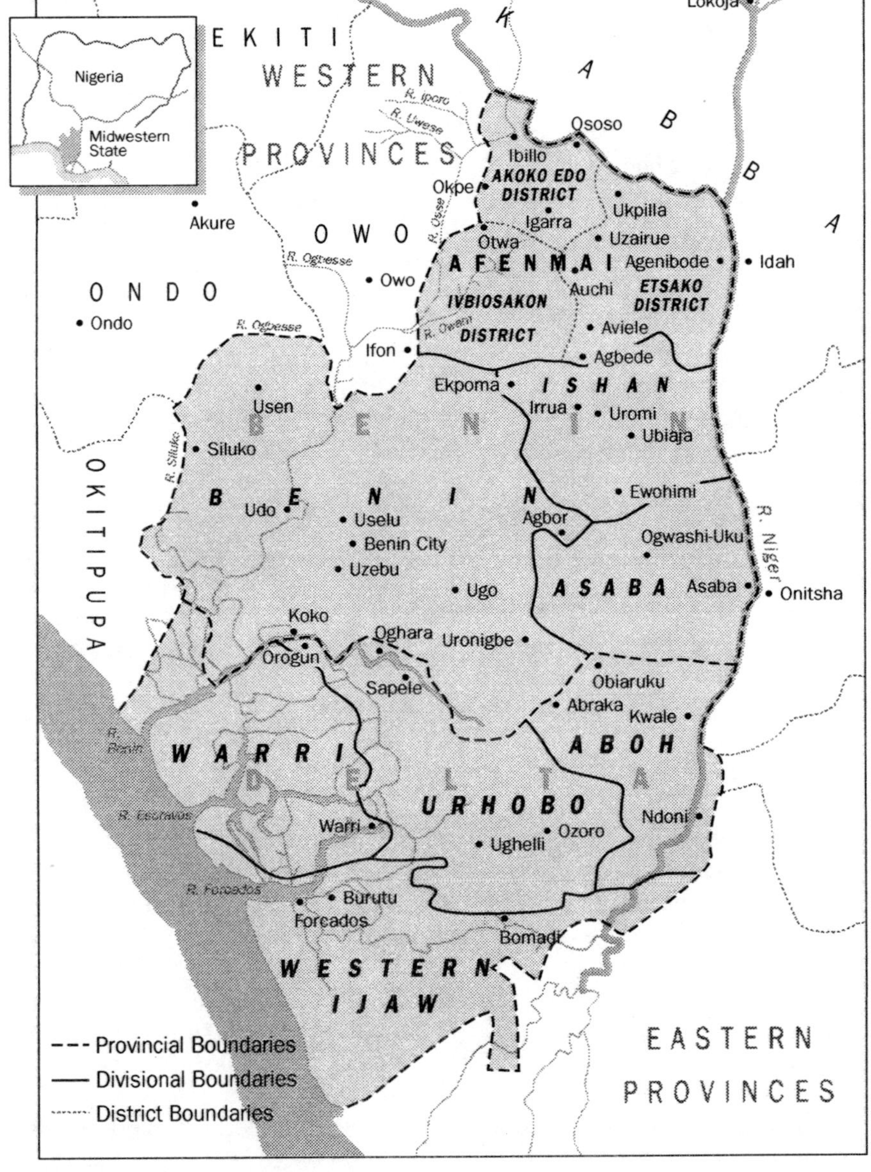

Mid-Westerners and Yorubas, the former frequently refer to this myth of origin. On the basis of this myth Mid-West peoples in general claim the position of "first among equals" with their Yoruba brothers. Further, this sense of superiority has been augmented by an awareness of the historical greatness of Benin and the Empire which once it controlled. As a great imperial power, the Bini once ruled over sizeable portions of Yorubaland.

> "The Benin Empire extended to Otun [the Ekiti-Yoruba boundary with the old Oyo Kingdom] in the North, the sea in the South, Asaba in the East and Lagos in the West".[8]

The capacity of the Benin Kingdom to emerge to greatness and to hold this position over a period of many centuries was not only the product of able leadership. Indeed, the capacity of the Bini to retain the support of peoples earlier subjugated—at least as Egharevba and Bradbury interpret oral traditions—was most significantly the product of the flexible, relatively participant system of government which gradually evolved between the fifteenth and eighteenth centuries. This system ensured a high degree of stability within the Bini heartland and permitted external objectives to be firmly secured.

During the 15th and 16th centuries, the Benin Empire reached its greatest extent.[9] At the same time the structuring of Bini society, particularly in the upper ranks, was effectively carried out. This comprehensive structuring brought into creation many of the palace societies which reflected so effective a balance between commoner and Royal elements; between personages who continued to fulfil symbolic roles and those who were functionaries.[10]

During the reign of Ewuare (about 1440-1473), the senior executive council called the *Eghaevbo n'Ore* was created. The major office it provided for was that of *Iyase*, the equivalent of Prime Minister. The *Iyase* rose to his position from commoner ranks; it was an earned and not a traditional title. In Bini political culture, the position of the *Iyase* which is next in power to that of the *Oba*, is symbolic of the representative and participant-democratic element which is built into the Benin political system. And even though the democratic channel brought threats to the security of reigning *Obas*, still it provided both informing and "safety valve" functions. In the latter instance, the *Iyase* when required served as spokesman for grievances generated within the ranks of the polity.

This relationship between Royal and commoner personages within the Benin Kingdom cannot be over-stressed. Yet, while these democratic channels were opened, the *Oba* and his traditional

MAP II

THE KINGDOM OF BENIN *

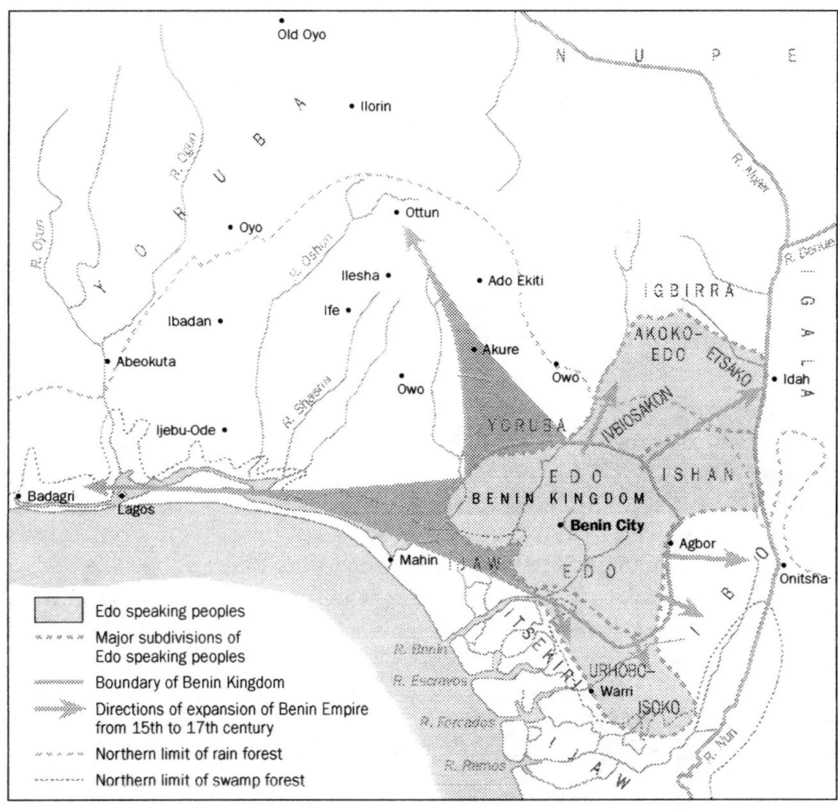

*** *Source*:** Adapted from D. Forde and P.M. Kaberry, (eds.), *West African Kingdoms in the Nineteenth Century*. London: Oxford University Press for the International Africa Institute, 1967. p.4.

officers of State continued to command a degree of habitual respect which permitted them to ride out many challenges. Indeed, though contemporary events tend to stress the near-calamities into which the *Oba* has fallen over the past 45 years, Egharevba emphasises that *Obas* in the past have had to face equally serious—sometimes far worse!—confrontations.[11]

In addition to the creation of the *Eghaevbo n'Ore*, with the structural benefits it brought, a number of additional innovations to the Benin governmental structure were introduced over a period of the next two hundred years which increased the flexibility of this relatively participant and responsive monarchical system.[12] The overall effect of these evolutionary innovations was to create a system of government under the monarchy of Benin which was to a very significant degree, "functionally democratic".[13] It ensured continuity of support and respect from those peoples in greatest proximity to the Bini heartland.

Bini Links with Neighbouring Groups   One of the oldest areas joined by traditional links with Benin City and the Bini, is Ika. This area is located about 30 miles southeast of Benin City and was founded by a Bini emigrant named Eka. The first settlers who moved out in waves to Ika were from Benin City. Later when the area was subdued by Agban, the *Ezomo* of Benin,[14] the major town in the area Evbo-Eka, was re-named Agbor; the town holds this name today. Even though the Bini influence was strong and successive waves of emigrants had come to the area from Benin City, the language of the Ibos who had migrated to the area from Asaba and across the River Niger, was dominant. Bini customs, institutions and styles of dress, however, were retained. The first *Obi*, it is said, was sent to Agbor by the *Oba* to be their ruler.[15] Overseers and local rulers likewise were delegated by the *Oba* to other towns in Ika.

> "All the *Obis* of Eka were installed in office by the *Oba* of Benin at Benin City in the early days, and given the sword of office... on special application. They owe allegiance to the *Oba* of Benin, their overlord at Benin City".[16]

Egharevba notes how, even in recent times, the traditional link with the *Oba* had been maintained. In 1933, *Obi* Obika of Agbor was sent to study local administration at Benin City; in 1934 the *Obi* of Owa, another important Ika natural ruler, was sent for the same training. Overall, Bini influence in the area was ensured through the persistence of Bini customs and institutions and

MAP III

ETHNOGRAPHIC MAP OF THE MID-WEST

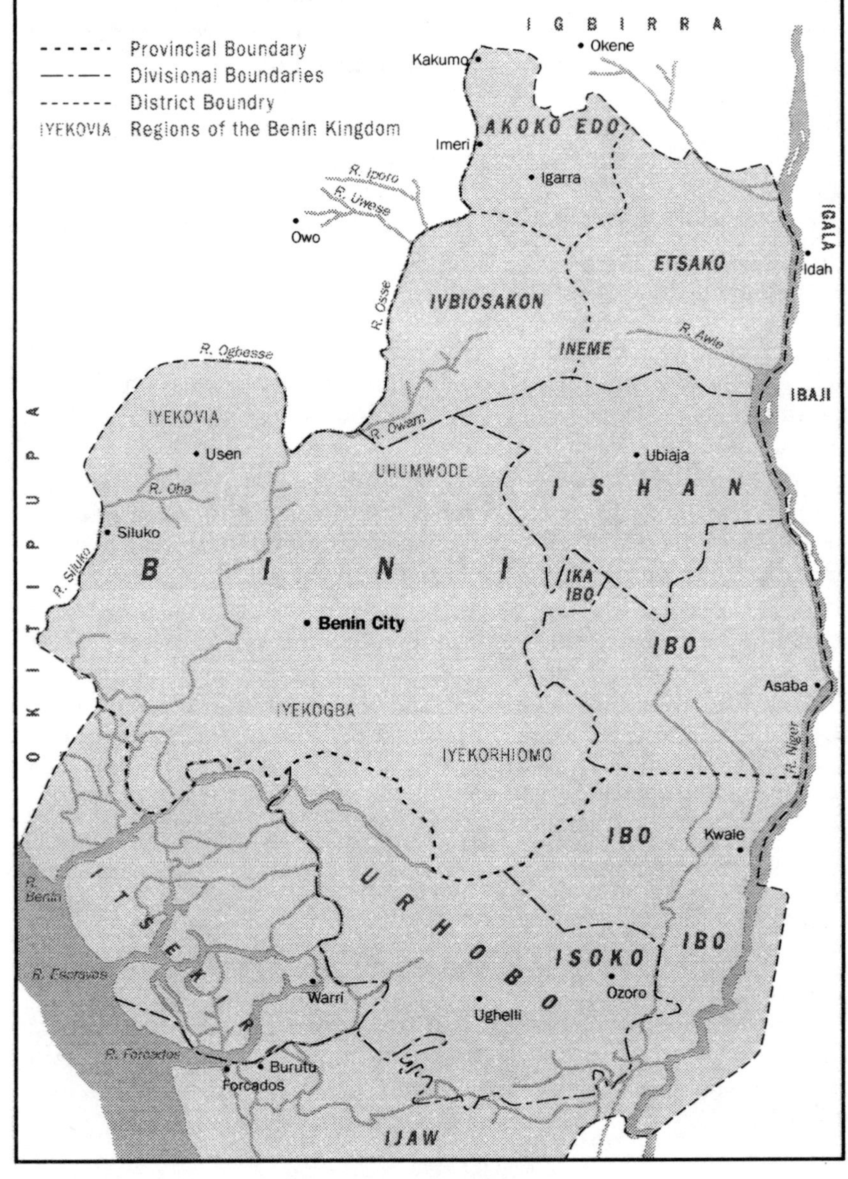

through the perpetuation of such important rituals as the installation of the *Obi*. It was largely through the influence of language, therefore, that the Ibo presence was felt.

The early people of Ishan are believed to have been Bini emigrants who moved into the area during the First and early Second Periods of the Benin Empire.[17] The name of the area, Ishan, is taken from the name of the Bini man who first moved to settle there. Other leaders who followed him—mostly princes of Benin—became leaders of the various Ishan localities. These leaders, traditionally called *Enije* (pl.), or ruling "Princes of Ishan" were installed in office by the *Oba* of Benin at Benin City. "Some are still given the sword of office... by the *Oba* of Benin, on special application." [18] The Princes of Ishan owe allegiance and tribute to the *Oba* of Benin. Further, Egharevba points out that this traditional link has been sustained by continuing participation of Ishan traditional personages in Benin activities and ritual.[19]

However, a significant degree of independence of mind and activity was present due to the fact that many of the early and later "...emigrants to Ishan from Benin are said to have fled from Justice or oppression".[20] A similar strain of independence is to be seen in the claims of origin which diverged from the standard claims of a Bini "Ancestor who dropped from the sky". Residents in Ishan localities including Uromi, Ewu and Ewohimi maintained claims of origin from an ancestor who emerged from the ground or rivers.

It would appear, therefore, from the accounts of these traditions given by Egharevba and particularly Bradbury, that there is a strong element of independence in the Ishan-Bini relationship. While it is clear that there was a due recognition of the *Oba* of Benin, and indeed, participation in ritual and obligations associated with this recognition, it would appear that distance from Benin City combined with Yoruba and Nupe[21] influence, had a great deal to do with the relatively autonomous existence evolved by the peoples in the area.

Ivbiosakon is located in the North-West of the Mid-West territory and borders on Yorubaland.[22] This area is said to contain 17 formerly autonomous or semi-autonomous tribes.[23] Despite proximity to Yorubaland and the considerable influence which Yoruba customs and language had on the area, Bradbury contends that, "in general, they have retained closer associations with Benin and a stronger allegiance to the *Oba* than the other Northern Edo groups".[24]

These Bini links however, were by no means founded on an amicable base. Egharevba states that Omorodion, one of the older sons of the Eweka I, who was a founder of the Ivbiosakon area, left Benin, like many of the founding emigrants to Ishan, with very hostile sentiments towards the Bini.[25] When his claim to the *Obaship* was passed over, he left Benin City. Furthermore, he declared he would find a home in the "bush" rather than be called a Prince of Benin. Ozolua also, before be became *Oba* of Benin, sought refuge in Ivbiosakon after he had been banished from Benin City. Still, despite the fact that many of the area's founders are believed to have been disgruntled Bini from Benin City, "Many of the tribes retained friendly contacts with Benin, and some... continued to pay tribute to the *Oba*".[26]

Over the centuries, however, and coming to modern times, it is evident that Yoruba influence became increasingly more significant.[27] Yoruba language and dress, customs and institutions all grew to become common in the area. Similarly, with the growth of Yoruba influence, parallel changes in the behaviour and attitudes of the people could be anticipated. Old attitudes of deference to the Bini authority structure were to be replaced by independent attitudes significant of greater autonomy. It is not surprising, therefore, that political affiliations which evolved in the contemporary period should have been more closely aligned with Ibadan than Benin City.

The origins and evolutionary development of the Etsako[28] peoples is very similar to that of the peoples of Ivbiosakon. The nine Edo-speaking ethno-linguistic units which comprise the Etsako, claim a common Bini origin. Similarly, the Etsako also have been subject to the considerable influence of the neighbouring Yoruba. Each of these nine ethno-linguistic units operates with a considerable degree of autonomy. The people of the Etsako seem largely to fall outside the disciplinary control of the Bini hierarchy of authority. It is maintained that the people in many of the principal areas of Etsako were from Benin, and that the people of Agenibode were the guard of the Benin Royal Troops during the Idah War. Stressing that the founders of the area came from among disgruntled Bini, Egharevba states that:

> "The founder of Okpe was a Bini who was sent to Ife on a special embassy. Having returned, he, in fury, left with his family and followers and became the ruler of Okpe".[29]

Like all Northern Edo peoples, the Etsako were subject to the onslaughts of the Nupe. All of the peoples in these Northern areas of the Mid-West territory ultimately "paid tribute" in the form of slaves, to the *Emir* of Bida, and Nupe agents were posted in some Etsako settlements.[30] In one area, Aviele, Nupe titles were introduced and ultimately replaced those of Benin origin. New culture and customs insinuated by the adjacent Yoruba, reinforced by new institutions and religious faith (Muslim) imposed by the conquering Nupe, were effective in weakening the Bini link and building associations and future political affiliations with peoples to the West and the North.

To the south of the Bini heartland lay areas populated by a number of different groups. Among these the main groups included Urhobo, Isoko, Itsekiri and Ijaw.[31] Of the Urhobo and Isoko peoples, many lived in the rain forest extending to the south and south-east of Benin City; others were settled in the creek and lowland areas further to the south and south-east. The Itsekiris, a small, well-integrated and very influential group in the Mid-West, together with the Ijaw, an equally small, significantly more isolated people, populated the coastal lowlands in the Niger Delta.

Of all the peoples in the southern territories of the Mid-West it would seem that the Itsekiris have evolved the greatest independence from remnant strands of their Bini heritage.[32] The contacts and business they were able to generate with coastal traders, together with traditions of origin which laid stress on a Yoruba heritage have contributed to their independence and evolution of an identity separate and distinct from Benin.[33]

It might therefore be assumed that the relationship between these two peoples has been superficial and slight. Lloyd suggests that in some instances this was so. Indeed, he emphasises that cultural and linguistic traditions render the term "proto-Yoruba" appropriate for describing the Itsekiri.[34] Still, when investigating the question of origin, he discovered that a founding Bini link was confirmed; most Itsekiri clans attributed their origins to the mythical god Ginuwa. Ginuwa they regard, as their founder and first *Olu* or King. This version of the Itsekiri tradition contends that he came to the Delta "escorted by numerous chiefs from Benin, where he was the son of the *Oba*, and settled near Ode-Itsekiri, later the Itsekiri capital".[35]

It is important to note this claim of an original Bini source by the majority of Itsekiris; for in contemporary times when politicians and traditional leaders have advanced arguments of historical connections stressing the Yoruba-Itsekiri link, this generally confirmed prior association of the Itsekiri with the Bini is frequently ignored or denied.

In turning now to the areas inhabited by the Urhobo and Isoko peoples, it is thought that an indigenous aboriginal population existed here long before the influx of the Bini and other Edo-speaking peoples. Referring to Hubbard's book, *The Sobo of the Niger Delta*, Bradbury contends that:

> "The distinctive characteristics of the various Urhobo and Isoko tribes are a result of the super-imposition of Ijaw, Ibo and later Edo-speaking emigrants upon aboriginal strata already speaking Edo-type dialects".[36]

Oral tradition is not clear about when the majority of the Urhobo and Isoko came under the rule of the *Oba* of Benin. It is known that many of the *Ivia* (or kings) of Urhobo and Isoko tribes had to seek confirmation of their titles from the *Oba*.[37] Further, Bradbury notes that the *Orodje* of Orerokpe (in Urhoboland) received ceremonial swords from the *Oba* as late as 1953.

Despite these persisting connections with the *Oba* and Benin City, it is obvious that the existence of an aboriginal people prevented the Bini founders from establishing communities firmly rooted to Bini customs and institutions, as with Ika and most areas north of the Bini heartland. The influx of an assortment of Edo, Ibo and Ijaw peoples did not, of course, improve the basis from which the Bini link might be strengthened. Further, the existence of different primary allegiances, like that of some of the *Ivia* who looked on the *Obi* of Agbor as their overlord, further dissipated existent Bini influence.

At the same time, however, a factor which served to bring the Urhobo-Isoko peoples closer to the Bini, was the exploitation which the former had suffered largely at the hands of the Ijaw and Itsekiri.[38] Both of the latter peoples were very active in the slave trade, frequently as agents for Europeans who were establishing their coastal contacts.

The final major ethnic group in the Mid-West which will be discussed here is the Ijaw.[39] The Ijaw peoples—that is, the section of these peoples who reside in the area known as the "Western Ijaw"—are found only partially within the territorial boundaries of the Mid-West. In terms of their identity with Mid-West groups and the Bini in particular, the links of the Ijaw seem slight. Talbot contends that their closest association is with the Ijo linguistic grouping of the Niger-Congo. He recounts how the Ijaw people,

> "...inhabit practically the whole coast, some 250 miles in length, stretching between the Ibibio and the Yoruba. The Niger Delta is, therefore, occupied by this strange people—a survival from the

dim past, beyond the dawn of history—whose language and customs are distinct from those of their neighbours and without a trace of any tradition of a time before they were driven southward into these regions of sombre mangrove".[40]

While more recent studies do not seriously challenge this contention of origin for the Ijaw people,[41] E. J. Alagoa is one modern scholar who suggests that while clearly defined historical links with the Bini may be few, the impact of "commercial, political and cultural contacts"[42] with Imperial Benin in the more recent past—15th to 17th centuries—left their mark on many Ive (separate primary ethnic groups) of the Ijaws. Furthermore, participation in certain aspects of the inland and coastal trade later stimulated by the European influx brought these Ijaws into closer contact with the Bini, as well as with the Itsekiris and Western Ibos of the Aboh area.

WEAKENING OF IDENTITY: THE COLONIAL INFLUENCE

It has been shown that each of the neighbouring Mid-West groups entered a fairly distinct and separable form of relationship with the Bini, but that each, at the same time, retained certain localised attitudes and affinities. Common to each group, however, was either a founding origin through the Bini, or an historical-cultural link representing significant Bini influence in guiding the evolution and/or development of the group.

Challenge to Bini Dominance   Following the advent of British Colonial influence in the late nineteenth century, however, this underlying identity amongst Mid-West ethnic elements started to wane. In addition, Bini traditional authority under the Mid-West overlord, the *Oba* of Benin, showed signs of a similar decline. The opening up of trading opportunities had a great deal to do with this. A number of trading associations controlled routes to the interior.[43] For those participating, the opportunities for gaining wealth and possible elite status at Benin were markedly increased. Gradually, and perhaps inevitably, many members of these associations came into conflict with the *Oba* and the *Iwebo* Society.[44] As this crisis grew, so developed a challenge to the traditional Bini governmental structure. Functions and loyalties started to overlap, and great difficulties were encountered in trying to maintain a governmental and administrative system based on the traditional form of centralised authority under the *Oba*.

At the core of this evolving challenge to the dominance of the Benin Traditional system was the growth of new tensions between the *Oba* and *Iyase*. From the time the British first sought to impose their control over the area following the events of 1897, this contest grew to become the prime focus of Benin political life—one which was severely to test the traditional system of government and administration. From the viewpoint of Mid-Westerners, these developments had a dual negative effect. They reduced respect for and effectiveness of Bini power and influence amongst Mid-West peoples.[45]

This developing conflict between *Oba* and *Iyase* grew out of the increased power and status which the British accorded to the latter. The *Iyase*, with whom the British had worked closely following the banishment of *Oba* Ovonramwen in 1897, was Agho. He proved to be compliant to their wishes as well as an effective go-between and administrator. As time progressed, therefore, he gained an increasing measure of power and status within Bini society. As in other African territories and areas of Nigeria, continual attempts were made by the British to work through people in the traditional order who were "reliable". Bradbury notes that most of these were in fact drawn from within the top two ranks in Bini society, *Uzama Nihinron* and *Eghaevbo n'Ore*. But it is significant that he adds:

> "They were not chosen or accorded authority with reference to their specific placement in the traditional orders of chieftaincy. It was to be many years before the British began to obtain even an approximate understanding of the traditional polity".[46]

The lesson was absorbed by the young chiefs. They saw that power and authority in the modern age would come to those who co-operated with the white man. A small elite of "reliable" chiefs therefore played an active part in the development projects initiated by the British.[47] Concessions on rubber, palm oil and palm kernel plantations, along with sizeable timber tracts were placed in the hands of these individuals. The final touch was applied on Agho's elevation to the title of *Obaseki*, following the *Oba*' s return from exile. The British sought increasingly to pursue their interests through him. Other members of the traditional Bini society were apparently quick to note this shift in power. Consequently, if they now wished to reach the Resident in regard to a pressing matter, it was to Agho they would go.

A Contrived Restoration   On the death of *Oba* Ovonramwen in 1914, the British sought to consolidate their gains. The death of the *Oba* coincided with the British desire "to inaugurate a native administration on the lines of those which had proven successful in the Northern Provinces".[48] In order to effect this policy the traditional structure, which the British in the past twenty years had been largely responsible for destroying, had to be resurrected; a "suitable" *Oba* called Aiguobasimwin succeeded to the throne. In accordance with these objectives, the British, while interested in "resurrecting the traditional system," made it clear to the new *Oba* that his powers were to be diminished sizeably.

To some extent, this contrived "restoration" created a new surge of Bini patriotism together with some movement back into traditional patterns of political behaviour. *Oba* Aiguobasimwin (called Eweka II following his installation in July 1914), gathered around him individuals who had not gained positions on the Provincial or District Councils. In a sense, he became the symbol of—if not the actual spokesman for—grievances arising from the traditional community. From 1914 to 1929, the *Oba* and the District Councils were locked constantly in bitter conflict. Gradually, the *Oba*'s renewed presence began to fade and the support he had been receiving subsided.

Thus, while a sustained effort had been made to restore a modified version of the traditional Bini Governmental structure, complete with a figurehead *Oba*, this effort, by the waning years of Eweka's reign (1926-1932), had clearly faltered. The *Oba* had lost a good deal of prestige both within the Bini heartland and the Mid-West in general. Nor from the British viewpoint had he been a success. For rather than remaining quietly in the background, he had served as a magnet to disaffected elements—elements which were blocking British objectives. He had hardly provided the impartial British-type figure-head monarch, which was the role the British had envisaged for him in the "restored" Benin Kingdom.

Advent of* Oba *Akenzua   When *Oba* Akenzua II took office in 1933, he was heralded as a progressive. He had attended King's College, Lagos from 1918 to 1921. Then for a year, 1922, he had served as a Transport Clerk in the Benin District Council Office. In subsequent years he served as a Judicial Council Clerk in the Benin Native Administration and a Confidential Clerk to his father. After a year's study of Egba Native Administration (in Yorubaland), he was appointed in 1927 as District Head of Ekiadolor District close to Benin City.[49] Certainly, his experience and education had been broader and more formal than any previous *Oba*; the people were justified in expecting much from him. Nor were these expectations in vain.

When he took office he implemented a number of reforms. He disbanded the harem; he freed girls from the obligation to marry him. He dispensed with many Palace attendants. At the same time, however, he restored the role of ceremony in the conduct of various aspects of Bini life. His installation was observed and performed in accord with traditional ritual; his mother was posthumously installed as Queen Mother (*Iyoba*). He re-constituted the order of body titles, whose members represented the physical and metaphysical components of his person, and whose duty it was to share his spiritual burden. And in addition to the changes which Akenzua brought into being, Bradbury stresses that the *Oba* was well aware of the effort which would be required of him to re-establish the authority of his office.

For the first years of his tenure, all went well for *Oba* Akenzua. He recruited many new men—clerks, teachers, merchants—into his camp. In 1935, however, the *Oba* entered into conflict with the *Iyase* over the "Great Water-Rate Agitation". It was contended by a number of Benin chiefs behind their spokesman the *Iyase*, that the *Oba* was misrepresenting his people in conceding to the British Administration that water-rates ought to be paid.[50] The *Oba*'s antagonists contended that water-rates had been paid from 1910-1920, and that when direct taxation was introduced, this water-rate had been stopped. The water-rate, it was held, was covered by the charges now levied through the direct tax.

In the ensuing controversy, it became evident that these men harboured grievances against the *Oba* that went much deeper than those expressed over the water-rate issue. In the re-organization of the BNA during 1936-37, many chiefs had lost their seats in the old Native Authority Council and courts. Further, when this re-organisation was completed, not only were the numbers of councillors drastically reduced, but a new regulation stipulated that new members selected to the council should not receive salaries. These acts had raised the wrath of those excluded, as well as those who felt that they were being deprived of legitimate earnings. Banding behind the *Iyase*, they sought to bring strong pressure against the *Oba*.

The seriousness of the crisis it produced was noted by the *Oba* himself. He declared that the "agitation which started in 1937 shook the constitution of Benin almost to its very foundation".[51] Once again, therefore, the gap had opened in ominous fashion between *Oba* and *Iyase*. Though the *Oba* had commenced his reign by generating a good deal of co-operation and good-will, the water-rate issue revealed the possibility of disintegration.

By the time the water-rate crisis had finally died down, following the death of the *Iyase* in 1943, one important point had clearly emerged. It was evident that the *Oba*'s traditional and symbolic influence, despite his efforts to re-generate respect for the office and its powers, was at a low ebb. At a time when a political movement was being formed which would seek to bring in not just Bini, but all "children of the Mid-West", this failure of respect for and authority of the *Oba* within even his traditional Bini stronghold, signified the extent to which his role in the prosecution of the Mid-West State issue might be minimised.

MID-WEST AUTONOMY: PROSPECTS AND LIMITATIONS

It was apparent that by the early 1940's there were certain trends which could have a considerable bearing on the future of the Mid-West State Movement. While the existence of a heritage of identity might serve as a basis for reminding disparate Mid-West peoples of their historical kinship, there was no guarantee that it could serve as a more effective mechanism for bonding these elements.

Since the advent of British interests in Nigeria, new concerns associated with the burgeoning social and economic opportunities of modernity had generated pressures which resulted in a sharp challenge to the sanctity and authority of tradition. Neither the predominance of the *Oba* nor the pre-eminence of the favoured Bini, as traditional "first among equals" in the Mid-West, was assured. Bearing in mind these factors the potential effectiveness of an appeal to common cultural association under Bini royal tutelage in any future pan-Mid-West context—an appeal which was, as we shall see in later chapters, to be frequently extended—seemed to offer dubious prospects.

Mid-West autonomy prospects at this early period in the awakening of separatist sentiments were, therefore, not quite so certain and assured as seemed superficially apparent. Certainly, general considerations suggested that there was no serious substantive factor which might detract from legitimising the concept of an integrated and autonomous Mid-West State.

Furthermore there could be no disputing the fact that an underlying heritage of identity did exist, and that this might well serve as the vital element to effect the bonding of disparate Mid-West ethnic elements in any future pan-Mid-West context.

Still it had to be recognised that there were basic centrifugal forces at work. These forces arose from the fact that a "family re-union" of Mid-West peoples might not so easily be achieved; that the surfacing of internal divisions strengthened perhaps by the expression of intra-Mid-West separatist aspirations, might well pose a sizeable obstacle to the securing of pan-Mid-West co-operation and to the pursuit of common Mid-West objectives.

———————————————

References

1. See Map I, below, p.19.

2. See Map III, below, p.23.

3. See "Memorandum on the Economic Viability of the Mid-West State", in *The Case for a Mid-West State*, mimeo., (Warri: 1957). (BAS).

4. The first National Census, conducted in 1952, set the total population of the Mid-West provinces at 1,492,000; this figure constituting about one-quarter of the total population of the Western Region (6,085,000). Of the Mid-West total, about 900,000 resided in Benin Province and 500,000 in Delta Province. (See *Population Census of the Western Region of Nigeria 1952*, (Lagos: Census Superintendent, 1956).) In area, the Mid-West provinces comprised two of the Region's eight provinces and about one-third (14,922 square miles) of the Region's total area. (See *Mid-Western Nigeria at a Glance* (Benin City: M.O.I., 1971).)

5. See "Memorandum on Economic Viability...", *op. cit.*

6. "The *Oba*'s Message", in *Circular*, dated 20 October, 1948, in file BP/2647. (INA).

7. R.E. Bradbury, *The Benin Kingdom*, (London: International African Institute, 1957), p.19.

8. Jacob Egharevba, *A Short History of Benin* (Ibadan: University Press, 1960), p.82. For location of Otun (or Ottun) See Map II below, p.21.

9. See R.E. Bradbury, "Chronological Problems in the Study of Benin History", *Journal of the Historical Society of Nigeria*, Vol.1, No.4 , (December, 1959). See also Egharevba, *A Short History of Benin, op cit.*, p.75; and P.A. Igbafe, "The Pre-Colonial Economic Basis of the Benin Kingdom", University of Ife, *History Seminar Series*, No.4, (1968-69), (mimeo.). The period of greatest expansion would appear also to have been the period of greatest diffusion and consolidation of structure in the upper ranks of the Bini hierarchy.

10. It is interesting to note that some of the greatest warriors— Ewuare, Ozolua and Ehengbuda—were also the greatest structural innovators. Each created new Palace Societies designed to fill a specific function in the Royal household. (See Egharevba, *op.cit.*, pp.75-81.).

11. *Ibid.*, pp.23-27.

12. See particularly R.E. Bradbury, "Continuities and Dis-continuities in Pre-Colonial Benin Politics: 1897-1951", in Michael Banton, (ed.), *History and Anthropology*, A.S.A. Series, No. 7 (London: Tavistock, 1968); and R.E. Bradbury, "The Kingdom of Benin", in D. Forde and P. Kaberry (eds.), *West African Kingdoms in the Nineteenth Century*, (Oxford: University Press, 1967). Additional seminal thoughts may be found in R.E. Bradbury, "Patterns of Political Incorporation in West African Kingdoms", (mimeo.), *Centre of West African Studies Seminar Series (1966-67)*, WA/1966-67, Nos.11 and 12.

13. Though monarchical with an hereditary aristocracy the Benin political system made provision for commoners to attain the benefits of status, wealth and political power; these largely through achieved positions in the *Eghaevbo n' Ore*. For details of the nature and ranking of the different Palace Societies, (See Egharevba, *op.cit.*, pp.78-79, and Bradbury, *The Benin Kingdom, op. cit.*, pp. 43-45).

14. The title of *Ezomo* ranked fourth below the *Oba* in the senior palace society, the *Uzama Nihinron*. (See Egharevba, *ibid.*, p.78). Generally regarded as the "generalissimo of the state" (Bradbury, *ibid.*, p.44), the *Ezomo* conducted most of the major military campaigns.

15. Egharevba, *ibid.*, p.85.

16. *Op.cit.*

17. These early migrations are thought to have taken place up to about 1000 A.D. (See Egharevba, *ibid.*, p.86, and Bradbury, *The Benin Kingdom, op. cit.*, p.63).

18. Egharevba, *op cit.*

19. *Ibid.*

20. Bradbury notes that other Bini who emigrated to Ishan at this early period included, "Warriors who did not return to Benin; relatives of the *Oba* and others who offended him; individuals placed by the *Oba* to guard the shrines; craft, trading and ritual specialists who came to seek their fortunes or were invited by the *Enige*; slaves or servants sent to farm for Benin chiefs." (*The Benin Kingdom*, *op.cit.*, p.64).

21. See Map II, above p.21, for location of the Nupe.

22. See Map III, above p.23, for details of ethnic groupings in the area. Also see Map I, above p.19, for Divisional and Provincial territories.

23. See, Bradbury, *The Benin Kingdom*, *op.cit.*, p.84.

24. *Ibid.* See also, M.O. Oloyo, "Afenmai Country in the Pre-Colonial Era", *University of Ife, History Seminar Series, No.8, (1968-69)*, (mimeo.).

25. See, Egharevba, *op.cit.*, p.87.

26. Bradbury, *op.cit.*, p.86

27. Both Bradbury and Oloyo infer that the growth of Yoruba influence was attributable not so much to any initiative of the latter, but to a noticeable decline of Bini influence in the area. (See Bradbury, *The Benin Kingdom, ibid.*)

28. See Map I above, p.19, for location of the Etsako area in Benin Province.

29. Egharevba, *op.cit.*, p.88.

30. See Bradbury, *The Benin Kingdom*, *op. cit.*, p.101.

31. See Map III above, p.23, for position of these groups in Delta Province.

32. See P.C.Lloyd, "The Itsekiri", in Bradbury, *The Benin Kingdom, op. cit.*, pp. 177-81. A.F.C. Ryder, in his article, "Missionary Activities in the Kingdom of Warri to the Early Nineteenth Century", *Journal of the Historical Society of Nigeria*, Vol. II, No 1 (December 1960), pp.1-25, suggests that a major reason for the success of Portuguese missionaries in the 16th century, was that the Itsekiris saw a God under whom they might gain protection and bring effective sanctions against the *Oba* and the gods of Benin.

33. See Lloyd, *op. cit.*, p.101.

34. See *ibid.*, p.174.

35. *Ibid.*

36. Bradbury, *The Benin Kingdom, op. cit.*, p.129.

37. *Ibid.*

38. The Urhobo and Isoko were raided by Ijaw and Itsekiri slaving

bands, (though also by Bini slavers as well). According to P.A. Talbot, *The Peoples of Southern Nigeria*, Vol. I, (London: Humphrey Milford, 1926), pp.317-342; and Obaro Ikime, *Merchant Prince of the Niger Delta*, (London: Hutchinson, 1968), the Ijaw and Itsekiri were the most aggressive in this regard.

39. The preferred modern spelling of this word (Ijaw) is Ijo. This is the name of the linguistic group within the Kwa branch of the Niger Congo family of languages. (See E. J. Alagoa, *A History of the Niger Delta*, (Ibadan: University Press, 1972), p.15). Throughout this study, however, the word "Ijaw" will be employed as it was the nomenclature current during the period (1948-63) with which this study is concerned.

40. F. A. Talbot, *Tribes of the Niger Delta*, (London: Sheldon Press, 1932), p. 5. For further detailed interpretations of Ijaw migrations, see R.K. Granville, "Notes on the Jekris, Sobos and Ijos of the Warri District", *Journal of the Royal Anthropological Society*, XXVIII, (1898), pp.104-126.

41. See E.J. Alagoa, *op.cit.*, p.84; and J.C. Anene, *Southern Nigeria in Transition*, (Cambridge: University Press, 1966), p.7.

42. Alagoa, *op.cit.*

43. See Bradbury, "Continuities and Dis-continuities...", *op.cit.*, p.198.

44. The *Iwebo* Society was at this time the Bini Palace Society responsible for the regulation of riverside trade. (See Egharevba, *op.cit.*, p.79). The head of the Iwebo society, the *Unwague* held one of the key offices of state; this office conferring great prestige and powers of patronage on its holder. (See Bradbury, "The Kingdom of Benin", in Forde and Kaberry, *West African Kingdoms...*, *op. cit.*, p.18).

45. See *Southern Nigeria Defender*, 18 December, 1952.

46. Bradbury, "Continuities and Dis-Continuities...," *op.cit.*, p.204.

47. *Ibid.*, pp.206-209.

48. Quoted in Bradbury, *ibid.*, p.215, from A. C. Burns, *A Short History of Nigeria*, (London: 1929), p.217.

49. For further details on the early life of Oba Akenzua, see R.M. Aitalegbe, *Profile: Oba Akenzua II, C.M.G.*, (Benin City: M.O.I., 1964), pp.3-5

50. See Ben Prof 2/BP/1472. (INA)

51. *Benin Province: Annual Report*, 1938, p.3, in file *ibid.*

CHAPTER 3

DUBIOUS BEGINNINGS

The general assessment in the previous chapter indicated certain obstacles which could impede both long and short term Mid-West prospects. Still, following the events of 1948 the future of the Mid-West cause seemed—at least to newly awakened Mid-West protagonists—to be filled with considerable promise. The pronouncements of the *Oba*, Chief Omo-Osagie and the RBC[1] had sounded a clear and forceful rallying call to all supporters and potential supporters of the Mid-West cause. Furthermore, statements made by the NCNC leader Azikiwe and the Yoruba Nigerian Youth Movement (NYM) leader Awolowo, made clear that Nigeria's major minorities, including the Mid-West peoples, would have the full support of Nigeria's most prominent political leaders. Finally, it seemed possible that even the British Colonial authorities might concede that their long established "three-pillar" policy was no longer practicable. They might now recognise that new states were needed.

In theory, there seemed good reason that Mid-West protagonists should view their future prospects with at least moderate expectation and confidence. In reality, however, there were certain basic factors which suggested that the Mid-West cause might not rise beyond even the level of the *Oba*'s and the RBC's 1948 pronouncements. At this early stage the Mid-West Movement *per se* had taken no concrete form. The Mid-West issue was an idea only. Although the *Oba* and Omo-Osagie clearly had plans to extend the reach of the RBC beyond the immediate locale of Benin Division, for the moment at least, these plans did not include the extension of a network of control beyond what might be effected through personal contacts and the general appeal of the Mid-West issue. Consequently, hopes for securing early success rested not only on the active backing of the NCNC at the forthcoming Constitutional Review Conferences, but also on a strong lead from the *Oba* and Omo-Osagie. This lead needed support from equally committed leaders in the Mid-West localities.

By mid-1948, it became apparent that the prospect of the strong lead needed from the *Oba* and Omo-Osagie was not likely to be forthcoming. Furthermore any hope of retaining the united support of the Mid-West leaders in the localities seemed also to be fast dwindling. In view of these developments it seemed that Mid-West prospects at the forthcoming Review Conferences might not be so good as the more optimistic of Mid-West protagonists believed.

Mid-West Leadership under Pressure

The most grave development in terms of future prospects for the Mid-West cause emanated from the perilous position, which by mid-1948, was occupied by the *Oba* of Benin and Chief Omo-Osagie. If these two leaders were to infuse the Mid-West cause with the requisite spirit, and provide it with the necessary energetic guidance and advocacy, it was vital that each should have a secure and prominent platform within the Benin heartland from which to advance his pan-Mid-West appeal and to organise support. As early as April 1948, however, it became apparent that both the *Oba* and Omo-Osagie, quite apart from fulfilling broader Mid-West commitments, would have a most arduous task merely to eke out some form of personal political survival. The Honorable Gaius Obaseki, the powerful Bini leader of the BTPA governing party in Benin Division[2] made clear during this period his determination to ensure that neither of these Mid West leaders should secure any position of prominence either within or outside the Division. Life was not to be easy either for the *Oba* or Omo-Osagie.

The Oba Challenged   The *Oba* of Benin, to a considerable extent, was the author of his own troubles. In Chapter 2, it was pointed out that within Benin Division—and indeed within the Mid-West as a whole—a serious rift, by the early 1940's, was developing. On the one side was the *Oba*, along with certain traditional rulers and "new men" excluded from positions of authority and/or personal benefit in the local authority; on the other side, the rising or already prominent "new men" and traditional rulers who had found favour with the powerful BTPA leader Obaseki.

Obaseki, the wealthy and influential son of the legendary Agho who had been so valuable an instrument of British interests during and after the restoration of 1914, had emerged as the dominant political figure in the Bini heartland. Thus, when in

1943 the former *Iyase* died, it was generally assumed that Obaseki would be selected by the *Oba* to fill this vacant title. Indeed, while his colleagues and supporters in the BTPA tended to assume that the choice of Obaseki would be automatic, there was a good deal of general non-partisan support amongst all Bini for the *Oba* to make such a choice. For, politics aside, it was an established tradition amongst the Bini people that the post of *Iyase* (or Prime Minister) should go to the most prominent Bini commoner.[3] At that time, there could be no question that Obaseki was such a man.

The *Oba*, however, viewed the situation rather differently. *Obas* in past Bini history had not always been keen on appointing a man who might become a powerful and independent spokesman of the people's interests. In olden times, lamented *Oba* Akenzua, an *Iyase* who had become troublesome could be "sent off to a war from which it was unlikely he would return".[4] Ruefully, he observed that this useful ploy was no longer available to him. In the absence of such controls, therefore, *Oba* Akenzua determined to resist the traditional and political pressures being applied to him. He opted not to select Obaseki. This decision was to lead to serious trouble for the *Oba*

In his first effort to evade the *Iyase* issue, *Oba* Akenzua, with the backing of the *Eghaevbo n'Ore* announced that in keeping with modern political trends he had decided that the traditional Bini hierarchy should be modified. Amongst the modifications proposed was one which would eliminate the post of *Iyase*.[5] This bold initiative failed to receive the reception for which he had hoped. All Bini were outraged by the *Oba*'s alleged unilateral efforts to tamper with established practice. The *Oba* was duly forced to withdraw his proposal. In its place he put forward another. This proposal called for the creation of the title *Obadeyanedo* to replace that of *Iyase*. Once again, however, there was uproar. This title, literally translated, meant "*Oba* rules over all Edos"; it implied virtual elimination of the powers associated with the Iyaseship. It was rejected, and in increasingly vociferous and forceful terms. Yet again, the *Oba* was pressured to withdraw his proposal.

Finally, and very reluctantly, the *Oba* agreed that the title of *Iyase* should be retained. He then announced in February 1948 that he had proposed, and the *Eghaevbo n'Ore* had endorsed, the nomination of the aged and illiterate *Esogban* of Benin to the post of *Iyase*. To many Bini, and to Obaseki and his BTPA supporters in particular, this was the last straw.

In the following weeks, the political situation in Benin City approximated that experienced during the Great Water Rate Agitation of 1937. There were clashes between BTPA and RBC supporters. The tide of feeling against the *Oba* was rising fast. There were demands for his deposition. According to rumour, his immediately junior brother was preparing to replace him. However, despite the displeasure of many Binis over the *Esogban*'s nomination and a risk of serious violence in the Mid-West heartland—to say nothing of the threat to his title and person—the *Oba* stood firm.

Only the timely introduction of the far-reaching Local Government reforms of 1948 prevented growing tension in Benin City and environs from worsening. So far as the *Oba* was concerned, these reforms eased the enormous pressures on him. But the relief was not secured without cost: the price the *Oba* had to pay was the virtual emasculation of his executive power in the BNA Council, together with a considerable curtailment of his powers within the previously inviolable traditional sector of his authority. The provisions of the new Benin Constitution made it clear that the days of the *Oba* as Sole Native Authority were now over. He was henceforth to fill the figurehead position of President of the crucial Administrative Committee of Council, and he was to have no control over appointments to the courts or administrative services. What made things worse for the *Oba* was that these crucial powers which had been taken from him were now going to be vested in the Chairman of the BNA Council; and the Chairman of the Council was none other than his old antagonist, Gaius Obaseki.

What followed in the wake of these Local Government reforms in Benin Division was probably inevitable. With Obaseki now in the dominant position in Council and the *Oba* reduced to a subordinate role, BTPA councillors pressed for the nullification of the *Esogban*'s nomination as *Iyase*. It was their leader Obaseki, they strongly contended, who should occupy this office. They impressed their views on the *Oba*; and though the methods they used were hardly subtle, they were effective.

As the *Esogban* had not yet been formally instated as *Iyase*, BTPA councillors secured the passage of a resolution by the BNA Council giving the Council, in the name of the Bini people, the right to put forward its own candidate(s). The *Oba* was prevailed upon to consent to this decision. Council then approved a motion that the final determination of the candidate to be selected as *Iyase* should be the responsibility of the *Oba and Council*. Reluctantly, the *Oba* also consented to this resolution. The rest was easy.

At a meeting of the BNA Council in early April 1948, the BTPA, its benches packed with party supporters, moved that Council approve the nomination and appointment of Gaius Obaseki to the title of *Iyase*.[6] This motion, according to witnesses present at this meeting, was met with the loudly voiced approval of Obaseki's supporters who constituted the overwhelming majority in Council.[7] Obaseki, thronged by his triumphant supporters, then left the Council Hall. This wholesale departure of Obaseki's supporters had the effect of bringing the meeting to a sudden and rather unexpected end. If the *Oba* or others had planned to bring forward the name of the *Esogban* or other candidates, it was too late.

At a meeting of the BDC on 19 April, 1948, the *Oba* finally capitulated. In an address to Council the *Oba* declared:

> "I approve and confirm the appointment of Gaius Obaseki as Iyase. By his appointment in the way we now do such things, I feel that our customs and traditions, which must be jealously guarded, have been modified in appropriate manner. I warmly congratulate the new Iyase. I hope it has been understood that the question involved in the Iyase tangle was... one of principle".[8]

In the outcome of the *Iyase* dispute, it was apparent that the *Oba*, by following the course he had chosen, had played directly into the hands of Obaseki, his BTPA supporters and the British Authorities. The British were committed to the democratisation of politics, starting from the grass-roots; they were now implementing this policy. Governor MacPherson, in his address to the BDC in May 1948, had declared that "if sound progress was to be made" it was "essential for those in authority at every level to take the people into their confidence".[9] It was in order to secure these "modern and progressive" goals, stated Sir John that changes in the structure of the BNA had been carried out. The dramatic cuts in the powers of the *Oba*, and the enhanced powers of democratically representative elements in Council, actions which were encompassed within the general framework of newly evolved British policy, happened to coincide almost perfectly with the rather more self-interested objectives of Obaseki and the BTPA.

Obaseki and his BTPA colleagues now wasted little time in asserting their authority. Immediate steps were taken to lower the *Oba*'s dignity and to curtail his prerogatives.[10] The *Oba*'s salary was slashed from £1800 to £800 p.a.; he was forbidden to confer any title without Council's consent. It was no exaggeration for Bradbury to declare that "the *Oba* [now] seemed almost as impotent as his father had been after the 1914 restoration".[11] This was hardly an advantageous position from which to initiate an effective Mid-West assault.

The *Oba* of Benin had clearly been humbled. Still Obaseki was forced to recognise that he should not push his assault too far. The *Oba* was, after all, the sacred embodiment of the Bini people. Thus, while Obaseki was at pains to demonstrate his authority over the *Oba*, and that in a secular context at least he would tolerate no challenge to his newly-won position, still the BTPA leader was aware that it was politic to demonstrate his deference to the spiritual and traditional authority which the *Oba*, of course, still retained. Accordingly, in his maiden speech as Chairman of the re-organised BNA Council, Obaseki "appealed to the *Oba*...[who] represents our system, our traditions, our institutions and the culminating will of our people" to give "the lead that would maintain and advance the prestige of our community".[12]

This was an impressive show of deference by the commoner Obaseki to his traditional overlord; it indicated that there were limits to the pressure he was prepared to exert. However, in relation to the other Mid-West nuclear leader, his arch political antagonist Chief Omo-Osagie, no such restraints were operative!

Omo-Osagie Challenged   It was at the local level within the BNA Council that Omo-Osagie, as leader of the RBC challengers, first began to feel the pressure of Obaseki and his BTPA colleagues. Indeed, Omo-Osagie himself facilitated the attack which Obaseki was about to launch. The RBC platform he chose was an exposed one. The progressive and militant stand of the Benin Community— predecessor of the RBC—from as far back as the Great Water Rate Agitation had ensured that its adherents would be viewed askance by the British Colonial authorities. The RBC had an established reputation of political opportunism and trouble-making. One British administrative officer referred to RBC supporters as a rabble of "trouble-makers, hoodlums and ex-convicts".[13] Omo-Osagie, therefore, could expect little help from the British authorities if he found himself in trouble as a result of his political initiatives.

It was again to fruitful provisions of the new Benin Constitution that Obaseki turned. Making full use of new BDC powers over the selection of sitting Members, Obaseki and his BTPA colleagues moved swiftly. In April, 1948, the BDC called for—and secured—the expulsion of Omo-Osagie and his four leading RBC colleagues on the technical grounds that these five men had been "neither appointed by their societies nor by the Community" and therefore represented no person or group except themselves.[14] This came as a severe blow to Omo-Osagie, his expelled colleagues and the RBC. Still, try as they might, the BTPA leaders could not prevent Omo-Osagie from exercising his right at least to sit in Council. This right existed because he was still a Member for Benin Province in the Western House of Assembly. It was stated, however, that while he might sit in the Central Council, as a special Extraordinary member, he would have no right to be appointed to any of its committees. Nor was Obaseki prepared to let the matter drop here.

At the *1948 Benin Provincial Conference*, on behalf of the BNA, he presented a letter to the Conference Chairman.[15] This letter, covering a copy of a petition to the Chief Commissioner of the Western Provinces, called for the removal of Chief Omo-Osagie from his position as Benin Provincial Member to the Western House of Assembly. The Resident, as Conference Chairman, maintained it was perfectly in order for the meeting to consider and report whether Omo-Osagie's representation had been satisfactory. When, however, the meeting was canvassed on this matter, it was maintained by Omo-Osagie's supporters, that as the petition was not addressed to the Provincial Council, it would not be in keeping with the accepted procedure for Conference delegates to comment on it. Chief Omo-Osagie expressed astonishment at the petition, and asked the Chairman that he, Omo-Osagie, be permitted to "state my defence and forward it to the Chief Commissioner with the petition". The Resident agreed.

A little more than a month later, at another Benin Provincial Conference, held this time at the *Oba*'s Palace,[16] Obaseki tried again to secure the expulsion of Omo-Osagie from the Western House. This time, he put the BNA Council case in much stronger terms. Obaseki declared that the RBC leader should be expelled for "inaction" in the Western House. Omo-Osagie, he maintained, "did not do what his constituents wanted" and because of this he should no longer be their representative.

When the Chairman of the Conference objected to Obaseki's apparent definition of a Member's responsibilities, Obaseki sought only to press forward his contention more strongly. The Benin Provincial representative in the Western House of Assembly, he maintained, sat as a representative. And if this representative did not represent the views of the Provincial Conference, whose views did he then represent? Obaseki felt the position of Chief Omo-

Osagie was perfectly clear. The latter's own Native Authority had expelled him from representing it at the Provincial Conference, and yet the Provincial Conference was apparently unable or unwilling to withdraw him from the Western House of Assembly.

The opponents of Obaseki's views asked that the whole matter be dropped. They held that as there had been no reply from the Chief Commissioner regarding the petition from the Benin Native Authority, and since the law officers had not made any statement on the power of the Provincial Conference to withdraw a Member, there was no point in further pressing the matter. Thus, once again the issue was allowed to lapse. Omo-Osagie's membership in the House of Assembly, for the moment, was secure.

By the end of 1948, Obaseki and his BTPA supporters had amply demonstrated the very considerable pressure they were now enabled to exert on their RBC opponents. BTPA leaders believed that with continued pressure on Omo-Osagie, his close associates and RBC supporters, they (the BTPA) might soon emerge as the unchallenged, controlling, and increasingly popular party in Benin Division. Indeed, Obaseki himself warned, in his inaugural speech on 23 April, 1948, as Chairman of the newly re structured Benin Council, and in language very thinly veiled, that "in future, anybody found trying to sow seeds of discord... shall be regarded as an undesirable... and will have no place in the onward march of Benin".[17]

Altogether, in terms of stature in their native Benin homeland, both the *Oba* of Benin and Omo-Osagie retained at this point only the most tenuous and insecure of positions. In addition, there was little to suggest that the worst was over. The *Oba* had been threatened with deposition in early 1948; the issue might be raised again, and with more serious consequences. As for Omo-Osagie, he too was vulnerable; he had been expelled from the BNA Council, and nearly ousted from his seat in the Western House of Assembly. Certainly, it was evident that neither the *Oba* nor Omo-Osagie had anything approaching a secure base from which to launch a firm and confident initiative on the Mid-West issue.

Fragmenting Leadership in the Localities   Since its inception in 1944, the NCNC had retained in the Mid-West the respect and loyal support of prominent local leaders. It had served as an umbrella political organisation drawing in all the leading political elements from the different districts and ethnic groups. Major and minor leaders in all Mid-West areas were proud to identify themselves with the NCNC because of the party's commitment to the great cause of National Liberation and all that they envisaged this would entail. Chief G. E. Odiase, later to become Secretary-General of the Mid-West State Movement, maintains that at this time, "We Mid-Westerners were all Nationalists; we all believed in the NCNC and Zik, its great leader".[18] The party's adoption of the *Freedom Charter*, said Odiase, served further to enhance popular affection and support for the NCNC and its leader.

It was essential that the NCNC should continue to retain the loyalty and support of prominent Mid-West local leaders, uniting the disparate ethnic and area elements of Mid-West leadership. Within the general framework of the NCNC, a united Mid-West leadership might then drive home with impressive effect a common pan-Mid-West policy at the forthcoming *Constitutional Review Conferences of 1949-50*. Obviously this united support, backed by the promised NCNC general initiatives on the New States issue, could force the Colonial authorities to recognise the strength of the pan-Mid-West position and hence the need for a separate state. Indeed, in the absence of a strong lead from the *Oba* and Omo-Osagie, which under the circumstances now seemed more than likely, it became evident that a united Mid-West leadership could assume a new and vital significance in advancing the Mid-West issue at these forthcoming conferences.

As early as mid-1948, not long after publication of the *Freedom Charter*, however, it became apparent that this requisite united front of NCNC support amongst Mid-West leaders was not to be retained. While Chief Odiase may maintain that during this period all Mid-West leaders were supporters of Azikiwe and the NCNC; in principle at least it became increasingly evident that some were more loyal than others. Many were dissatisfied with the leadership of Azikiwe and the policies of his party; and some were now giving serious thought to abandoning both him and the NCNC. These developments and their bearing on the unity of Mid-West leadership did not augur well for Mid-West prospects.

There were three main reasons for increasing dissent amongst many prominent NCNC leaders in the Mid-West districts. First, there were growing doubts about the capability and character of Azikiwe. As the Itsekiri leader, Chief Prest, put it: "In the early days, Zik was a good talker and a dreamer; from this viewpoint, he was a good politician".[19] But, Prest added, by the end of 1948 it was generally accepted amongst many Nationalist leaders, that Azikiwe would start a fight and not finish it; that when in trouble he would try to run away from it. In support of their arguments, dissenters pointed to the alleged "Assassination Plot" against Azikiwe, and to the position assumed by the NCNC President in relation to the fiery address, "A Call to Revolution", given by Zikist, Osita Agwuna.[20] In both instances it was held that Azikiwe's behaviour had been at best, indecisive, at worst cowardly. Indeed it was from about this time that Azikiwe started to drop sharply in the esteem of the more radical and militant elements in the Nationalist Movement, of whom a number were Mid-Westerners.[21]

While this general conviction that Azikiwe was lacking in commitment and courage was gaining greater acceptance amongst militants, Mid-West dissenters shared with other radicals a growing sense of unease about other aspects of his politics. Prest, along with Enahoro, noted with some alarm Azikiwe's apparent pan-Ibo leanings. These fears were shared by many Nigerians of non-Ibo origins, particularly the Yoruba people of Lagos and the West. They were deeply troubled by the meteoric rise of Azikiwe, his unprecedented popularity among politically conscious Nigerians and the growing militancy of the Ibo settler community at Lagos, which was said to support its "favorite son" to a man.[22]

The more conservative Mid-West leaders were also unimpressed by Azikiwe's political style. Gaius Obaseki was sceptical of the effect which Azikiwe's "American-style" politics might have on the gradually evolving politics of Nigeria. Obaseki, a wealthy man with great influence amongst legislators and British administrators at Ibadan and Lagos, was convinced that the volatile politics of mass participation preached by Azikiwe presented serious dangers for the country as a whole.[23] In his capacity as a senior Itsekiri statesman, Chief Arthur Prest confirmed this view of Obaseki. He added that it was his own view in 1948, that if the Nationalist Movement continued along the path on which the NCNC directed it, the result would be the sudden elevation to positions of political authority, of "small boys of unproven worth and questionable integrity and character".[24]

The sudden appearance of Chief Bode Thomas, the political emissary of Chief Awolowo, in the Mid-West provinces during May 1948, enhanced the increasing polarisation of opposing elements within the Mid-West leadership. Chief Thomas, on his "friendly and informal" tour met with a number of disgruntled political leaders. At Warri, Chief Thomas spoke with Itsekiri leaders including Chief Prest, O.N. Rewane, Chiefs Begho and Edukugho. Thomas spoke of

Awolowo's interest in forming a new political party with a leadership drawn from men of "proven ability and integrity". Its objective would be to retain "principle in politics" and to provide "dynamic and decisive" direction.[25] At Benin too, Thomas received a favourable reception from Gaius Obaseki.

Altogether, Thomas' visit to the Mid-West stirred a good deal of interest amongst both "established" and "youthful" elements. His proposal that the new party should have a "Yoruba orientation" actually strengthened the appeal of his proposition. Itsekiris in particular were aware of their kinship links with the Yorubas; and so far as Obaseki was concerned, a Yoruba emphasis was preferable to the growing Ibo emphasis of the NCNC. From the viewpoint of building Mid-West unity, however, the impact of Thomas' visit was serious. Political divisions were growing, and prospects for maintaining a united political leadership were fast diminishing.

With the *Oba* and Omo-Osagie in political limbo and with the unity of Mid-West leadership in the outlying districts showing ominous signs of fragmentation, prospects for the Mid-West issue at the forthcoming Constitutional Review Conferences looked poor. Still there was external support. Nigeria's leading Nationalists were united in support of the new states issue; furthermore the British Authorities might be more accommodating than their past policies tended to suggest. Although it seemed any appeal now launched by the *Oba* and Omo-Osagie would be muted, the impact on indigenous leaders would not be known until tried.

SHOCK OF REALITY: THE CONSTITUTIONAL REVIEW CONFERENCES

The lengthy consultation processes on the Richards Constitution, soon revealed that the anticipated unified local support for the Mid-West issue was not going to materialise. Indeed, these Constitutional Review Conferences demonstrated the extent to which opinion was divided on—even flatly opposed to—the creation of a Mid-West State. For supporters of the Mid-West cause these Review Conferences were most demoralising.

The *Benin Provincial Conference* opened on 5 July 1949. It was convened at the Council Hall, Benin City, with the *Oba* of Benin as Chairman. Following procedure laid down by the Chief Secretary to the Government, Hugh Foot, the Conference was instructed "to find answers to a series of questions, each one of which", Mr. Foot pointed out, "demands the most careful examination".[26] The questions on which attention focused were the first two:

> "1. Do we wish to see a fully centralised system with all legislative and executive power concentrated a the Centre; or do we wish to develop a federal system under which each different Region of the country would exercise a measure of internal autonomy?

> "2. If we favour a Federal system, should we retain the existing Regions with some modification of existing Regional boundaries, or should we form Regions on some new basis, such as the many linguistic groups which exist in Nigeria?"

In answer to question one, the Conference delegates expressed their preference for a federal system under which each different state in the country would exercise a measure of autonomy.[27] However, in response to the second question, separate groups advanced views which supported autonomy, but in two very different forms.

The representatives of the Kukuruku (Afenmai) and Ishan peoples along with Bini and other Edo-speaking delegates, called for a radical modification of existing Regional boundaries to accommodate the demands of Mid-West ethnic groupings for a unified and autonomous Mid-West State.[28] Asaba Division (Western Ibo) representatives, however, put a rather different position. These delegates expressed strong preference either for alteration of Regional boundaries to incorporate territories inhabited by West-Niger Ibos within the Provincial structure of the East Region, or as a last resort, for creation of a West Niger Province within the existing West Region. They vehemently opposed any plan to include them within a future Mid-West State.[29] Ultimately the *Benin Provincial Conference* adopted the resolution put forward by the Edo-speaking majority. Nevertheless the Western Ibo position had been made clear. Indeed this position, had been advanced with even greater intensity at the Warri Provincial Conference of May 1949.

At this Conference, the Warri National Union, "mouthpiece of the Itsekiri Nation" declared that "Itsekiris wholeheartedly support the system of Federation of States in which the various ethnic or linguistic groups are directly represented, to form the United States of Nigeria".[30] The Union further asserted that Itsekiris were opposed to the "principle of Regionalisation, in any shape or form". Neither the present arrangement of grouping the Itsekiri in the Western Region, nor any proposal to form a separate Region called Benin-Warri Region has our support in the 1950 constitution".[31] Indeed, at the end of its lengthy list of resolutions, the Warri National Union memo went on to demand a separate Itsekiri state whereby Itsekiris would be represented by their "sons and daughters," in "all the councils or committees of the country".[32] Union members, the memo concluded, re-affirmed their loyalty to the NCNC and adopted, in principle, the NCNC *Freedom Charter*.

The Warri Conference received memos from many ethnic elements in the Province. Each was equally intent on asserting its claim to autonomy, and to this end—and in close accord with the provisions of the much-heralded NCNC *Freedom Charter*—each demonstrated its support for a "New Nigeria". This would be organised into a commonwealth of autonomous states founded on a national and linguistic basis. Typical was a statement received from the Aboh Union, Lagos Branch, which resolved that "the Aboh people, in support of the Ibo State Union and Western Ibo Union, accepts the NCNC Freedom Charter as the basis of 1950 constitutional reforms."[33] Similar statements expressing support for the *Freedom Charter*, and demands for sub-regional autonomy were made by the Isoko Youth Patriotic Association, the Aboh Union of Warri, the Igbuku Group Council and the Ukwani Improvement Union, a group with Ibo affiliations. Ijaws called for creation of a separate state which would comprise the riverain areas of both the East and West Regions, areas which Ijaws regarded as their native domain.[34]

Memos presented to the Warri Provincial Conference showed there was little support from non-Edo-speaking groups for a Benin-Delta, or Mid-West state. Conversely, each ethnic and ethno-linguistic group gave full backing to proposals that would support creation of more "ethno-specific" states. Itsekiri people demanded a separate Itsekiri State, while Western Ibos, Ijaws and Isokos sought similar objectives. Each contended that new micro-states should be created in accord with the more specific demands of ethno-linguistic units, and in keeping with the NCNC *Freedom Charter*. Only Urhobo delegates maintained that an "autonomous Benin-Warri State" could best advance the interests of the Mid-West peoples.[35]

At subsequent Regional and General Conferences on the Constitution the intensity of debate on the Mid-West issue was greatly reduced. The *Oba* of Benin was one of the few delegates to press the Mid-West issue. At the West Regional Conference, his request for a full airing of the Mid-West issue was rejected by the Conference Chairman. The response of the *Oba*, in company with many Mid-West delegates, was to walk out of the Conference and return to Benin.[36]

The last that was officially heard of demands for a "Central" or Mid-West state at this stage occurred at a meeting of a Select Committee of the Western House of Assembly which was convened in April 1950, after the General Conference. This Committee, however, was empowered only to consider decisions of the General Conference; it could not recommend changes. Hence, no action was taken in relation to final demands made by Mid-West Committee members.[37]

The majority of demands made by Mid-West elements at the *Constitutional Review Conferences* pressed for creation of *smaller states settled on the foundation of ethnic or low-level ethno-linguistic units. Itsekiri, Western Ibo, Isoko and Western Ijaw demands focused on the creation of separate micro-states within the Mid-West territory. Only the Bini and Edo-speaking peoples along with the Urhobos in the Delta indicated any significant commitment to the larger territorial concept of a Mid-West state.* Yet, despite divisions, there was one issue on which all were agreed: none wished to be subjected to Yoruba rule from Ibadan. On this issue alone Western Ibos, Itsekiris and Edo-speaking peoples, at this point in time, shared a common concern.

THE MID-WEST CAUSE: FEARS AND HOPES

The *Constitutional Review Conferences* showed that more than common identity and assumed common interest was needed to secure advancement of the Mid-West cause. Other home truths too had been learned.

Active support by NCNC and Yoruba nationalists had been assumed; it had not materialised. At the General Conference the more militant Nigerian political elements were represented by only 12 of the 50 delegates; and of these 12 only six identified themselves with the NCNC.[38] Most were either anti-Nationalists or conservative-Nationalists. Furthermore, any NCNC initiatives on the New States issue at the General Conference, were severely handicapped by the absence of the NCNC President, for Azikiwe, though an official delegate to the General Conference, did not attend its proceedings.[39] His colleagues who did attend managed only to agree a Minority Report recommendation that the new Constitution should make provision for a "federated Nigeria with local government based on natural and not artificial geographical boundaries".[40] This did little to alleviate the impression that the NCNC was less than sincerely committed to the minorities issue.

At the *West Regional Conference*, the performance of the Mid-West's Nationalist champions had been equally disappointing. Azikiwe had been present, but in the end, he and his NCNC delegates, along with Awolowo and his NYM colleagues, were prepared to endorse recommendations, "that there shall be a federal responsible government consisting of states formed on an ethnic and/or linguistic basis; there shall be three states, namely, Western, Eastern and Northern".[41] The ambiguity of this statement so angered the *Oba* of Benin that he boycotted the subsequent General Conference.[42]

Still it was not just their Nationalist allies who had disappointed Mid-West protagonists. Contrary to expectation the British clearly were intent on maintaining the existing three Region structure. The *1947 Despatch*[43] had stipulated this structural commitment, and from it the Colonial Authorities had shown little propensity to deviate.

In the instance of the West Regional authorities, this structural commitment was emphasised graphically in policy papers issued by the Secretary to the Governor of the Western Provinces before the Review Conferences were convened. On the one hand, the Regional authorities indicated their concern to hear the widest range of minority opinion: "Opportunity should be given to all sections of the public as well as to the Native Authorities themselves to express their views and minority opinion".[44] On the other hand, when it came to *action*, these same authorities were adamant in their resolve to resist demands for structural devolution. It was held that while "some people" had proposed a further division of Regions into tribal or linguistic groups, such proposals originated from "personal ambition or strong local feeling". Such fragmentation, it was explained, would be "impractical and create insurmountable problems of administration".

By early 1950, only a little more than a year following the formal launching of the Mid-West cause, the Mid-West issue was virtually subsiding into an "also ran" issue. Clearly, if it was to be successfully advanced then some form of effective organisation to integrate Mid-West elements within a coherent united structure was vital. Much more than an appeal to Mid-West sentiment was needed. At the same time, it was necessary to devise a strategy to deal with problems raised by external elements: active support from the NCNC was required, and attempts must be made to "neutralise" the British influence.

There were, however, more immediate and pressing problems to be dealt with. The Local Government and inaugural West Regional General elections to be held in 1951, were fast approaching. If the Mid-West cause was to retain viability, then it was vital that everything possible be done to ensure that, at the Regional level, the NCNC went into office at Ibadan. With an NCNC Government ruling in the West, Mid-West protagonists would be in a good position from which to press their NCNC "Champions" for appropriate action.

As for the Local Government elections: their outcome, and particularly in Benin Division, would have a vital and fundamental bearing on the Mid-West issue. It was clear that Obaseki and his anti-Mid-West BTPA colleagues must be ousted from BNA office. Only then might the Mid-West's nuclear leaders, the *Oba* and Omo-Osagie, be lifted from their current political obscurity and thus be afforded the platform in the Bini heartland from which to breathe new and much-needed life into the Mid-West cause.

— — — — — — — — — — — —

References

1. See Chapter 1 above, pp.6-7.

2. For details of Obaseki's background and leadership of the BTPA see above p.11, n.17.

3. See above, pp.18-20.

4. File No. BNA 730/1, Addendum 3, p.2 (BCA).

5. For details on this and later postures of the *Oba* and Obaseki on the *Iyase* issue of 1948, See Bradbury, "Continuities and Dis-continuities...", *op. cit.*, pp.119-21.

6. See File No. BNA 730/2, pp.76 and 88 (BCA).

7. See interview with Chief Lawal Osula, Int.II, p.33.

8. *Benin Native Authority: New Constitution, 1948*, (Benin City: Two Brothers Press, 1949), p.17, in File BNA 730/2, *op.cit.*

9. *Address by Governor MacPherson to the BDC, 25 May, 1948*, in file *ibid.*, p. 208.

10. See Bradbury, "Continuities and Dis-Continuities...", *op.cit.*, p.63.

11. Ibid.

12. *Address by Obaseki to the BDC, 23 April, 1948*, File BNA 730/2, pp.71-72.

13. *Benin Province Annual Report, 1950*, Ben Prof BP/1170/1 (INA)

14. See File BNA 730/2, p. 85, and *ibid.*, *Order on Removal of Omo-Osagie and Four Others from the BDC, 23 April, 1948*, p.193.

15. See *Report of the Benin Provincial Conference, Auchi. December, 1948*, in File Ben Prof BP/2328 (INA).

16. See, *Report of the Benin Provincial Conference, Oba's Palace Benin City, January 1949*, in file ibid.

17. BNA 730/2, pp.71-72.

18. Odiase, Int.II, p.10.

19. Prest, Int.III, p.1.

20. For details of these incidents see Sklar, *Nigerian Political Parties, op.cit.*, pp.64-78; Coleman, *Nigeria: Background to Nationalism, op.cit.*, pp.285-99; and E.A. Enahoro, *Fugitive Offender*, (London: Cassell, 1966), pp.89-97.

21. Included amongst this more radical element were: O.N. Rewane and E.N. Begho, Itsekiris from Warri; Nduka Eze and O.I. Dafe from Western Iboland; Ja' Isuman of Agbede, Afenmai; and E.A.(Tony) Enahoro, at this time still a young journalist working on newspapers owned by Azikiwe.

22. See Sklar, *Nigerian Political Parties, op.cit.*, p. 68.

23. See interview with Judge Andrew Obaseki, Int.V, p.15.

24. Prest, Int.III, p.3.

25. See Interviews with Prest and Rewane, Int.VI, p.23 and Int.III, pp.1-2.

26. For details of these questions see *Nigeria Legislative Council Debates, 11 March, 1949*, (Lagos: Government Printer, 1949), p.320.

27. For details of delegates' positions see file on *Proceedings of the Benin Provincial Conference on Constitutional Reform. Held at Benin City, July 1949*, Ben Prof BP/2678/1 (INA), and file section on *Provincial Conference on Constitutional Reform. 1949*, correspondence between Benin and Warri Provinces' political and ethnic group organisations and the Resident, Benin Province, *loc.cit.* See also file of *Official Correspondence Not to be Communicated to Private Persons, 1932-52*, Ben Prof BP/742 (INA).

28. See *Proceedings of the Benin Provincial Conference*, BP 2678/1.

29. See *Ibid.*

30. *Memorandum of the Warri National Union, 1949*, in file Papers Relating to the Warri Provincial Conference on Constitutional Reform, 1949-50, Warri Prof WP/569/1 (INA). For further details see *Annual Report for Warri Province, 1949*, Warri Prof WP/235/2 (INA).

31. *Memorandum of the Warri National Union, op.cit.*

32. *Papers Relating to the Warri Provincial Conference, op.cit.*

33. *Ibid.*

34. See *Memorandum of Western Ijaw Peoples*, in file Warri Prof WP/569/1, op.cit.

35. See *ibid.*, Memoranda 13-15.

36. See D. C. Rothchild, "Safeguarding Nigeria's Minorities", in *African Reprint Series*, (Pittsburgh: Duquesne University Press, 1964), p.37.

37. See, *Report on West Regional Conference on Constitutional Reform*, in file section, *Benin Provincial Conference on Constitutional Reform, 1949*, Ben Prof BP/2678/1, *op. cit.*

38. See Coleman, *Nigeria: Background to Nationalism, op.cit.*, p.472-73, n.4.

39. *Ibid.*

40. *Nigeria: Proceedings of the General Conference on Review of the Constitution, January, 1950*, (Lagos: Government Printer, 1950), p.244 (INA).

41. *Nigeria: Review of the Constitution — Regional Recommendations*, (Lagos: Government Printer, 1949), p.18 (INA).

42. See Rothchild, *op.cit.*, p.37.

43. *Despatch from the Secretary of State for the Colonies to the Governors of African Territories*, (London: H.M.S.O., 1947). In this document a comprehensive plan for the development of responsible government from the grass-roots upwards, was laid out.

44. Ben Prof BP/2678/1, *op.cit.*

CHAPTER 4

STRATEGIES FOR SURVIVAL

By early 1950, the Mid-West cause and its protagonists had been given their first exposure to the rigours of modern political competition. The point had been fully, even brutally driven home, that the future of the Mid-West issue, indeed its very survival, would depend largely on Mid-West protagonists alone and the efforts they could muster. Fully aware of the formidable task now facing them Omo-Osagie and his RBC colleagues set to work with a will and it was at the local level in Benin Division that they first concentrated their efforts. In a very real sense, the past deeds and misdeeds of Obaseki and his BTPA were to make the job of raising an effective RBC challenge surprisingly easy. All the old issues which had rankled during the 1947-50 period were now resurrected by the RBC and used with effect against Obaseki.

RBC TAKES THE OFFENSIVE

In the assault which they launched on the BTPA, Omo-Osagie and his colleagues gave prominent place to the *Iyase* dispute. Obaseki was vilified for his role in it. Many Bini, while conceding that the *Iyase* title should go to a man "who is in the prime of life",[1] were not prepared to overlook the methods he had employed; methods which had virtually amounted to his "usurping"[2] the post. Although powerless at that time many Bini had deeply resented Obaseki's "lordly and high-handed" behaviour.[3] As one BDC Councillor, put it:

> "Gaius seemed to feel that he was *Oba*; at least his reserved, autocratic behaviour seemed to suggest this. The people, of course, resented this. Only one man has the right, by our traditions, to conduct himself in this way, and that is the *Oba*! Obaseki was not the *Oba*! He was a commoner! The common

people viewed him as such; tradition runs deep in the Bini man. We sometimes thought he was trying to outdo his father! [the late Agho]".[4]

In accord with this interpretation of the *Iyase* dispute the *Oba* was now projected as the innocent victim of the affair; that he, the office of *Oba* and sacred Bini tradition had been subjected to an unforgivable assault by Obaseki. Using the *Iyase* issue as a springboard, Omo-Osagie broadened his attack on Obaseki and the BTPA. Obaseki, with the active support of his "*Ogboni* henchmen," was accused of causing disruption in the Division.

"The Hon. Gaius Obaseki is not the Local Government of Benin, or the Benin Native Authority, but an individual in the state. Notwithstanding this, the *Ogboni* have dominated the Native Administration of Benin in the interest of their secret *Ogboni* cult".[5]

Indeed, *Otu Edo* supporters went so far as to declare that the Benin Native Authority Police Force was being used by *Ogboni*s as the vehicle for pursuing a "ruthless policy to ensure the continuance of an *Ogboni*-dominated Native Administration".

In order to lend added impetus to combative rhetoric Omo-Osagie set into operation a plan for a "punitive expedition" against his BTPA opponents in Benin Division. This expedition was to take the form of a march on Benin City, by RBC/*Otu Edo* and anti-*Ogboni* elements. Fortunately, "in the interests of peace and the prevention of bloodshed",[6] details of the plan were leaked to the Colonial Authorities. The Resident at Benin City, despatched Native Authority and Nigerian Police units to each of the main gathering points; at Benin City, the detachment was strengthened and put in a state of readiness.[7] The fact that the element of surprise had been removed soon became known to Omo-Osagie. The march was called off.

By mid-1950, there were unmistakable signs that a political change in Benin was imminent. Clearly, Omo-Osagie's appeal to the common man had started to have its effects. It was now not just in Benin City that the ordinary citizen had come to regard Obaseki's government of the Division, as un-representative, high-handed, and *Ogboni*-dominated. Omo-Osagie's message had gained a positive response from elements as far afield as Ishan and Asaba divisions.[8] Nor was his appeal without attraction to Natural Rulers in the districts. As guardians of Edo culture, the allegations of Obaseki's *Ogboni*-orientation constituted a challenge they could hardly ignore.

Indeed as the prospects of an increased challenge to BTPA rule at Benin steadily grew, so too did prospects of a parallel growth in lawlessness approach ominous proportions. Although no future march was to be organised of the size and violent potential as that of the aborted March 1950 "punitive expedition", still, during the next year and a half, an increasing amount of small-scale violence was to characterise politics in Benin Division. In almost all these instances, the violence followed Omo-Osagie's "revenge attacks" against *Ogboni* administrators and politicians.[9]

As the *Otu Edo* campaign gained momentum during 1950 and early 1951, Omo-Osagie and his supporters brought increasing pressure to bear on the BTPA and the British Administration in the Division. No opportunity was lost to embarrass the Colonial Authorities and, where possible, to allege and imply collusion with the BTPA. It was clear that Omo-Osagie felt he now had the opportunity to get his own back on his two old antagonists—and furthermore that he could use these "revenge attacks" to advance *Otu Edo* interests at the same time.[10]

AN EMERGING ACTION GROUP PRESENCE

With the Local Government elections fast approaching, and with Omo-Osagie and his *Otu Edo* supporters retaining the momentum they had generated over the past year, the BTPA presence in Benin Division noticeably waned. Even Obaseki seemed to fear the force of the *Otu Edo* assault as he frequently failed to attend meetings of the Central Council, of which he remained Chairman. Although it was continually maintained by Omo-Osagie's supporters in the districts, that BTPA/*Ogboni* elements were still victimising *Otu Edo* men through the various organs of the BNA, it seemed that such efforts were having little effect on their intended victims.[11] Morale remained high in the *Otu Edo* camp.

Despite promising prospects in Benin Division, within the broader context of Mid-West politics certain serious obstacles were becoming apparent. Since mid-1948 there had been much restlessness amongst Mid-West leaders of greater and lesser prominence; these leaders, as earlier noted, were dissatisfied with and increasingly suspicious of the NCNC and its leader Azikiwe. In April 1951, this restlessness and dissent took concrete form when the majority of these dis-satisfied Mid-West leaders opted to join the newly-inaugurated Action Group party. The party itself was brought formally into existence at the historic Owo Conference of 28-30 April, 1951.[12]

The first serious indication in the Mid-West that the embryonic Action Group party was on the point of creation was revealed at a meeting of "invited leaders and public men"[3] from Benin and Delta Provinces. This meeting which was convened at Sapele on 21 April, 1951, under the Chairmanship of Anthony (later Chief) Enahoro, appeared to be an innocent enough gathering. Delegates from most of the Mid-West districts were in attendance; prominent amongst these were Obaseki, Prest, Okorodudu, Festus Sam Edah (later Chief Okotie-Eboh) and S.O. Ighodaro. The general topic for discussion was "the solidarity of the peoples of the Mid-West under the new constitution of 1951".

Close consideration was given by the Sapele Conference delegates to the position of the Mid-West as a minority area within the Yoruba-dominant West Region. Many delegates maintained that the sovereignty of the Yorubas could only result in discriminatory and repressive acts being initiated by any Yoruba-controlled government at Ibadan. In an editorial, the *Star* observed that the Sapele meeting was long overdue, and called on Mid-West leaders to act, just as leaders of other areas had acted, to claim what was rightfully theirs. The *Star* declared:

> "There is a general feeling amongst our people that their support in the past has been used by some of our brothers in other parts of the country to further their sectional interests, and when we notice how well other regions and zones have come out in the race for progress, we can't deny that there is some ground for this feeling.... If we fail to correct the situation in the circumstances arising from the new constitution, we shall have only ourselves to blame". [14]

These were fine and supportive sentiments. However, it did not take long for alarmed Mid-Westerners to recognise that the Sapele meeting had a rather more suspect intent. Two *Otu Edo*/NCNC leaders, E.O. Imafidon and Chike Ekwuyasi, who had been sent to the meeting by Omo-Osagie, were not long there before hurriedly returning to Benin City.[15] They informed the *Otu Edo* leader that the meeting was being attended by a large number of Mid-West "dissenters". In addition, they reported that after discussions, during which strong anti-Mid-West sentiments were expressed, the matter of invitations to and attendance at the forthcoming Owo Conference (the formal founding Conference of the Action Group) had been raised.

When only a week later, the Owo Conference was held, it soon became apparent that the suspicions of Omo-Osagie and his colleagues had not been misplaced. Of the many Mid-Westerners who had attended the Sapele Conference, six of these secured positions on the new party's 13-man National Executive Committee. Benin and Delta provinces were represented on the Action Group Executive by three members each: for Benin Province, Hon. Gaius Obaseki, Vice-President; S.O. Ighodaro, Treasurer; Tony Enahoro, Assistant Secretary; for Delta Province, Chiefs Arthur Prest and W.E. Mowarin, Vice-Presidents; and M.E.R. Okorodudu, Legal Adviser.[16]

This nucleus of prominent Mid-West leaders, put the Action Group in a position to threaten seriously the hitherto unchallenged political authority of the NCNC. Whether it could effect any major inroads into the Mid-West was, of course, another matter. It was, after all, a new party. Although its leaders had been busy over the past two years attempting to gain support and lay some kind of structural foundations for the party, there was little to indicate that it had achieved adequate success to create any effective opposition base. Still, the threat was there, and to this Omo-Osagie and his *Otu Edo*/NCNC colleagues were swift to respond.

Less than a week after the Sapele Conference, and before the Owo Conference had begun, the *Otu Edo*/NCNC sponsored a "Giant Rally" at Benin City. The "rally" which started on 24 April, lasted five days. It concluded on 29 April, the day that the Action Group Owo Conference was adjourned.[17] The Benin City rally was attended by crowds, said to have exceeded 50,000, and many prominent NCNC personalities were present. The NCNC National President Azikiwe was joined by Alhaji Adelabu and A.M.F. Agbaje from Ibadan, T.O.S. Benson from Lagos, together with many Eastern Region NCNC leaders.

Though Omo-Osagie escorted his guests around the principal towns of Benin Division only, he maintains that residents from all Divisions in the Mid-West travelled to attend. Azikiwe, Omo-Osagie and their entourage, it was said, met everywhere with an enthusiastic response.[18] It was Omo-Osagie's hope that this "giant 5-day rally" within his home Division would counteract any Action Group "infections" which might spread within the localities under his most immediate supervision.

VICTORY AND ITS AFTERMATH

Despite Otu Edo/NCNC initiatives in the period preceding the Local Government elections of 1951, Omo-Osagie and his colleagues remained anxious and uncertain. The eventual outcome of these elections, however, made clear that *Otu Edo* preparations had been more than adequate. The party won majorities in 18 of the 20 outlying District Councils; in Benin City it gained control in all twelve of the city's wards.[19] At the level of the BDC, therefore, Omo-Osagie and his *Otu Edo* had secured an overwhelming majority.

Post-Election "House-Cleaning"   What followed this *Otu Edo* victory in Benin Division was, perhaps, inevitable. It was now the turn of the BTPA to experience the bitter aftermath of defeat. Prior to these local elections, the *Otu Edo* had released a four page manifesto. The manifesto enumerated all the benefits which awaited electors if the party was voted into power. However, in another document issued at this time,[20] the *Otu Edo* indicated that once victory had been gained, it was its intention to remove *Ogboni* Government in Benin. It declared, "We shall not be satisfied with anything less than the total annihilation of *Ogboni* influence in Benin Politics".[21]

In the period following the elections the *Otu Edo* were true to their word. There was widespread violence within the Division. Jubilant *Otu Edo* supporters were believed to be the prime instigators of this lawlessness. Following a tour of the affected areas in Benin Division, the Resident confirmed acts of violence and lawlessness. He then reported that he had confronted *Otu Edo* leaders in Benin City and told them that "personally and morally", if not officially and legally, he held them responsible for lawlessness in the District.[22]

These admonishments, however, had little effect in damping the "enthusiasm" of the new *Otu Edo* "masters" of Benin Division. Indeed, by mid-August, 1951, when the Primary Tier Elections[23] to the Western House of Assembly were under way, *Otu Edo* stalwarts were alleged still to be exceedingly active in their "house-cleaning" exercises. On 27 August, 1951, the General Secretary of the BTPA reported to the Resident that at Usonigbe,

> "Over 35 houses were demolished and properties therein looted; the owners of these houses with their families were driven into the bush. Very many more of the non-*Otu Edos* are still in Usonigbe bush, ambushed by the *Otu Edos*".[24]

At Usen, a former local councillor on 1 September, 1951, petitioned against what he called "unlawful expulsion and brutality".[25] The petition appealed for immediate assistance to "rescue their life [*sic*] and their unfortunate fellows from the hands of *Otu Edo*... who for about a week have carried out riot of the first order". The *Otu Edo*, the petition maintained, were "destroying houses and commonly displaying [*sic*] arson". Another petition from Councillor Atitu, of Okha Village, alleged that he and his people had been suffering bitterly at the hands of the Otu Edo.[26] His unfortunate fellow villagers whom the *Otu Edo* had suspected to be *Ogboni*, had been "mercilessly beaten and rendered homeless".

The phased elections to the Western House of Assembly which now followed were conducted in an atmosphere fraught with tension and political violence. It further appeared that such conditions served to the advantage of the *Otu Edo*. After securing an overwhelming victory at the Primary Tier elections, and after further selections at the Intermediate Tier, Omo-Osagie delivered six *Otu Edo* candidates—himself among them—to occupy the seats allocated to Benin Division in the Western House.[27] Five of these six subsequently declared for the NCNC.[28] Of the remaining 18 seats allocated to Mid-Westerners, at the final Tier, 16 of these went ultimately to the NCNC. Only Chief Prest of Warri and Tony Enahoro of Ishan Division opted for the Action Group. This left the NCNC with 21 of the Mid-West's 24 seats in the Western House.

By the end of September, 1951, Mid-West protagonists had secured the two major objectives in their quest for "survival". In Benin Division, Omo-Osagie and his *Otu Edo* party had soundly thrashed Obaseki and his BTPA. Victory provided for Omo-Osagie, now the undisputed "political petrel" and new "Master of Benin," the vital platform from which to pursue with new authority and vigour the Mid-West cause.

The *Otu Edo* victory also served to restore the spiritual leader of the Mid-West Movement, the *Oba* of Benin. As Bradbury notes, the result of *Otu Edo* efforts to see that the *Oba* be restored to his rightful position, was that "many of those who had vilified him three years before, now gave him their unstinting praise".[29] Once in office, the *Otu Edo* took "immediate steps to restore the *Oba* 's dignity by raising his salary and re-affirming his prerogative of conferring titles".[30] Clearly, the *Oba* too was now in a much-improved position from which to undertake the vital leadership role which had been envisaged for him.

The results of the West Regional elections had been equally gratifying for Mid-West protagonists. It was now for the 21 new Mid-West NCNC members in the Western House to ensure that the NCNC Mother party carried out its promises. While the House of Assembly was not scheduled to hold its opening session until

January 1952, early counts by NCNC leaders during September and October 1951, following the Final Tier elections, produced confident predictions that Azikiwe and his colleagues would be entering office at Ibadan.[31] Thus, with what seemed a good prospect of the NCNC and Azikiwe securing control of the Government of the West, Mid-West protagonists were justified in looking forward to an early and favourable resolution of their demand for a separate Region.

Receding Mid-West Prospects   Sadly, for Mid-West supporters, this envisaged advantage was not to last long. Although in Benin Division, the hold of Omo-Osagie and his *Otu Edo* colleagues remained secure, at Ibadan evolving political events put the situation in a different light.

When the inaugural session of the House of Assembly was convened it became clear that it was not the NCNC, but rather Awolowo and his Action Group, who commanded the support of a majority of the 75 members. At the beginning of the sitting, on 7 January, 1952, 49 members had declared for the Action Group; by the end of the sitting this number had risen to 51.[32] The meaning of this development was obvious enough: the *NCNC, the party to which Mid-West members had given overwhelming support would not be in a position to implement the Mid-West mandate.* Any NCNC championing of the Mid-West cause would now have to be conducted from the Opposition benches.

Still, despite the recent anti-Yoruba campaign of Mid-West NCNC candidates at the 1951 Regional Elections, there was always the possibility—even though this now seemed an outside chance— that Awolowo might still be prepared to view the Mid-West issue as one of "principle" and hence "above politics"; that accordingly he would provide the necessary Governmental initiative to bring the Mid-West State into being. He was on record as being strongly in favour of a multi-state federation, even if specific support for particular minorities like the Mid-West was implied rather than stated. Furthermore, if Awolowo did implement such an undertaking, while this would probably mean that his party would lose much of the unsecured and largely *anti*-Mid-West support it had to this point gained, still it could serve to bring the majority of Mid-West voters over to the Action Group. As the party had aspirations of developing a national rather than simply a regional body of electoral support, such backing might in future prove valuable.

For most Mid-Westerners, however, any prospect of such a venture being undertaken by Awolowo, either in the immediate or distant future, was soon obliterated. This was the result of a most impolitic and—from the vantage point of future Action Group prospects in the Mid-West area—most unfortunate statement by the old *Alake* of Abeokuta at the opening ceremonies of the new House of Assembly. Following the Speech from the Throne by Sir Hugo Marshall, Lieutenant-Governor of the West Region, the *Alake* rose to speak. A great hush fell over the gallery and the crowded lawns and grounds outside the Assembly building. In measured tones and with dignified flourish, the *Alake* commenced his fateful address: "On my right sits the *Oni* of Ife.... On my left, the Leader of our Government, Obafemi Awolowo.... The voice of the West is complete"![33]

So far as Mid-West NCNC legislators were concerned, and in particular their many supporters who had arrived from their various localities to be present at this historic occasion, nothing more needed to be said. The *Alake* had said it all. He had, in essence, confirmed their fears and deep-seated suspicions of a West Regional Government under the control of "alien Yorubas".

As Chief Oweh, one of the (Urhobo) Mid-West legislators in attendance at these opening ceremonies put it, "if before it had not been made sufficiently clear, the evidence was now before us. There was no place for the Mid-West minority peoples within a Yoruba-dominated West".[34] Indeed, at this early juncture in West/Mid-West relations, it could be said that Mid-West protagonists, had now stepped into the settled context of what was to become a relationship of hostility and mistrust; a relationship which was gradually and then more sharply to increase as the 1950's progressed.

However, while Mid-West protagonists had been disappointed in their expectations at the Regional level, nevertheless within the Mid-West heartland, their newly-won position of prominence was secure. A promising base was therefore available from which to pursue Movement organisational initiatives. Rather curiously, however, no such serious initiatives were forthcoming from the pro-Mid-West camp. Omo-Osagie and his colleagues appeared content to wait on events. Indeed, for most of the next year and a half (January 1952-August 1953), the Mid West issue, to a very considerable extent, faded from public and official view.

NCNC as the Party Medium   Any formal efforts made to advance the Mid-West issue during this period were extended through sporadic statements of support by Mid-West NCNC MLA's in the House of Assembly, and through the medium of two rather *ad hoc* bodies—each strongly NCNC—whose members were drawn largely from the ranks of Mid-West members at the Provincial Conference and House of Assembly levels. While neither of these two bodies, the *Central State Congress* and the *Committee of the Mid-West Organisation*, did anything of note to enhance the existing level of Mid-West popular support, still each did make a useful contribution—the *Congress* in further evolving the Movement ideology; the *Committee* in providing a timely warning of "conservative restraints within".

The Central State Congress was formed following consultations amongst Mid-West political leaders and Natural Rulers attending the annual *Benin Provincial Conference* held at Ogwashi-Uku, on 23 June, 1952. At the Provincial Conference, the new Congress leaders, under the approving eye of their *de facto* chairman, the *Oba* of Benin, voiced their support for Mid-West goals, together with a more modified concern over alleged discriminatory practices on the part of the Action Group.[35]

J.O. Odigie, an Ishan NCNC MLA, contended that Benin and Delta provinces were being discriminated against in the House of Assembly. The population of Benin Province, he pointed out, was approximately 624,000, while the figure for Ijebu Province was 383,000. Yet the expenditure by the Western Regional Government was £225,000 for Ijebu Province as against £169,000 for Benin. Benin, therefore, was receiving about £55,000 less in government expenditure than Ijebu, a province with only slightly greater than half the population of Benin. In addition, Odigie further indicated that of the nine Ministers at Regional level, only one was from Benin Province. This minister was the Bini lawyer, S.O. Ighodaro. Odigie was supported in his statements by Chike Ekwuyasi. Ekwuyasi stressed that there was a danger that the Yoruba bloc in the Western House of Assembly would discriminate against their area.

The Western Ibo MLA, and future leader of the Mid-West State Movement, Dennis Osadebay, then told some personal stories of the ethnic discrimination he had suffered while at Ibadan. Osadebay ended his speech by demanding a mandate from the Conference to agitate for the creation of a Central, or Mid-West State. He gained near unanimous support. The one dissenter was J.

W. (later Chief) Amu, the representative for Kukuruku (Afenmai) Native Authority. Amu emphasised that Benin Division *itself* should become "peaceful and united" *before* any demand was made for a Central State. His comments were met with derision by other Conference delegates.

After discussion was concluded, the delegates agreed to a resolution which held that:

> "In view of the general clamour and desire of the people of the Benin and Warri Provinces; in view of the fact that the creation of a Central State would not in any way prejudice the working of the new Constitution; in view of the fact that one Region outnumbers all other Regions; in view of the fact that the Revenue of a Central State would be sufficient to pay its own Lieutenant–Governor and maintain its government;

> "It is hereby resolved by this Provincial Conference now in session: To demand a Central State and to request that all Representatives of Benin Province in the House of Assembly, as well as the House of Chiefs, go with the Resolution as a mandate to demand the creation of a Central State, and that all delegates to the Conference return to educate their people to demand a Central State".[36]

There was little evidence in the course of the next year to suggest that Congress members had, in fact, returned to their respective districts "to educate their people to demand a Central State". However, a number of Mid-West NCNC MLA's did at least take up the Congress' charge to promote the Mid-West cause in the House of Assembly. During this period, NCNC members from all divisions in the Mid-West provinces advanced the arguments which were to become the standard assertions of Mid-West protagonists in the years to come.

In February 1953, the second *ad hoc* body designed to promote the Mid-West cause, the *Committee of the Mid-West Organisation*, was brought into existence.[37] The Committee was a rather curious creation. Its avowed aim was to serve as a form of "underground organisation" comprising leading Mid-West MLA's at Ibadan. They were charged with promoting the objectives of the Central State Congress, and ensuring that Mid-West demands were effectively advanced to the Awolowo Government. The Committee, under its *pro-tem* Organising Secretary, the Bini NCNC Member, R.O.A. Odita, was also charged with the task of moderating the rather random assaults being launched by Mid-West (NCNC) protagonists. The Committee put emphasis on "working towards the possible rather than the ideal". Demands for better representation, or as a last resort for a separate legislature, were —as the Committee saw it—within more realistic reach than a separate state. The Committee cautioned Mid-West legislators to exercise "care and common sense in advancing Mid-West demands".

The Mid-West Cause: Neglect and Betrayal

By mid-1953, the Mid-West cause was seriously ailing. The Movement needed an organisation with "teeth", one which would provide a solid platform from which to extend an appeal of which the Action Group Government would be compelled to take note. However, no such organisation had emerged. Only the *Central State Congress* and the *Committee of the Mid-West Organisation* had been inaugurated; and it was clear that neither was capable of doing much more than keeping the idea of the Mid-West alive in the political forums of the West. Much more was required. Yet Mid-West leaders, since their triumphs of 1951, had shown themselves to be consistently reluctant to tackle the essential tasks.

At the same time, since the completion of the inaugural West Regional elections in September 1951, it had become clear that neither the Action Group nor the Mid-West's NCNC "champion" was prepared to put its "New States" policy into practice. Just as at the Regional and General Conferences on the Constitution in 1950, so during this 1951-53 period the NCNC and the Action Group had shown themselves to be evasive and non-committal. Indeed, it was becoming increasingly clear that the Action Group now regarded support of *anti*-Mid-West sentiment within the Mid-West provinces, as its best line of action.

In the midst of these most unsettling developments, Mid-West protagonists were afforded yet another opportunity for securing a favorable resolution of their demands, without having to resort to more rigorous and militant measures. In July and August 1953 a Conference to discuss changes to the 1951 Constitution was to be held in London. Each of Nigeria's main political parties was to be represented by a separate delegation. This London Conference would provide the NCNC "champions" of the Mid-West with the opportunity to make up for the party's "oversights" at the last round of constitutional negotiations in 1950. Indeed, as the Conference was to give much of its attention to matters relating to proposed alterations in governmental structure, Mid-West leaders stressed that "every effort must be made to ensure that a Federation comprising *at least eight states*, be substituted for the existing three

Region structure".[38]

The London Conference, however, duly showed that the major parties had distanced themselves even further from the minorities issues. Both the Action Group and the NCNC demonstrated in the course of the Conference's proceedings, that their greatest concern was in securing maximum power for the *Regional governments* which each controlled. No serious consideration was given to the Mid-West or minorities issues. Only the National Independence Party which represented East Regional (COR) minority interests, dissented from the Conference's decision to vest residual powers in the Regional Governments.[39]

The Mid West's NCNC "champion" was conspicuous by its silence. As for the Action Group; its performance at the Conference made clear that Awolowo and his colleagues were more than ever concerned to secure the territorial interests of the West within the grip of the Government they controlled at Ibadan. The Action Group leader was, to say the least, displeased over the Conference's decision to excise Lagos from his sovereign domain.[40] He made it clear that *the West would tolerate no further territorial encroachments.*

From this point in mid-August, following completion of the *1953 London Conference*, events moved swiftly for Mid-Westerners. Chief Omo-Osagie, on his return from the London Conference, brought a first hand report of its proceedings to the *Oba* of Benin. He gave vent to his frustration and bitter disappointment. It had indeed been true, as the NCNC leader Dr. Azikiwe was later to observe, that the *1953 London Conference* "marked the first time in our history when Nigerian political parties acting through their leaders, decided on the type of constitution under which Nigeria should be ruled".[41] But, as Omo-Osagie now outlined in some detail, this "historic break-through" in the participation of Nigerian leaders provided no solace for the Mid-West minority.

Each of the major substantive decisions of the Conference had served only as further proof of the relentless shift in the direction of entrenched and militant regionalism. It had been agreed that the Federal Authority should be vested with limited and specific powers; but residual powers, which were now alarmingly enhanced—so far as Mid-westerners were concerned—were to rest with the respective Regional Authorities. Furthermore, Omo-Osagie and his Mid-West colleagues—with the notable exception of Festus Sam Edah, (later Chief Okotie-Eboh) whose silence on the matter was conspicuous—felt a good deal of uneasiness over the

Conference decision to grant "full internal self-government" as early as 1956, to "those Regions desiring it". Still, the provision which allowed for the convening of another Conference for the purpose of reviewing the progress of the 1953-54 agreements provided some re-assurance.[42]

During the third week of August an Executive meeting of the *Central State Congress* was called. Omo-Osagie once again expressed his disappointment over the Conference outcome. It was, he declared, quite evident what the Action Group and NCNC party leaders had in mind: their own "security and welfare". Mid-Westerners, therefore, would have to start seriously to organise in order to advance their own interests.[43] A proposal, calling for an "Inter-Provincial Conference to decide what form the struggle for the new Mid-West State should take"[44] was duly agreed, and 18 September, 1953, set as the date it should be convened.

—————————————

References

1. *Resident's Address to the Benin Divisional Council. 19 April, 1948*, in file BNA 730/2, p.46, (BCA).

2. *Edo National Union Memorandum. 20 May, 1948*, in ibid., p. 86.

3. *Ibid.*

4. Interview with E.O. Imafidon, Int.II, p.33.

5. Quoted from correspondence in file of *Papers Relating to Activities of the Otu Edo Union,. 1951-54*, p.5), Ben Prof BP/1170/2 (INA).

6. Interview with Chief H.O. Emokpae, Int.VI, p.42.

7. See Interview with Mr. H.L.M. Butcher, at this time Acting-Resident, Benin City. (Interview and correspondence with writer, June 1972).

8. See *Papers Relating to Activities of Otu Edo...*, *op cit.*, p.15.

9. *Ibid.*, p.22

10. Ibid.

11. See J.A. Brand, "The Mid-West State Movement in Nigerian Politics", *Political Studies*, Vol.XIII, No.3 (1965), p.351.

12. See Sklar, *Nigerian Political Parties*, *op.cit.*, p.106.

13. *Nigerian Star*, 17 April, 1951.

14. *Ibid.*

15. See Interview with Chief Omo-Osagie, Int.I, p.21.

16. See Sklar, *op.cit.*, p.106; also p.104, where Sklar refers to the Sapele Conference as being "the first meeting of the Mid-West Zone of the Action Group".

17. See *Nigerian Defender*, 30 April, 1951.

18. See Omo-Osagie, Int.I, p.28-29.

19. See *Report of Local Government Elections*, in file BNA 730/2, Appendix III (BCA).

20. See *Otu Edo / Benin Action Group Alliance Bulletin No. 3. 18 June, 1951*, in file BP/1170/2.

21. *Ibid.*

22. See *Report of the Resident, Benin, to the Secretary, Western Provinces*, in file BP/1170/3 (INA).

23. See *Papers on Phased Elections Leading to the Western House of Assembly, 1951-55*, in file BP/2678/11 (INA).

24. Correspondence in file BP/1170/2.

25. *Usen Petition to the Resident, Benin*, in file BP/1170/3.

26. *Okha Village Petition to the Resident, Benin, ibid.*

27. See *Papers on Phased Elections...*, *op. cit.*

28. The sixth, S.O. Ighodaro, declared for the Action Group after his selection at the final tier elections.

29. Bradbury, "Continuities and Dis-continuities ...", *op.cit*, p.68.

30. *Ibid.*

31. See Sklar, *op.cit.*, pp.115-16.

32. *Ibid.*, n.64

33. *Western House of Assembly Debates*, 7 January, 1952.

34. Interview with Chief Oweh, Int.VI, p.24.

35. See *Report of the Benin Provincial Conference. 1952*, in file BP/2328/1 (INA).

36. *Ibid.*

37. *Nigerian Defender*, 12 February, 1953.

38. *Nigerian Defender*, 26 May, 1953.

39. See *Report of the Conference on the Nigerian Constitution, held in London, July-August. 1953*, Cmnd.8934, (London: H.M.S.O., 1953), p.4.

40. See, Obafemi Awolowo, *Awo: The Autobiography of Chief Obafemi Awolowo*, (Cambridge: University Press, 1960), p.247.

41. *West Africa,* 7 July, 1956, p.47.

42. A full account of the decisions reached as a result of the London and Lagos meetings is given in the *Report by the Resumed Conference on the Nigerian Constitution held in Lagos, January-February, 1954,* Cmnd. 9059, (London: H.M.S.O., 1954).

43. See, *Pilot,* 23 August, 1953.

44. *Ibid.*

CHAPTER 5

BDPP—A PAN-MID-WEST PARTY

THE OBA'S INTER-PROVINCIAL CONFERENCE: BIRTH OF THE BDPP

Invitations to the 18 September Benin City Inter-Provincial Conference were issued by the *Oba* to all leading Natural Rulers and political personalities in the Mid-West provinces. There was, as a result, a large attendance. Many Natural Rulers, with the notable exception of the *Olu* of Warri, rallied to the *Oba*'s call; all Mid-West legislators—once again with the exception of the Action Groupers, Prest, Enahoro and Ighodaro—were present, together with a number of councillors from the Mid-West local authorities. The Conference, it seemed, had all the makings of a "Mid-West family reunion".

In his opening address, the *Oba* said he knew that all the people in the Mid-West would like the idea of Benin-Delta State because all

> " ...want to get freedom, not only from the white man, but from foreign African Nations. ...I hope everyone will pull his weight in this National Struggle, [because] at this critical time when all the Nations of this country called Nigeria are fighting hard to assert their National status, it will be unwise for Benin-Delta to do nothing about asserting its own".1

The *Oba* described as "nonsense" the argument that the provinces were small and weak, and noted that this was the kind of argument used by "those who do not want to be dominated, but are fighting to dominate and overshadow others". He contended that:

> "The unity of Old Nigeria can only be maintained by the type of regionalisation it [the London Conference] has recommended. [Furthermore] Benin-Delta was a sovereign Nation before the occupation of the country by the British; that is why Britain cannot annex it to the Yoruba State".2

In concluding his address, the *Oba* maintained that past events had shown beyond any doubt, that a political party to represent solely Mid-West interests was now essential.

After applause for the *Oba* had died down, a number of Mid West Natural Rulers and politicians rose to add their support. The central issues, together with a number of peripheral ones relating to Mid-West demands, were voiced. The humiliation felt by Mid-Westerners at the opening session of the Western House of Assembly was recounted; the attempt by the Regional Government to gain control over Mid-West forestry resources; the selection of Adegoke Adelabu to replace Dr. Azikiwe as leader of the Opposition in the Western House of Assembly, instead of Dennis Osadebay; each along with many more issues were brought to the attention of the Conference. Chief Omo-Osagie, the dominant political personality during the early and later stages of the Conference, reminded delegates that "no one is going to hand us autonomy on a silver platter, if we want it, we are going to have to fight for it! We must have a party which will serve as the vanguard in our battle for the Mid-West!" [3]

Mid-West Party, or Movement?   With these opening formalities completed, the Conference now proceeded with the serious business. The *Oba* as Chairman of the Conference and leading Patron of the cause, withdrew from the meeting at this point. Omo-Osagie, taking over as *pro-tem* Chairman, observed that delegates had expressed unanimous approval of the *Oba*'s call for Mid-West autonomy. The question was about the *form* the struggle should take.

This discussion revolved around a single point: the title and function of the proposed pressure group-party. Omo-Osagie, backed by his Bini colleagues and most of the Edo-speaking delegates—including most noticeably, the fiery *Enogie* of Ewohimi—maintained that the *Oba*'s suggestion should be followed up; a Mid-West party, which would elevate the Mid-West autonomy issue "above politics" and which would recruit "without prejudice and without prejudicing" supporters already committed to either the NCNC or the Action Group, should be formed.[4]

Omo-Osagie then provided a brief *resume* of the treatment meted out to Mid-Westerners at the hands of both the Action Group and NCNC. If Mid-Westerners were to ensure the attainment of their objectives, they must provide a forceful initiative. A *political party* which would perform this function was the logical answer. Omo-Osagie called for the creation of a Mid-West political party, to be named the Benin-Delta Peoples' Party (BDPP).[5]

To others, however, this logic was not so clear. The leading delegate from Western Iboland, Chief J.I.G. Onyia, stated that he could see no reason why a political party to represent exclusive Mid-West interests should be formed; it could serve no useful purpose.[6] There were already two established political parties claiming the allegiance of political partisans in the Mid-West. Surely then it would be best to form a *political movement*—rather than a political party—*which could apply pressure both within and on these parties as required*. To form a political party which would inevitably be viewed as a challenge or threat to the existing parties, would, argued Onyia, be "folly in the extreme". What was needed was a *non-party* organisation. Chief Onyia called for the creation of a "Mid-West, or Central State Movement". There was a ripple of support for Onyia's proposal. However, a vote of Conference delegates showed that the overwhelming majority supported the creation of the BDPP. A list of Honorary Members or Patrons was then agreed. In the week following the Conference a second list of Executive Committee members was released.[7]

The BDPP was now formally in existence. Chief Onyia's objections, however, showed the fundamental reservations of Western Ibos, together with others not affiliated with the Bini Mid-West protagonist group. The Conference had served merely to enhance non-Bini uneasiness about prospects for all Mid-West ethnic elements under the guidance of the *Oba* and his Bini adherents. It took very little to awaken suspicions which, in any case, were only partially dormant.

The Organisational Plan   Undaunted, Omo-Osagie, together with the BDPP Secretary-General, G.E. Odiase, now pressed on with the tasks of party organisation. Basically, the organisational plan of the BDPP was simple. The Party was formally committed to its impartial and bi-partisan stance. This commitment alone, however, still might not be adequate to ensure that BDPP organisers would be able to gain entry to the localities. The NCNC was by no means fully supportive in its attitude towards the BDPP; thus, it could be expected that there might be local resistance to the visits of BDPP teams in districts where NCNC loyalties remained strong. Similarly, there might be even greater resistance to BDPP organisers in Action Group strongholds. Thus, in order to ensure relatively open access to all Mid-West districts, the BDPP organisers hit on a simple plan.[8]

The *Oba* of Benin would undertake a series of tours of the Mid-West districts for the informal and public purpose of calling on his fellow Chiefs and Natural Rulers. Indeed, just to ensure that everything might be seen to conform with this plan, the *Oba* would *only* visit particular districts at the formal *request* of the local Natural Ruler. Such invitations could be—and were—easily arranged. Organisers travelling with the *Oba*, in concert with local political

---

TABLE I

BENIN/DELTA PEOPLES' PARTY: LIST OF OFFICERS

I PATRONS
President-General: the *Oba* of Benin
First Vice-President: the *Ogirrua* of Irrua
Second Vice-President: Chief Emeni of Obiaruku
Third Vice-President: the *Ovie* of Ughelli
Fourth Vice-President: Chief Momodu of Agbede
Fifth Vice-President: the *Ovie* of Effurun
Sixth Vice-President: the *Ogenieni* of Uzairue

II EXECUTIVE COMMITTEE MEMBERS
Secretary-General: G. E. (later Chief) Odiase
Administrative Secretary: T. O. Elaiho and
the Hon. Chief G. Brass Ometan
Benin Province Organising Secretary: Chief J.W. Amu
Delta Province Organising Secretary: Rev. J. D. Ifode
Publicity Secretary: Jackson Igben
Joint Auditors: Martins Adebayo and John Uzo
Political Adviser: H.O. Uwaifo
Legal Adviser: Barrister G. E. Longe

—————————————————————————————

* *Source:* See File Ben Prof 2/BP/3022 (INA)

Note: It is interesting to note the *absence of Omo-Osagie* from this list of BDPP executive members. Although he was to exercise dominant control over the party, he never assumed a formal executive office. Also no Western Ibo is named in this list; nor later was any Western Ibo to assume an Executive Committee office.

leaders who in most instances had been deputised previously, would get on with the business of explaining the Mid-West cause, recruiting members and, hopefully, securing financial commitments. In this way, moving from district to district throughout the provinces of the Mid-West, Omo-Osagie and his BDPP stalwarts hoped to generate a powerful ground-swell of support emanating from the very roots of the Mid-West localities.

Action Group Anxieties   Alert to these developments, Action Group leaders in Benin began to feel increasingly anxious. In letters to the Action Group Secretariat at Ibadan and the British Resident, Benin City, they expressed their fears and called for action to curb what they contended was a growing "crisis" in Benin Division. Chief H.I. Osula, in a letter to the Resident, Benin, maintained that a crisis like that of 1951, "is now in the offing, and it is the duty of every law-abiding person to call the attention of Government to it, before it assumes an uncontrollable magnitude".[9] At the centre of events, serving to foment this crisis, was, it was asserted, the *Oba* himself.

If, in fact, the British and Action Group authorities did attempt to bring pressure on the *Oba*, it apparently had little effect. For the *Oba*, seemingly warming to his "impartial activist" role, now brought the BDPP cause to the attention of his fellow Natural Rulers in the Western House of Chiefs. The *Oba* declared:

> "It is a pleasure for me to inform this House of the formation of a new political party called the Benin/Delta Peoples' Party. Like the *Oni*'s Action Group, the BDPP is out to fight by all constitutional means for the solidarity and establishment of the Benin/Delta State".[10]

Proceeding in the face of a flurry of objections on "points of order," the *Oba* continued determinedly.

> "The Benin/Delta Peoples Party will declare the national status of the Benin/Delta State in a federal or unitary Nigeria, and in this respect it believes that all peoples of goodwill everywhere will give it their full support. I think that the Benin/Delta State can succeed very well without being tied to the apron strings of the Yoruba state".

The *Oba* went on to remind the House that what the BDPP was seeking, a Benin/Delta State, had already received the committed support of nationalist politicians. Concluding his statement with a show of tactful finesse the *Oba* shifted the focus of attention from himself and the BDPP. "The decision of Her Majesty's Government," he declared, "to free the Benin/Delta State from this unfortunate bondage before they surrender the reins of government will be regarded, like the decision to separate Lagos from the Western Region, as a very wise one".

The time for talking, for the moment, had now passed. The *Oba* and his entourage, under the direction of Omo-Osagie and Odiase, were now ready to undertake their sortie into the districts of Benin Province. If all turned out as Omo-Osagie believed, the mandate which the *Oba*'s antagonists in the House of Chiefs had contended was non-existent, would soon be proved.

The Oba's Tours and Political Recruitment

Triumph for Tradition   The *Oba*'s first tour into the outlying districts of Benin Province was a whirlwind affair. In the course of three days and two nights away from his Palace at Benin City (11-13 December), the *Oba* covered well over 300 miles. In company with Chiefs Omo-Osagie, Odiase and a substantial BDPP entourage, together with Palace retainers, the *Oba* managed to visit his fellow Natural Rulers and address meetings at Irrua in Ishan Division; Agbede and Jattu, in Afenmai Division; and Afuse and Sabongidda-Ore, in the old Ivbiosakon (now Owan) Division. He even ventured into Owo Province in Yorubaland in response to a request to meet the people of Ifon. His first circuit tour complete, the *Oba* returned to Benin City.

In general, the BDPP leadership was well pleased with the tour outcome. The strategy employed by the party organisers had counted on the *Oba* attracting big crowds in the localities. This goal had been fully realised. As Omo-Osagie put it: "When the *Oba* moves around, the whole country moves with him".[11] Certainly, there could no longer be any serious doubt: the *Oba* of Benin *retained a continuing and very sizeable measure of influence and respect—at least in the main centres of the districts he had visited in Benin Province.* The first step in the BDPP plan, that of *penetrating* the districts had, therefore, been accomplished. The BDPP organisers also were satisfied that the *approach* to the districts had proved successful. In accord with their hopes, the local Natural Rulers had provided the most favourable conditions under which to convene the "meet the people" assemblies.

In his second tour, the *Oba* moved into the districts of Delta Province. He and his BDPP entourage held meetings at Sapele, Orerokpe, Ughelli, Oleh and Ozoro.[12] Odiase and the BDPP leadership were again pleased with the turnout of area residents which these meetings had attracted. Still, Oweh reminded Omo-Osagie and Odiase that while they might enjoy the support of "whole villages"—as Odiase was fond of contending—there was a big difference between support "in principle" and commitment "in practice". While the Party might realistically expect to gain a good measure of support in Urhobo Division, and from the Urhobo and minority migrant areas of Warri Division, Oweh warned that Warri Township—which along with Western Ijaw Division had not been visited by the *Oba* and his entourage—must be watched carefully. This area could serve as the nucleus of Action Group infiltration efforts into neighbouring divisions.[13]

' In February 1954, the *Oba* and his BDPP entourage set out on their third "meet-the-people" tour, this time to Aboh Division. In the course of three days, well attended meetings were held at Obiaruku, Amai, Kwale and Ashaka. Finally, in May, the *Oba* completed his first series of visits with a tour of Asaba Division. In keeping with party policy, the *Oba* and his entourage avoided areas where known support for the Mid-West cause was not already established. As a consequence a "giant rally" was held at Agbor, followed by a swift non-stop tour of villages in the immediate area of Agbor. It was not thought that "any useful purpose" would be served by moving on towards Ogwashi-Uku and Asaba Town on the River Niger. In fact, no invitations had been extended by the Natural Rulers in these areas. Accordingly, the entourage circled north through Ekpon and Ewohimi in Ishan Division where brief meetings were held; then after another brief stopover at Igueben in Benin Division, it returned to Benin City.[14]

Political and Ethnic Reservations   While these four tours, comprising the first round of "meet-the-people" visits by the *Oba* and his entourage were officially considered a success by Omo-Osagie and his BDPP leadership, it was obvious that this "success" was qualified. True, the first tour into the Northern Edo districts had generated an impressive popular response. But what of the other three tours?

The party's venture into the Delta Province had resulted in impressive turnouts for the *Oba*'s meetings. T.O. Elaiho, Odiase's assistant at Benin, confirmed that these meetings had resulted in approximately the same number of membership enrolment applications (500) as had been received following the Northern tour. Omo-Osagie expressed confidence that the inter-ethnic hostilities which had broken out between Urhobo and Itsekiri elements during 1952, would ensure that the "Urhobo people would continue to give strong support to the Mid-West issue and the *Oba*".[15] However, one could not help wondering whether the Urhobo people too, like Western Ibos, might not also develop a more guarded stance in relation to Mid-West objectives as espoused by Omo-Osagie and his Bini vanguard.

The Delta spokesman in the BDPP nuclear leadership, Chief Oweh, was quite ready to accept that there was extensive support in Urhoboland arising—as in the Northern Edo districts—from the Natural Rulers of the area. "Natural Rulers", Oweh stressed, "consider it a privilege to sit and talk with the *Oba*. Also [in accord with the demands of tradition] they are obliged to follow his lead".[16] Indeed, Chief Oweh reminded his colleagues of the obvious: "For many of the Mid-West's Natural Rulers, these visits of the *Oba* have become the high spot in their lives. The *Oba*'s visits have done much to boost morale and prestige of Natural Rulers in the eyes of their people". *Oweh, however, warned his colleagues not to equate the support of Natural Rulers with popular support for the Mid-West cause.*

The tour to Aboh Division also appeared to generate a reassuring response. But it was difficult to understand how Omo-Osagie could claim of the tour into Asaba Division, that "there were no problems there".[17] Clearly, the BDPP was encountering little other than serious problems in Western Iboland. It has been indicated in earlier sections that most Western Ibos distrusted Binis, and Omo-Osagie in particular. This basic situation had not altered. Indeed, there now were indications that Bini/Western Ibo relations were further deteriorating.

As Chief Odiase notes, "the Action Group had been busy. They seemed to be making some headway in convincing Western Ibos of the advantages of supporting rather than opposing the [West Region Action Group] government".[18] The Action Group also, he maintains, had managed to heighten Western Ibo anxieties over the future they might anticipate under any future "Bini dominant" Mid-West state. Indeed, in examining more closely the wavering position of the Western Ibo community in the next section of this chapter, it will be shown how their central concerns appeared to focus on other matters bearing little or no relation to the BDPP. To most Western Ibos, the BDPP was, as Chief Onyia put it, "an underground party"—though "paper party" might in this instance, have been more appropriate.[19]

This rather gloomy prognosis was further strengthened by developments in other quarters. The Conference (Resumed) on the Nigerian Constitution convened at Lagos in January 1954 had given no consideration to the issue of new states. The party delegates had quietly gone about the business of securing the constitutional bases of authority for their respective Regional governments.[20] It had been anticipated that the Conference might provide the scene for yet another vitriolic outburst from Chief Awolowo. As leader of the Action Group he had, in the preceding months, expressed outrage at the decision of the London Conference (1953) to separate Lagos from the West. In the event, however, the Action Group delegation was notably subdued and co-operative.

Still, co-operative or not, it was well known to Mid-West leaders that the Lagos issue had served to destroy any practical prospect of the Action Group conceding to Mid-West autonomy demands. The party was still very bitter over the loss of Lagos, which it regarded as a "71 per cent Yoruba" area; secession of the West from the Federation, it seemed, was still not out of the question. In the contest for national political control, therefore, it seemed likely that the Action Group would take all steps necessary to secure its existing territorial authority—and this would *include* the Mid-West.

A Second Triumph for Tradition   Despite increasing indications of renewed Action Group interest in the Mid-West districts—and Benin Division in particular[21]—the *Oba* and his BDPP entourage set out on May 13 for a second three-day tour of the Northern Edo districts. The tour followed a familiar pattern. The *Oba* received enthusiastic welcomes from the Natural Rulers and local peoples. The tour moved first into the districts of Etsako Division. Passing by Auchi, the *Oba* held meetings at Jattu where he and the entire entourage were feted by the *Ogieneni* of Uzairue, an enthusiastic supporter of the Mid-West idea, and an arch-rival of his neighbour, the *Otaru* of Auchi. After subsequent meetings at South Ibie and Fugar, home of the stalwart BDPP organiser, E.A. Lamai, the tour moved on into Akoko-Edo, where the *Oba* again was enthusiastically received by the local rulers at Igarra and Okpe, both areas where Action Group influence under the leadership of Olatunji Oye, was known to be strong. Finally, during the last leg of the tour through Ivbiosakon (now Owan) Division, meetings were held at the small towns of Otwa, Sebe, and Worrake, then at Afuse and finally a second visit was made to Sabongidda-Ora.[22]

There was little doubt that the popularity of the Mid-West cause had been enhanced considerably as a result of the *Oba*'s visits. The *Oba* had been well-received in the opposition areas of Etsako and Akoko-Edo in particular. Not in all instances, however, had the *Oba* been successful in penetrating opposition districts. The *Olotu* of Ososo and the *Olokpe* of Okpe stubbornly resisted the efforts of Odiase and local NCNC leaders to have a visit arranged. Indeed, the *Oba* of Benin urged the *Olokpe* to visit him in Benin City, where the *Oba* himself could explain the reasons for a visit to the *Olokpe*'s district. In due course the *Olokpe* came to Benin City and had talks with the *Oba*, but the latter then failed to reciprocate the visit while harassment of the leading BDPP sympathiser in the area, Martins Adebayo, continued.[23]

G.E. Ogedengbe of Afuse put the general BDPP predicament as well as any, when he commented that "most leaders and people in Ivbiosakon, preferred to back the Mid-West cause, behind the banner of the NCNC"[24]—*not* behind Omo-Osagie and his "Bini-dominated" BDPP. Ogedengbe stated that while he and most Northern Edos revered and respected the *Oba*, the same sentiments did not extend to Omo-Osagie, whom he regarded as a powerful and very dangerous man.

Recruitment and the Appeal of Tradition   By the end of these tours there were many hopeful signs to be noted by Omo-Osagie and his colleagues. The strategy they had agreed upon had proven most effective. The invitations which now flooded into the Benin Secretariat made it abundantly evident that the Mid-West districts, whether or not these were NCNC-orientated, were eager to have the *Oba* visit their respective areas.

Similarly, the BDPP organisers had made progress in establishing local branches. Though the initial enrolment applications for membership represented only a fraction of the total numbers attending the respective tour meetings—indeed card-carrying membership never exceeded 28,000[25]—still Odiase and his Secretariat staff were not unduly concerned. To those doubters, who suggested that the relatively small numbers of membership enrolment forms completed indicated that district residents had turned out primarily to catch a glimpse of the *Oba*, Odiase maintained simply that the party had only made a start; it would grow.

While there was, perhaps, good reason for retaining optimism in relation to the party's prospects at this stage, there were other difficult facts to be faced. First, the BDPP Constitution required that the *Oba* and all Natural Rulers retain a totally "impartial" political position. Furthermore, *no Natural Ruler*—the *Oba* included—*was to hold an active (as against honorary) executive post*. It was, however, already apparent that the *Oba*, for one, was by no means restricting himself to an honorary post. Though at this point, it was possible partially to disguise his active participation in BDPP decision-making, there was no way that his frequent statements could be interpreted as anything other than partial. Thus, it seemed that the *Oba* either was compromising the party's neutrality—and that of his fellow Natural Rulers—from the very outset, or perhaps that the party had no real intent of fulfilling its policy commitment in this regard. In either case, such a course was fraught with danger.

The second, and perhaps more disturbing point was that the BDPP connection with the NCNC was an open secret. The party was dependent on NCNC organisational resources in the districts, to say nothing of the alleged financial support which the NCNC mother party was providing.[26] It took no great intelligence, therefore, for NCNC and Action Group leaders to recognise the implications of this association. Certainly, the BDPP's apparent efforts at duplicity were anything but subtle.

GROWING DISSENT IN WESTERN IBOLAND

Before formation of the BDPP, Western Ibos, though uneasy about the Mid-West initiative, were still prepared to co-operate with Omo-Osagie and his Mid-West protagonists. At the *1952 Benin Provincial Conference*, held at Ogwashi-Uku, F.H. Utomi, one of the leading Western Ibo-spokesmen, assured delegates that while his people were still intent on attaining a separate Western Ibo Province, this would *not* affect Western Ibo "co-operation in the campaign to secure a Central or Mid-West state".[27] Both Onyia and Osadebay supported Utomi's contentions, stressing that Western Ibos had no desire to join their Eastern Ibo ethnic brothers; that they preferred to remain within the context of the Western Provinces. Before the Conference adjourned, a motion proposed by Utomi and seconded by Osadebay, calling for the creation of a new Western Ibo Province *within* the proposed Central (Mid-West) State, was carried by a large majority.

This commitment was soon to evaporate in the aftermath of the BDPP formation. We have seen how Western Ibo delegates to the inaugural party gathering in September 1953, came away feeling that their suspicions of Omo-Osagie and his Bini compatriots were well-founded. Discussions between Western Ibo leaders followed and on 19 December 1953, a Conference attended by Natural Rulers and political leaders in the Western Ibo divisions was held at Isele-Uku. At this Conference a resolution was passed which marked the final death-knell for BDPP prospects in Asaba and Aboh divisions. It declared that:

> "A demand be immediately made for the creation of West Niger Province comprising the peoples of Asaba and Aboh division; that the creation of the Benin-Delta State should be suspended; and that all people from Asaba Division who attend the BDPP should cease attending further meetings of the said party".[28]

This resolution triggered a flurry of outraged response. The *Defender*, in its persisting role as champion of Mid-West interests castigated the Asaba Divisional Natural Rulers for their "lazy" decision. It warned that the "carving out of Benin Delta Provinces into a Mid-West State is a foregone conclusion".[29]

Nor did criticism emanate solely from partisan BDPP quarters. In Western Iboland itself the Ika Federal Union was highly critical of the statement by Asaba Natural Rulers. Mr. O. Nwanwene, Publicity Secretary of its Ibadan Branch, issued a declaration against the resolution of the "so-called Natural Rulers and leaders of Asaba Division".[30] The declaration read:

> "We hereby dissociate ourselves from the irresponsible statements issued by an unorganised and, therefore, unauthorised Natural Rulers organisation of Asaba Division The statement is diametrically opposed to the views of my people—all Ika-speaking elements of the Mid-West. What we want is a West Niger Province in which we Ikas will be given our own Division—*all within the Mid-West State*".[31]

Finally, the *Oba* of Benin himself issued a statement as a rejoinder to the Asaba declaration. The *Oba* simply re-iterated the positions of the Movement and the Western Ibos, as these already were known. "The demand for the Creation of [a Western Ibo] Province", he maintained diplomatically, "is not surprising, because it is in keeping with the decision of the Benin Provincial Conference held at Ogwashi-Uku in 1952".[32]

Demand for a West Niger Province   In very short order, however, it became clear that Utomi and Onyia, the leading political spokesmen for Western Iboland were little moved either by these pro-Mid-West outbursts by their fellow Western Ibos, or by the *Oba*'s efforts at appeasement. Utomi decided that the time had come to secure a Western Ibo Province; it would be foolhardy and dangerous to first await the creation of a Mid-West state. Accordingly, on 16 February, 1954, Utomi introduced into the Western House of Assembly a motion requesting:

> "That this House recommend to His Excellency the Governor to use the offices vested in him by the Nigerian (Constitution) Order-in-Council, 1954, Chapter I, Part 2, Territorial Divisions, Section 6(1), to incorporate the Ibos of Asaba Division, Benin Province and Aboh Division, Delta Province, and create a Province to be designated either Western Ibo or West Niger Province".[33]

In the course of the debate that followed, the House was informed that the Regional Government was not unsympathetic to the motion, but it was pointed out that there were "difficulties of implementation".[34] First, there was the problem of finance, since the creation of a new Provincial Headquarters was likely to be a costly business. Further, with regard to the siting of the Provincial Headquarters, there was likely to be great difficulty. After lengthy debate the motion gained majority support in the House of Assembly. No executive action was possible, however, until it was known whether the Lieutenant-Governor of the Region had decided to accept the recommendation of the House and given the necessary instructions.

In the months that followed, the Western Ibos continued to move away from any involvement with the Mid-West cause, and to engage themselves solely with the problems to be surmounted in gaining their own province. The Asaba and Aboh leaders, joined now by others from Ika Division convened a meeting at Agbor on 6 June, 1954 to take further the matter of a Provincial Headquarters. They concluded that the Governor, as referee, should act to resolve this issue which was "bringing only a heightening of conflict within Western Iboland".[35] Following up this conclusion, the Conference resolved that "the Governor be entrusted... with the siting of the Headquarters". In due course the Governor's reply was received. He instructed the Chief Secretary that no further action should be taken on the Resolution of the House already cited, until an agreed proposal for the site of the new Headquarters had been resolved.[36]

On 4 July, 1955—nearly a full year later—legislators representing Asaba and Aboh Divisions in the Western House of Chiefs, House of Assembly and the House of Representatives, Lagos met at Amai, Aboh Division. Also present were "24 councillors from the two Divisions, the accredited representatives of the people".[37] After long and strenuous debate, it was agreed that Alidinma, which is situated at the boundary between Asaba and Aboh Divisions, should become the headquarters. On the basis of this agreement, the Governor of the West was asked to implement the House of Assembly Motion of 16 February, 1954, to create West Niger Province. Having reached this point, however, the consensus which earlier had been attained only with the greatest difficulty, started to dissolve as rifts once again opened between rival Western Ibo factions. As a result, further action by the Regional Government was suspended.

It was, only at this point (July 1955) still more than a year away, that Western Ibos once again were to re-consider their position and potential prospects within the context of the Mid-West Movement. In the interim, the BDPP had to press on with other matters and attempt to secure the support it had generated in the areas of Benin and Delta provinces where its prospects seemed most promising.

AUTONOMY AND DEPENDENCE

In order to ensure that further losses might be minimised and existing gains be secured and perhaps extended, Omo-Osagie supervised a programme designed to maintain BDPP momentum. Benin City, says Omo-Osagie, became the "nerve centre". He put at the party's disposal the *Otu Edo* fleet of 40 motor cars. This way the party leadership was able to remain in close contact with district BDPP branches. "Every week", contends Omo-Osagie "we sent round four or five cars on tour to different spots".[38] Sometimes the cars were sent in response to a branch request, but most often to troubled areas, "where we tried to bring as much support as possible to local leaders who often were working under heavy pressure". Frequently, Omo-Osagie drew on his *Otu Edo* organisers in Benin City to accompany party officials on trips into the districts. He contended that leaders from the 12 Benin City wards which his party now controlled, served as "a very useful reserve of organisational expertise". These wards were commonly recognised as the best organised districts at either the local government or Regional level in the Mid-West.

Constant contact was also kept with the divisional—or in some instances "area", i.e. covering more than one division—Organising Secretaries. Two upon whom the party heavily depended were: E.A. Lamai in Afenmai, and Rev. J.P. Ifode (replaced in September 1954 by the BDPP Executive member Chief Oweh), in Urhobo Division. Each month the party's organising secretaries, together with as many branch leaders as could arrange it, met with other members of the Executive Committee in Benin City. The monthly Central Executive meetings, however, were little more than a forum for the discussion of problems: the Central Executive had no effective authority. Chief Odiase indicates that if a Branch Executive became delinquent in its duties, there was little that the party leadership could do. Sanctions were extremely limited.

Despite the brave words of BDPP leaders, who continued to maintain that a Mid-West State was now only "a matter of time", there could be little question of the precarious and tenuous condition of the party. Mid-West leaders and supporters began to wonder "how much time?"

As for the "political autonomy" of the BDPP, the *Oba* of Benin and Omo-Osagie had declared an official and public "independence" from the NCNC when they undertook the 1953 founding of the party. In the year that had since passed, however, it had been made abundantly clear to the BDPP leaders themselves that the party was deeply dependent on the financial and organisational resources of the NCNC. From the very outset, the BDPP leaders had made the use of NCNC local Branch Executives an integral part of the party's campaign strategy. Whether the party leaders then thought that once the BDPP branches had been established that the party would be able to generate and maintain its own momentum and initiative in the districts, is unclear. Certainly, it is evident that some such plan was envisaged. What happened in fact was that the BDPP continued to depend on NCNC resources. The BDPP needed the NCNC.

Viewed from this perspective it was hardly surprising when at the First Annual Conference of the BDPP, an overwhelming majority of delegates voted for the two parties to unite.[39] In terms of objective political realities, this official and public merger was long overdue. Yet, while the majority of BDPP leaders showed themselves prepared to come to terms with "NCNC reality", there remained one notable dissenter. And this, to the considerable surprise and alarm of Mid-West protagonists, was none other than the *Oba* of Benin!

In a personal statement to Conference delegates, in which he sought to explain the reasons for his action, the *Oba* asserted that "After a very long and careful, deep and serious thought, I have come to the conclusion that party politics cannot and will not do this country any good at the present time".[40] He went on to state:

"I have also come to the conclusion that self-government for Nigeria now or in 1956 is an ill-conceived proposition or experiment. Consequently, I have decided without prejudice, to dissociate myself and withdraw my patronage and presidentship from all political parties in Nigeria, *except the BDPP*, whose main aim is to achieve a separate state for the Benin-Delta provinces within the Federation of Nigeria. *I hereby also declare myself un-equivocally as an independent Nigerian nationalist and politician*, who is ready at all times to contribute his quota to the progress of Nigeria generally and the Benin-Delta State particularly".[41]

This decision of the *Oba* to "go it on his own" raised obvious vital questions about both the leadership and the official party auspices under which BDPP leaders and supporters might now operate. Certainly, as the year 1954 came to a close, it did little to re-assure Mid-West loyalists of the future of their cause.

--- --- --- --- --- --- --- --- --- ---

References

1. Ben Prof 2/BP/3022 (INA).

2. *Ibid.*

3. *Ibid.*

4. See *ibid.*

5. See *ibid.*

6. See interview with Chief Onyia, Int IV, p. 5.

7. For lists of BDPP patrons and Executive Committee members see p.74, below.

8. It should be noted that this plan was very similar to that employed by the Action Group, when in 1950-51, the *Oni* of Ife, in company with party organisers toured the Yoruba West.

9. *Report of Divisional Action Group President, Chief H.I. Osula, to the Resident, Benin City, 8 October, 1953.* (IGH)

10. *Western House of Chiefs Debates*, 20 October, 1953, p.21.

11. Omo-Osagie, Int. I, p.44.

12. See *Report of BDPP Tour in Delta Province, January, 1954*, mimeo. (In possession of the writer).

13. See Oweh, Int.VII, pp.31-34.

14. See Odiase, Int.II, pp.20-22.

15. Omo-Osagie, Int.I, p.46.

16. Oweh, Int.VII, p.33.

17. Omo-Osagie, Int.I, p.45.

18. Odiase, Int.II, p.20.

19. See Onyia, Int.IV, p.4. It was O.N. Rewane who used the term "paper party" in reference to the BDPP. (See Int.VI, p.26).

20. See *Report by the Resumed Conference on the Nigerian Constitution..., op.cit.*

21. During April to June, 1954, Omo-Osagie and his BDPP colleagues had their suspicions raised by a (West Regional) Governmental enquiry into local government in Benin Division. (See *Report on the Application of the Western Region Local Government Law to Benin Division*, mimeo., dated 22 July, 1954, at Benin City. (IGH)). The Report, amongst other recommendations, called for certain Administrative District boundary changes, and alterations in the system of appointing chiefs to local councils.

22. See *Report on Oba's Tour to Afenmai, 13-15 May, 1954*, mimeo. (In possession of the writer).

23. Shortly after the *Olokpe*'s return, Adebayo was charged with "grievous bodily harm", following an alleged fight with local cocoa growers, and with "non-payment of taxes". Appearing before the Customary Courts, he was found guilty on both charges. (See Odiase, Int.V, p.25-26).

24. G. E. Ogedengbe, Int.III, pp.67-68.

25. See, Odiase, Int. II, p.22; also pp.16-17.

26. While Chiefs Omo-Osagie, Odiase and Oweh acknowledged that money was received from the NCNC National Branch, they did not specify amounts. It was, however, the contention of the Western Ibo leader, F.H. Utomi, that from January 1952 through to February 1955, the NCNC financed local Mid-West party operations—and indirectly BDPP operations—to the amount of £9,000 per month. (See F.H. Utomi, Int.VI, p. 33).

27. Ben Prof BP/2328/1 (INA).

28. Ben Prof BP/3254 (INA).

29. *Defender*, 8 January, 1954.

30. *Defender*, 11 January, 1954.

31. *Ibid.*

32. *Defender*, 22 January, 1954.

33. *Western House of Assembly Debates*, 16 February, 1954, p.86.

34. This was an argument which the Action Group government in the West Region was to advance on many future occasions; it constituted a major device for warding off Mid-West pressures.

35. Ben Prof 2/BP/3254 (INA).

36. See *ibid*

37. *Ibid*.

38. Omo-Osagie, Int.I, p.46.

39. See, *Defender*, 10 September, 1954.

40. *Pilot,* 14 September, 1954.

41. *Loc. cit.*, (Italics added).

PART II

RECKONING WITH REALITY

CHAPTER 6

DEMISE OF THE BDPP

Viewed from the perspective of BDPP prospects following its initial campaigns, the best that could be said was that the party had managed a beginning. While it might be able to retain a generous measure of support in Benin and Ishan divisions, and in Delta Province amongst the peoples of Urhoboland, such a position remained distant from its objective. Despite BDPP efforts, there was little change in the polarisation of sectional interests within the Mid West provinces.

Itsekiri and Western Ijaw peoples together with ethnic elements in Akoko-Edo, and to some extent Afenmai and Ivbiosakon districts in northern Benin Province, were building and strengthening links with the Action Group. Though Western Ibos at this point appeared ambivalent in their allegiance—they too might swing away from the NCNC and in behind the Action Group—still their desire to remain aloof from Omo-Osagie and the BDPP was clear enough. Omo-Osagie and his party leadership had yet to convince these dissenting elements that the BDPP was something greater than a Bini, or at most, Edo-speaking "family reunion".

Prospects for the party were seemingly further undermined by the decision of its leaders—with the notable exception of the *Oba*—to enter into formal alliance with the NCNC. It was one thing to *employ* NCNC resources under the formal posture of an independent political stance, but quite another to *formalise* these links and so publicly shatter this official non-partisan stance. In making the party's alliance with the NCNC official, the BDPP leaders were risking the forfeit of any gains they had managed in Action Group areas. From the viewpoint of these BDPP/NCNC leaders, the fight for a Mid-West State would now be on a *politically partisan* basis. The Action Group was the declared enemy.

Finally, one has to ask how the party could hope to press forward with confidence and some security and coherence, when a serious breach had opened in its leadership. The initial plans and initiatives for the BDPP had been the product of joint activity by the two dominant Mid-West leaders, the *Oba* and Omo-Osagie. A successful outcome would depend largely on a continuing united effort. Yet, despite these obvious requirements these two leaders appeared bent on pursuing divergent paths—Omo-Osagie in linking the BDPP with the NCNC; and the *Oba* in supporting a far more active political role for himself.

Viewed from any perspective, the plight of the BDPP was grave. The party, it seemed, had merely lived up to the expectations of its detractors and other sceptics. It had, at various points been referred to as a "paper party", as a "party within a party", an "underground party", a "movement within the NCNC party", a Bini "Family Reunion". As the months passed in 1955 its condition further deteriorated. By November 1955, Chief Odiase, Secretary-General of the BDPP, was winding up the party's affairs. The BDPP was no more.

ACTION GROUP ENCROACHMENTS

While all these factors undoubtedly contributed to the party's demise, there was another vital consideration. After nearly three years of off-hand interest, the Action Group towards the end of 1954 started to show serious concern for its position in the Mid-West provinces. Its attention focussed on Benin Division—"Heartland of the Mid-West".

Elections were again forthcoming: Local Government in 1955, and Regional in 1956. Action Groupers fully recognised the importance of securing electoral control of the "Heartland", for it was often said "as goes Benin, so goes the Mid-West". And victory at Benin, could bring an important bonus: removal of the prime driver of the Mid-West cause, Chief Omo-Osagie. The defeat of Omo-Osagie could in turn mean that the existing strength of the NCNC in the Mid-West provinces would suffer accordingly. Thus, a successful Action Group assault on Benin Division at the Local Government level could have beneficial results for the party not only within the Division itself but within the Mid-West provinces as a whole. These, then, were objectives which held promise of lucrative political returns, and it was to their attainment that the Action Group, now devoted its energies.

Take-over Tactics and Role of the Oba

While the Action Group had made a promising start to building support in a few Mid-West districts before the General Elections of 1951, these efforts had noticeably declined after the party took Office at Ibadan. For party leaders in the Mid-West the two years which followed were filled with anxiety and frustration. The pleas of S. Y. Eke, Osula and their Action Group colleagues in the "Benin Heartland" appeared to fall on deaf ears at Ibadan.[1] But just when it seemed they had reached the point of no return, the pendulum started to swing in their favour.

Towards the end of November 1954, it became known that a most astonishing event had taken place. The *Oba* of Benin had made a "secret pact" with Awolowo and his Action Group.[2] *It was understood that the Oba had agreed to use his influence — largely through the break-away BDPP faction over which he exercised control — to generate support for the Action Group, in return for a guarantee from the party that it would give legislative support to the Mid-West demand for a separate state.*

The first "material" indications, which signified to alarmed NCNC/BDPP leaders that the *Oba* was implementing the designs of his new Action Group masters, occurred in December 1954. At this time, it was learned through "reliable sources" close to the *Oba*, that he had approached three Urhobo Division members of the Western House of Assembly. These men, Yamu Numa, James Ekpre Otobo and Sam Isekiri were all NCNC'ers who were known to be disenchanted with the Eastern mother party.[3]

The proposition which the *Oba* put to these men was said to be explicit and simple: if they would declare for the BDPP, the *Oba* would pay to each £1,000.[4] The only binding stipulation on the part of the recipients was that each must make his declaration public prior to or immediately following the dissolution of the Western House of Assembly, then set for October 1955. When this formality was completed, each would receive his payment in full.[5]

Where this money was coming from was not officially known. Omo-Osagie and his NCNC colleagues, however, knew that the *Oba* did not personally possess this kind of wealth. Thus, they contended, there could be only one logical answer: this money was being supplied by the Action Group; the *Oba* serving as the Western party's instrument, was using the BDPP as a screen behind which to draw disgruntled Mid-West NCNC leaders over to the Action Group.

Splitting the Otu Edo   The plot thickened further when, in January 1955, the *Oba* appointed "a Representative Committee drawn from [the two rival factions within the *Otu Edo*] on 25 January, 1955, to go into the affairs of the *Otu Edo* and submit its report".[6] The Committee was appointed, ostensibly, to carry out an inquiry which might serve to resolve certain differences which had grown between Omo-Osagie and a rival *Otu Edo* faction headed by A.G. Bazuaye. To carry out this inquiry, three members from each faction were appointed to sit on the committee; the *Oba* appointed a separate chairman, Hawden O. Uwaifo, a commoner well-versed in the internal intrigues of Benin politics.

In the course of its hearings the Committee received much detailed evidence from both sides. But when in due course the Report of the Committee's findings were released, it became obvious that the entire proceedings had been undertaken simply to discredit the President-General of the *Otu Edo*, Omo-Osagie, and to reinforce the split which had developed within the party.[7] The *Oba* could have intervened, but he did not. Instead he allowed the Report to be released despite its one-sidedness and potential destructiveness to party harmony and stability.

Although Omo-Osagie's closest supporters were incensed by the Report, the leader himself was not noticeably distressed. Even while the Committee hearings were in progress, Omo-Osagie acted to keep at least one move ahead of his antagonists. In a circular released 7 February, 1955, he reminded *Otu Edo* members and prospective candidates that local government elections in the Division were soon to be held. These elections were set for May, and Omo-Osagie pointed out that it was his intention to complete all necessary arrangements as soon as possible, as he would be departing for Lagos by the end of March to take up his appointment as Parliamentary Secretary to the Ministry of Finance.[8]

However, before a month had passed, Omo-Osagie and his supporters received a very rude jolt. On 11 March, a letter from the Resident informed both *Otu Edo* and BTPA leaders that the BNA Council was to be dismissed forthwith. The Resident explained that he was acting on the instructions of "the Minister of Justice and Local Government, Chief Rotimi Williams". Chief Williams, he said, had declared that it was "not the intention of the Regional Government to extend the life of the present Native Authority, which has already expired".[9]

In order to carry out the day to day business of the Division during the interim until completion of the local government elections, it was announced that the Regional Government intended to appoint a Provisional Council as a "Caretaker" Native Authority. The vital provisions regulating appointments to the Caretaker Council were laid down.[10] It was specified that the *Otu Edo* and BTPA parties should each submit a list of 24 members, each showing "sufficient similarity of candidates appointed to suggest agreement [between *Otu Edo* and BTPA] on membership had been reached". What these provisions meant in practical terms was that an "acceptable" list would be one which included twelve *Otu Edo* and twelve BTPA members.

A Rival Challenge   The impact of the Council dissolution on Omo-Osagie's plans was shattering. He and his faction—which still retained control over the Bazuaye faction within the party—had started preparations for the local government elections set for May. There was now no guarantee this date would hold. Chief Williams had been vague about the tenure of office of the Provisional Council. If the tenure was long, then whichever list was accepted, the control and authority of Omo-Osagie and the *Otu Edo* would inevitably be weakened. Certainly, it was obvious there was no way that Omo-Osagie and his *Otu Edo* faction could hope to benefit from the installation of the Provisional Council. Whether the tenure of the Provisional Council was long or short; whether the BTPA or *Otu Edo* list was accepted, Omo-Osagie stood to lose.

The provisions governing the appointment of members to the Provisional Council also provided little cheer for Omo-Osagie. It was evident that Bazuaye and his faction would submit a separate list. And if Bazuaye, under the instructions of the *Oba*, was in as close an association with the Action Group as Omo-Osagie and his supporters believed, then it was almost a foregone conclusion that his list would be accepted at Ibadan.

This in fact is what happened. The Bazuaye list was accepted by the Regional Government. It comprised the required 12 BTPA and 12 *Otu Edo* appointees. It was interesting to note that along with Bazuaye and his factional loyalists, the names of S. Y. Eke and V. O. E. Osula, the Action Group leaders in Benin Division, appeared in the list of Provisional Council members.[11]

It was not difficult to interpret what the installation of this Caretaker Council in Benin Division meant. The delight of the Bini Action Group stalwart, Osula, was perhaps the single most graphic indicator. In a letter to the Action Group Secretariat at Ibadan he exultantly declared, "Believe me, if there were to be an election just now, most of the present members would not smell the portals of the Council chambers"![12]

Finally the Action Group had gained a significant foothold in Benin Division. Although it was only a Provisional Council; nevertheless, with an adequate extension to its life, it was possible that the party might now be able to use its influence to build popular support with an authority it had not hitherto possessed. This had been the strategy suggested by Osula and Eke to the Ibadan party, as early as March 1953. For Omo-Osagie loyalists, anxiety was also provoked by the obvious Action Group leanings of the now-dominant (in Council terms, at least) Bazuaye faction of the *Otu Edo*.[13] It seemed that Bazuaye was not simply intent on displacing Omo-Osagie from the *Otu Edo* leadership, but in addition was constructing links with the "alien Yoruba" Action Group.

Tightening the Action Group Links   During April and May, the Bazuaye faction moved into a co-operative association with the BTPA. BTPA men who retained prominent Action Group allegiances were appointed to the leading positions on Committees re-created by the Provisional Council. Gaius *Oba*seki and S. Y. Eke, each occupying several key posts, emerged as the most powerful men in the new Council. Following these appointments, significant financial concessions were made to certain members of Council. The *Oba* was voted an annual stipend of £2,400 together with a £600 allowance for entertainment; *Oba*seki was granted a £600 annual salary; Council voted also that each member of the Provisional Council be allocated an annual salary of £240; finally, provisions were agreed to for the payment of stipends to the Extra-ordinary members (i.e. the *Olotu*, recently appointed by the *Oba*) of Council.[14]

The Action Group had now placed its local stalwarts in the controlling positions of the BNA Council. Leading members who had fallen in behind the *Oba*'s initiatives, or those who had shown—or could be expected to show—loyalty to the party, had been financially rewarded. Eke and his Action Group colleagues now had the base they sought in Benin Division, and there was the possibility of further assistance from Ibadan.

By the beginning of June, 1955, there were unmistakable signs that the party was preparing to supply this assistance. Chief Oweh, now Parliamentary Secretary to the Ministry of Trade at Lagos following his "promotion" up the NCNC hierarchy after successfully contesting the 1954 Federal Elections in Urhobo

Division, finally expressed feelings which most Mid-West protagonists had been harbouring for more than eight months. Should the *Oba* of Benin, declared Oweh, accept an Action Group ministerial post in the West Regional Government, such an undertaking "would be an act amounting to the greatest political defection of our time".[15] Oweh, apparently privy to undisclosed and very specific information, warned the *Oba* that:

> "Your acceptance and eventual appointment to the Action Group Cabinet will precipitate the dissolution of the BDPP and impede the Party's hope for a separate state".[16]

These were strong words from Oweh, a man who before the *Oba*'s split with the BDPP hierarchy, had served as one of the *Oba*'s leading political advisers. They had, however, little effect. The *Oba* moved relentlessly on. He announced the appointment of A.G. Bazuaye to an *Olutu* title. It was from these *Olotu* (traditional rulers in Benin Division) that traditional members for the Divisional Council would be selected. Along with the pro-Action Group Bazuaye, the *Oba* declared he was going to appoint a full new slate of *Olotu* to fill posts left vacant. This, of course, afforded the *Oba* a useful opportunity to select those men who would adhere to the political course which he proposed to steer.

Shortly thereafter, Yamu Numa, one of the three Urhobo members who, it was alleged, had had earlier dealings with the *Oba*, delivered an impassioned address in the Ibadan House of Assembly and declared for the "*Oba* and the BDPP". In his speech, Numa pretty well summed up the case against the NCNC. Although Oweh and Otobo maintain that Numa's speech simply fulfilled the terms of the agreement he had struck with the *Oba*, and that as a result of it he was £1000 richer, even so, Numa provided excellent value for monies expended![17]

The Mid-West Motion "Delivered"   The day following Chief Numa's address, the Action Group moved forward to fulfil its part of the bargain. On 14 June, 1955, M.S. Sowole introduced a Motion from the Action Group benches into the Ibadan House of Assembly calling for the "Creation of a Separate State for Benin and Delta Province".[18]

The Sowole Motion reflected an unusual element of goodwill. Sowole pointed out how Awolowo, in his presidential Address at the Warri Annual Congress of the party in 1953, stated that he would welcome the creation of a separate state for the Mid-West peoples. Chief Awolowo then made a brief but extremely important statement to clarify the nature of the Mid-West Motion. He announced that "the Government adopts no official attitude whatsoever" towards the Motion. Secondly, he declared the Motion open to a free vote: "Members of the Government and of the Opposition who wish may support it without any restriction whatsoever".[19]

After lengthy initial sparring with their Action Group opponents Mid-West members settled down to serious debate. James Otobo moved directly to the point at issue. If the Itsekiri, Western Ijaw and perhaps Western Ibo peoples withheld their support for a Mid-West State, would the Action Group then set into operation, what he referred to as the "all or none law?"[20] The practical meaning of this "law" was that unless all Mid-West peoples, including these recalcitrant groups, supported the creation of a Mid-West state, there would be no State created. Action Group spokesmen made no response.

Otobo went on. In order to reassure Mid-West members of the Government's good intent, he suggested the Action Group consider two proposals. First, he contended that Mid-Westerners would be greatly re-assured if "the Benin and Delta provinces shall be fully represented separately from the West Region at the 1956 constitutional talks". Second, it would be in keeping with the spirit of the Sowole Motion, if the Government were to "find its way clear to setting up a separate Committee on Mid-West Affairs"—a Committee which would be comprised only "of members from the Mid-West in this House".

In a speech which in more explicit terms underlined Chief Awolowo's adherence to a non-committed posture on the Mid-West issue, Enahoro assured Otobo "on the behalf of the Government, that a most serious consideration will be given to the request made up of very, very sound points".[21] The Motion was then put to a vote and passed with unanimous support.

RECKONING WITH REALITY

These two days, 13 and 14 June, 1955, were certainly action-packed, and with a far-reaching meaning and impact. Despite the very precise and coherent *provisos* which Awolowo had appended at the outset, the debate provided his NCNC rivals with a vital piece of documentary evidence which ultimately, in 1961, they would use against the Action Group with devastating effect.

Yet, there was ample justification for this Action Group initiative, albeit a potentially risky one. Anthony Enahoro was one leading Action Grouper who had made it clear to the Leader that if any headway was to be made against the NCNC in the Mid-West, then the Western party must appeal more directly to local interests and loyalties.[22] Also the 1956 West Regional elections were rapidly approaching. It was vitally important, therefore, that the Action Group make use of every available tactic in order to improve its chances in the Mid-West provinces. Certainly, it could not afford another loss like that it had suffered in the Mid-West at the Federal elections of 1954 when all ten seats were won by the NCNC.

Finally, it was not to be forgotten that Awolowo allegedly had struck a bargain with the *Oba* of Benin. Short of rendering formal support for the Action Group party, the *Oba* clearly had lived up to his end of the bargain. To fulfil his promises and to ensure that the *Oba* might finally deliver himself and his converts to the Action Group, it was therefore essential that Awolowo render the legislative support to the Mid-West issue, which, it was claimed, he had earlier promised. Thus it was not difficult to appreciate why the Action Group had taken the bold step of giving legislative support to the Mid-West cause at this time.

Battle for Benin   At the local level too, vital opportunities were available. On direct orders from Chief Rotimi Williams, the Action Group-controlled Provisional Council which had been ruling in Benin Division since March 1955 was to be dissolved. This was to take place in September 1955. Local Government elections in the Division's 22 local council areas would—at long last—follow. Elections had already been conducted in the other seven Divisions of Benin and Delta provinces during the April-June period. In each instance the NCNC, had secured majority control.[23] These BNA elections would thus provide the "acid test" to all the party's complex and largely covert preliminary manoeuvrings.

When finally, on 16 September, the balloting in Benin Division was completed, the result showed that the Action Group challenge had failed badly. Chief Omo-Osagie and his *Otu Edo*/NCNC faction remained the indisputable political masters of Benin Division. They succeeded in winning majorities in each of the Division's District and Local Councils. Although BTPA candidates made a modest showing, the *Oba's BDPP candidates had no success*. Any contest had been between old *Otu Edo* and BTPA rivals.[24] For Omo-Osagie, the victory was particularly sweet. For even though he had spent most of his time since the end of March 1955 in Lagos, he had now demonstrated that his strength, and the organisational strength of the *Otu Edo*, was as great as he had always contended.

This overwhelming success of *Otu Edo*-NCNC candidates was a bitter disappointment to the rivals and enemies of Omo-Osagie and his faction. The Action Group, in particular, had been dealt a severe blow. Substantial inroads into the elected councils of the BNA had been regarded as the first step in securing an increasing hold within the Mid-West districts as a whole. Under the assault of the *Otu Edo*-NCNC machine, however, such plans had crumbled.

It was evident that *it would take a great deal more than "Caretaker Councils", the distribution of a few benefits and the exploitation of factional and personal animosities, to effect any meaningful political change in the Bini heartland.* Clearly, Omo-Osagie was in full control and it seemed the *electoral process would serve as an inadequate and ineffective medium through which to challenge him.*

Post-Election Tactics and Defection of the Oba   Despite this depressing assessment (for Omo-Osagie's opponents) and as if to demonstrate that approaches other than electoral must be employed, in December 1955, at the first meeting of the full new Divisional Council—comprising 80 members!—the 20 chiefs selected to fill the quota for Traditional members on the Council all retained BTPA affiliation.[25]

The *Oba*, had done his job well; the approved *Olotu* had been installed. Thus, while the Action Group's BTPA ally had failed *electorally*, its voice might at least be heard through *appointed traditional* representatives on Council.

The political situation, at least for the moment, had now been resolved in Benin Division. The *Otu Edo* was dominant. The NCNC—so long as it allowed this Benin party a certain independence—could expect to retain it as a valued ally in an increasingly broad Mid-West context. The Action Group on the other hand remained in a weak position. It had to re-consider its tactics. The BTPA and the *Otu Edo* under Bazuaye had proven ineffective allies. Amongst the vanquished, the one person who had emerged as the most conspicuous figure was the *Oba* of Benin. The *Oba* had plotted against Omo-Osagie and his *Otu Edo*-NCNC. After achieving what appeared to be a series of significant pre-electoral successes, the *Oba* had been humiliated by the election outcome. One was left to wonder what course he would now pursue.

Any further doubts about the *Oba*'s political allegiance were finally resolved when on 25 October it was announced that he had been appointed a West Regional Minister without portfolio in the Action Group Government.[26] He succeeded the *Odemo* of Ishara who had resigned the post earlier in the year. After the Ibadan swearing in ceremony, the *Oba* left for Benin City.

One of the first persons to see the *Oba* on his return, was G.E. Odiase, Secretary-General of the BDPP. The news first reached him while he was on a party funding drive in the Eastern Region. Odiase at first discounted the reports as evil rumours. In a statement which he released to the press at that time, Odiase declared that he was "currently on tour on the *Oba*'s mandate", and that he "could not believe that the *Oba* would act against this mandate".[27] In due course, said Odiase, he would check these reports for himself, but he was certain the *Oba* would not accept what he termed "a Greek horse".

In the course of his audience with the *Oba*, Odiase learned the bitter truth. Odiase states that he then had "some very hot words" with the *Oba*.[28] The *Oba* maintained that he wanted to "remain with the Government of the West" and through this membership pursue Mid-West objectives. Odiase was furious. He pointed out that he had been prepared to follow the lead of the *Oba* and indeed had devoted all his time and energies to the cause of the BDPP. The *Oba*, however, had now gone too far. Odiase was not prepared to follow the *Oba* into the Action Group. He would continue to pursue the creation of a Mid-West State outside the Government of the West.[29] The *Oba* raised no objection when Odiase then stated that as the officer in charge of the party's administration, he would now see to those depressing matters connected with terminating the existence of the BDPP.

DEPENDENCE AND DEMISE

The *Oba*'s declaration for the Action Group now closed the second phase in the history of the Mid-West Movement. During the 1948-53 period, Mid-West protagonists had been prepared to posit faith exclusively in the NCNC and the assurances given by its leader Azikiwe. It took until mid-1953 for these supporters to accept that NCNC promises were little more than rhetoric. At this point it was finally recognised that if the Mid-West cause was to be advanced, stronger measures must be taken. Accordingly, the BDPP was created as a non-partisan and Independent party, designed solely for the purpose of promoting Mid-West interests.

This was the idea of the party. In practice, however, it was gradually revealed that BDPP aspirations to the principles of "independence and impartiality" could not stand up to the demands of political reality. We have seen how the BDPP was brought increasingly to recognise its dependence on the NCNC. The hard fact was that the party was dependent on a variety of NCNC resources and support. Chief Oweh, it would seem, classified the BDPP most accurately when he termed it a "Movement within the body of the NCNC party".

While by the end of 1954, the majority of the BDPP leadership had reconciled itself to this situation and had entered into formal alliance with the NCNC, we have seen that the *Oba* chose to strike out on a separate path. Distressed by the lack of concrete support from Azikiwe and the NCNC, the *Oba* proceeded with a series of clandestine acts designed to bring his faction and, it was hoped, all of the BDPP under the political control of the Action Group. It was the *Oba*'s view that with the *support* of the Government party in the West, the envisaged Mid-West State might more swiftly be brought within reach. Although it was too early to judge whether this course of action was generating the envisaged returns, one thing was quite apparent. The *Oba*'s action had precipitated the demise of the party which had been created to champion the Mid West cause, the BDPP.

Both BDPP politicians, and the *Oba*, its President-General and chief patron, had it seemed learned the hard way that the retention of an independent stance was simply not possible; collaboration in one form or another must be entered into with one or the other, or possibly both, of these Southern National parties. Just as these Mid-West leaders had earlier learned at very considerable cost not to trust the good intentions of a National party, so now they had been forced to recognise that independent initiatives would achieve little. It was possible that somewhere between these extremes an effective initiative might lie.

References

1. See *Letter from S.Y. Eke, Benin City Branch of the Action Group, to the Parliamentary Committee of the Action Group, Ibadan, dated 13 March,1953.*(IGH) In this letter, Eke indicated a number of specific grounds upon which dissolution of the BDC (by the Regional Government) could be justified. No Government action followed.

2. Together with S.Y. Eke and Osula at Benin City, Oweh and Otobo confirmed that the Oba-Action Group pact was sealed at this time. (See Int.VI, pp.48-53 and Int.VII, pp. 24-25) .

3. See Otobo, Int. VI, pp.49-50.

4. See Oweh, Int. VII, pp.38-39.

5. In interviews with Otobo and Oweh, the writer was unable to discern the precise terms of the agreement. It is possible that a small "down payment" was received when the agreement was first made, with the balance to follow on formal declaration. Also, it would seem the agreement between the *Oba* and these recipients was verbal only. And, while both Otobo and Oweh indicated their awareness of the *Oba*'s Ibadan link, it was not apparent whether this knowledge was gained before, during, or after their respective meetings in December 1954.

6. *Confusion in the Otu Edo*, (mimeo.), 4 March, 1955, circulated by the Otu Edo Secretariat, Benin City. (IGH).

7. See, *Comments on the Report of the Otu Edo Special Committee*, (mimeo.), dated 12 February, 1955.(IGH).

8. *Local Government Elections, 1955*, 7 February, 1955 (mimeo.). (IGH).

9. *Letter from the Resident, Benin City, to Secretary of the Otu Edo and Secretary of the BTPA, 11 March, 1955.* (mimeo.) (IGH).

10. See *Defender*, 9 March, 1955.

11. See, *Inaugural Meeting of the Provisional (BNA) Council at Conference Hall, Benin City, 2 April, 1955*, BNA 730/4, (BCA).

12. *Letter from V.O.E. Osula. Benin City to Action Group Secretariat, Ibadan, 18 March, 1955.* (IGH)

13. See, Sklar, *Nigerian Political Parties, op.cit.*, p. 255. Sklar notes the emergence of an "*Otu Edo* wing of the Action Group" in 1955; and that its membership comprised "a small minority of Benin people who supported the *Oba*", and who now followed him into the Action Group.

14. See, *Minutes of the Provisional Council Meeting of 5 May, 1955*, BNA 730/5, (BCA).

15. *Defender*, 8 June, 1955.

16. *Loc. cit.*

17. For details, see Chief The Honourable Yamu Numa, *Why I Break Faith with the NCNC, being the text of a speech delivered on 13 June, 1955, in the House of Assembly, Ibadan*, (Ibadan: Action Group Bureau of Information, n.d.). (In possession of the writer).

18. See *Western House of Assembly Debates*, 14 June, 1955.

19. *Ibid.*, col.59.

20. *Ibid.*, col.66.

21. *Ibid.*, col.73.

22. See Mackintosh, *Nigerian Government and Politics, op.cit.*, p.509.

23. At the District Council level, however, the Action Group had secured a notable post-election victory when victorious BDPP candidates belonging to the Oba's faction in Western Urhobo District Council declared for the Action Group. These declarations enabled the Action Group to rise from its minority position in Urhobo Divisional Council to one of majority control. (See, *Case for a Mid-West State, op.cit.*)

24. BDC 2 (1955), p.52a, (BCA).

25. See, *Minutes of the Benin Divisional Council Meeting held, 15-17 December, 1955*, BDC2/127, (BCA).

26. See, *Pilot*, 25 October, 1955.

27. *Pilot*, 26 October, 1955. Also see, Odiase, Int.II, pp.23-24.

28. See, Odiase, *op.cit.*

29. *Ibid.*

CHAPTER 7

NEW PROSPECTS IN THE MID-WEST

By the end of 1955 the Movement for a Mid-West State was in a most curious position. Formally, it was no longer in existence. The last remnants of the Movement's organisational structure had been destroyed when the *Oba* of Benin, President-General and Chief Patron of the BDPP, had declared for the Action Group in October 1955. In the circumstances, it was understandable that stunned and demoralised Mid-West supporters should label the *Oba* as a traitor to the Mid-West cause for carrying out what Chief Oweh declared to be "the greatest political defection of our time".[1]

There was, however, another side to the ongoing Mid-West saga. Between June and December 1955, the Mid-West issue had risen from its customary embattled position to a prominence and favour which was quite unprecedented. The Action Group having initiated the historic Mid-West Bill of June 1955 in the Western House of Assembly, had now emerged to pose an impressive challenge to the NCNC as "leading champion" of Mid-West interests. However, James Otobo added the vital *caveat*: only "the material implementation of the Benin-Delta state" would convince Mid-West supporters of the sincere commitment of the Action Group and the NCNC to the Mid-West issue.[2]

As matters now stood at the end of 1955 it seemed to many Mid-West supporters that two excellent opportunities would be available during 1956 finally to create the new state: the first in the period around the West Regional elections set for May; and, failing this, the second at the *London Constitutional Conference* set for September.

The West Regional Elections and
Party Competition in the Mid-West

The Regional elections were an event of great importance, particularly for the two main political competitors in the West, the NCNC and the Action Group. Each party was fighting to attain a particular objective. The Action Group, harassed and by no means secure as a result of the events of the past three years, was faced with doing electoral battle in order to consolidate its dangerously tenuous grip on government office at Ibadan.[3] Thus, for the Action Group, this electoral contest was concerned essentially with securing immediate Regional objectives. For the NCNC, the election had a different significance. The party possessed a secure home base in the Eastern Region. However, if it could secure victory in the West Region, it could then control politics and government in the whole of Southern Nigeria. Thus, in the context of escalating rivalry between these two parties, the importance which each came to attach to support from the Mid-West districts can readily be recognised.

Previous Action Group electoral endeavours in the Mid-West provinces had not been impressive. The party had been able to make progress in a few areas apart from the Itsekiri districts in Delta Province and Enahoro's stronghold in Ishan. Through exploiting factional differences in Western Ibo country,[4] and between rival clans in the Western Urhobo area, the party had brought pressure on the controlling NCNC. At the 1955 Local Government elections in Western Urhobo, for instance, the Action Group gained control of the District Council when the BDPP majority declared for the Western mother party following the defection of the *Oba*.[5] Elected BDPP members made a similar declaration in Isoko to reduce the NCNC margin in Council to 23-15.[6] While Action Group prospects in Northern Edo country improved it would not be until January 1957 that electoral prospects would be tested.[7] In Western Ibo territory, the Action Group had gained a valuable ally in the embittered former Zikist, Nduka Eze. Still it was to be July 1956 before the Action Group could mount an effective challenge to NCNC dominance in Asaba Division.[8]

The position of the Action Group in the Mid-West at the end of 1955 was, therefore, insecure. The party seemed content simply to draw off what amounted to the anti-NCNC vote; it appeared unwilling, and there is good reason to believe that it was ill-prepared, to make a positive and coherent appeal to potential Mid-West supporters. The party did, of course, have the support of the *Oba* of Benin. Still, it would take time to see whether this manoeuvre would actually enhance its position in Benin and the Mid-West.

In contrast, the NCNC was well entrenched in the Mid West districts. Through its Mid-West leaders the party retained a commanding presence. This had been proven at the 1951 general elections, the 1954 federal elections and the 1955 Local Government elections. Nor had the party been loath to extend a number of concessions which might serve to consolidate its position. The NCNC had been prepared not only to continue funding the party's Mid-West efforts through the leadership of Omo-Osagie and his Otu Edo/NCNC, but also it had endorsed the selection of Mid-West members to fill two key posts in the NCNC Opposition at Ibadan. Dennis Osadebay had served as Leader of the Opposition in the Western House of Assembly since November 1954, while V.I. Amadasun, one of Omo-Osagie's close associates in Benin, was Chief Whip. Similarly, despite reservations expressed from Enugu, the NCNC had been prepared to support the BDPP. At Lagos Omo-Osagie had been appointed Parliamentary Secretary to the Minister of Finance following his election to the House of Representatives in 1954; and Chief Okotie-Eboh had been selected as Minister of Labour

As the time for the Regional Elections drew near it became apparent that neither the Action Group nor the NCNC was injecting much energy into its respective Mid-West campaign efforts. The Action Group was largely content to let the Mid-West Bill (Sowole motion) serve as its major persuasive instrument— though it appeared dis-inclined really to capitalise on the electoral potential it possessed.

During a visit to Benin City, Alhaji Dauda Adegbenro, then Parliamentary Secretary to the Minister of Justice and Local Government at Ibadan, did stress in an indirect and rather sinister way the importance of supporting the controlling Action Group party at Ibadan. In an Address to the Benin Divisional Council on 17 January 1956, he emphasised the dangers of the Council Executive Committee assuming powers for which it had no authority. The massive re-shuffle which Omo-Osagie had been supervising in the BNA since the *Otu Edo* return to power following the 1955 Local Government elections, had involved many new appointments and "re-assignments" in an effort to purge the administration of Action Group sympathisers installed during the brief reign of the Provisional Council. After noting these developments, Adegbenro stressed that "Appointments and assignments of staff, particularly Secretaries or Council Clerks, Treasurers and Secretary/Treasurers must receive prior approval of the Regional Authority".[9] Not to adhere to this authorised procedure, said Adegbenro, could lead to "embarrassments" of which the Council already had experienced quite an adequate number in the past year.[10]

Certainly, if Mid-West protagonists believed the Action Group would implement the Mid-West Bill *before* the Regional elections, these apathetic efforts were a fair indication of the extent to which these hopes would fall short. While Chief Awolowo, Enahoro, Rotimi Williams and other Action Group leaders were quoted frequently and at length in the Nigerian press,[11] they gave no indications of advancing beyond the "principled" support of their NCNC rival. And though the NCNC leader Adelabu assailed the Action Group for waging "four years of terror" in the West, and of turning Chiefs into political "brokers and Commission Agents"[12]— amongst other things—there was little to suggest that such tactics were causing the party to alter its approach. It seemed the Action Group was prepared to continue in its role as "spoiler" in Mid-West opposition areas.

The NCNC too demonstrated little serious concern with the Mid-West. Though zonal leaders in the Mid-West organised "Operation 80" (the number of constituencies in the West), meetings were few, enthusiasm not readily apparent; indeed it seemed that the NCNC was inclined to take Mid-West support for granted. Clearly the party was more concerned with attempting to enhance its prospects in the Yoruba Provinces where in the 1951 elections it had managed to secure only 13 of 56 seats, and only 13 of 31 seats in 1954. Leading Yoruba NCNC'er, Chief Kola Balogun warned colleagues that success could only be secured by "a very solid registration campaign. The party must march forward. It is imperative"![13] But could it? And would the punishment meted out to Alhaji Adelabu by Azikiwe—when Adelabu had been forced to resign his position in the Lagos Council of Ministers following the findings of "financial impropriety" by the *Nicholson Inquiry*—serve to ensure the loyalty of the fiery Adelabu and his vital eight *Mabolaje* seats to the NCNC?[14]

When on 26 May, the West Regional elections were finally conducted, the result showed that the NCNC had been quite correct to vest confidence in a clear victory in the Mid-West provinces: the party won 16 of the 20 Mid-West seats.[15] In terms of the total popular vote, in Benin Province, the NCNC secured 58 per cent and the Action Group 34 per cent, (Independents, 8 per cent); in Delta Province, the NCNC portion was 72 per cent and the Action Group only 27 per cent (with Independents, one per cent).[16] Close contests were fought in the two Warri Division constituencies. There the Action Group won both with margins of less than 500 votes. The Action Group also managed to gain a victory in the newly-delimited Kukuruku North constituency, where Olatunji Oye defeated the former BDPP loyalist, A.O. Orisaremi, by a two to one margin. Finally, in Benin East, S.O. Ighodaro learned to his chagrin that the Benin environs remained strong in their defiance of the Action Group, even if the *Oba* had become Awolowo's supporter. Ighodaro lost to G. I. Oviasu, a promising young NCNC leader. Oviasu polled 21,841 votes and Ighodaro the incumbent, only a humiliating 9,080.

The NCNC had won a decisive victory in Benin and Delta provinces. In order to bring the party into Government at Ibadan all that was needed was for the NCNC to capture 25 of the 60 remaining seats in the provinces of the Yoruba West. The NCNC challenge, however, fell short by 9 seats. The party managed to secure only 16 of these seats—seven coming from Adelabu's eight *Mabolaje* constituencies. The Action Group, rising above various organisational and tactical difficulties, had therefore emerged triumphant, taking 48 of the West Region's 80 seats. As for the NCNC: having failed in its bid for office in the West Region, there was nothing it could now do to fulfil its electoral promise to Mid-West protagonists—if, in fact, this had been the party's real intent.

NEW MID-WEST INITIATIVES AND RE-BIRTH OF THE MOVEMENT

The failure of the Action Group to create a Mid-West State before the elections, and the electoral defeat of the NCNC, meant that Mid-West protagonists now came to pin their hopes on the deliberations of the London Constitutional Conference, set for September 1956.

There were several reasons why Mid-Westerners felt new confidence in their prospects. The terms set out in the *Report of the 1953 Constitutional Conference* had specified that at the *1956 Review Conference* provision must be made for the "representation of *all shades of political opinion*".[17] It was further stipulated that the grant of Regional Self-Government would be subject to the proviso that such an undertaking would *not* "in any way *make the continuance of federation impossible*".[18] Within the limits of these specified provisions the envisaged Mid-West plan, as seen by Mid-West protagonists, was obvious enough. Mid-West delegates to the mooted *1956 Conference* need simply contend that so long as the Mid-West issue remained outstanding the 'continuance of the Federation' in its existing form would indeed be 'impossible'. The Conference must *first* see to the creation of the promised Mid-West state; *then* the question of Regional Self-Government for the West could be considered.

While this reasoning constituted a plausible legal-constitutional foundation on which to press their claims, Mid-Westerners felt also that they had promising political grounds on which to anticipate strong backing from the NCNC. In particular, the NCNC favoured any initiative which would serve to diminish the Regional territory over which the Action Group might exercise control; and the creation of a Mid-West State would have this effect. Finally, there was still the possibility that the British Colonial Authorities might give support to the Mid-West demand. As the British had authorised the cession of Lagos from the West in 1953, there was no reason to believe they might not extend equal favour to the Mid-West demand.

Although restored to new confidence in their prospects, there were many tasks to be completed if Mid-Westerners were to achieve their objective at the London Conference. Not only would it be necessary to apply continuing pressure to the Action Group and the NCNC, but a unified effort would be required to press Mid-West demands and to raise the new state autonomy issue to a position of political prominence. In order to move towards these objectives, the Mid-West State Movement—successor to the BDPP—was founded.

The Movement—An Altered Emphasis   Inaugurated 5 May, 1956, the Mid-West State Movement was established for the purpose of "carrying out the objectives of the BDPP".[19] It was to help raise and retain a high level of popular support; to assist in unifying and rendering more effective the pressure which Mid-West leaders planned once again to bring to bear on controlling authorities and "reluctant Mid-West Champions" alike. Plans, in addition, were set in motion to undertake tours both within the Mid-West provinces and throughout the Federation to raise funds and secure support.

The Movement, like the BDPP, was at pains to retain an *ethnic and area balance* within its leadership; hence the representation of each Division (with the exception of Western Ijaw) by at least one person on the Movement Executive.[20] However, while much was made of the new organisation being a "political movement" rather than a "political party"—hence its potential capacity to effect greater pressure upon and secure greater co-operation from *both* the Action Group and the NCNC—in fact it was from the outset a "movement within the body of the NCNC".[21]

TABLE II

MID-WEST STATE MOVEMENT OFFICERS *

PATRON: THE *OBI* OF AGBOR

EXECUTIVE OFFICERS

LEADER: Hon. D.C. Osadebay, M.H.A., Asaba Division

DEPUTY LEADER: Chief H. Omo-Osagie, M.H.R., Benin Division
SECRETARY: Hon. J.E. Otobo, M.H.A., Urhobo Division
ASST. SECRETARY: G.E. Odiase, Ishan Division
FINANCIAL SECRETARY: Chief O. Oweh, M.H.R., Urhobo Division
TREASURER: Hon. F. Oputa-Otutu, M.H.A., Aboh Division
PUBLICITY SECRETARY: M. A. Kubeinje, B.L., Warri Division
LEGAL ADVISERS: Hon. J.M. Udochi, M.H.R., LL.B., Afenmai Div'n
       Webber Egbe, B.L.,Warri Division
       Hon. M.J.O. Edewor, M.H.A., B.A., B.L., Urhobo Division
       A. Atake, B.L., Urhobo Division
       G. E. Longe, B.L., Afenmai Division

---

* **Source**: Case for a Mid-West State (Warri: 1957) mimeo.

The Agbor Inaugural Conference served not only to specify the form which the Mid-West Movement would now assume together with its NCNC affiliation, but in addition, it revealed significant changes in the Movement leadership. Both the *Oba* of Benin and Omo-Osagie had been replaced. The *Obi* of Agbor now filled the position of Chief Patron of the Movement and Dennis Osadebay became its official Leader. Indeed, the *Oba* came in for a certain amount of guarded criticism. F.H. Utomi put it this way: "Though most of us recognised the *Oba*'s devotion to the Mid-West cause, there was, quite understandably, a good deal of hard feeling towards him".[22] Both Chief Oweh and Odiase voiced their disappointment in the *Oba*. Each was prepared to allow that while the *Oba* still might retain the interests of the Mid-West at heart, the methods to which he had resorted during 1955 had generated much bitterness.[23]

Perhaps of greatest significance in this change in leadership was the *prominence given to Western Ibos*. The Agbor Conference gave unanimous support to the candidacy of Osadebay as Leader of the new Movement.[24] While Osadebay's credentials were impressive—he was, up to 2 May, Leader of the Opposition in the Western House of Assembly, National Legal Adviser of the NCNC, a member of the party's NEC and Western Working Committee (WWC)—his selection over other possible candidates, including Omo-Osagie, demonstrated the suspicion with which most *non-Bini* Mid-Westerners continued to regard leadership centred on Benin. The initiative, it seemed, had now swung to the Western Ibo element.

Finally, it appeared the Movement had managed to secure comprehensive support from various Mid-West elements. Joining Western Ibos in the Movement leadership,[25] were Itsekiris co-opted through the efforts of Okotie-Eboh and the NCNC. After securing victory for the NCNC in Warri Division at the 1954 Federal elections, Chief Okotie-Eboh took an active part in supporting the NCNC challengers in Warri Division during the 1956 West Regional elections. As a result, both NCNC candidates came very close to victory. M.A. Kubeinje, who had come within 435 votes of ousting the successful Action Group candidate, Chief Reece Edukugho, was now elected to the post of Publicity Secretary on the Movement Executive. In the Northern Edo districts, Chief Odiase, was confident that interest in the Mid-West issue would be maintained.[26] There would, he stated, be a "carry-over influence" from the earlier efforts extended by the BDPP. Indeed, while Odiase did not say as much, it was apparent that a Mid-West cause under the guidance of Osadebay would be much more palatable to the peoples of the Northern Edo districts than the BDPP under Omo-Osagie. Already it has been shown in previous chapters that it was fear of 'Bini dominance' and Omo-Osagie himself that was a major cause of the party's limited effectiveness in these northern districts.

While the Movement appeared to be in a position to bring new life to the Mid-West cause, much would depend on the effectiveness of Dennis Osadebay as Movement Leader. It was no secret that many Bini delegates at the Agbor Conference had been outraged by the selection of Omo-Osagie to fill only the secondary position of Deputy Leader.[27] Even so, Osadebay had many political as well as personal credentials to recommend him for the job. For not only was he by now known and well-respected throughout the Mid-West but, in addition, his stature in the NCNC hierarchy afforded him the opportunity of extensive influence on the party.[28] Also, as the Mid-West cause was now to be advanced through the complex network of legal-constitutional negotiation; in this context, a leader who was trained and respected by both parties for his skills as legal craftsman and arbitrator was an appropriate choice. Delicate negotiations and coherent technical argument were *not* areas in which Omo-Osagie was known to excel!

Movement Prospects and the NCNC   There was a certain risk involved in making a full commitment to the NCNC. It was possible the party might again baulk when the time arrived for it to take a more active role. Such a possibility in the context of 1956, however, seemed unlikely. Mid-West leadership in the NCNC West Regional and National party hierarchies was strong; the NCNC had a vested interest in ensuring that the Action Group's West Regional territory was diminished; and Osadebay and Otobo were influential with Action Group leaders.

In the aftermath of the 26 May Regional elections, however, an event followed which reminded Mid-West leaders once again that the NCNC was still to be closely watched. Dennis Osadebay, was Leader of the NCNC Opposition in the Western House up to its dissolution on 2 May. In the interval between the dissolution and the elections, Alhaji Adelabu, fresh from his disgrace and humiliation at Lagos had settled back into his Ibadan stronghold. He had expressed confidence in becoming Premier if the NCNC was victorious. When the party lost he laid claim to the post of Opposition Leader—a claim duly supported by NCNC legislators gathered on 30 May. Indeed, when it was suggested that Osadebay had a superior claim to the position, Chief Sodipo "threatened to take the Yorubas out of the NCNC if a Yoruba man was not made leader of the Opposition in the Western Region".[29] When the meeting was adjourned, Adelabu had been elected Leader and J.O. Fadahunsi, another Yoruba, Deputy Leader. Only Otobo, elected Secretary, and V.I. Amadasun returned as Chief Whip, represented the Mid-West in the leadership of the

Parliamentary Party.[30] Osadebay, by far the highest ranking NCNC officer amongst them had by this act of exclusion been relegated to the status of an ordinary member.

It was humiliating and unsettling that Yorubas should now clearly control the NCNC in the West. This feeling was exacerbated by the fact that the meeting of NCNC legislators had been held in the presence of the National President, Azikiwe, who had himself been prepared to endorse the selection of Adelabu. Only a few months before, Azikiwe had been the instrument of Adelabu's political demise. For Mid-Westerners, this was yet another indicator that they were as much 'second class citizens' to the NCNC/West as they were to the Action Group.

The Movement on Tour   Putting this latest humiliation behind them, Leader Osadebay and his Movement colleagues prepared for a tour into the Mid-West districts in early August. Even before it began, however, there were doubts about its prospects. One of the main purposes of this tour was to raise funds; money was needed to cover the expenses of delegates to the forthcoming *London Constitutional Conference*.[31] The Movement application to the Regional Authority for a Public Collections Permit was, however, rejected. Thus, fund-raising could not be officially undertaken.[32] In addition, the appearance at the Benin City starting point of only four of the 12 Mid-West leaders originally selected to lead the tour did nothing to bolster confidence.[33]

Departing 18 August, Osadebay and his three Movement colleagues travelled first through the districts of Delta Province. At Orerokpe and Sapele, Osadebay addressed large, enthusiastic meetings where "purse gifts"—a way round the Public Collections ban—of £10 guineas and £3 guineas were accepted. In Sapele also, the delegation was joined by G.I. Oviasu, new Member for Benin Central in the Western House of Assembly.

At Warri the tour enountered its first setback. Though accompanied by the Itsekiri NCNC leader, Kubeinje, together with Chief Akiri, P.K. Tabiowo and Chief Obahor, all prominent Urhobo Warri residents, efforts to hold a meeting in Warri Town came to nothing; it was all, "a most embarrassing and regrettable affair".[34] A rally, first scheduled to be held on the evening of 18 August had been cancelled; it was re-scheduled for the next evening. However, next day, following his return to Warri from moderately successful sorties to Oleh and Ughelli, Leader Osadebay was then informed that, "due to campaigns going on for a bye-election to the Warri Urban District Council", their meeting could not be held. However, a dinner given by Tabiowo, "did a lot to soothe the feelings of delegates", and the tour moved on next day into Aboh Division minus Kubeinje and Oweh, but supplemented by Oviasu.

Despite rumours that the tour had been postponed, the Movement delegation had few problems in organising *ad hoc* gatherings: "Surprisingly, the people were most responsive and enthusiastic, very frequently besieging [the delegation]... on the way". Meetings were held at Ogume, Amai, Ashaka and Utagba-Ogbe. Osadebay led his team next day into Asaba Division. At Agbor, the first stop, the delegation was met by Chief Odiase, J.I.G. Onyia and also by Chief Oweh, who now re-joined the tour. After a "reasonably successful" meeting at Agbor Town Hall and also after receiving a number of purse gifts, the strengthened delegation moved on to Ogwashi-Uku, where Osadebay and local NCNC dignitaries, including F. H. Utomi, MLA, addressed a large local audience. At Asaba on the banks of the River Niger, where there was an equally impressive gathering, the Movement team made its last stop for the day.

On the morning of 22 August, Osadebay led his Movement team into Ishan Division. Here, again, "unfounded allegations" were abroad that the tour had been postponed. Still at Ewohimi a meeting was held in the Court Hall, presided over by Osadebay and the stalwart Mid-West supporter, *Onogie* Enosegbe II. The local NCNC Branch showed some coolness to the delegation at that meeting. S.O. Odigie, the Branch Chairman, stressed that while he was prepared to participate "in the move for a separate state", he must, "play safe by leaving the decision to the people". These words were applauded by a local "Action Grouper in a voluminous striped coat" who rather startled the gathering, when he "put in a bit of a speech". At Igueben, Ekpoma and Irrua, large meetings were held; at Uromi, home of Action Group Minister Tony Enahoro, and Ubiaja, meetings were cancelled. In each of these towns, however, a purse gift was presented to the touring delegates.

On 23 August, the delegation entered the Northern Edo districts of Afenmai Division. Once again, there were rumours that the tour had been cancelled. As a consequence, "no person expected the delegates, even at the first place of call".[35] At Auchi, a recognised Action Group stronghold, tour leaders met with K.S.Y. Momoh, the leading local politician—and one who was to become a sizable thorn in the side of future Movement efforts in the area—

and held a brief audience with the local natural ruler, the *Otaru* of Auchi. The *Otaru*, said a few words in general support of the Mid-West State, then presented a purse gift to Leader Osadebay. After addressing a large, rather sceptical gathering at Agenebode, the Movement team set off for South Ibie. Here a large meeting was convened and purses received. Following an enthusiastic send-off, the delegation travelled now to Afuse where another crowded meeting was held in the Town Hall. This gathering was only slightly marred by the absence of G.A. Ogedengbe, the local NCNC MLA, who was not present because of what he termed "security reasons". Though the tour entered the town of Sabongidda-Ora, it was decided that the scheduled meeting should not be held. Instead, the Movement team, now comprising only four delegates— the same number with which it had set out—returned to Benin City *via* Ifon.

A final assembly presided over by Movement Leader Osadebay was held the next morning (25 August) at the Divisional Council Hall, Benin City, with representatives from all Divisions except Western Ijaw in attendance. This meeting, which was regarded as "more of a conference than anything else, the large attendance being typical of the usual Edo support for the Mid-West State creation", provided Osadebay with an opportunity to give a brief account of the tour. In his final comments he referred to the forthcoming *Constitutional Conference* in ominous terms.

> "It would be a national calamity and a blow to democracy if in the face of the clear popularity of the demand for the Mid West State, this state was not accepted by Her Majesty's Government in the United Kingdom".[36]

The British Government, he stressed, must act to ensure that the Mid-West peoples received their "rightful" autonomy; further delay might mean that the West Region would be blocked in its bid for Self-Government. However, Osadebay was prepared to give way a little. Opponents of the Mid-West State, he declared, should hold a plebiscite on the issue "now", if they had any doubts about the sentiments of Mid-West peoples.

A Reserved Response   James Otobo, in assessing the outcome of the tour, summed up the situation when he stated that "but for the spontaneous nature of the demand for a separate state the tour might have been a failure".[37] All in all, it seemed that grass-roots political loyalties in the Mid-West districts had changed very little over the past two years. In 1953 and 1954 the BDPP had encountered resistance in Itsekiriland, in Western Ibo territory and in the Northern Edo districts. In August 1956, this response seemed little changed. And if Odiase and his organisers had felt that bringing Osadebay and other Western Ibos into the Movement leadership might serve to raise the popular appeal of the Mid-West cause in Western Iboland, they now had their answer. The response of both Natural Rulers and ordinary citizens had been, at best, luke-warm.

The behaviour of Movement leaders and their so-called local support organisations was most disturbing. The touring team had set off with only four of 12 gathering delegates. In the course of the tour it became apparent that all, with the exception of Osadebay and Otobo, were reluctant to extend their commitment to Movement goals any further than the boundaries of their respective home districts. Kubeinje remained with the delegates only until after the Warri fiasco; Chief Oweh departed after the Movement visits into Western Urhoboland, to re-join the delegation only briefly for its tour through Asaba Division; J.I.G. Onyia, also one of the original 12 selected delegates toured with the Movement only in Asaba Division. In Ishan and Afenmai Divisions, the job was left to Osadebay, Otobo and Odiase only; the absence of Omo-Osagie and his *Otu Edo* colleagues was most conspicuous—just as the presence of Oviasu, the NCNC-Pure MLA for Benin Central, suggested the continuing influence of Osadebay on the NCNC-Pure faction in the Mid-West.

At the Agbor inaugural meeting emphasis had been given to the "new all-inclusive" character of the Movement. The recent tour, however, demonstrated that the divisions between localities and ethnic sections persisted with equal intensity. Mid-West protagonists had suffered a grievous blow when the *Oba* of Benin had defected to the Action Group. While it was highly unlikely that Omo-Osagie would lead his *Otu Edo* in the same direction, still the loss of his committed support could be a crushing blow

By the end of August it was apparent that the Mid-West issue, yet again, was in a perilous position. During June and July, both Mid-West legislators and the NCNC Parliamentary Party at Ibadan had maintained strong pressure on Awolowo and his Action Group Government. Osadebay and his Mid-West colleagues had been vigilant in their efforts to hold the Action Group Government to its pledge on the Mid-West state; their warnings that inaction or dilatoriness could result in the nullification of Self-Government for the West had been clear and consistent. Adelabu also had given the issue greater visibility and force by including it as one of the four major problems which the Ibadan Government must resolve. Despite these efforts, however, there was still no concrete indication that the Action Group was moving closer to making the concessions sought.

At the same time, Adelabu, the new Opposition Leader in the West, was himself now concerned with shaping and advancing the demands of Ibadan Yorubas for a Central Yoruba State. Would not this new commitment now come first? Mid-West supporters also could not help feeling uncomfortable about their minority position in the Opposition party.

However, more serious problems threatened within the Mid-West itself. The Movement tour had shown not only that old sectional rivalries and suspicions remained, but also that a very damaging cleavage had opened up between the new Western Ibo and old Bini leadership. Neither Omo-Osagie nor any of his *Otu Edo*/NCNC colleagues had participated in the tour; with the exception of Oviasu, the Binis had been unrepresented. If differences within the "Mid-West family" hierarchy surfaced now, the result could be disastrous for the Mid-West cause.

Perilous Path to London

During the remainder of 1956, the condition and prospects of the Mid-West issue appeared to alter little. Non-Bini Movement protagonists together with a variety of NCNC National leaders continued to champion the Mid-West cause; Adelabu and his Yoruba NCNC hierarchy at Ibadan remained aloof; and, while the participation of Bini elements was conspicuous by its absence, still by the beginning of December it appeared that Omo-Osagie and his *Otu Edo* colleagues were moving towards a more co-operative posture. As for the decision of the British Authorities to defer the proposed *Constitutional Conference* to 1957; this provided both Yorubas and Mid-West protagonists with more time to manoeuvre.

During the early months of 1957, Movement leaders made much of statements of support emanating from Action Group strongholds in Warri Division and Northern Edo.[38] In addition the *rapprochement* of rival Bini and NCNC-Pure elements within the Movement leadership seemed still to be holding. Emphasis also was given to the importance of resolving the Mid-West issue *before* the Action Group delegation left Nigeria for the London Conference.

For the past year Mid-West protagonists, backed by their NCNC allies, had threatened to block the grant of Self-Government to the West Region, if the Action Group Government did not create the Mid-West State *before* the start of the Constitutional Conference.[39] The Action Group's response to these threats had been to procrastinate and to insist on the prior fulfilment of various conditions. About two of these the Action Group was adamant: a *Boundary Commission* to determine the limit of the proposed Mid-West State; and *a plebiscite* to ensure the willingness of all peoples inhabiting this Mid West territory to participate within the proposed state. Indeed, so confident of his position was Awolowo, that despite increased warnings of dire consequences, he chose to depart Nigeria "without any clear-cut statement on the Mid-West issue".[40]

Reduced to simplest terms, the success of Mid-West strategies at the *1957 London Conference* rested on the full co-operation of the NCNC. The plan was simple enough: Mid-West protagonists under the umbrella of NCNC support would insist on creation of the Mid-West State *before* the Conference moved on to consider the question of Self-Government for the Regions; if the Action Group baulked, Mid West protagonists had the assurance that their NCNC allies would provide the requisite voting bloc to ensure that Awolowo and his party would *not* achieve the Conference consensus they needed.

There were, however, drawbacks to this strategy. Suppose the Action Group should adopt *similar* tactics and seek to block the grant of Self-Government to the *Eastern* Region? Would the NCNC continue to hold to its Mid-West commitment? And if such a situation should arise, on which side would the loyalties of such men as Osadebay, and Adelabu—now elevated to First Vice-President of the NCNC—fall?[41] Under pressure, might their loyalty fall on the side of the NCNC and result, therefore, in abandonment of the Mid-West cause? As for the British, what position would they take? It was well recognised that the Colonial Authorities wished to see the existing Regional boundaries persist unaltered. Would they, therefore, attempt to forestall Mid-West efforts?

These questions, and many more, provided much upon which the sole Mid-West (voting) delegate, Osadebay, and his Advisers, official and unofficial, were to deliberate during the final days before arrival in the United Kingdom and the start of the Conference at Lancaster House. The answers, in time, would come.

References

1. *Defender*, 8 June, 1955.

2. *Western House of Assembly Debates*, 14 June, 1955, col.66.

3. Only a last-ditch effort by Action Group leaders at the final tier of the phased elections of 1951 allowed the party to enter into government office at Ibadan with a 10 seat majority (45-35) over the NCNC. (See particularly, Sklar, *Nigerian Political Parties*, *op.cit.*, pp. 115-16 and n.64). At the first federal elections in 1954, the Action Group was defeated in the West Region by the NCNC (23-18).

4. During the 1954-55 period, former Zikist, the Western Ibo Nduka Eze, was becoming a valuable asset to the Action Group. Though soundly beaten by J.I.G. Onyia at the 1954 federal elections, Eze as leader of the *Nnebisi* (after the founder of Asaba) party, saw his party secure 5 of 29 seats at the 1955 local government elections; he and his *Nnebisi* colleagues then declared for the Action Group at the first meeting of the Asaba Divisional Council. (See, Onyia, Int. IVa, p.13).

5. See, *Case for a Mid-West State*, op. cit., p.10.

6. *Ibid.*

7. *Ibid.*, p.11.

8. See, Onyia, Int. IVa, pp.12-13 and pp.16-17.

9. *Address by D.S. Adegbenro to the Benin Divisional Council, 17 January, 1956*, in file BDC 2/110 (BCA).

10 . See *ibid.*

11. See issues of the *Defender* and *Pilot*, 15 January-21 March. In these two (NCNC) newspapers, Awolowo's statements were frequently derided and used to launch indictments against his "subversive and hypocritical" activities in the Mid-West.

12. K.W.J. Post and G.D. Jenkins, *The Price of Liberty: Personality and Politics in Colonial Nigeria*, (Cambridge: University Press, 1973), p.303.

13. *Ibid.*, p.295.

14. See, *Report of the Commission of Inquiry into the Administration of the Ibadan District Council*, (Abingdon: 1956). See also Post and Jenkins, *op.cit.*, Chapter 11, and Sklar, *Nigerian Political Parties*, *op.cit.*, pp.300-301, for consequences of the *Inquiry* for Adelabu and the NCNC.

15. Following a new constituency delimitation undertaken by the Action Group government in 1956, the number of seats allocated to the Mid-West provinces was reduced by 4 (from 24 to 20). These 4 seats were then re-allocated to the Yoruba West, bringing the total for these provinces to 60. The NCNC complained bitterly about this "gerrymandering", particularly after its election defeat. (See *Defender*, 1 June, 1956).

16. See *Report of the Holding of the 1956 Parliamentary Elections to the Western House of Assembly*, (Ibadan: Government Printer, 1956), *passim*.

17. *Report of the Nigeria Constitutional Conference Held in London, May-June, 1957*, Cmnd. 207, (London: H.M.S.O., 1957), p.5.

18. *Ibid.*, p. 6.

19. Oweh, Int.VII, p.40.

20. See *Table II* below.

21. Otobo, Int.VI, p.4 and E.A. Lamai, Int.VII, p.47.

22. Utomi, Int.VI, p.32.

23. See Oweh, Int.VII, p.41; Utomi, Int.VI, p.32; and Odiase, Int.II, p.36.

24. See Oweh, Int.VII, p.39.

25. Chief Onyia maintains that Western Ibo leaders came to the conclusion by December 1955, that they could expect little consideration from Ibadan; on the other hand they had no assurances of better treatment if they should come under the control of the Government at Enugu. Thus, a Mid-West Movement seemed the most sensible available option. Though still very wary of the Bini presence, Onyia regarded the Mid-West situation this way: "We supply the brains and the trained manpower"; these, at least, would serve to secure Western Ibo prospects within any future autonomous Mid-West context. (See Onyia, Int.IVa, p.9; also, Lamai, Int.VII, p.46).

26. See, Odiase, Int.V, p.28.

27. V. I. Amadasun, M.L.A., one of Omo-Osagie's *Otu Edo* lieutenants in Benin, spoke of angry exchanges between Omo-Osagie and his *Otu Edo* colleagues following the Agbor Conference. Omo-Osagie, contended Amadasun, held that conceding the Movement leadership to Osadebay was the price Binis must pay for retaining Western Ibo support for the Mid-West issue. (Interview with V. I. Amadasun, Benin City, August 1969; also see, Omo-Osagie, Int.I, p.28). Though certainly there is logic in this contention, it should also be remembered that Osadebay was held in far higher regard by most non-Binis than the much-feared *Otu Edo* leader.

28. One very good reason for selecting Osadebay Leader was that for the first year of the Movement's existence he was prepared to finance its activities out of his "own pocket". (See D. C. Osadebay, *We Build a Nation*, [unpublished *mss.*, 1972], pp.271-72). Chief Odiase confirms Osadebay's statement. (See, Odiase, Int.II, p.36). One is left to wonder, however, precisely, what Osadebay meant by "his own pocket". In a later selection in his unpublished *mss.* (pp.430-31), he declared that the existence of the Mid-West Region was only made possible by the "self-sacrificing part played by the people of the.Eastern Region and their bank, the African Continental Bank, ...and also some trading companies".

29. Osadebay, *ibid.*, p.309.

30. See, *Defender*, 31 May, 1956.

31. In fact, the responsibility for meeting the expenses of official delegates was that of the West Regional Government. (See *Letter from Adelabu to Awolowo, dated 11 April, 1957*, entitled *London Delegation*, [ADELP]). Funds ultimately raised—officially and unoffic-ially—were presumably applied to covering expenses of "unofficial" Movement delegates attending the Conference (see n.41 below), and to meeting costs of preparing position papers, and in particular the lengthy and well-researched *Case for a Mid-West State, op.cit.*

32. The permit was finally issued on 27 August, two days *after* completion of the tour. (*Public Collections Ordinance*, Reg. No. WR/45/1956, mimeo. Copy in possession of the writer.).

33. See, *Mid-West State Movement: Report of the Tour of Benin and Delta Provinces, 18-25 August, 1956*, p.1, (mimeo.), referred to hereafter as the *Tour Report*. (Copy in possession of the writer.) The four who led off the Tour were Osadebay, Otobo, Oweh and Kubeinje.

34. *Ibid.*, p.2

35. *Ibid.*, p.5

36. *Ibid.*, p.7

37. Otobo, "Comments on Tour", appended to *Tour Report*, pp.7-8.

38. See, *Pilot*, 10 and 16 March; and 4 and 5 May, 1957.

39. See *Pilot*, 14 March, 1957.

40. *Pilot*, 13 May, 1957.

41. Chief Okotie-Eboh and James Otobo attended the *1957 London Conference* as "advisers", or unofficial delegates, *only*. (See *Cmnd. 207*, p.36).

CHAPTER 8

THE MID-WEST AND THE LONDON CONFERENCE OF 1957

As the time drew near for the start of the London Constitutional Conference, one journalist, noting the large-scale preparations being completed by various delegations observed that "By May 20, it looks as if Nigeria will be virtually empty of politicians".[1] Perhaps, he wryly added, this would afford "officials a chance of showing whether Nigeria's Government can still be carried on".

Certainly, when the Conference commenced, there was no shortage of Nigerian politicians and traditional rulers in attendance. The number of *official* delegates to the Conference, however, was relatively small. These totalled only 40—ten from each of Nigeria's three Regions, together with another ten British administrative officials and leading Regional Chiefs. These official numbers, however, were supplemented by Regional quotas of "official advisers", and large numbers of "unofficial advisers". Lancaster House was the scene of much activity.

While the Conference was primarily concerned with the British pledge of Self-Government to the three Regional Authorities, and to the Nigerian demand for "Independence within the British Commonwealth in 1959",[2] there could be little doubt that much of the Conference time would be given to the question of "separate states". Both Southern National parties, the Action Group and the NCNC, had prepared their respective strategies accordingly. And while it was apparent the NCNC would provide much of the running, it was equally evident that when it came to consideration of minorities' demands from within the East Region itself, the NCNC was prepared to mount no less formidable a defence than the Action Group in the West. Each party was determined not to give any concession which might result in a unilateral territorial encroachment by the other.

As for the NPC, though it was now at least prepared to recognise that "a measure of democratic autonomy"[3]—in keeping with measures for a "provincialisation" plan outlined in the *Hudson Report*[4]—was necessary, still, such recognition was not to be interpreted as in any way lending support to the demand for more states. Despite a number of reported statements by Tafawa Balewa which suggested an element of sympathy for minorities, the *Sardauna* of Sokoto, Premier of the North and Leader of the NPC, remained firmly committed to the Regional *status quo*, and, of course, to "one North."

British officials too were well aware of the impact which the new states issue could have on the Conference. Indeed, they too had made their plans accordingly. It was well-known that Whitehall and British field officers were in general agreement that the existing three-Region structure should be retained intact—a position which had persisted largely unaltered since 1946. Press reports preceding the Conference, provided ample evidence that Her Majesty's Government did appreciate the numerous coherent and forceful arguments advanced by aggrieved minority elements. Nevertheless, it was equally apparent these officials intended to stand their ground, contending that "all reasonable demands of Nigerian minorities" could, for the time being, "be met within the existing governmental framework".[5]

Still, there was the precedent of the separation of Lagos from the West. Mid-West protagonists, with a recognised and well-established claim, could hope that the British once again might relent and grant a special concession.[6]

Autonomy Demands and Conference Deliberations

After completing opening formalities on 23 and 24 May, the Conference settled down to business on Monday 27 May. At a morning Plenary Session, delegation leaders discussing the primary issue of Regional Self-Government, brought up for the first time the question of new states and the Mid-West demand. Awolowo and the Sardauna agreed that Self-Government should be discussed first, *before* any consideration of the new states issue. Azikiwe, however, stated that he felt the questions of Regional Self-Government and the creation of new states were so closely integrated that it would be best to grapple *first* with the problem of new states.[7]

Alhaji Adelabu and Osadebay gave strong support to Azikiwe's statement. Adelabu, addressing his remarks to the particular question of Self-Government for the West, now made specific reference to Mid-West claims.[8] He explained that the demand for a Mid-West state had not only a strong foundation in popular support, but more important, it had received legislative sanction by the Awolowo Government. This legislative approval had been given long prior to passage of the motion on Self-Government for the West, yet the Awolowo Government had consistently refused to honour its pledge. "A mandatory obligation" he declared, must be placed on the Western Government to implement the Mid-West Bill once the grant of Regional Self Government had been confirmed. In a final appeal which was clearly directed at eliciting the sympathy of British officials, Adelabu called on the Conference to recognise the unquestionable need to endorse the Mid-West demand:

> "The Western Regional Government should not be placed in a position to treat the legislative sanction for the creation of the Mid-West State as a mere scrap of paper. The legislative sanction has become a solemn pledge which at this Conference must be honoured, just as Her Majesty's Government is being called upon now to honour her [*sic*] own pledge to Regions desiring Self-Government".[9]

Osadebay now followed on with an address on behalf of the Mid-West State Movement. In this address, however, little was added to what Adelabu had already said.[10]

As Movement leaders had feared, Awolowo, supported by another prominent Action Group delegate, Chief F.R.A. Williams, did not accept these points. Chief Williams, put forward the position of the Action Group Government. Advancing a technical point first, Williams asserted that:

> "A distinction should be drawn between Regional Self Government on the one hand, which was the acceptance of an offer by Her Majesty's Government, and a request for the creation of more states, on the other, which was the subject of an invitation to Her Majesty's Government to make an offer".[11]

This legal technicality referred to the fact that the British Government, at the 1953 London Conference, had committed itself to considering ways and means and the *de facto* grants of Regional Self-Government at the mooted 1956 Constitutional Conference, while no such commitment had been made with respect to the creation of states. In this reasoning put forward by Williams, the new states issue had yet to be put in the form of a request to the British Government; only when this had been done would the latter be in a position to consider advancing an offer to meet these demands. Williams went on to advance his second point. The distinction between the Self-Government and New States issues, he declared, was, "the more valid, since the motion passed by the

Western House of Assembly on the Mid-West State had been initiated by a back-bencher, and no expression of the Regional Government's attitude had been made towards it.[12]

The Action Group was adamant: Self-Government for the Regions should be decided *first*; then the issue of new states could be given consideration. Nor were Action Group delegates amused when K.O. Mbadiwe, a leading NCNC figure at the Conference suggested that if Awolowo and his colleagues were so vehemently opposed to primary discussions and settlement of the new states question in general, then the Mid-West State issue might be considered separately by the Conference.[13] Williams asserted coldly, that all new State demands must be considered only after the Conference had disposed of the matter of Self-Government for the Regions.

From these statements by Williams, it was clear that the Action Group had no intention of "co-operating" on the Mid West issue. If Mid-West protagonists wanted their new state they once again were going to have to fight hard for it. Osadebay and his Mid-West colleagues Otobo and Chief Okotie-Eboh could only hope that the NCNC would honour its pledge and maintain its backing for Mid-West demands.

In the course of the next three days, the Conference went on to consider provisions for the immense range of functions for which Self-Governing Regions and the Central Government would be responsible. After preliminary deliberations on these and other matters, however, the Conference, on Friday, 31 May, turned once again to the new states issue, and to the primacy of the Mid-West demand.

SUPPORT FOR NEW STATES

The NCNC Position

The NCNC presented an impressive case in support of the new states and Mid-West issues. Outlined in some detail in a series of memoranda submitted to the Conference, it provided ample indications that the NCNC was determined to try to live up to its now rather tarnished title of "Minorities Champion". The general position of the party was that the prospects for Nigeria achieving future success as an Independent country rested largely on actions which might now be taken to reduce the size of her "monster regions".[14] Many people it was maintained, "believe that the present Regional Units are so large that they make the operation of the Federal Government a futile exercise". If the Federation itself was not to be jeopardised, then attention must be given to ways and means of creating more states "each of which [would be] less powerful than those that exist today". The memorandum went on to point out there were many who held that the "old provinces" should be converted "into States within the Federation".[15] But, this would mean tackling the staggering tasks needed "to give us some 25 odd States in all". While it was recognised that this undertaking would be in concert with the NCNC "new states" policy commitment, and indeed, in line with "the usual evolution of Federal Government in other countries", nevertheless a more "cautious and responsible" approach was counselled.

The NCNC contended that eleven new states were "definitely practicable and highly desirable at the current moment".[16] In addition to breaking down the "monster Regions", the general advantages of effecting the creation of these eleven states would be two-fold.

> "First, those people who are keen on the social services which touch intimately the lives of the people will find ample scope in the Legislatures of the states where such matters as Education, Health and Social Welfare are dealt with. Since the country is very big, the greater the degree of decentralisation the better the quality of social services for the people.

> "Secondly, those people who are interested in National politics... will find ample room for their political ambition in the activities of the House of Representatives and the Council of Ministers".[17]

In contrast to this rather philosophical and flexible presentation, the contentions of the NCNC National Party on the question of Self-Government for the West were direct and uncompromising.[18] Attention focused on "the method and circumstances" by which legislative sanction for this request was passed through the Western House of Assembly in December, 1955. "Six months before the Motion for Self-Government", it was pointed out:

> "A motion for the creation of a Mid-West State was passed unanimously. The passage of the Mid-West motion, along with a Prayer to Her Majesty's Government to take measures to implement same at the present Constitutional conference, made the NCNC members in the Western House of Assembly believe that the new State would be created before the request for Self-Government was granted and no doubt influenced them in joining hands in passing the Self-Government motion".[19]

The memorandum went on to state that the NCNC Delegation would raise no objections if the issues of a Mid-West State and Regional Self Government for the West, were dealt with in the order in which their respective Motions were passed. If these two issues were not treated in this order, "the grant of Self-Government to the Western Region would be opposed". The NCNC delegation could fight employing legal tactics. The particular legal loop-hole related to the interpretation of "any Region". Should the British Government declare that it would grant Self-Government to any Region that desired it, then the NCNC Delegation maintained it must establish a precise definition of the term. A second NCNC tactic was based on a legal-contractual argument.[20]

These initiatives by the NCNC National delegates, received forceful support from Adelabu and his NCNC colleagues from the West (which included, of course, both Osadebay and Otobo). In a memorandum submitted by NCNC West delegates, emphasis was given to the primacy of the Mid-West claim, as distinguished from claims made by all other minority elements at the Conference, for Regional status. "The demand for the creation of a Mid-West Region must be treated as an issue separate and distinct from demands made by or in respect of other areas and groups of population in the other Regions".[21]

The Movement States Its Case

While NCNC National and NCNC West delegates contributed extensive and persuasive support to the Mid- West issue, it was the Mid-West State Movement, represented by Leader Osadebay and James Otobo which provided the most detailed and comprehensive backing for Mid-West autonomy demands. The details of the Movement's contentions were laid out in a memorandum entitled *The Case for a Mid-West State*.[22]

At the outset of the memorandum, Mid-West protagonists emphasised that the demand for a separate state by the peoples of Benin and Delta provinces was

> "... not a sudden, emotional or seasonal conception; it is a spontaneous, growing, persistent and... active political aspiration. It is not the dream of 'a few frustrated politicians'; it is a mass agitation well understood by all and forming the basis or goal of political aspirations of the peoples of these two provinces". (p.2).

Ethno-Cultural Considerations   Following a historical summary of the development of the Movement, consideration was next given to the "Causes of Separation"—that is, the causes creating the desire of Mid-West peoples to separate from the West. Socio-cultural causes were explained in simple terms, terms which conveyed differences far more effectively than earlier, over-worked and far more complex explanations. It was maintained that:

> "We [Mid-Westerners] have our own way of life [and this] is not a theoretical, empty and academic claim; it is real. One has only to look at the similarities in dress, in farming methods, in handling cutlasses and hoes, in such things as eating and bathing habits, in music and musical instruments, in physical strength and courage of the various peoples of the Benin and Delta Provinces to know that in the Western Region there are two groups the Yoruba and Mid-West peoples".(p.3).

In reference to the position of Mid-Westerners as a down-graded minority in the West Region, it was stated that the 1,250,000 residents of the Mid-West[23] were treated with disdain and indifference by the majority Yoruba group. Those from the Mid-West area were disparagingly referred to as "Kobokobos" or barbarians. The giant tribal organisation, the *Egbe Omo Oduduwa*, was created, it was held, "for the express purpose of upholding Yoruba tradition... and improving the way of life of the Yoruba people". Further, it was asserted strongly that, "The interest of us, the minority section, can only be safeguarded by ourselves. The present federal constitution can correct this situation by constituting Benin and Delta Provinces into a separate Mid-West State or Region".

TABLE III

POPULATION TOTALS OF MID-WEST PEOPLES (1952)[24]

Benin	292,081
Urhobo	248,210
Asaba	212,382
Afenmai	204,229
Ishan	192,194
Aboh	130,121
Western Ijaw	82,284
Isoko	75,105
Itsekiri	54,284

In support of this demand, it was pointed out that if such a state was created, there would be a sound balance between cultural sections, "where no single tribal group can dominate the other". Drawing again on figures from the 1952 Census, it was held that this relatively even distribution of group numbers within the Mid-West area, amply satisfied one of the "grounds for a federal constitution".

The memorandum went on to cite instances, which it maintained demonstrated graphically the exclusivist interests of the Yoruba-dominated West Regional Government. These allegations were based on current claims of Yoruba discrimination against Mid-Westerners. It was alleged that on occasions, "even in the Western House of Assembly, Members from Benin and Delta Provinces have been referred to as 'the extraneous elements in the House'." Further, it was added that:

> "The *Alake*'s of Abeokuta's remark on one occasion on the premises of the Western House, '...that is the Oni of Ife, that is Awolowo the Premier, and this is myself—the voice of the Western Region is complete,' in utter defiance of even our own natural rulers then present, was a lesson". (p.8)

Economy and Infrastructure   Turning then to matters of more material concern, it was stated in the memorandum that in 1954:

> "The Western Government set up a Road Development Planning Committee to recommend which roads should he tarred with the £4 million set aside for this purpose. In spite of repeated questions and demands by two Mid-West legislators on the relevant spending committees of the House, no report on all the roads in the Mid-West was prepared and well over seven-eighths of that money had been allocated to the Yoruba West... preliminary work was already going on on what was called essential 'cocoa roads,' as if the Mid-West forbade the construction of 'rubber,' 'timber,' and 'palm oil' roads". (p.11).[25]

From 1952 to 1955, there had been a strong demand by Mid-West legislators for the creation of a Rubber Marketing Board or at least a Rubber Representative Committee.[26] The memorandum noted that these Mid-West demands, which called for a specific organisation which could be charged with the functions of producing and marketing rubber, had been ignored by the Government. "Instead it has come out with much fanfare with schemes for rubber processing factories—as if the answer to cocoa production and marketing would be the setting up of a chocolate factory!" (p.13).[27]

Finally, an effort was made to outline overall economic discrimination against the Mid-West through an *Analysis of Approved Estimates Between the Benin-Delta Provinces and the Rest of the West Region, for the Years 1954-55 and 1955-56.*[28] These estimates provided figures on an overall *Summary of Revenue and Expenditure*; in a second section specific attention was given to Revenue and Expenditure relating to Board Funds.

The overall Summary of Revenue and Expenditure showed nothing startling. In accord with the comparative population figures, an equitable distribution would see the Mid-West area, as against the rest of the West Region, operating on the basis of a 24.5 per cent to 75.5 per cent ratio. During 1954-55, Revenue allocations to the Mid-West area amounted to £2,444,000, or 18.5 per cent of the Regional Total. The Revenue figures for 1955-56 differed very little; the allocation to the Mid-West was £2,339,000 or 18 per cent of the Regional Total. Thus, so far as Revenue was concerned Mid-Westerners could contend that they were receiving slightly less than one-fifth instead of nearly one-quarter of the total Regional Revenue allocation[29] to which they were entitled. Expenditure figures showed little of use to the Mid-West argument. The Mid-West totals were 22.5 per cent and 23.8 per cent of the Regional Expenditures for the financial years 1954-55 and 1955-56. Also, the supplementary (Expenditure) Estimates on public utilities and community amenities indicated that an equitable balance with the Yoruba Provinces had been retained. Thus, with the exception of the small discrepancy in total Revenue figures, and Expenditure figures that showed the Mid-West was engaged to a small degree in deficit financing in each of the years considered,[30] no startling revelations could be drawn from the Overall Approved Estimates of Revenue and Expenditure.

The allocation of Board Funds revealed the major discrepancies. In looking at Capital allocations to the Production Board, it could be seen that the Mid-West had received only about one-ninth of the total Regional Capital allocation, instead of about one-quarter to which it was entitled. Similarly in the allocation of Marketing Board Funds, it received only about one-tenth, or £3.7m. as against £33.3m. for the rest of the West Region. As for Development (Loans) Board funds, the figures indicated that the allocation to the Mid-West was equitable.

It was the allocation of Board (Production and Marketing) Funds which gave Mid-West Movement leaders the opportunity

TAB

ANALYSIS OF APPROVED ESTIMATES
AND THE REST OF THE

SUMMARY OF REVENUE

| | POPULATION IN 000's | PERCENTAGE OF REGIONAL TOTAL | 1954 | |
			REVENUE IN 000's	PERCENTAGE OF REGIONAL TOTAL
BENIN-DELTA PROVINCES	Benin 901 Delta <u>591</u> TOTAL 1492	24.5%	2,444	18.5%
REST OF REGION	4595	75.5%	10,758	81.5%
TOTALS	**6087**		**13,202**	

NOTES:

1. **REVENUE FIGURES** determined by the division of all items of Revenue in proportion to the populations of the two areas, except in the case of Export produce which was divided on a derivation basis.

2. **EXPENDITURE FIGURES** determined by Derivation break-down.

3. (a) Expenditure provided for from:
   Urban Water Supplies, Roads, Education
   Buildings, Medical and Road Development

LE **IV**

AS BETWEEN THE BENIN-DELTA PROVINCES WESTERN REGION

AND EXPENDITURE

-1955				**1955-56**	
EXPENDITURE IN 000's	PERCENTAGE OF REGIONAL TOTAL	**REVENUE** IN 000's	PERCENTAGE OF REGIONAL TOTAL	**EXPENDITURE** IN 000's	PERCENT OF REG'L TOTAL
2,780	22.5%	2,339	18%	2,493	23.8%
<u>287</u> (a)				<u>1,806</u> (a)	
3,067				4,299	
9708	77.5%	10,672	82%	9,302	76.2%
<u>849</u> (a)				<u>4,427</u> (a)	
10,557				13,729	
12,448				**11,795**	
<u>1,136</u> (a)				**<u>6,233</u> (a)**	
13,624		**13,011**		**18,028**	

they sought. It was held that in particular "The Marketing Board Analysis is an eyesore... and emphasises the need for a permanent organisation to be charged with the production and marketing of our produce".(p.7) The unequal division of Marketing Board Funds played right into the hands of Mid-Westerners who had contended consistently that greater attention must be given by the West Regional Government to the production and marketing of Mid-West commodities. From an assessment of the allocation of Board Funds, it was stated that:

> "It is clear that sufficient investment is not being made in the Benin-Delta Provinces. For, how could an area be expected to improve and show adequate returns without adequate application of funds? It must be remembered, too, that most of the schemes... e.g. Road Development... have not even begun".(p.8).

Summary consideration next was given to what were felt to be the "most significant aspects" of the political demand for a separate Mid-West State. It was made clear that the Mid West Movement was prepared to accept the implementation of a plebiscite in the affected (Mid-West) areas. Though Mid-West leaders hitherto had consistently held that any plebiscite must be conducted *prior to* the London Conference, they were now prepared to allow that this might be undertaken afterwards. To be acceptable to Mid-Westerners, however, any such plebiscite would have to be conducted by British Officials or the Federal Government. It was stated, however, that political demands could be measured by other means; not least important was the "persistence and tenacity," with which the Mid-West State issue had been pursued. "The personalities connected with the Mid-West Movement might change, but the demand itself—the basic factor—goes on".(p.9) The results of elections conducted in the Mid-West territory reflected, it was held, the separatist wishes of the Mid-West peoples.

Perhaps the most difficult and vital question with which the Mid-West Movement had to deal related to economic viability. In a *Special Memorandum* submitted by the Economic Committee of the Mid-West State Movement to the 1957 London Conference, this matter was given sole attention.[31] Emphasis was first placed on the capacity of a separate Mid-West State to support financially the administrative structure of an autonomous state. In order to demonstrate this capacity an analogy was drawn with the Southern Cameroons.

TABLE V

ANALYSIS OF APPROVED ESTIMATES AS BETWEEN THE BENIN-DELTA PROVINCES AND THE REST OF THE WESTERN REGION FOR 1955-56.

BOARD FUNDS

A. PRODUCTION BOARD

	TOTAL £000s	BENIN-DELTA £000s	REST OF REGION £000s
CAPITAL EXPENDITURE			
PROJECTED	11,379	1,137	10,242
ACTUAL	10,724	2,290	8,434
Over-Expenditure	1,153		
Under-Expenditure		1,708	

NOTE: Figures exclude any projected expenditure on technical education.

B. DEVELOPMENT (LOANS) BOARD

TOTAL	BENIN-DELTA	PERCENTAGE OF TOTAL	REST OF REGION	PERCENTAGE OF TOTAL
610,483	146,773	24%	463,710	76%

NOTE: The proportion of loans made in the two areas corresponds within one-half *per cent* of the relative populations proportions of the two areas.

C. MARKETING BOARD

TOTAL £M	BENIN-DELTA £M.	REST OF REGION £M.
£37m.	£3.7m.	£33.3m

In 1953, The *Report* of the Fiscal Commissioner on Financial Effects of Proposed New Constitutional Arrangements, set out an item by item listing of the estimated cost of establishing separate departments for the proposed Southern Cameroonian Region. Using these figures as a base from which to draw comparisons, it was contended the Mid-West provinces possessed more than enough revenue capability to establish an equivalent administration. To bolster this argument, it was pointed out that major export commodities, including rubber and timber, had produced increased revenue between 1954 and 1955.[32] The memorandum added that by examining "the relative proportions of the economically significant parts of the population of the Mid West State," and in comparing these to other parts of the Western Region, the 1952 Census figures revealed that the Mid-West possessed 1.7 more persons in the economically active category. Considering, the above factors, the memorandum went on to declare:

> "It is hard to see why the revenue of the Mid-West State as compared with the rest of the Region should indicate both a fall and a smaller contribution to the Region's revenue as a whole. Either... the human resources are not being fully utilised or... the economic administration has been inefficient".(p.30).

Agricultural and Industrial Capacity   Attention next was given to the capability of the Mid-West to produce staple crops. In each of the three staple crops—yams, cassava and rice—the Mid-West provinces showed their capacity to produce these commodities in greater proportional quantity (pounds *per* acre) than nearly all of the other Provinces in the West Region. In livestock, Benin Province showed a greater capacity for the raising of sheep and goats than Delta Province, but the balance, it was maintained, provided adequate totals that would serve to meet Mid West area consumption needs. Further, it was added that the potential capacity of Warri Province to produce fish, (which, it was hoped, would result from the development of a full-scale fishing industry), would help considerably to make up for its low production of live stock. The memorandum held that, overall,

> "Because of its high potential as a food producing state, the Mid-West State stands as the bulwark of any industrial enterprise in the Western Region; along with other food producing areas of Nigeria it provides the basis of Industrialisation anywhere in the Federation of Nigeria".(p.32).

One of the greatest strengths of the Mid-West, in terms of its export resources, was said to lie in the fact that the "Mid West alone specialises in more than one of the major agricultural commodities that is exported from Nigeria".

> "The Mid-West State has practically a monopoly in the production of Rubber for export in the Western Region. The same is true of Timber for export, the bulk of which comes from the thick rain forests of Benin; the production of Timber from the rest of the Western Region is devoted mostly to the needs of local consumption. The Mid-West State and the Eastern Region share the production of Palm Oil for export".(p.32)

Taking into consideration the value of export commodities produced in the Mid-West together with population density, it was estimated that the value *per* head of production fell within the range of "£10 and over *per annum per* head." It was pointed out that "In the Cocoa parts of the West, and in fact in the rest of the West outside the Mid West State, the highest figure for Export Production of Agricultural Commodities is within the range of £5 to £6 *per* head".(p.34)

The Mid-West's economic viability also rested largely on the exploitation of the area's industrial potential. It was pointed out that requisite raw materials were plentiful. Brown coal and water resources in Asaba Division were available to serve as a power generating source.

> "Palm Oil, to undertake a Chemical and Soap,... industry; Timber products for Paper and Furniture Industry; Rubber for the various ranges of Rubber Goods... and above all, the state has the largest River Front in the Region and a coastal belt to provide the location for a Fishing Industry on a National scale". (p.34).

Estimates of basic costs for establishing basic industries would run at: electricity £2.15m.; vegetable oil refinery £2.3m.; pulp and paper, £1.6m.; chemical £3.5m. The total expenditure would be close to £10m., "an amount about half the value of exports from the Mid-West State in a single year." The memorandum stressed that above all it should be remembered that the "most heavily capitalised industry in Nigeria... is the African Timber and Plywood Company situated within the Mid-West State [at Sapele]".(p.35). It was maintained that within the framework of this large enterprise, the building up of subsidiary paper and furniture industries would not prove difficult. After some mention of the value of Mid-West Ports, both to the Mid-West and the Federation in general, the memorandum moved on to consider its final argument.

Ultimately, it was pointed out, *the economic viability of any area must rest on the desire of the people concerned to make their economy viable*: "the will of the peoples concerned is of the greatest importance".(p.36). Once again the instance of the Southern Cameroons was referred to:

> "Their [Southern Cameroonians] desire for [autonomous] status was so overpowering, that they imposed on themselves extra taxes. In a matter of about one week they almost tripled their normal revenue. That is what invariably happens where there is a will, as distinct from an idle wish."(p.36).

On paper, the Mid-West Movement had argued a strong, logical and rational case for the creation of a separate state. Over the past five years and more, it had been made abundantly clear there was a "will" amongst most Mid-Westerners for the creation of a separate State. Little concerted attention, however, had been given to the economic realities. The Movement submission had reversed this emphasis. This was timely, important and justified the insistence of Osadebay, Otobo and Okotie-Eboh that the Mid-West issue should receive primary consideration.

QUALIFIED SUPPORT FOR NEW STATES

The Action Group Position

Speculation now turned to how the Action Group delegation would meet the formidable challenge of the NCNC and Mid-West protagonists. In the event, Awolowo's approach was relatively straight-forward. Seeking first to expose weaknesses in Mid-West and NCNC contentions, he pointed out that at the Conference, "concrete demands" had been made for the creation of altogether, 17 new states. All these, except the COR State demand, had been supported by the NCNC and its allies. "The creation of states in this number, was", he declared, "a frightful prospect." and could prove fatal to the integrity of the Federation. However, if delegates accepted the necessity of Federalism, they must also be prepared to accept its implications, namely that

> "All the Governments in the Federation [Regional as well as Federal] must be equal in status and independent of one another within the sphere of the functions assigned to them and in the derivation of their Revenue".[33]

Awolowo went on to hint darkly that "the NCNC was aware of the implications of its proposals and had put them forward to achieve purposes other than those openly stated".[34] Since 1953,

NCNC spokesmen had openly admitted that their acceptance of federalism was a temporary expedient, and that in due course they hoped the country would revert to a unitary form of constitution. The movement for the creation of new states was therefore being used as a device for "achieving the objectives of a unitary constitution", since the creation of so many new states must inevitably result in their subordination to the Central Government. Awolowo also alleged that the NCNC was exploiting the new states movement in an attempt to secure dominance in the Upper House of the Federal Legislature.[35] COR demands, he declared, were being equally strongly opposed by the NCNC because *the Government of the Eastern Region knew that oil was likely to be found in commercial quantities in that area.*

Awolowo brought forward a further important argument which was bound to hold the attention of the Sardauna and particularly Azikiwe. There were many practical problems involved in the creation of new states, and these, he stated, "could not be reconciled with the request for Nigerian Independence in 1959". The Conference could only set up machinery to examine the claims. Each would then have to be examined in the light of a plebiscite and financial viability. It would be impossible, declared Awolowo, "for the various Nigerian [separate states] claims to be fully examined and for reports to be submitted within two years". For these reasons, the Action Group opposed strongly demands for creation of new states, with the exception of three: Mid West, COR, and Middle Belt.

Support "In Principle"   This was the first mention of specific minority demands by Awolowo. The Action Group Leader allowed cautiously, that his party supported "in principle" the creation of these three states, provided that each could satisfy the following four principles:

"1. No new state should be created within the jurisdiction of any other state, nor any state be created by the joining of two or more states or parts of states without the consent, signified by a two-thirds majority, of the legislatures of the states concerned as well as the Federal Parliament.

2. No ethnic or racial group in any of the existing Regions should be split in the process of creating new states. The bonds which existed between the various tribes of Nigeria and which had been fostered by the British had, in fact, served as a stepping stones towards the creation of a common feeling of Nigerian Nationality and nothing should be done to weaken these bonds.

3. Any ethnic group which did not elect to join the proposed state to be permitted to stay out and to remain with the original state, unless such a group was not geographically contiguous with the original state. If the principle of Self-Determination was to be considered in the creation of new States, then each ethnic unit should be allowed to decide whether to go with the new state or to remain with the old.

4. The creation of a new state should satisfy the test of viability. Both the new state and the residue of the old state should be viable, and the viability of the Federation as a whole should not be impaired. Moreover, the new states should be able from the outset to maintain all the services and amenities provided for the people, by the Government of the original state; and must be capable of developing such services progressively in the future. Nor would it be fair to the people concerned to maintain existing services by imposing heavier taxation; the Conference should oppose the creation of a new state where this would invoke the immediate imposition of heavier taxation".[36]

These stipulations made the Action Group's position known once and for all. Clearly, it was not possible that any aspirant area within the Nigerian Federation, would be able to meet all the conditions specified. As far as the Mid-West was concerned, hopes for a separate state would be dashed by the first principle. The requisite two thirds consent of the West Regional legislature would never be secured so long as Awolowo and his Action Group Government remained in power.

Awolowo went on to state that these four principles should be entrenched in the Constitution. In a generous gesture, however, he held that the claims for the creation of Mid-West, COR, and Middle Belt states were worthy of consideration by the Conference, since these claims were of relatively long standing; had formed part of the election issues at the 1956 Regional elections; were reasonably in accord with what appeared to be practicable in the present circumstances; and consideration of these claims would go a long way towards assuaging the feelings of those now claiming separate state status. He further suggested that, if the Conference felt the claims of these three areas merited investigation, the following procedure should be applied.

First, a Boundary Commission should be appointed to delimit the boundaries of each state in accord with principles 2 and 3 above. The Fiscal Commissioners who were to be appointed for other purposes should then be required to examine the viability of the areas as delimited by the State Boundary Commissioner. The Reports of the Commissions when prepared should be submitted either to a further meeting of the Conference or to the Secretary of State for the Colonies, who should then obtain the comments of the Governments of the Regions concerned and of the Federation. If the area had been correctly delimited, and the proposed states were found to be viable, directions then should be given for the state(s) to be created—subject to the *proviso* that the supporters of the proposed state(s) should win a majority of seats in the area of the new state at the subsequent Federal or Regional elections, whichever were earlier.

Should, however, any of the three proposed States fail to satisfy these tests, then, Awolowo declared, it should not be created. If such a fate should befall the Mid-West State demand, the Leader "guaranteed" that the Action Group, would undertake to adopt either the "Welsh arrangement"[37] or the Provincial Authority Scheme proposed by the Northern Regional Government,[38] with such modifications as were deemed necessary. Finally, Awolowo asserted that if the Conference should decide that new states were to be created, it was also then the duty of the Conference to lay down principles which would prevent the complete disintegration of the country and to set up adequate machinery for the application of these principles.[39]

This, then was Premier Awolowo's reply to his rivals. It provided a terse, rigorous and—to minority and Mid-West aspirants— profoundly shattering statement. Awolowo had made no effort at all to deal with the "Case for a Mid-West State". Indeed, the conspicuous absence of any detailed comment on Mid-West contentions made a mockery of all the initiatives which had been so fully and laboriously advanced by the NCNC delegates and Mid-West protagonists. There was little consolation for Mid-west leaders in the declaration by Awolowo of his interest in the Welsh arrangement or the Provincial Authority Scheme; such a concession would obviously fall far short of the requirements of the Mid-West demand. The inflexibility of Awolowo and his party on the Mid-West issue had now been fully demonstrated. Though a Conference recess *communique* released on 3 June stated that "preliminary examination of the question of Regional self-government"[40] had been completed, the reality was that the NCNC and the Action Group were in a stalemate. The question now was, which party would give way? The fate of the Mid-West issue hung in the balance.

MID-WEST AND MINORITIES BETRAYED

When the Conference re-convened on Friday, 14 June, it was quickly obvious that the Nigerian delegates had mixed a good deal of business with pleasure during the holiday interval. Clearly there had been some hard bargaining amongst the major party delegations and a major decision reached. The NPC, NCNC and Action Group parties had come to an agreement on the New States issue. The details of this agreement were given in a statement on joint proposals now submitted to the Conference.[41] A quick perusal of this document was enough to tell the story: the Mid-West cause, once again had been betrayed. For Mid-West protagonists Friday, 14 June, was indeed "Black Friday".

The Statement asserted that it was "desirable for the Conference to lay down principles and to set up necessary machinery for dealing with [new states] claims", not only as they currently existed, but whenever they might be made in the future. The proposals asked that:

> "A State boundary Commission be set up by the Secretary of State in the first instance, and by the Government of the Federation after Independence, to consider claims for the creation of new states".[42]

In considering such claims, it was held that the Boundary Commission should observe that:

> "(a) The wishes of the people of the area be ascertained by a plebiscite.

> (b) No ethnic group should be split into new states except with the express wishes of a 3/5 majority of the people in the ethnic group as determined by a plebiscite.

> (c) The creation of a new state should be consistent with the principle of viability.[43]

> (d) All competent units of the new states should be geographically contiguous".[44]

There was in this statement, no mention of the Mid-West claim—or the claim of any other Nigerian minority. The cold, impersonal wording of this brief document was somehow both outrageous and astonishing. It was difficult to believe that it had been issued by rival parties which only a week before had been submerged in impassioned debate on just this issue. The debates of the past were, however, now history. The present document on the new states issue revealed the determination of the three major Nigerian political parties to secure *first* the vital objective of National Independence in 1959; and for the East and West Regional Governments *immediate* confirmation of the British grant of Regional Self-Government. The question of more states would have to wait.

This new synthesised position of the major party delegations was now elaborated in the course of discussions at the Twelfth Plenary Session. Basically, each recognised the convenient "cover" which the British delegation's proposals provided. In a major memorandum submitted to the Conference, the British outlined the approach which they considered would best meet the problems raised by the new states issue.[45] The main contention was that to deal justly and effectively with minority claims, a Commission to investigate and assess these should be appointed at end of the Conference. Attention, however, should initially be given only to the three areas—Mid-West, COR and Middle Belt—from which well-recognised demands had been forthcoming; to do otherwise would be to exacerbate to dangerous levels the number and intensity of minority claims, and possibly even delay the proposed date of 1959 for Nigerian Independence.

Finally, at the close of this very eventful day a *communique* on the "Separate States" issue was released by the Conference.[46] To Mid-West supporters this document represented the collective betrayal they had suffered at the hands of their "fair-weather Champions", the NCNC and the Action Group in collusion with the British Governmental Authorities. This *communique* which is quoted below in its entirety, provided a precise and vivid picture for Mid-West and other Nigerian minority elements, of the complex, and indeed very dubious context within which they must now work in order once again to approach their respective objectives. The communique stated that:

> "The Conference recommended the appointment of a Commission of Inquiry to ascertain the facts about the fears of minorities in any part of Nigeria and to propose means of allaying these fears, whether well or ill founded.

> "Though the desire for the creation of new states in part arises from the fears of minorities it would be impracticable to meet all these fears by the creation of new States. There are many different ethnic groups and peoples in Nigeria and, however many States were created, minorities would still inevitably remain in each. It

will therefore be the task of the Commission to propose *other means of allaying these fears and to consider what safeguards should be included for this purpose in the constitution.*

"However if, but only if, no other solution seemed to them to meet the case, the Commission would be empowered as a last resort to make detailed recommendations for the creation of one or more new states, specifying the areas to be included and the governmental and administrative structure most appropriate.

"Before agreeing to any such recommendation as might be made, Her Majesty's Government would have to take into account the effect of the establishment of any such new state on the existing Regions in the Federation and on the Federation as a whole. They would also have to be convinced (and the Commission would have to satisfy them on this point) that any such new state would be viable both from the economic and administrative point of view. In this connection it is the present view of Her Majesty's Government that administrative and other practical reasons will inevitably limit most severely the possibility of further sub-division of Nigeria into states modelled on the present Regional system.

"It is also the present view of Her Majesty's Government that, while the creation of even one more state in any Region would create an administrative problem of the first order, the creation of more than one such state in any Region cannot now be contemplated.

"The Conference invited the Secretary of State for the Colonies to establish the Commission as soon as possible and to determine its precise terms of reference along the foregoing lines.

"The Commission's report will be submitted to the Secretary of State for the Colonies, who will then consult with the Federal and Regional Governments on whether it can be dealt with by correspondence or otherwise or whether the Conference should be re-convened to consider it.

"Following this agreement, the Secretary of State for the Colonies stated that, subject to the adoption by the Conference of the report of the Committee on Public Services, the item of the agenda dealing with Regional self-government was now satisfactorily concluded. In view of this, he formally announced that steps to implement the undertaking on this subject given by Her Majesty's Government at the Conference on the Nigeria Constitution held in London during 1953 would be taken forthwith in respect of the Eastern and Western Regions of Nigeria".[47]

Although the provisions specified in this *communique* raised hopes that the proposed Commission of Inquiry might recommend the creation of a Mid-West State—possibly before the year was out—still the views of the major parties were only too clear. Each was pre-occupied with the problem of territorial control. And now that the British had confirmed their grants of Regional Self-Government to the East and West, it seemed inevitable that minority prospects would be correspondingly diminished. The future for Mid-West protagonists and their minority compatriots throughout Nigeria once again, seemed bleak.

The Nigerian Delegations, having surmounted the Mid-West and new states hurdles, with what had in the final analysis proven to be relative ease, now pressed on with other vital business. For minority representatives, however, the Conference was over; their cause, once again, had been lost. For many, the next hurdle could prove most formidable: what explanations could be given to their faithful followers at home? Neither the new promise offered by the proposed "Minorities Commission", nor the prospect of National Independence in 1959 would necessarily ease the inevitable anger and disappointment of local supporters in the minorities areas.

Osadebay, though a participant in the inter-party meetings which had shaped and finally agreed on the "Joint Proposals", now expressed his distress and deep disappointment. "We are the only people whose case for a separate state has been passed by a Legislature".[48] And now, he lamented, the Conference had, in effect, endorsed the right of this legislature—controlled by the Action Group Government—to *evade* its (1955) legal obligation on the Mid-West issue.

As for the decision of the Conference to set up a "Minorities Commission," the Mid-West Movement leader merely observed that to his mind, this represented "a step back".[49] James Otobo, the Mid-West Movement Secretary and Official Adviser to Leader Osadebay in the West Regional Delegation, was more forthright in his comments. The Action Group, declared Otobo, had given every indication that it intended to circumvent Mid-West demands; the "Joint Proposals" and Conference decision on "Separate States" now provided a graphic demonstration that it had been successful.[50] The only Mid-West voice not to be heard at this time was that of Chief Okotie-Eboh. Chief Festus, who like Osadebay, had participated in shaping the "Joint Proposals", clearly regarded silence to be the best policy.

————————

References

1. *West Africa*, 27 April, 1957, p.395.

2. *Loc cit.*

3. *West Africa*, 25 May, 1957, p.480.

4. See, *The Hudson Report on Provincial Authorities*. (Kaduna: Government Printer, 1956).

5. "Secession or Safeguards?", *West Africa*, 23 March, 1957, p.266.

6. See interview with James Otobo, Int.VI, p.57.

7. See *Minutes of the Third Plenary Session*, 27 May, 1957. NC (57), Third Meeting, (IGH).

8. See *Statement by the Hon. Adegoke Adelabu Concerning Self-Government for the Western Region*, 27 May, 1957, Third Plenary Session, (ADELP).

9. *Ibid.*, p.3.

10. See *Minutes of the Third Plenary Session, op.cit.* p.6.

11. *Ibid.*, p.7.

12. *Loc.cit.*

13. See *ibid.*, p.8.

14. See NC(57) Memorandum No.2, *The Units of The Federation of Nigeria*, submitted by the NCNC (National party) delegation to the Conference, (ADELP).

15. Reference was made here to appropriate provisions in the recently completed *Hudson Report, op.cit.*, which called for extensive strengthening of the powers of existing provincial authorities.

16. These were: 1. The Colony State; 2. The Yoruba State; 3. The Mid-West State; 4. The Ibo State; 5. The Calabar-Ogoja State; 6. The Rivers State; 7. The Cameroons State; 8. The Ilorin-Kabba State; 9. The Middle Belt State; 10. The North-Eastern State; 11. The Hausa State. See *The Units of the Federation of Nigeria, op.cit.*, p.2.

17. *Loc. cit.*

18. See *Self-Government for the Western Region*, Memorandum by the NCNC (National Party) Delegation, submitted to the 1957 London Constitutional Conference, (ADELP).

19. *Ibid.*

20. For details, see memorandum *Self-Government for the Western Region, op.cit.*

21. NC(57), *Mid-West Region*, Memorandum submitted to the Conference by Opposition Members of the Western Region Delegation, (ADELP).

22. See, *The Case for a Mid-West State, op.cit.* Further references below to this document are by page number only.

23. See, *Population Census of the Western Region of Nigeria. 1952*, (Lagos: Census Superintendent, 1956).

24. *Ibid.*

25. See also *Western House of Assembly Debates*, 9 September, 1954, pp.339-54, for contributions of Mid-West Members on the proposed annual expenditure allocation for the Ministry of Public Works.

26. See *Western House of Assembly Debates*, 4 September, 1954, particularly pp.51-56. Here Mid-West legislators, including Osadebay, Omo-Osagie, Oweh, Otobo and Edah (Okotie-Eboh) argued strongly, but in vain, for the inclusion of rubber within the purview of the Marketing Board Bill provisions.

27. In *Western House of Assembly Debates*, 8 March, 1955, the West Regional Minister for Development, Chief C. D. Akran stated, that it was hoped that when the Ikpoba (Benin) and Delta Provinces processing facilities were operating efficiently, "they will help to improve the economy of the areas substantially".(p.119).

28. See below, *Tables IV* (pp.132-33) and *V*.(p.135).

29. Although the proportional difference between slightly less than one-fifth and slightly less than one-quarter of total regional revenue might appear slight, in monetary terms this meant the Revenue Allocation to the Mid-West area was £856,000 short—no small sum to a lean budget.

30. In the memorandum it was contended that the deficit balance for the Mid-West during the two years examined in the Western Regional Government's *White Paper* was "designed to show that the Mid West has been parasitic on the Yoruba West". (p.7).

31. See *Case for a Mid-West State*, Appendix II, *op.cit.* Further references to this appended document are by page number only.

32. See *Tables IV* and *V* above, for details of fluctuations in Exports during 1954 and 1955. It will be noted in particular that each of the major Mid-West export commodities—that is timber, plywood and veneers, and rubber—showed export *increases* in 1955 over the 1954 totals. At the same time, the major (Yoruba) West Export commodity, cocoa, showed a significant *drop*; this decrease amounting to nearly £13m., or about one-third of the 1954 export total.

33. The issue of revenue allocation and distribution became highly contentious at this Conference. A Commission appointed to consider these questions presented its *Report* to the Resumed Constitutional Conference in London, 1958. (See, *Report of the Fiscal Commission*, Cmnd. 481, (London: H.M.S.O., 1958) In this *Report*, the outline of the revenue allocation system later to be developed was put forward, and in it Awolowo's wish to retain Regional control of Regional revenue was recognised. One of the major recommendations of the *Report* was that the principle of derivation should be given primary consideration in revenue distribution.

34. NC(57) *Minutes of the Ninth Plenary Session*, p.12 (IGH).

35. If the NCNC was able to retain the allegiance of new states' leaders, it would be in a strong position to control selection of states' candidates to the Upper House (Senate). Selection to the Senate was to be on the basis of appointment by the Federal Authority from lists of candidates supplied by the respective Regional or State governments.

36. *Minutes of the Ninth Plenary Session, op. cit.*, pp.13-14.

37. The United Kingdom *Ministry of Welsh Affairs* was at this time— June 1957—a second portfolio under the Minister of Local Government and Housing, Mr. Brooke. The Action Group Minister, Chief Tony Enahoro had been impressed by this "doubling" arrangement, and held strongly to the view that a similar doubling of his Home Affairs portfolio with a proposed Mid-West Affairs Ministry could effectively meet the exigencies of the Mid-West situation. (See, *ibid.*, p.16). It was this "Welsh arrangement" which Leader Awolowo was duly to accept and implement later in 1957.

38. See the *Hudson Report, op.cit.*

39. See *Ninth Plenary Session, op.cit.*, pp.9-11.

40. *West Africa*, 8 June, 1957, p.539.

41. See *Joint Proposals by the NPC, NCNC and Action Group Delegations: The Creation of New States*, mimeo., (IGH). Statement submitted to the Nigerian Constitutional Conference, London, June 1957.

42. *Ibid.*

43. No apparent attention was paid to the carefully developed viability argument presented to the Conference by the Economic Committee of the Mid-West State Movement. (See, Appendix II, *Case For a Mid-West State, op. cit.*) One would have thought that the principles laid out in this memorandum would have been incorporated, to some extent, in the (c) clause above. As it stood, this clause was left open to broad interpretation.

44. *Joint Proposals..., op.cit.*

45. See NC(57) *Self-Government and New States*, memorandum submitted by the British Delegation to the 1957 London Conference (IGH).

46. See *West Africa*, 22 June, 1957, p.590.

47. *Ibid.*

48. *West Africa*, 22 June, 1957, p.579.

49. *Ibid.*

50. See interview with Otobo, Int.VI, p.55.

CHAPTER 9

THE MID-WEST AND THE MINORITIES COMMISSION

Following completion of the London Conference, Mid-West leaders were in a quandary. Where should they go from here? The first reaction of Movement Leader Osadebay and his Official Adviser at the Conference, James Otobo, was to break once and for all with the NCNC.[1]

Osadebay and Otobo had, in anger and frustration, come to the conclusion that the NCNC would never become anything more than a "champion in principle" to the Mid-West peoples. Consequently, it was their intention on arrival at Lagos to announce their resignations from the NCNC. Osadebay was also to outline provisions for a "Blueprint for Nigerian Minorities" that he and Otobo had been working on during the London-Lagos voyage.[2] Finally, Osadebay was to announce the formation of a new, militant and exclusively Mid-West political party.

When Osadebay released his statement on arrival at Lagos, Otobo was astonished to find it differed radically from what had been agreed on ship-board. The Mid West Leader clearly had had a change of heart.[3] In his initial statement Osadebay emphasised the disappointment of Mid-West participants at the failure of the London Conference to grant Regional autonomy to the Mid-West. He said he regarded the Conference decision to appoint a Commission to enquire into the fears of Nigerian minorities as a retrograde step but thought that the Mid West peoples should regard the Commission as a "challenge."[4] Osadebay made no mention of the NCNC; nor did he allude to the proposed militant Mid-West party. The following day he repeated over the wireless what one Mid-West leader referred to as his "self-deceptive statement".[5] He maintained that the Mid-West Movement was "satisfied with the arrangement to appoint the Minorities Commission"; the Movement, he declared, would now work to ensure that the Commission would make "our Mid-West dream a reality".[6]

Chief Omo-Osagie, lending forceful support to these statements by Osadebay, skillfully shifted attention to the role of Lennox-Boyd and the British governmental authorities at the Conference. With characteristic flourish, he roundly abused the United Kingdom Government. By not having "the courage to do the right thing" in taking the requisite steps to secure the creation of the Mid-West, declared Omo-Osagie, Lennox-Boyd and his British colleagues had committed "a most grievous act [which would] deal a death-blow to Democracy in Nigeria and particularly in the West".[7] Continuing in a similar vigorous vein, he maintained that:

> "The UK Government has created a state of anarchy and despotism, disorganised society, kindled with hate, bitterness and antagonism and has perpetuated oppression of the minority by the majority. The Nigerian Constitution has failed before it has gone half-way in its deliberations".

Omo-Osagie warned that "the people of the Mid-West would willingly submit to the use of nuclear weapons, devastating bombs or machine guns to annihilate them, rather than remain in a Self-Governing West". Like Osadebay, he made no mention of the NCNC, merely conceding that the decision of the Colonial Secretary was, at least "a challenge". Mid-West protagonists would seize upon the opportunities it offered.

These statements by Osadebay and Omo-Osagie said all that really needed to be said about the policy which the Mid-West Movement was now bent on pursuing. No unfavourable reference was to be made to the NCNC; and criticism relating to the failure of the Mid-West cause should be directed at the United Kingdom Government. The elaboration of this basic posture was simple and straight-forward. Mid-West protagonists were assured it was "a foregone conclusion"—just, it should be noted, as Mid-West supporters had been assured *prior* to the London Conference—that the Commission would "without fail" recommend creation of a Mid-West State.[7] In order, therefore, to present the most convincing case to the Commissioners, the Mid-West peoples were called on to provide full backing for a new and wholly independent campaign.[9] The Mid-West Movement, though a "non-political party Movement", was nevertheless "a political entity in its own right" and would fight "a political battle with all the materials at its disposal".[10]

THE MINORITIES COMMISSION AT BENIN

When the Minorities Commission arrived on 8 December at Benin City *en route* from their second official Public Hearings at

Oyo, it was in the company of something approaching a triumphal procession. Mid-West Movement supporters, on being informed of the approaching Commission entourage, rushed to the outskirts of Benin City to greet the Commissioners and provide a cheering, tumultuous escort.[11]

The mass of Movement supporters was confident that the Mid-West State was now within close reach. Statements issued by Movement leaders over the past four months had made it clear that the Minorities Commission would "without fail" recommend the creation of a separate Mid-West State. Indeed, though Movement supporters had been encouraged to prepare a vast quantity of evidence for both oral and written submissions, it was generally considered that the presentation of such evidence would be a formality only; it would merely serve to confirm the established Mid-West claim which had been virtually accepted in both principle and practice by the Commission. This, at any rate, is what Movement supporters had been led to believe.

The truth of the matter was, however, rather different. Basically, the terms of reference under which the Commission had been appointed made it abundantly clear that it was unlikely that *any* new state, let alone the Mid-West state, would be recommended by the Commission. These terms called for the Commission:

"1. To ascertain the facts about the fears of minorities in any part of Nigeria and to propose means of allaying those fears, whether well or ill-founded.

2. To advise what safeguards should be included for this purpose in the Constitution of Nigeria.

3. If, but only if, no other solution seems to the Commission to meet the case, then, as a last resort, to make detailed recommendations for the creation of one or more new states, and in that case:

a) to specify the precise area to be included in such state or states;

b) to recommend the governmental and administrative structure most appropriate for it;

c) to assess whether any new state recommended would be viable from an economic and administrative point of view and what the effect of its creation would be on the Federation.

4. To report its findings and recommendations to the Secretary of State for the Colonies".[12]

Section three of the terms of reference stipulated that "*If but only if,* no other solution seems to the Commission to meet the case, then *as a last resort...* [it should] make detailed recommendations for the creation of one or more new states."[13] The two italicised phrases in this section said all that was necessary about these terms of reference. Mid-West and other separate state protagonists would have to bear an immense burden of proof if they hoped to substantiate their claims. For, according to these terms, *they must first be able to prove conclusively that no other form of legal and/or constitutional safeguard could serve effectively to allay their fears; only when—and if—the Commission was satisfied that such safeguards would be inadequate would it then be in a position to call for the creation of a new state.*

The harsh truth was that these terms of reference militated *against* the creation of new states; nor was there anything to suggest that the Mid-West cause in particular might elicit a more favourable response. Indeed, it seemed most unlikely that Mid-West protagonists would be able to prove what George G. Baker, the Mid-West Movement leading counsel, had termed "a negative proposition". Yet this was the objective at which Movement protagonists must aim. Certainly they faced rather more than a sporting challenge.

Movement Preliminaries   In proceeding with the Movement case, Baker's approach was bold and systematic. It was clear from the outset that he was well aware of the limits within which he must work. The terms under which the Commission was constrained to operate, as we have earlier noted, placed a heavy burden on Mid-West Movement representatives at the hearings. If Baker was to approach fulfilment of these requirements in strict accord with the terms of reference, he must first demonstrate that fears of Yoruba domination amongst all (not just certain districts or factional elements) Mid-West peoples, clearly existed; he must then be able to show that these fears were well founded. He must then demonstrate the inadequacy of existing and proposed legal and constitutional safeguards; finally, having convinced the Commission of the inadequacy of these safeguards, he must show not only that a separate Mid-West State would be the sole measure which could serve to protect adequately Mid-West interests, but provide concrete evidence that such a state would be both acceptable and viable in economic and administrative terms. Not only was appropriate evidence required to be presented in full, but the majority of it was to be submitted within approximately six days—the time allocated to Baker for presentation of the Mid-West case at the Benin and Warri sittings.

In view of these heavy and demanding requirements, it was hardly surprising that in his introductory remarks before the Commission Baker revealed he had decided on a more direct approach. Ignoring the formally stipulated requirement that "other safeguards" must first be shown to be inadequate, Baker moved directly to the Mid-West claim. He declared that he represented "an ethnic minority... who considered that the only way their fears could be allayed would be by the creation of a Mid-West State".[14]

The case he would be presenting, he continued, would be aimed at "getting at the root of Mid-West fears and at the heart and mind of the people". In completing his case outline, Baker stated bluntly, that following submission of Mid-West Movement evidence he then would "invite the Commission to say that there were no safeguards other than the creation of a Mid-West State which would adequately protect the interests of these people".[15] Though the Commission was later to indicate it was displeased with this unorthodox manner of proceeding, no effort was made to caution Baker; he was allowed to proceed.

After providing a summary account of the common historical and cultural roots of the Mid-West peoples Baker pointed out that their fears were largely those generated by apprehension of "increasing colonisation" of the Mid-West area by the Yorubas. In general terms, he stressed that these fears were substantiated by the fact that "99 per cent of the Civil Service was Yoruba, and that the Regional Marketing Board was completely Yoruba with the exception of one member";[16] further, in the Executive Council, Baker declared there was one Mid-Westerner only [Tony Enahoro]; "Government doctors in the Mid-West were predominantly Yoruba, although there were equally well-qualified Mid-Westerners available". It was to these and other "general fears", he declared, that much Movement evidence would be directed.

Movement Testimony from the Bini "Heartland"   Moving on now with the presentation of substantive evidence, Baker called on a succession of traditional rulers who held hereditary office in the various Palace Societies of the Bini. Amongst these, four expressed grievances which provided specific—if not very pointed—evidence which supported the general allegations of Yoruba domination and neglect. Three of the four traditional rulers also described themselves as "supporters but not members" of the Action

Group, thus giving credence to statements made earlier by Baker that the Mid-West Movement was "non-party" and embraced all elements in the Mid-West provinces. Although none of these witnesses was vehement in his denunciations of Yoruba "colonialism" and "neglect", each indicated dis-satisfaction with the existing system of control exercised in the Mid-West through the Ibadan Government. Chief Lawal Osula, the *Arala* of Benin, stated that the Mid-West, which was a "large producer of rubber, still waited for the West Regional Government to respond to the demands of Mid-West protagonists for improved "Marketing and Processing facilities." Chief Ezomo, one of the seven hereditary *Uzamas* under the *Oba* of Benin, declared that he was "dissatisfied with the present state of development in the Mid-West; taxation was exorbitant and the greater part of tax collected was sent to Ibadan". Chief Oliha stated that the development of the Mid-West area "had suffered since the present Government assumed office some six years ago; roads were bad, water supplies inadequate and the city of Benin itself was extremely dirty".[17] When it was pointed out to Chief Oliha that the Divisional Council was responsible for the cleanliness of the town the old chief once again pointed the finger of blame at Ibadan. It was, he said, because the Divisional Council had been kept short of funds that it had been unable to do its work effectively. Finally, Chief Ineh brought this modest list of allegations by Bini natural rulers to an end when he maintained there was discrimination against Mid-West people in favour of Yorubas particularly in the allocation of scholarships.

Baker next summoned three prominent Bini women. Amongst these, Madam Eweka, President of the *Otu Edo* Ladies Section, put forward the most coherent and detailed statement about alleged Yoruba discrimination and neglect. She declared that "the revenue from forest products [in the Mid-West area] was not used for Mid-West development"; and expressing a more specific grievance of Benin women traders, she alleged that the latter were "treated badly" when they attempted to trade at Ibadan, and that unlike their Yoruba sisters and brethren, Mid-Westerners received no loan funds for the development of their farms.[18] Madam Eweka also voiced another general grievance. "Mid-Westerners", she declared, were often dismissed from "good Government jobs and replaced by Yorubas". Though Madam Eweka stated that she did not know the "manner in which they were removed", she maintained that this seizure by Yorubas of Mid-West jobs was the basis for a great deal of the ill-feeling and fears against the Awolowo Government.

Chief Omo-Osagie, the next witness called by Baker, took a different line with his initial evidence. Taking advantage of the terms of reference, which specified that the fears of *religious* as well as ethnic minorities should be considered by the Commission,[19] Omo-Osagie alleged that the introduction of Yoruba cults such as the *Ogboni* and *Ifa*—the latter being a "cult of divination"—was having an "insidious effect" on Mid-West peoples.[20] Neither cult, he stated, was in any way associated with traditional Bini and Mid-West deities; yet both were gaining increasing influence in the area. The *Ogboni* Society,[21] he said, was particularly feared, and was "far more dangerous than Freemasonry" to which it had been likened. Omo-Osagie said that he feared that when Independence was granted to Nigeria, laws would be passed making membership in it compulsory; already, he felt it was widely accepted in the West that *Ogboni* membership was a requisite qualification for gaining governmental appointment at any level.

Omo-Osagie now turned briefly to the recent passage of the *Western Region Chiefs Law No. 20 of 1957*—about which Opposition elements throughout the West were very apprehensive. Sections 4, 5, 6 and 7 of this Law dealt with procedures now to be followed in the election of an *Oba*. This law, declared Omo-Osagie, effectively placed the authority for selection of an *Oba* under the control of the Regional Government. According to traditional practice in the Mid-West (and elsewhere in the Western provinces) the *Oba* is elected by a committee of traditional chiefs; the new law now altered this procedure since the committee of traditional chiefs was now to be "subject to the direction of a Regional Minister".[22] Furthermore, declared Omo-Osagie, Mid-West fears of Yoruba meddling with this "sacred indigenous institution" were not lessened by the additional provision in the new Chiefs Law which gave to the Minister the authority to "over-rule the committee of traditional chiefs in the making of a Chieftaincy appointment".

At this point, and for the first time in the course of Mid-West Movement evidence, attention was briefly given to the question of safeguards. Chairman Willink, addressing Omo-Osagie, said the Commission had now heard much evidence indicating that Mid-West fears of Yoruba domination of a fundamental, as well as a more instrumental nature did exist. The Chairman then asked Omo-Osagie what safeguards would serve to allay these fears.

Without hesitation, Omo-Osagie replied that he felt there were two alternatives: either there should be a return to a unitary system of Government where representatives from all parts of the country would be elected to a single central government, or a new state for the Mid-West area should be created. Omo-Osagie rejected outright the suggestion of Chairman Willink that a restriction on the power of the Regional Government, accompanied by a parallel increase in the power of the Federal Government, might be acceptable.

Mid-Westerners, asserted Omo-Osagie, would resist any attempt to leave the peoples of Benin and Delta provinces under even a drastically modified West Regional authority. Indeed, he maintained, it was because Mid-West people felt this way, that the new Ministry of Mid-West Affairs was considered entirely unacceptable; under its newly selected minister, Enahoro, the Ministry and its subordinate Mid-West Advisory Council were viewed by most Mid-West residents as instruments for extending the "dominance and colonisation" of the Mid-West provinces by the Ibadan Government.

Omo-Osagie now moved on to stipulate what he alleged were specific instances of Yoruba domination. The Senior Police Officers in the Mid-West area were, he stated, "all Yorubas"; nor did he know of "any Benin man" who held a responsible police position in the Yoruba provinces. The membership of Government Boards was comprised "almost entirely of Yorubas", as was the staff of the Western Region Office in London; and indeed, added Omo-Osagie, nearly all scholarships awarded went to Yorubas. He gave the example of Ijebu Province, no larger than Benin Division, where 17 candidates had been awarded scholarships by the West Regional Government while no applicant from the Benin/Delta area had been successful.

Moving on with his catalogue of grievances, Omo-Osagie asserted that in the Public Service of the West Regional Government discrimination against Mid-West applicants and in favour of Yoruba applicants was rife and well-known. So far as Economic and Industrial Development in the Mid-West area was concerned, Omo-Osagie maintained that the Awolowo Government was guilty of "consistent neglect". Appeals for the establishment of a Rubber Marketing Board had been ignored "until recently, when the Western Region Government announced that such a board was under consideration". And although a grant of over £4m. from *Colonial Development and Welfare* funds had been made to cocoa farmers, no comparable sum had been made available for the rehabilitation[23] of rubber in the Mid-West. And to make matters even worse, declared Omo-Osagie, the recent development of rubber plantations in Ijebu Province (Yorubaland) was considered concrete evidence by Mid-West residents of the West Regional Government's intention to "kill the rubber industry" in the Benin/Delta area. This impression was further strengthened by the apparent electoral strategy of the Awolowo Government at the time of the 1956 West Regional elections. Following renewed agitation for the creation of a Mid-West state, the Awolowo Government had undertaken the construction of a rubber processing factory at Ikpoba (Benin Division). Shortly after these elections, however, the factory had been shut down, for reasons which Omo-Osagie declared, had yet to be fully known.[24] This "devious strategy", he maintained, was very similar to that employed by the Action Group Government in the Delta, where, prior to the 1956 regional elections, it had had voted £100,000 for the development of Koko Port. In the event, however, no funds had been provided after the election.[25]

For his final examples of "Yoruba domination" Omo-Osagie turned to his own Benin Divisional Council; he referred to two acts which, he maintained, clearly demonstrated that the West Regional Government had grossly abused its powers in its efforts to assert its authority over the BDC. The first act concerned Chief R.O.I. Iyamu, the former Assistant Secretary of the BDC. The Council had recommended to the Ministry of Local Government, Ibadan, that Chief Iyamu be dismissed. However, "owing to the fact that he is a member of the Action Group", alleged Omo-Osagie, not only was this BDC recommendation ignored but Chief Iyamu was "offered a transfer to another Local Government Council in the Province and his designation changed to Deputy Secretary".[26]

The second act to which Omo-Osagie referred involved the March 1955 dissolution of the BDC. This act of dissolution, he stated, had been a tremendous jolt to BDC councillors; the dissolution had followed an extra-ordinary meeting of the BDC attended by the Ministers of Justice and Local Government, and Home Affairs; and no reason had been given for the decision to dissolve the BDC.[27] These acts, Omo-Osagie maintained, had been but a small part of an overall plan which the Awolowo Government had been attempting to implement since late 1954 and which was designed to secure for the Government party the support of Benin Division, "heartland of the Mid-West."

In leading the testimony of the remaining Mid-West Movement witnesses from Benin Division, Baker concentrated on drawing evidence from each which would strengthen earlier contentions of Government pressure tactics being applied to the BDC. It was alleged that in addition to the direct measures, which Omo-Osagie had outlined previously, another more indirect but equally punishing tactic had been employed: Awolowo and his Action Group Government had engaged in "overt discrimination" against the BDC and its constituent councils in the matter of local appointments to the Loans Board and in the allocation of Local loans. It was generally recognised that the capacity of local communities to initiate or perpetuate development programmes depended to a large extent on substantial financial support through the Local Loans Board of the Regional Government. As a consequence, the withdrawal or decrease of support in this area of expenditure could be viewed as one of the most effective methods of making localities aware of the Regional Government's presence.

In Benin Division, Mr. Adonrin, Chairman of the Iyekovia District Council expressed his bitter disappointment over the treatment his Council had received from the Local Loans Board. He pointed out that his Council had submitted to the Regional Government at the invitation of the latter, the names of persons whom it had nominated to serve on the Local Loans Board at Ibadan. These persons had not been appointed and others who were not nominated by the local Council had been substituted for them.[28] A.E. Atohengbe, Chairman of the Uhunmwode District Council, an area within which there was majority support for the creation of a Mid-West state, complained that his Council had received similar treatment. His Council had received a request from the West Regional Finance Corporation to nominate persons to serve as members on the Local Loans Board. Accordingly, the Council had put forward ten names. Of these, he declared, only one ultimately was appointed to the Board.[29] Farmers in the area, said Atohengbe, had applied for loans. It was thought, however, that "there was little prospect for non-supporters of the Action Group receiving them".

Benin City had also been allegedly subjected to similar discriminatory treatment. D.P.I. Ogbebor, Chairman of the Benin City Council since the NCNC had been voted back into power at the local government elections of 1955, declared that, while "not a single person nominated by his Council had been approved", it was significant that "other persons, most of whom were Action Group members, had been appointed".[30] Awolowo and his West Regional Government, he stated, were bent on winning over support in the Mid-West heartland, and to achieve this, the Action Group leader was prepared to use all requisite measures.

Movement Testimony From the Outlying Divisions   In evidence submitted by witnesses from the other three divisions of Benin Province, emphasis was given to the common cultural and historical links of Mid-West peoples, together with additional allegations of Yoruba domination, discrimination and neglect.

The first witness from Ishan Division, G.O. Ebea, Member for Ishan in the Federal House of Representatives, contended that the Ishan Divisional Council(IDC) had been subjected to the same basic assault from the Awolowo Government, as had the BDC, and for the same reason. The IDC had been dissolved on the instructions of the Minister of Justice and Local Government in April 1957. Although the reason given by the Awolowo Government was that the dissolution had been ordered to facilitate the "setting up of nine new District Councils upon which appropriate powers formerly held by the IDC would be devolved",[31] Ebea maintained that the real reason was quite different: the Government had simply wished to eliminate this NCNC-controlled council.

The decision to create these new District Councils had been, he pointed out, the result of a recommendation by a "Committee presided over by Mr. Enahoro, the present Minister of Home and Mid-West Affairs"; but this recommendation, he declared, had no basis in fact. The IDC, he stated, was solvent, and as matters now stood with the District Councils, "even with the additional revenue they might derive as a result of taking over certain functions of the IDC", these councils still would have "insufficient funds to meet the cost of their staff, let alone to carry out any development work". He felt that this was another example of Yoruba efforts to dominate the people of the Mid-West through abuse and manipulation of local government institutions.

As evidence of further attempts at domination and discrimination by the Regional Government, Ebea and subsequent Ishan witnesses provided testimony of pressure applied to the Opposition IDC through manipulation of chieftaincy appointments. It was pointed out by Ebea that the "appointments of the *Onogie* of Idoa and the *Onogie* of Ubiaja" had been terminated "without the consent, consultation or demand of the people".[32] The *Onogie* of Idoa, he stated, had been appointed as one of five traditional members of the IDC; the appointment had been made official in *Western Region Legal Notice No. 212 of 1955.* Less than a year later, however, and for no specified reason *Western Region Legal Notice*

No. 252 of 1956 announced the termination of his appointment. Ebea stated that the reason for the removal of both *Onogies* was simple; each had rendered support to the dominant party in the IDC, the NCNC. The Awolowo Government was determined to remove them and so had revoked their appointments. Chief Shaka Momodu put it more directly when he declared these *Onogies* were "removed because they would not change over to the Action Group".[33]

While Baker's Ishan witnesses levelled many complaints against the West Regional Government and the Action Group, alleging abuse and manipulation of chieftaincies, very little was said about discrimination over patronage and benefit allocations. The single major complaint presented in evidence referred to the fact that "until recently there were no medical facilities" in the Division. A.I. Ibhazo, who possessed the impressive title of "parliamentary secretary" to the Ibadasa District Council, said that the Ibadasa people themselves had decided to build a medical centre at Iruekpen "with their own labour and no government assistance".[34] They had spent about £6,500—all applications for Government assistance, it was contended, had been turned down.

This Ishan evidence had neither the range nor depth of that produced by Benin Division witnesses. Indeed, Ishan witnesses called had been few; evidence from area chiefs had been sparse; in fact only the stalwart Mid-West protagonist Enosegbe II, *Enogie* of Ewohimi had been prepared to come forward. One of the Ishan political leaders, Ibhazo, was hardly of any great prominence in the divisional community. These factors, allied with the slightness of evidence actually produced, were not re-assuring to Mid-West prospects.

However, if the strength of Mid-West Movement evidence had diminished in the course of the Ishan Division testimony, the deterioration in the submissions from the remaining two Benin Provincial Divisions of Afenmai and Asaba, was little short of alarming. Beginning evidence for Afenmai Division, the *Oba* of Agbede, a minor chief in the division, attested to the historical and cultural links which he contended existed between Afenmai and Benin. He said that he recognised the *Oba* of Benin as his ruler.[35] Further, he stated that his people "understood the Edo language as spoken in Benin, and some of them were also able to speak it". Subsequent witnesses called by Baker were able to provide further historical and cultural information for the Commission, but little else.

With time now rapidly running out for the submission of Movement evidence at the Benin sitting, Baker called forward two witnesses from Asaba Division. Both were prominent local politicians who had held leading posts in the Movement since its inception under the BDPP in 1953. The first was Chief F. H. Utomi.

Utomi, who was at this time Chairman of the Asaba Divisional Council and a Member of the Western House of Assembly, stated that the evidence he would submit to the Commission would be "representative of the Councils of the Asaba Divisional Authority".[36] Dealing solely with allegations of "discrimination and neglect", Utomi spoke first about the dearth of Government support for the development of Medical Facilities in the Division. He stated that though the Divisional Authorities had received a £10,000 Government grant to assist in the founding of a hospital at Ogwashi-Uku (Utomi's home-town), this figure, "compared unfavourably with much larger capital grants to similar combined hospitals in the Yoruba areas". The hospital at Agbor, he further stated had been built in 1906 and was "completely inadequate, being without light or water". The Divisional Council had applied several times for Government assistance in developing this facility, but without success.

On the subject of roads, he said that the Council had been invited by the Government to submit recommendations for the expenditure of funds totalling £4.5m. voted for the road programme. He maintained that none of the Asaba Council's recommendations had been accepted, and "the greater part of the money had been used to tar cocoa roads in the Yoruba areas". As for Water Supplies, Utomi stated that the Government grants allocated to Asaba and Ogwashi-Uku had never been received and that no water supplies in these two places had been developed. In relation to educational facilities, Utomi stated that the Divisional Council had applied for an Elementary Teachers' Training Centre, in connection with the Government's newly implemented primary education programme. This application, however, had not been accepted; thus the Division remained without the Training Centre.

In concluding his testimony, Utomi referred to two final instances of what he felt were examples of overt discrimination by the Regional Government; one at Asaba, the other at Ibadan. At Asaba, "a palm oil mill run by the Western Region's Production Development Board had been handed over to a private individual who was a party [Action Group] member". Once in the hands of this person, he stated, the mill had failed after only one year of operation. At Ibadan, Utomi alleged, "over 150 lower-paid hospital employees who were mostly Western Ibos" were dismissed without any adequate explanation.With a final assurance that his 212,000 fellow Western Ibo and Ika residents of Asaba Division were committed to joining the Edo-speaking people in a Mid-West State, Chief Utomi now made way for Asaba's, Chief J.I.G. Onyia.

Chief Onyia referring to a memorandum submitted by his Western Ibo colleague, C.O. Odiakosa, directed his remarks to one of the eight examples of alleged West Regional Government discrimination cited in the Odiakosa memorandum. This example dealt with the removal of names of NCNC supporters from Voters Lists[37] prior to the 1956 West Regional Elections. Onyia stated that the original Voters Lists had been made up and approved in the Division, "but after printing by the Action Group at Ibadan, it was discovered that some 600 known supporters of the Honourable A.E. Isede, NCNC Member of the House of Assembly for Asaba West, had been omitted". Though Onyia confirmed that this irregularity had not been raised with the appropriate Government and legal authorities "since Isede was successful at the election, having gained a majority of some 12,000 votes over his Action Group opponent", still, he stressed, the time had now come to reveal the kind of behaviour to which the Action Group had all too often been resorting.

The Mid-West Movement under the guidance of its leading counsel Baker had been anxious to secure its position at these Benin hearings. It was, however, now obvious that the Movement case—in so far as it had to this point been revealed—was dangerously weak. Certainly, a degree of blame rested with Baker. His unwillingness to deviate from the set Movement strategy which gave no consideration to "other safeguards" short of a Mid-West State, had not only irritated Sir Henry and his colleagues, but also meant that the Movement submission was consistently falling short of the requirements specified in the terms of reference.

Still, it was possible that this decidedly bold approach by Baker might in the end be successful, *if the quality and quantity of evidence supporting Movement contentions of "fears" was convincing*. Here again, however, the Movement case had been shown to be astonishingly weak. Movement evidence from Benin Division appeared to be adequate, if repetitious and often irrelevant to the demonstration of "fears", but evidence from the outlying districts of Ishan and Afenmai in particular had deteriorated. Baker's witnesses were few, and of dubious credibility; the evidence submitted scanty and frequently of only peripheral relevance to stated "fears".

Opposition Testimony   It was now the turn of opponents of the Mid-West cause. Their evidence was led by Chief R.A. Fani-Kayode, leading counsel for the Action Group at these Benin hearings. His submission was thorough and effective and cast doubt on much Movement evidence while raising serious doubts about the credibility of witnesses.[38] The thrust of Fani-Kayode's submission for Benin Province was to show that the peoples of Afenmai, Ishan, Asaba and Benin divisions harboured greater fears of Ibo than Yoruba domination. Ibos, it was pointed out, already monopolised trade in these areas, and if political power were added to this monopoly there would be "a real danger of complete subjection". I.A. Aderemi, counsel for the Action Group "front" body, the Anti-Mid-West State Movement, claimed that, contrary to the evidence of Movement witnesses and Chief Omo-Osagie in particular, there was a close affinity between the Edo and Yoruba peoples, and indeed that the West Regional Government had done everything possible to encourage Edo culture.[39] In support of these contentions, the Action Group counsel paraded before Sir Henry and his colleagues a seemingly endless procession of witnesses.

Fani-Kayode meanwhile stressed continually that the Action Group supported wholeheartedly the concept of a Mid-West State; that the party was in fact ready to give *de facto* support for its immediate creation. There was only one small reservation which, he said, the party retained: this was that *"those intra-Mid-West peoples who wished to opt out of such a construct should be allowed to do so"*.[40] Fani-Kayode maintained that his clients were adamant that any future Mid-West State should not include Afenmai and Ishan divisions; nor should it encompass the Western Ibo peoples of Asaba Division—*in other words, three of the four divisions of Benin Province*! The Mid-West Movement, he reminded the Commission, was committed to the principle of self-determination: obviously, then, it must recognise the responsibility it now had to the smaller groups within Benin Province.[41] "The large group comprising the people of Benin", he stated, must, therefore, surely grant to smaller groups within Benin Province the opportunity either to opt out of a Benin State and form a smaller unit of their own, or to give their allegiance to the people of their choice.

Fani-Kayode and his Action Group lawyers now stepped aside, leaving Chief F. Rotimi Williams, leading counsel for the West Regional Government, to proceed with his clients' case—which also was "in support" of the creation of a Mid-West State. Chief Williams, in short order, made clear that the West Regional Government supported, with minor variations[42] the Action Group concept of a "residual Mid-West", (that is to say, Benin Province, less Afenmai, Ishan and Asaba divisions).

With the basic position of the Awolowo Government on the Mid-West issue established, Chief Williams launched a penetrating two-pronged assault on the Movement submission. The object of this assault was not only to demolish Movement contentions of "discrimination and neglect" by the West Regional Government, but also to impress upon the Commission in broad, positive terms the extent of Government industry and application in relation to a range of activities within the West Region as a whole. To this end, Williams called forward an impressive array of "calm, quiet" British administrators who testified on the policies, functions and actual operations of their respective departments.

These witnesses provided lengthy, detailed evidence on the supply of amenities (water, roads, electricity); the allocation of educational facilities and resources (primary, secondary, training college and university levels); the provision of Medical services (dispensaries, health and maternity clinics, hospitals); the allocation of Government appointments through the Public Service Commission, together with the procedures employed for appointments, dismissals, discipline and promotion.[43]

Chief Williams, with the assistance of his legal associate Mr. Fatayi Williams, then turned his attention to refuting a few of the most significant Movement allegations. Once again he made full use of the Regional Government's British administrators. On this occasion, the attention of these witnesses was given to refuting allegations of "discrimination and neglect" in relation to: economic and industrial development; rubber development; Local Government authorities, with particular reference to the Benin and Ishan Divisional Councils; and the staffing of West Regional Boards and Corporation.[44]

As a result of this combined effort by Fani-Kayode and Chief Rotimi Williams, the Movement case, by the end of the Benin hearings, had been reduced to a precarious condition. From the vantage point of Mid-West protagonists, the obvious and critical question was: 'What steps might now be taken to *salvage* the Mid-West cause?'

This was not an easy question to answer. The Movement task at Warri would at best be no less taxing. With the exception of Urhoboland it has already been shown that the other districts of Delta Province were neither consistent nor enthusiastic in their support for the Mid-West cause. But one thing at least was clear. Baker must concentrate on ensuring a high standard of evidence. This evidence must be relevant, relate *directly* to specified "fears", and be presented by prominent and reputable witnesses. Furthermore, Movement counsel needed to think seriously about the risks involved in advocating a Mid-West State as the "only adequate safeguard"—a tactic already shown to be fraught with danger.

Still, there remained one final factor which might, in the end, swing the balance in the Movement's favour: this was the active support of the NCNC at the remaining Mid-West hearings. Although developments during the course of the Benin sitting suggested that such an eventuality would be unlikely, still there was hope. It was not too far-fetched to suggest that on the fulfilment of this hope rested the fate of the Mid-West cause.

The Minorities Commission at Warri

As Baker proceeded now to outline the case which he was presently to submit to the Commission at Warri, it became immediately evident that the Movement yet again could be in serious trouble. Baker, it seemed, was not only content to persuade the Commission of the moderation of his clients' position, he was even prepared to grant concessions. With astonishing casualness he was prepared to allow that the Mid-West State would not be weakened if the Western Ijaws and the Akoko Edos were not included within its bounds; and, indeed, that even if the Warri Division remained outside any such Mid West construct, the new Mid-West State would remain a "viable entity".[45] Baker did, however, maintain one rather significant reservation: should Asaba and Aboh divisions be excluded from the proposed state, then, he said, "the picture might be very different". All this seemed a strange way to bring a forceful and convincing case to bear.

Certainly, judging from his past performances, Chief Williams would be quick to turn Movement moderation and concessions to the advantage of his clients; nor was it likely that a gentler and more accommodating approach to Chairman Willink and his colleagues would compensate for the dearth of requisite evidence. Baker up to this point had given no indication that he was prepared to conform to the requirements of the Commission's terms of reference; the Movement apparently still intent on adhering to the position that only a separate state would provide adequate safeguards for Mid-West interests. Finally, there was the matter of NCNC support. Here also the indications were not encouraging. So far, no member of the NCNC hierarchy had indicated whether the party intended taking any formal part in these proceedings.[46] It could only be assumed, therefore, that the Movement once again must be prepared to fight it out alone against the combined might of the West Regional Government, the Action Group and their satellite organisations. Certainly, it was not a promising prospect which the Movement faced at these forthcoming hearings.

Movement's Warri Division Testimony   In the course of Baker's first presentation at these Warri hearings—that for Warri Division—it soon became apparent that the Movement submission once again was falling short of its objectives. The main thrust of Baker's presentation did not focus on the Mid-West issue *per se*; rather, emphasis was on why Warri Division should be included in a Mid-West State, if a separate Mid-West State was, in fact, created. Baker was, however, at least fortunate to have at his disposal two prominent witnesses, Chiefs Arthur Prest and Festus Okotie-Eboh. Though a good deal of ill-feeling still existed between these two—largely as a result of Chief Festus' victory over Prest in the bitterly contested 1954 Federal elections[47]—still a shared antipathy towards the Action Group now allowed both to find common cause.

The basic position of Baker's witnesses at these Warri hearings was clear enough: the interests of all ethnic elements in Warri Division, particularly the Itsekiris, would best be served by ensuring that the Division would be included in any future Mid-West State. Not to follow this course would be to risk renewed outbreaks of ethnic hostility together with the dislocation and likely deterioration of the Division's prosperous yet fragile economy—a subject of particular concern to wealthy, land-owning Itsekiris. Movement evidence was submitted to confirm that all non-Itsekiri ethnic elements endorsed this position: Urhobos and Ibos in the Division were said to be "99.9 per cent behind the Movement for the creation of a Mid-West State";[48] and though Baker produced no spokesman for the Ijaws of Warri Division, Chief Festus somewhat weakly maintained that as the Member representing Warri Division in the Federal House, and who "enjoyed the confidence of the whole Division" he was speaking for Ijaws too, in calling for the inclusion of Warri Division within the Mid-West State. As for the Itsekiris, Baker's witnesses stated that there was currently a majority in favour of including Warri Division in any future Mid-West State[49]— though this confident estimate was later to be subjected to sharp challenge from Action Group witnesses.

Altogether a fair body of evidence was presented in support of the position calling for the inclusion of Warri Division within any future Mid-West State. However, much less attention was given to dealing with *fears* of Yoruba domination and to contentions of discrimination and neglect by the West Regional Government, the primary considerations of the Commission. Both Prest and Okotie-Eboh provided general support for the standard Movement allegations of *discrimination and neglect* in relation to the development and maintenance of amenities in the Delta Province, and in relation also to the issues of rubber development and the Koko Port project; however, they supplied no detailed backing for these allegations, nor did Baker's other witnesses show any greater interest in providing it.

There were two further and rather unsettling developments for Mid-West protagonists to be noted in the Movement's Warri submission. So far, Baker still had given no indication that he was prepared to consider the vital matter of "other safeguards." It was also significant that the NCNC as a party had yet to take a formal part in the proceedings. Although Chief Okotie-Eboh had advanced briefly the NCNC position on new states in general; for the rest he made it clear he was advancing solely the views of those he represented in Warri Division.

Testimony from the Outlying Divisions   While these developments in the submission for Warri Division were hardly encouraging to Mid-West supporters, the presentations now made on behalf of Aboh and Urhobo divisions—with not even a gesture of attention to Western Ijaw Division—clearly indicated that the Mid-West case was slumping into rapid decline. The presentation of the remainder of substantive evidence was completed in just a little over two hours on 20 December, only the second day of the Warri sitting!

The submission which Baker led for Aboh Division which, with Asaba Division, made up what was known as Western Iboland, was particularly weak. Though the two witnesses called were both prominent—Chief Frank Oputa-Otutu was the MHA for Aboh

West, and J.I. Izah, MHR for the Division—neither gave anything more than the most cursory attention to the Mid-West State issue and nothing was said about "fears". This Aboh Division evidence amounted to nothing more than a token submission. Why had not such influential witnesses as Movement Secretary James Otobo, Chief O.I. Dafe and the *Obi* of Obiaruku amongst other prominent Aboh leaders, come forward to bolster the Mid-West claim?

The final Movement submission, this time from Urhobo Division was equally disappointing. Of the four Movement witnesses called forward, three of these, P.K. Tabiowo, Chief J.G. Mariere and the old *Ovie* of Oghara (all, it was to be noted, "staunch" Movement leaders of long standing) preferred to restrict their testimony to allegations of "discrimination and neglect" in relation to the development of roads and the allocation of medical facilities in Urhoboland and the Mid-West provinces in general.[50] Each of these allegations was set out in only the most general terms. Indeed, efforts by Chairman Willink to secure evidence of a more specific nature brought only the assurance from Mariere that he "strongly suspected" that the alleged discriminatory acts had and were continuing to take place.

Even Chief Oweh, the sole Movement witness to address the contentious issue of "Yoruba domination", was hardly less vague in his testimony. Yoruba domination, he contended, was shown by the simple fact that the Yoruba people were entrenched as the "eternal majority" group controlling the Government in the Western Region; that since this was the case, there was "no possibility of a Mid-Westerner, however loyal to the party, ever becoming Premier". Oweh was on rather stronger specific grounds when he alleged that the Regional Government had discriminated against the Urhobos when the number of MLA's returned from the Division had been reduced from six to three. This took place in 1956 following the discovery that the population figures on which the seat allocation for the Division had been made were vastly inflated. Oweh alleged that this drastic reduction in the Division's seats had been effected solely to deprive the NCNC of three seats—the NCNC controlled all six seats in the Division at that time. On the basis of this noticeably limp testimony, the Movement presentation at these hearings concluded.

Opposition Contentions　　　As the hearings turned now to consideration of submissions by Movement opponents, it became apparent why, in the instance of Western Ijaw Division, the

Movement had neglected the claim of Mid-West protagonists for the inclusion of the Division within a Mid-West State. The position put by A.O. Allaghoa, and later by Mr. Ozeki, counsel for the Ijaw State Union, was clear and categorical. *Western Ijaws did not wish to be included in any future Mid-West State; nor did they wish to continue within the territorial jurisdiction of either the East or West Region. Western Ijaws wished to join with their fellow Ijaws of the riverine areas of the East and West regions in a separate pan-Ijaw Rivers State.*[51]

Moving to the Warri Division evidence, O.N. Rewane, counsel for what were, in effect, pro-Action Group Itsekiris, led off the case. Rewane's presentation was forceful and thorough. Examining the "essential plight" of Itsekiris in Warri Division, he managed clearly to show why most Itsekiris were so strongly opposed to inclusion in any future Mid-West State.[52] The Movement submission for Warri Division had stressed the ethnic identity of Itsekiris with their Urhobo antagonists and other Mid-West "neighbours". Chiefs Prest and Okotie Eboh had emphasised that the interests of Itsekiris could best be secured through a policy of accommodation with their former rivals, and that this could most easily be achieved within the confines of a Mid-West State. These contentions were now shown to be tenuous at best. Rewane outlined Itsekiri claims to kinship with the Yorubas and to an identity separate and quite distinct from their ethnic "neighbours" in the Delta and the Mid-West as a whole. He then traced the history of increasingly hostile relations between Itsekiris and the numerically dominant Urhobos leading up to the present time.

Rewane constructed a most persuasive argument to explain why the "good neighbour policy" advocated by Baker and his Movement witnesses would offer no security to Itsekiris. He stressed evidence showing that Itsekiris had been under growing pressure from increasing numbers of Urhobos and other "stranger" elements over the past twenty years. Non Itsekiris it was stressed, now dominated the Warri Urban District Council (WUDC); also in 1954 Chief Festus had drawn heavily on non-Itsekiri support to wrest the Division's Federal seat from the incumbent Chief Prest. It was further maintained by Rewane's witnesses that Mid-West non-Itsekiris were now well on their way to achieving similar objectives at the Regional level of government and administration. Under these circumstances, therefore, it was quite understandable that Rewane's Warri Division clients should express a strong desire to create even closer, more direct links with the Ibadan Government and the Yoruba West. Certainly, it was obvious that neither a Mid-West State nor even the existing constitutional arrangement would alleviate fears.

It was now the turn of Chief Rotimi Williams, on behalf of the West Regional Government, to lead off what was to be the final major submission at the Commission's Mid-West hearings. While Chief Williams introduced some new evidence, his case served mainly to strengthen the primary contentions which he had earlier advanced at the Benin Sitting, and once again to impress upon Sir Henry and his colleagues the initiative and industry with which the West Regional Government had been carrying out its many and varied undertakings, not just within the Mid-West provinces, but indeed within the whole Region.

In relation to the Supply of Amenities, Chief Williams gave further brief consideration to the provision and development of Medical Facilities, Roads and Water Supplies in the Mid-West provinces. Once again it was Chief Williams' "calm, quiet" British administrators who provided valuable testimony in support of Government contentions.[53]

Chief Williams then turned his attention, if only briefly, to two specific allegations of discrimination which had been raised at these Warri hearings: the first related to Urhobo grievances over the reduction of Urhobo divisional seats in the Western House of Assembly; the second concerned Itsekiri (Action Group) complaints about their loss of control of the WUDC.

The Urhobos, stated Williams, had benefited in the 1951 allocation of Regional seats due to a serious failure in the system used to estimate divisional populations throughout the Region. By taking the number of taxpayers and multiplying it by a factor,[54] rough population estimates had been established. In Urhobo Division the resulting estimate had been shown to be grossly inaccurate when the figures from the 1952 Census had become available. Urhobo Division had in 1951 been allocated six seats in the House of Assembly on the basis of a 600,000 population estimate; when the 1952 Census revealed that the enumerated population was closer to 300,000, the Urhobo Divisional seat allocation had been reduced by half for the 1956 Regional elections. Chief Williams said he could sympathise with the "disappointment and disillusionment" of Urhobo leaders; nevertheless, he called on them to recognise that the 1956 allocation of three seats to the Division was a "just act by the Delimitation Commission, even if it was one generating much understandable distress".[55] As for the plight of Itsekiris in the WUDC, Chief Williams pointed out that the statutory instrument for the Council made provision for the representation on it of six traditional members; each of these six members, he added, owed allegiance to the Itsekiri overlord, the *Olu* of Warri. These members, along with the *Olu* "gave the Itsekiris a certain representation on the Council", but, he observed, the Warri Division demand put forward by Rewane and his witnesses for overall Itsekiri control of the Council was one which would be difficult to secure under the democratic system of "one man one vote".

MID-WEST STATE: "CAUSE" OR "CASE"?

The Mid-West hearings, which lasted more than two weeks, had now finished. Movement protagonists under the guidance of their long-suffering and dogged British counsel, G.G. Baker, had set forward extensive evidence in support of their claim. But what was the strength of the case? At the Benin Sitting Baker had set forward a case which could only be regarded as mediocre. While Movement evidence from Benin Division had been thorough and persuasive, the subsequent submissions for Ishan, Afenmai and Asaba divisions deteriorated markedly. The Movement case at Benin had been further weakened by impressive Action Group and West Regional Government submissions. Still, the Movement had stood a good chance of improving its prospects at the Warri hearings, if it could manage to attain certain vital objectives, including: an improvement in the quality and quantity of evidence ahhering more closely to the requirements of the Commission's terms of reference; the use of prominent and reputable witnesses; greater attention to "other safeguards"; and finally the active, support of the NCNC.

Unfortunately for Mid-West protagonists, the Movement effort fell considerably short of these objectives. In essence, the evidence submitted by Movement witnesses at Warri showed no improvement; the quality as well as the quantity of pertinent testimony was not impressive. As for "other safeguards", Baker and his witnesses again preferred to steer clear of this issue. Apparently unwilling—and perhaps unable[56]—to set forward evidence that other measures would be inadequate to afford protection of Mid-West interests, Baker continued to adhere to the Movement contention that "no other safeguard than a Mid-West State"[57] would be acceptable.

Finally, if Mid-West leaders had hoped the NCNC would come to their support, it was now clear that such hope was in vain. Neither the NCNC National nor the NCNC West Opposition party made any appearance at the Mid-West hearings. And while the NCNC West under the guidance of their British counsel, Dingle Foot, did make a showing at the Lagos hearings on 31 January, this appearance came *only after* the recess in Proceedings following the *completion* of evidence bearing on the Mid-West case.[58] Indeed, as Foot outlined the submission he was shortly to present before the Commission, it was painfully clear that he was under instructions which studiously avoided any reference to the Mid-West State issue. Adelabu and his NCNC West colleagues were clearly determined to press on with their attempts at an *expose* of the Awolowo Government, along with advancing their demands for a Central Yoruba State. Yet again, the NCNC had deserted the Mid-West cause.

In addition to these weaknesses in the overall Mid-West case as presented at Warri and Benin, the credibility of much Movement evidence had been extensively undermined by the strength of the submissions at Warri and Lagos led by O.N. Rewane and Chief Williams. Rewane had been able to refute much if not all of the Movement evidence presented by Baker's key witnesses, Chiefs Prest and Okotie-Eboh. The submission led by Chief Williams on behalf of the West Regional Government, though not as rigorous and detailed as his Benin presentation, was competent and impressive.

Once again the combined presentations of Rewane and Williams had produced a formidable front against any residual encroachments which the Mid-West Movement might have achieved at the Warri hearings. The Commission, of course, had yet to deliberate on its findings, and ultimately in its Report to present its views on the Mid-West situation along with its recommendations. However it now seemed clear that while the Movement did indeed represent a "cause", it was doubtful whether in fact it had proved a "case."

——————————————

References

1. See interview with Otobo, Int.VI, p.58a. Also, in an open letter to Mid-West NCNC leaders dated 10 September, 1957, Ja' Isuman states it was an "open secret" that when the Mid-West NCNC leaders at the Conference, "became disappointed... they made up

their minds to break away from the NCNC and form a militant Mid-West political party". (Quoted from J. U. Isuman, *Facts About the Mid-West State*, (Lagos: Amalgamated Press, 1960), p.19).

2. Many of the details included in this "Blueprint for Minorities" had been gleaned from discussion papers circulated at an *ex officio* meeting of minority representatives attending the 1957 London Constitutional Conference. This meeting, convened by Dr. Udo Udoma considered in some detail the problems facing all Nigerian minority elements; a joint statement submitted subsequently to the Conference presented a brief summary of the topics discussed. (See NC(57) *New States and Nigerian Minorities: A Joint Statement Submitted by Minorities Delegates to the London Conference*, (IGH)). James Otobo states that Leader Osadebay left this meeting at the point when he (Osadebay) was to present an address to the gathered delegates; Otobo had then to speak on Osadebay's behalf. (Otobo, Int.VI, p.58a). Otobo was suspicious. He feared that Osadebay was re-considering his rebellious behaviour. Chief Okotie-Eboh had earlier warned both Osadebay and Otobo that it would be "extremely unwise" for either to associate with other minorities representatives or to attend their unofficial meeting. (See Osadebay unpublished *mss.*, *op.cit.*, p.286).

3. Otobo was quite convinced that Osadebay's sudden reverse was the result of pressure applied by other NCNC delegates with whom Osadebay had been meeting on the return voyage to Lagos. (See Otobo, Int.VI, p.58a).

4. *Pilot*, 11 July, 1957.

5. Isuman, *Facts About the Mid-West State, op.cit.*, p.19

6. *Pilot*, 13 July, 1957.

7. *Pilot*, 14 July, 1957.

8. See *Pilot*, 21 July, 1957. See also circular report of *Mid-West State Movement: Benin Mass Rally, 30 November, 1957*. (BAS)).

9. See letter from an unidentified Mid-West leader to Ja' Isuman dated 4 October, 1957, in Isuman, *Facts about the Mid-West State, op.cit.* p.44.

10. *Ibid.*

11. See *Daily Times*, 10 December, 1957.

12. *Report of Commission Appointed to Enquire into the Fears of Minorities and the Means of Allaying Them*, Cmnd. 505, (London: H.M.S.O., 1958), pp.1-2.

13. *Ibid.*, p.1, (Italics added).

14. *Minorities Commission Proceedings*, 10 December, 1957, p.4 (IRL).

15. *Ibid.*

16. *Ibid.*, p.6.

17. *Minorities Commission Proceedings*, 11 December, 1957, p.2 (IRL).

18. *Ibid.*, p.3.

19. The word "minorities" was intended to mean "permanent minorities" of an "ethnic or religious nature". See *Statement Read by the Chairman at Benin Public Sitting, 10 December, 1957* (IRL).

20. See *Minorities Commission Proceedings*, 11 December, 1957, p.6.

21. For *Ogboni*, see above p.13, n.17

22. *Minorities Commission Proceedings*, 11 December, 1957, p.6.

23. See *Minorities Commission Proceedings*, 12 December, 1957, p.2 (IRL). During World War II rubber trees in Mid-West plantations had been over-tapped to supply latex for the war effort. Mid West planters had unsuccessfully made applications for *C.D.& W.* (Commonwealth Development and Welfare) funds to rehabilitate these plantations.

24. See *ibid.*

25. See *ibid.*

26. *Minorities Commission Proceedings*, 11 December, 1957, p.7.

27. See *Minorities Commission Proceedings*, 12 December, 1957, p.1.

28. See *ibid.*, p.4.

29. See *loc.cit.*

30. *Ibid.*, p. 5.

31. *Ibid.*, p. 6.

32. *Ibid.*

33. *Minorities Commission Proceedings*, 13 December, 1957, p.2 (IRL).

34. *Ibid.*, p. 3.

35. See *ibid.*, p. 4.

36. *Ibid.*, p. 7.

37. See *ibid.*

38. See *Minorities Commission Proceedings*, 14 December, 1957, pp.2,3 and 5 (IRL).

39. See *Minorities Commission Proceedings*, 16 December, 1957, p.7, (IRL).

40. *Minorities Commission Proceedings*, 14 December, 1957, p.2, (Italics added).

41. See *ibid.*

42. Chief Williams was, for instance, prepared to qualify the Action Group position by declaring that of the various peoples of Afenmai Division—those of the Akoko-Edo area in particular—would "more appropriately be placed under the rule of a Yoruba state". (*Minorities Commission Proceedings*, 17 December, 1957, p.4).

43. For details relating to each of these areas of evidence, see *Minorities Commission Proceedings*, 17 and 18 December, 1957; also see *Memorandum submitted to the Minorities Commission by the West Regional Government*, (Ibadan: 1957), Part III, (INA). This document is referred to hereafter as *WR Memo*.

44. For details see *Minorities Commission Proceedings*, 19 December, 1957; and *WR Memo., op.cit.*

45. *Minorities Commission Proceedings*, 19 December, 1957, p.5.

46. In meetings between Chairman Willink and leading NCNC politicians at Lagos shortly after the arrival of the Commission in Nigeria at the end of November 1957, the party's position on the steps it intended to take in relation to the new states and Mid-West issues at the Mid-West hearings was shown to be characteristically ambivalent. Both Dr. Mbadiwe and Chief Okotie-Eboh in separate interviews with Chairman Willink indicated clearly enough that the NCNC National Party would argue strongly the general case for the creation of "more and smaller States in the Federation"; (Quoted from *Notes of a Meeting held on 27 November 1957, with Dr. K.O. Mbadiwe, Federal Minister of Commerce and Industry*, (copy), p. 1 (IGH)) but on the issue of active support for the Mid-West cause, even Okotie-Eboh would only evasively contend that "the case for a Mid-West State should be considered on its own merits". (Quoted from *Notes of a Meeting with Chief Festus Okotie-Eboh. on 27 November, 1957*, p.1 (IGH)). The NCNC West Opposition Party had released no public statement about its position on the presentation of these issues at the Commission's hearings. The NCNC, therefore, remained uncommitted on the question of actively supporting the Mid-West cause.

47. It is Prest's contention that Chief Festus spent in excess of £50,000 on his election campaign in 1954, (Prest, Int.III, p.7) and that the latter was prepared to "use all means" in his efforts to secure not only the Urhobo and Ibo "immigrant vote", but a large enough section of the Itsekiri vote to dislodge Prest who was then the incumbent. The Prest/Okotie-Eboh rivalry had grown increasingly bitter since 1952. For details on the complexities of "tribal politics" in Warri Division and the roles of Chiefs Okotie-Eboh and Prest, see K. W. J. Post, *The Nigerian Federal Election of 1959*, (London: Oxford University Press, 1963), pp.410-414; and P.C. Lloyd, "Tribalism in Warri", in the *Proceedings of the Fifth Annual Conference of the West African Institute of Social and Economic Research*, University College, Ibadan, 1956).

48. *Minorities Commission Proceedings*, 20 December, 1957, p.8.

49. One of the Movement's Warri Division witnesses, A.T. Rerri, maintained that increased taxes and the failure of the Action Group Government to fulfil a variety of election and other promises, including Government aid for Industrial and Agricultural Development, supply and maintenance of public amenities and safeguards to ensure adequate representation of Itsekiri interests in the Legislature and Government at Ibadan, had contributed towards reducing Itsekiri opposition to the Mid-West cause. Though prepared to hazard no precise estimate, Rerri maintained that "there was now a clear majority of Itsekiri support for the Mid-West State". *Ibid.*

50. *Ibid.*, pp.11-12.

51. See *Minorities Commission Proceedings*, 21 December, 1957, p.1.

52. For details of Rewane's *Warri Division* submission, see *ibid., passim.*

53. See *Minorities Commission Proceedings*, 30 December, 1957, *passim.*

54. See *Minorities Commission Proceedings*, 23 December, 1957, p.6.

55. *Ibid.*

56. George G. Baker (the Movement's leading Counsel) states that he was pressed hard at the Warri hearings to organise the basic evidence relating to alleged "discrimination and neglect". He states that he and John A. Baker, the Goodman-Derrick solicitor who assisted him throughout his period in Nigeria, "never knew from day to day who would or would not be available to give evidence." Furthermore, in his advance preparations, he points out that he had "no proofs and few statements, save those we secured by interviewing potential witnesses far into the nights before they were called on or discarded". (*Letter and notes from G. G. Baker to the writer, dated 9 September, 1975*). Under these pressured circumstances it is quite possible that even had he wanted to follow up the question of "other safeguards" and had been able to persuade Movement leaders that this should be done, time and opportunity were simply not available.

57. *Ibid.*

58. *Minorities Commission Proceedings*, 31 December, 1957, p.6.

CHAPTER 10

COMMISSION AFTERMATH AND THE
1958 LONDON CONFERENCE

The anxiously-awaited *Minorities Report* was officially released on 30 July, 1958. The result was not a happy one for minorities supporters. Sir Henry and his colleagues did not call for the creation of a Mid-West State, nor were they prepared to afford more lenient treatment to other Nigerian minorities. The Commission declared categorically, that "in each Region, we came to the conclusion that... a separate state would not provide a remedy for the fears expressed".[1]

THE COMMISSIONERS REPORT

It was the view of Sir Henry and his colleagues that "it could not be asserted with confidence that broadly-based majorities in each of the proposed states actually favoured the separatist solution".[2] In fact, quite to the contrary, as Sklar observes, "it seemed to the Commission that new minorities problems might well flow from the creation of new states". There was, it was stressed, also the problem of viability: new states "would be comparatively weak with respect to financial resources and trained administrative manpower".[3] Finally, in providing the fundamental justification for the general decision it had arrived at, the Commission, with an eye to the country's future, maintained that "tribal separation should [not] be embodied in the structure of Nigerian Government". Real and lasting security for Nigeria's minorities would be ensured by what the Commission envisaged as "the inevitable shift of political gravity from the regional governments to the federal government"[4] where, it was conjectured, "no single nationality group" could predominate.

Turning to *general* safeguards for Nigerian minorities, the Commission called for the institution of a Nigerian Police Force under the control of the Centre Government, together with provisions for securing Fundamental Human Rights. And what of *specific* safeguards? In order to protect specified minority areas, the Commission made the following recommendations. First, it called for the area in the Niger Delta inhabited mainly by Ijaws, of both the East and West Regions, to be designated a "Special Area" due to the problems of development in this territory of creeks and mangrove swamps; a Special Board, with a Chairman and Vice-chairman chosen by the Federal Government would be in charge of the area. Second, and of particular interest to COR and Mid-West supporters, the Commission called for the creation of a Calabar Council in the East Region and an Edo Council in the West; neither, however, to be empowered to do more than "consult and advise".[5]

In calling for the creation of an Edo Council, the Commission pointed out it was fully appreciative of steps the West Regional Government already had taken to establish the Mid-West Advisory Council under the Chairmanship of Chief Enahoro. This Council, however, had not appeared to "inspire confidence" in the Mid-West localities. Such confidence, the Commission suggested, might be more readily forthcoming "if certain modifications were made in the present arrangements".[6]

> "In the first place we suggest that the proposed [Edo] Council should be made more representative of opinion in the area with which it is concerned. It is not, we think, enough that the Government should nominate persons from the area; they must include men who are ready to criticise, and we consider that an element in the Council should be elected or nominated by local bodies in the area. We do not think that it is necessary that special elections should be held".[7]

In considering the areas within the Edo Council's jurisdiction, the Commission suggested that Western Ijaw and Warri divisions, along with Akoko-Edo district should be excluded; on the inclusion of Aboh and Asaba divisions, the Commission was ambivalent. "On the whole, we would confine the operation of the Council to the Edo-Speaking districts, that is to say, Benin Division, Urhobo Division, the two remaining districts of Afenmai and the Ishan Division". It would then be this area for which the Council should exercise its "special responsibility"; the Mid-West Advisory Council should, however, be re-named the *Edo Council* and the Minister for Mid-West Affairs become the *Minister of Edo Affairs*; the Edo Council, it was further stressed, should retain its "advisory responsibility for the development and welfare of the Edo-speaking peoples, and in particular, for the preservation of Edo culture".[8]

Moving on, finally, to consider the Council's actual statutory powers, the Commission stated that "the Council should be required to produce an Annual Report which should be debated in the Western House of Assembly"; and to further ensure that expressed Council demands and grievances could not be suppressed at the Regional level of government, the Commission in its concluding recommendation contended that the ultimate safeguarding of Edo people's interests could be ensured by requiring that "the Report of the Council for Edo Affairs should also be laid on the table of the House of Representatives and that an opportunity should be given there for debate".

An Impressive Document   These were the conclusions at which the Commission had arrived. Certainly, at first glance, the *Minorities Report*, was an impressive document. It was apparent to anyone even remotely aware of the immense complexity of the minorities issue in Nigeria that the Commission had managed a most masterful assessment; and all this (i.e. the final deliberations and writing) it had completed in the incredibly short period of just nine weeks.[9]

The *Report* provided a wealth of detail relating to the conditions of Nigeria's minorities along with the nature and foundations of their alleged fears. Also by considering submissions which fell well outside the formal limits set by its terms of reference, the Commission gave ample opportunity to minorities to put their respective cases in their own way which, in each of the main submissions by minorities representatives, meant by-passing "other safeguards" and calling solely for the creation of separate states. In justifying this manner of proceeding, the Commission explained that while "it would have been logical and in accordance with our instructions to consider *first* the constitutional safeguards and to discuss the creation of new states *only if* the constitutional safeguards seemed insufficient",[10] this approach "would certainly not have satisfied the minorities which appeared before us; in each Region, it was the case for a new state which they wished to argue". As a result, the Commission had decided instead to follow "the arrangement which the evidence suggested" and thus first to consider the creation of new states, "not so much as a last resort, but on their own merits".[11]

In plainer language, what this explanation really meant was that if the Commission had been so inclined, it would have been acting fully within its terms of reference, if it had rejected outright the cases advanced by the various minorities claimants.

Certainly, this gesture was one which appeared to demonstrate the generous and sympathetic consideration which Sir Henry and his colleagues were prepared to extend to the minorities.

It was also clear that Sir Henry and his colleagues had come directly to terms with the main issue which confronted them: whether or not to call for the creation of new states. The Commission had stated categorically that in view of the evidence it had received it was satisfied that in each Region, based "on its own merits—*a separate state would not provide a remedy for the fears expressed*".[12] The Commission's basic contention, that it could not assert with confidence that "broadly-based majorities in each of the Regions actually favoured the separatist solution"[13] clearly represented a fair and accurate assessment of the minorities' submissions—one which was quite adequate, and well within its terms of reference, to justify its eventual decision *not* to call for the creation of new states.

Certainly there was no shortage of support amongst majority elements for this conclusion which the Commission had reached. Although, understandably, a little cautious about making any public statements to this effect, both the Nigerian Regional and British Colonial Authorities were clearly pleased with most aspects of the Report and relieved about its decision not to call for the creation of new states. Governor-General Sir James Robertson summed up the reactions of his British colleagues in Nigeria when he observed that "in spite of the babble of talk and criticism we are bound to hear, I believe [the *Minorities Report*] has pointed the way to a satisfactory solution of a very difficult problem".[14] As for the Regional Government leaders, though each retained certain reservations about particular aspects of the *Report*,[15] it was obvious all were content, at least privately, with the stand taken by the Commission against the creation of new states. Indeed, when Sir Robert de Stapledon, the Governor of the East Region observed, following a meeting with Azikiwe, that it was his "impression that the satisfaction" over the *Report* to which the Premier had given "public expression" was "but a pale reflection of the delight which he privately feels",[16] Sir Robert might well have been expressing the sentiments of Azikiwe's fellow Premiers at Ibadan and Kaduna; each was much relieved that the Commission had seen fit to reject the respective claims for a Mid-West and Middle Belt State.

A Less Favourable Assessment   This generally favourable appraisal of the *Report*, however, tended to fade in the light of closer examination. In particular, it was not readily apparent what actual protection would be afforded minorities by the "other safeguards" (in place of separate states) which the Commission had set forward. *Sir Henry and his Commissioners, it seemed, had been most reluctant to direct their attention to the obvious source of the immediate and profound fears of minorities: the Regional Governments.*

The overwhelming balance of evidence had made it quite clear that the Mid-West minority, for one, harboured profound fears for its future security under an Independent West Regional Authority, and of this the Commission was well aware.[17] Strong and effective controls on the West Regional authority would be required if the apprehensions of the Mid-West minority were to be diminished, but the Commission had proposed safeguards which approached, but in no serious way provided for, these requirements. The proposals calling for creation of a Federal Police Force appeared adequate to provide the basic *minimum* of protection for minorities from the more oppressive acts of their Regional masters.[18] Similarly, the inclusion of Fundamental Human Rights[19] as a separate section in the Independence Constitution could constitute an avenue for appeals against alleged governmental abuse—even though the Commission stressed that such appeals would have little chance of success, since Human Rights provisions were notoriously difficult to enforce, and often "difficult [even] to interpret".[20]

When it had come down to substantive safeguards, however, the Commission had not been prepared to go beyond making minor proposals. In the instance of the Mid-West, it maintained that the West Regional Government had amply demonstrated its "good intentions"[21] towards the minority; and this combined with what the Commission was convinced would be the future "decrease of tribalism"[22] led it to the logical position that "tough" safeguards were therefore unnecessary. Hence its proposals for the creation of a Special Area, and two Minority Areas; these, in its view, being quite adequate to meet minority needs. Indeed, the Commission did not envisage that either the proposed Niger Delta Development Board or the Calabar and Edo Minority Councils should have authority extending beyond the power to consult and advise. The proposal that the Annual Reports of the Edo and. Calabar Councils should be submitted to the Federal House of Representatives held out the prospect that in the *last resort* the Federal Government might be persuaded to come to the aid of a beleaguered minority, but such an eventuality seemed unlikely in the extreme. Not only was the proposed Edo Minority Council, for instance, to be under the firm control of the Minister of Home and Mid-West Affairs at Ibadan, but, in addition, it would probably be only in an appended dissenting minority report, that any strong grievances could be voiced. Even then, it was to be remembered that it was the Minister of Home and Mid-West Affairs as Chairman of the Edo Council who would be responsible for framing the Annual Report in its final form. Furthermore, it was to be noted that the Commission was silent on specific powers for the Central Authority, should the latter body consider that an action of redress against a Regional Government was called for.

Summary   In summary, these proposals set out by the Commission left Nigeria's intra-Regional minorities little, if any better off than they already were. These minorities had stressed the fears they harboured of their respective Regional masters; further, they had emphasised that these anxieties would increase sharply should the Regional Authorities *not* be made subject to a range of effective restraints *before* the advent of Independence. The response of the Commission had been to recommend what could only be regarded as a set of "toothless" safeguards. It was, therefore, hardly surprising that Mid-West supporters should refer to the *Report* as "a cowardly document;"[23] that its recommendations should be regarded as "window dressing only";[24] and that these recommendations, rather than affording any token of real and effective protection to the Mid-West minority would serve only to "sanction continued Action Group domination"[25] in the minority area.

The Commission's *Report* and recommendations, by and large, satisfied Nigerian governmental elements and their British administrative and political counterparts in Nigeria and London. Furthermore, the Commission's provisions were to prove adequate for bringing the major contending participants safely and successfully through the forthcoming *1958 Constitutional Conference*. In this sense, the Commission had admirably fulfilled the primary objective of its intense labours. But insofar as *it failed to confront the root issues facing Mid-West and other Nigerian minorities, and to propose effective safeguards which would serve to ease the real and profound fears of these minorities*; in this sense it failed in its task. It is sad, but nevertheless true to say, that the Commission's Report and recommendations were to serve mainly to legitimise the oppressive assaults which in the course of the next few years the Action Group Government in the West, and its Regional counterparts in the North and East, were to bring to bear with increasing vigour on their respective intra-Regional dissenting minorities.

The 1958 London Conference

On 29 September, 1958, the Resumed Conference on the Nigerian Constitution (the *1958 London Conference*) was convened at Lancaster House. The eventual outcome of the minorities issue was in no serious doubt. Nevertheless this did not deter certain minorities' representatives entering the Conference proceedings with an initial surge of vigour and optimism.

Dr. Udo Udoma, General Secretary of the COR Movement in Eastern Nigeria had already made his feelings known about the *Minorities Report*. He had bitterly attacked the Commission for completing a *Report* that offered little hope to the COR peoples, or for that matter any other Nigerian minority. Its provisions, he maintained, would only encourage Nigeria's Regional Authorities to extend further their oppressive and discriminatory behaviour. At a COR Convention prior to his departure for London, Udoma's supporters had made their feelings clear about their COR State: "No COR State, no Independence".[26] The COR Movement had mandated the UNIP (United National Independence Party)—for which Udoma was the *1958 London Conference* delegate—and the Action Group, to press for the creation of separate COR, Middle Belt and Mid-West States. If the COR State was not created, Udoma warned that the Conference would be plunged into "deadlock". The "only solution", he declared, would be "a plebiscite" in the COR minority area.[27] In the North, Patrick Dokotri, General Secretary of the UMBC/Action Group Alliance, and a leader of the Middle Belt Movement, had stated bluntly that the provisions in the *Minorities Report* were "totally unacceptable"[28] and that Joseph Tarka, UMBC delegate to the London Conference, had been mandated to press their demand for a Middle Belt State. As for the Mid-West Movement: in keeping with its expressed opposition to the major provisions in the *Minorities Report*, a meeting of the Central Executive Committee, held 30 August at Benin City, endorsed a joint resolution for Mid-West Movement and NCNC delegates to the London Conference to secure "once and for all" a Mid-West State.[29]

As the Conference proceeded, however, it once more became apparent that the Mid-West and other major-minorities would have little opportunity to bring their objectives within closer reach. The Agenda agreed to by the three Nigerian Governmental delegations (though, in fact, formally, representation was by political party) and the British Authorities placed the major issues dealing with minorities well down the list. This reflected an uncomfortably similar course to the proceedings of the *1957 London Conference.*

Thus, before the Conference arrived at the main issues concerning minorities, agreement had already been reached on a number of major items, including: provisions to safeguard fundamental rights; provisions to secure the re-organisation of Police under a unified Federal Authority; the date—15 March, 1959—for the Northern Region to become Self-Governing; the transfer of a number of responsibilities from the Federal Government to the Lagos Town Council; provisions relating to the security of judicial tenure; and the main proposals set forward in the *Fiscal Commission Report.*[30] Indeed, the fact that the Conference had managed to get through such a large quantity of business with such little delay, together with the apparent reality that the "whole atmosphere" of the Conference was regarded as "fairly relaxed"[31] did not augur well for minorities' prospects. The Nigerian national party delegations seemed—understandably—intent on getting through the business at hand as quickly as possible. Barring unforeseen major obstacles, they could count on British confirmation of the mooted 1960 Independence date.

A Final Mid-West Thrust

When, finally, the Conference did turn to the minorities issue, Mid-West Movement representatives in the NCNC delegation, with the conspicuous absence of James Otobo, moved quickly to the offensive. In a memorandum submitted to the Conference, Mid-West grievances over the analysis carried out by the Minorities Commission and the proposals it had made in its *Report* were forcefully and thoroughly aired. The memorandum started off mildly enough. The Mid-West Movement, it held, "welcomed the Commission's recommendations for safeguarding fundamental rights by provisions in the Constitution", and for strengthening the powers of the Federal Government.[32] The memorandum then went on to stress that Mid-westerners strongly disagreed with the Commission's implied notion that the provisions for the protection of fundamental rights and for strengthening the power of the Federal Government were adequate reasons for not creating a separate Mid-West State. Such provisions, it was felt, would be necessary even in a Mid-West State. In moving on to the key points in the Movement attack it was pointed out that the Commission had observed quite correctly that:

> "What is feared is a permanent Action Group majority in the Western House of Assembly. The Action Group drawing its inspiration from a Yoruba Society, the *Egbe Omo Oduduwa* expressing itself... through the *Ogboni* Fraternity, controlling Boards, Corporations and Commissions, eventually even the Magistracy and Judiciary, aiming at the obliteration of all that is not Yoruba. That is what is meant by Yoruba Domination".[33]

In the economic field, the Commission had found there was anxiety over the treatment of the Mid-West's rubber plantations and the West Regional Government's policy towards rubber. The Commission had found evidence to confirm these anxieties. As for roads, although allegations of neglect in upkeep and construction were termed "vague, generalised and exaggerated", the Commission had felt it important to note that there had been no extra effort to keep roads in repair, and it would, therefore, be necessary to increase expenditure, "If the Government... were convinced it was necessary for them to keep the good-will and the votes of the Mid-West".[34] Indeed, the Commission had, it was pointed out, become convinced that fears did, in fact, exist among Mid-Westerners and that in some instances, these fears were well-founded. But having made this assessment the Commission had then gone on to conclude, that so long as the Government's intention was "to seek re-election by popular vote" it would become increasingly its object to show that it was impartial in the treatment of the different sections within its territorial grasp. This, it was held, was a most curious conclusion and had clearly evolved from a "mis-reading and mis-interpretation of the facts leading up to it.

It was pointed out first, that the Commission had overlooked perhaps the critical point in its concluding comments. "The West Regional Government", the memorandum emphasised, "is not dependent on the votes of the Mid-West for its majority".[35] The Action Group, it was pointed out, held at that time (September 1958) only four of twenty seats in the Mid-West, but still had an overall majority of 48 to 32 in the West Regional House of Assembly. Further, it was added that "Any attempt to remedy the present [Mid-West] grievances or allay the fears of the Mid-West might rather lose the Government the votes of their supporters elsewhere".[36] Secondly, and perhaps of greatest fundamental importance, the Movement's memorandum maintained that fears, grievances and abuses experienced under the existing system, and for which the peoples of the Mid-West had failed to obtain "remedy or redress", were "utterly unlikely to be allayed or remedied under any future system of government". The memorandum stated flatly, *"There will be no means of preventing the Western Region Government doing as it will; there will be no sanctions within the power or reach of the minority, nor will there be any incentive for the Government to pay any heed to the Mid-West peoples; indeed the reverse will apply"*.[37]

In the final section of its memorandum the Movement, now apparently reconciled to the inevitable, laid out its last card. If the Conference should reject the creation of a Mid-West state, the Movement demanded that the following alternative should be adopted: "There should be established and written into the Constitution of Nigeria, a Provincial Assembly with a Commissioner for the Benin and Delta Provinces". Appropriate articles should provide for an "Assembly to... consist of all members representing the Provinces in the Federal and Regional Houses" together with "Chiefs in the Provinces who are members of the House of Chiefs". In addition, the Commissioner "should be appointed for a period of five years". It was further stipulated that the Assembly should have deliberative and executive control over Local Government, Customary Courts, Chieftaincy, Communal land rights tenure and Finance and a budget-share of funds allocated on population and/or other basis from the Revenue of the existing Western Region.[38]

This final demand in the Movement memorandum provided a most interesting revelation. *In the last resort, Mid-West leaders had demonstrated that they were prepared to lower their sights and accept the "second best" solution.* To their chagrin, however, the representatives of Nigeria's majority elements at the Conference were now to show that they were no more amenable to this proposed "second best" solution than they had been to the option of a new state.

Party Positions: Support "In Principle"

The NPC delegation was in theory prepared to consider the prospect of creating new states in accord with the "four-fold principles" agreed by the Regional Premiers at the *1957 London Conference*.[39] Nevertheless, it was still unwilling to give *de facto* consideration to general minorities claims and was opposed outright to any specific new state demands. The Action Group, however, conscious of its new image as "Minorities Champion", had a more elaborate pattern of explanation to follow in order to arrive at a position which, in essence, was very little different from that set forward at the *1957 London Conference.*

A memorandum submitted by the Action Group delegation upbraided the Commission for rejecting in its *Report*, the Action Group/West Government concept of a "viable Edo Speaking State".[40] The Commission, it pointed out, had argued that an Edo-Speaking State would be too small to permit it to survive as an autonomous, viable unit. This contention the Action Group hotly disputed. The fact that Mid-West protagonists had no interest whatsoever in this Action Group "mini-Mid-West" concept was, of course, not raised. However, while the Action Group memo went on to castigate the Commission for not even specifying "mechanisms and procedures" for the future creation of new states, it did stress that the creation of more than one state from any existing Region could not at the moment be contemplated. Having put this point, the party, having come full circle, now arrived at the position which it had finally reached by the end of the *1957 Conference.* The All-Party Agreement secured at that time, it was maintained, provided through its "Four Principles" an excellent guideline for resolving new states demands which might arise at any time following Independence.[41] In addition, the Action Group memo advanced two further propositions.

"a.   The issue of whether or not there is support for a Middle Belt State, COR State or Mid-West State in the areas concerned, should be put before the electorate at the coming Federal Elections.

b.   That the decision of the Secretary of State should be in accordance with the views of the majority of elected Representatives in the areas concerned".[42]

These additional proposals, served as little more than an obvious electoral inducement to minorities protagonists to vote Action Group at the forthcoming Federal Elections. Action Group support of minorities claimants was largely an exercise in rhetoric.

As for the NCNC, while it continued to retain its established position on the new states issue—adherence to the terms of the All-Party Agreement, support for the Mid-West State issue, and rejection of COR State demands—it preferred to let the Mid-West delegates at the Conference speak for themselves, the party keeping a discreet distance from the views expressed. In the event, however, there was little in the submissions of Osadebay and Chief Okotie-Eboh which could have exposed the NCNC National party to any distasteful and possibly embarrassing interchanges with their new confederates, the British Authorities. After the Colonial Secretary, Lennox-Boyd, had briefly observed that the findings of the Commission had come as "no surprise"[43] to him, Movement Leader Osadebay chose this moment to rise and take issue with the British viewpoint. He pointed out that the Commission had given its reasons for not recommending the creation of a Mid-West State,[44] but, added Osadebay, "I will [contribute another] namely, *the wording of the terms of reference, which were so designed as to make it an uphill task for proponents of new states to persuade any Commission that the creation of a new state was possible*".[45]

Furthering these criticisms, Chief Festus, commenting on the matter of including Itsekiris within the proposed Mid-West State, noted that the Commission had accepted as proven the Mid West contention that the *Olu* of Warri was an agent of the Action Group. Yet, bearing this proof in mind, he pointed out, the Commission had made no allowance for the fact that this "influential Itsekiri Traditional leader spoke as an Action Group man and not for the Itsekiri people". It was obvious, therefore, that "the Itsekiris had little opportunity to make their legitimate demands for the creation of a Mid-West State known" when their major traditional spokesman was "an agent of the party which was seeking to block its creation". Referring then, to the northern territories of the Mid-West, Chief Okotie-Eboh pointed out that the Action Group witnesses had maintained that Ishan Division should be excluded from any future Mid-West State. This position, he stated, was advanced "not apparently on ethnic grounds, but mainly because it contained Action Group supporters".[46] In rounding out his criticisms Chief Festus concluded by stating that "The Action Group wishes to create a monolithic Yoruba State, larger than the others and designed to occupy the dominating role in Nigeria". This desire, he stated, was nothing more than "unrealistic hypocrisy"[47] and inevitably was doomed to failure.

Closing the Door" on Minorities and the Mid-West

With general discussion on the Mid-West and minorities issues exhausted, the Conference now moved on to secure agreement on proposed constitutional provisions for the creation of new states, and to additional specific provisions designed to "safeguard" the interests of the Mid-West and COR minorities. In order to encourage the two Southern party delegations to support the proposals he now set forward, Lennox-Boyd pointed out that the British Authorities were prepared to endorse one of two possible courses of action on the minorities issue.

First, if the Nigerian delegations felt that the new states issue should be resolved *before* Independence, then Her Majesty's Government would be prepared to accede to this demand. However, he emphasised, in that case 1960 could no longer be accepted as the date for National Independence; the date would have to be re-negotiated at a time when the minorities issue had been satisfactorily resolved. Secondly, Lennox-Boyd stated that Her Majesty's Government was prepared to confirm *"now"* the offer of a 1960 Independence date, if the Nigerian delegations could see themselves free to endorse the proposed constitutional provisions and procedural safeguards. *Put in this way, what self-respecting "Nationalist" in the NCNC or Action Group delegations could do other than accept the terms of the second proposition?*

Accordingly, with a minimum of delay, consensus of Conference participants was first secured on constitutional provisions relating to the creation of new states. It was agreed that the creation of new Regions and major boundary changes between Regions should involve a special procedure to be written into the Constitution. There would, first, have to be a resolution passed by a two-thirds majority of all members of each House in the Federal Legislature, approving any proposed change. Secondly, approval of this resolution either by a simple majority in both Houses of the Legislatures in two Regions, of which one must be the Region from which the new state was to be created, or by "each House of the Legislatures of a bare majority of the Regions",[48] must then follow. The third step, "enactment of the necessary legislation... by a simple majority of the Federal legislature", would require further approval "by resolution of the legislative Houses of at least two Regions".[49] Finally, on fulfilment of all the above requirements, the law creating the new Region could come into effect if, following a referendum "in the area which it is proposed to convert into a Region... at least 60 per cent of those who in fact vote are in favour of the proposal".[50]

Clearly, these were complex measures. Outraged minorities declared bitterly that the Conference had not only turned its back on immediate new state demands, but that by virtue of these complicated provisions to be written into the Independence Constitution, the British Authorities and Nigerian majority elements had effectively combined forces to "close the door" on any successful new state demands in the post-Independence era. The response of the minorities' opponents to such allegations was, perhaps, predictable. To "close the door" on minorities, it was stated, was certainly not the object of these constitutional procedures. Indeed, it was held that "this was never likely",[51] since it was conjectured that the minorities problem would be a major feature of Nigerian politics for many years to come. However, hope was expressed, that the agreed constitutional provisions would discourage "perpetual, frivolous agitations" and ensure that the only sort of agitation that could hope for success would be "one that is sustained, well-organised and assured of genuine support in the area concerned".[52] Certainly, minorities' protagonists could only ruefully recognise that the Conference decision had indeed achieved this objective—and with a vengeance.

With the prospect of the immediate creation of new states now safely beyond their reach, minorities protagonists were afforded two final opportunities for a "last stand". At the 26th Meeting of the Conference, consideration was given to the establishment of a Special Area Board in the Niger Delta, in accord with recommendations made in the Minorities Report. This proposed Special Area Board was ostensibly designed for the purpose of assisting "the people, mainly Ijaw, in the swampy country along the coast between Opobo and the mouth of the Benin River".[53] However, it did not receive a warm response either from the Rivers (Ijaw) delegate Harold Biriye, or the Action Group representatives. Biriye maintained that, "it would not give the minorities in the area... the opportunity to solve their own problems, but would simply put them in the position of begging for help from three different [Federal, Western and Eastern] Governments. The Board would thus be a source of fear rather than of hope to the minorities".[54]

Biriye was strongly supported by the Action Group leader, Chief Awolowo, who declared that, "The people of the [Western Ijaw] area concerned would have nothing to do with the Special Area proposal". He argued that the Minorities Commission had admitted that under-development in the area was not the fault of man, or his Government. Thus, "To pursue the proposal for a Special Area Board", he asserted "constitutes an attack on the efforts which the Western Region Government has made during the past six years to solve the problems of the area".[55] In backing Awolowo's position, Chief S. L. Akintola argued that, "The proposed Special Area Board would be able to put its recommendations to the Regional Government concerned, but the Regional Government would be open... to ignore completely the Board's findings. This rendered the whole scheme futile".[56]

Despite this spirited if brief opposition to the proposed Special Area Board, the Conference soon agreed to accept the constitutional provisions set forward by the Secretary of State. In accord with these provisions it was agreed that: A Niger Delta Development Board should be established with an initial term of ten years; the Board should consist of a Chairman appointed by the Federal Government, one representative each of the East and West Regional Governments, and a number of representatives of the inhabitants of the area; the Board should be responsible for the survey of area needs and for proposing appropriate development schemes to meet these needs, to the Federal and Regional authorities; and the funds for carrying out these functions should be supplied by the Federal Government.[57]

In turning finally to Conference deliberations on the creation of the Mid-West and Calabar Minority Areas, it was not so much the minorities delegates who attempted to muster for a "last stand"; rather it was the Action Group leadership which once again sought vigorously to press home its views. While Dr. Udoma, Osadebay and Chief Festus continued to protest that the Minority Area concept would not in any way alleviate the "fears and apprehensions" of the COR and Mid-West peoples, the Action Group, concentrating its attack, bore down hard on the Mid-West issue. Awolowo and his "minorities champions" were adamant that the proposed Mid-West Minority Area should be strictly limited to the area suggested in the Action Group/West Government proposals, and not be extended to include "extraneous non-Edo speakers"[58] in Western Iboland, Warri Division and the northern territories of Benin Province. As for the earlier Mid-West Movement/NCNC proposal of a "second best" solution, this proposal the Action Group rejected outright. The idea of a separate Mid-West Assembly with deliberative and executive functions, "a Government within a Government",[59] was totally unacceptable.

At this point, Awolowo and his colleagues drew the attention of the Conference to the proposed provisions set out in the *Minorities Report* for a Mid-West Advisory Council. The Advisory Council was to serve as the representative body of the proposed

Mid-West Minority Area, providing an "effective" avenue through which the Mid-West peoples could "express their views and make their criticisms". The Action Group stated that it would undoubtedly, "contribute substantially towards allaying the fears" of the Mid-West minority,[60] and would meet the needs of the area "quite adequately".

Following this brief discussion in which only the Action Group appeared to have taken a spirited part, the Conference arrived at the following agreement with regard to the creation of a Mid-West Minority Area:

> "A Minority Area should be created in the Western Region and it should consist of the whole of the Benin and Delta Provinces excluding Warri Division and Akoko-Edo Districts, on the understanding that:
>
> a. The position of Warri Division in relation to the proposed area should be further considered after local consultation between the Western Regional Government on the one hand, and Chief Okotie-Eboh and other concerned interests, on the other;
>
> b. This decision should be without prejudice to the Conference's later discussions regarding the Ijaw Special Area Board".[61]

It further was agreed that the proposed Council should be composed of Members of the House of Assembly, House of Representatives and House of Chiefs, elected or appointed within the Area. A *proviso* was added that the West Regional Government would not be committed to this proposed composition if the general principles enunciated by Chief Awolowo (which called for similar composition and structure for Minority Areas in the East and North Regions) were not accepted by the Conference for general application to the whole of Nigeria.

As for the functions of the proposed Council, the Conference agreed that:

> "The functions... should be, broadly, to foster the well-being, cultural advancement and economic and social development of the Minorities Area and to bring to the notice of the West Regional Government any discrimination against the area, and to exercise such executive powers as might be delegated to it from time to time by the West Regional Government".[62]

Finally, on reaching agreement also that "the Province of Calabar should be made a Minority Area and that a Calabar Minority Council should be appointed" with composition and functions "the same as those agreed in respect of the Mid-West

Council in the West Region",[63] the Conference had now completed its elaboration of the basic constitutional formulae designed to accommodate the needs and "allay the fears" of those Nigerian "Minority" and "Special Area" peoples, whom it felt were deserving of being so designated.

BETRAYED AGAIN!

By the close of the *1958 London Conference* on 27 October, it was apparent that the distance between support "in principle" to the Mid-West cause and active commitment "in practice" was just as great as ever. Mid-West protagonists had started the Conference with strong and confident verbal commitments from both the Action Group and the NCNC. In the course of the Conference proceedings, however, this "assured support" had evaporated and the two Mid-West activists Osadebay and Chief Okotie-Eboh found very quickly that they had been left to make the best use they could of their own resources.

Outside of a jointly-sponsored NCNC/Mid-West Movement memorandum, the NCNC preferred to retain a discreet distance from the Mid-West representatives and their few rather dis-spirited pronouncements. No word or gesture of support for the Mid-West cause was forthcoming from Dr. Azikiwe or from members of the party's National hierarchy, with the exception of Osadebay and Chief Festus (both members of the NCNC NEC).

Mid-West supporters had also discovered that Action Group "fighting words" had not been translated into action. Indeed, shifting very little from the position they had taken at the Mid-West hearings of the *Minorities Commission*, Action Group spokesmen revealed the extent of their continuing opposition to Mid-West demands. *In principle*, the party backed the demand for the creation of several new states before Independence; *in practice*, however, the pre-conditions they set for any aspirant minority area put *de facto* creation well beyond immediate reach. Similarly, while Action Groupers agreed, in principle, to the creation of a Mid-West State; in practice the party's concept of a mini-Mid-West, which had earlier been elaborated before Willink and his colleagues, was quite unacceptable to Mid-West Movement supporters. As for the Movement's final proposal of a "second best" solution, the extent of Action Group sympathy for this proposal— one which was designed to afford Mid-Westerners at least some measure of legislative and executive control over their own affairs—was made unmistakably clear. Awolowo and his associates rejected outright this Mid-West proposal.

Thus, abandoned by their eloquent "champions", Mid-Westerners, together with Nigeria's other major-minorities, had succumbed to the weight of overwhelming odds at the Conference. The result was that Mid-West and minority interests in general were now to be "protected" by what were all too obviously "toothless safeguards". *The three-Region Federation, with dominant power resting with the Regions, was to constitute the fundamental pattern of future Nigerian Government.* For Mid-Westerners, the newly-initiated Ministry of Mid-West Affairs and the newly-endorsed Mid-West Advisory Council would, for the foreseeable future, provide the greatest opportunity for participation and representation in the activities of the Regional Government which would continue to dominate their lives.

––––––––––––––––––––

References

1. *Report of the Commission Appointed to Enquire into the Fears of Minorities and the Means of Allaying Them*, op.cit., p.87. This document will be referred to hereafter as the *Minorities Report*.

2. Sklar, *Nigerian Political Parties*, op.cit., p.139.

3. *Ibid.*

4. *Ibid.* See also, *Minorities Report*, op.cit., pp.88-89. In this section (Section I, Chapter 14 of the *Minorities Report*) the Commission provided its extensive rationale for advancing its hypothesis that the future shift in power would be from the Regional to the Central or Federal Government.

5. See *Minorities Report*, op.cit., Sections 3 and 4, Chapter 14 for details of the Commission's recommendations relating to "Special Areas", and "Minority Areas".

6. *Loc.cit.*

7. *Ibid.*

8. *Ibid.*

9. This nine week period refers to the interval between the return of the Commission to London in the third week of April 1958, and its completion of the draft *Report* during the first week of July. It should be pointed out, however, that a great deal of the

background ethnic, political and legal constitutional materials had been consolidated by Colonial Office officials in Whitehall operating under the guidance (for the Secretary of State, Alan Lennox-Boyd—now Lord Boyd of Merton) of an Assistant Under Secretary of State, C. G. Eastwood. (See *Minorities Commission Papers*, particularly letters exchanged between Eastwood and the Commission's Chairman, Sir Henry Willink (IRL)). The reason for the rush was that it was essential that the *Report* be released in time for all interested elements to have the opportunity to read and assess its contents before the start of the *London Constitutional Conference* due to commence 20 September, 1958.

10. *Minorities Report, op.cit.*, p.87.

11. *Ibid.*

12. *Ibid.*

13. Sklar, *Nigerian Political Parties, op.cit.* p.139.

14. *Letter from Sir James Robertson to Sir Henry Willink, dated 25 August, 1958 at Lagos, Nigeria*, in "Correspondence File", *Minorities Commission Papers* (IRL).

15. Though all Regional Government leaders were obviously relieved with the Commission's decision not to call for new states, there were other aspects of the *Report*—and, of course, particularly its conclusions—about which they were not so pleased. In the East, Azikiwe publicly expressed his disappointment at "the failure of the Commission to call for the creation of a Mid-West State" (*Pilot*, 13 August, 1958)—though privately, it was contended, he had no real interest in the Mid-West creation anyway. (See "Correspondence File", *op.cit.*, *Letter from Sir Robert de Stapledon, Governor East Region, to Eastwood, Colonial Office, Whitehall, dated 26 August, 1958, at Enugu* (IRL)). In the North, the delight of the NPC leadership over the Commission's decision against the Middle Belt Movement was only slightly diminished by the Commission's proposal that a plebiscite in Kabba and Ilorin provinces *might* be held to determine whether these areas should remain in the North or go to the West. (See *Minorities Report op.cit.*, Ch.15, p.105). In an interview with Sir Gawain Bell, Governor of the Northern Region, Alhaji Abba Habib, General Secretary of the NPC, declared that his party would strongly oppose "the idea of a plebiscite when it was discussed at the Constitutional Conference". ("Correspondence File", *op.cit.*, *Letter from Sir Gawain Bell, to Eastwood, Colonial Office, Whitehall, dated 23 August, 1958 at Kaduna, Northern Nigeria* (IRL)). Finally, in the West Region, Awolowo and his Action Group at Ibadan dismissed as being "impracticable... the proposed Special Area for Ijaws". ("Correspondence File", *ibid.*,

Letter from Sir John Rankine to Eastwood, Colonial Office, Whitehall dated 30 August, 1958 at Ibadan (IRL)). In addition, "the omission of the Middle Belt from the recommendation for Minority Areas", (*loc. cit.*) was strongly criticised. And finally, while the Action Group maintained that the creation of new states (in principle and in the "future") could serve as the "only means of satisfactorily allaying the fears of minorities", it was stressed that the Commission had got things off to a very bad start in this direction by not calling for a plebiscite in the "Mid-West, COR and Middle Belt areas, as they did in the case of Ilorin-Kabba". (*Ibid.*, p.2.)

16. *Letter from Sir Robert de Stapledon...*, in "Correspondence File", *op.cit.*

17. In its conclusions, the Commission openly stated that "In each of the three Regions... we found a minority or group of minorities who described fears and grievances which they felt would become *more intense when the present restraints were removed*". (*Minorities Report, op.cit.*, p.87. (Italics added)). Indeed, even allowing for some exaggeration in these alleged grievances, the Commission was prepared to concede that *"there remained a body of genuine fears and that the future was regarded with real apprehension"*. (*Ibid.*) (Italics added).

18. The Commission maintained that "a first essential of any scheme" for allaying the fears of minorities would entail the provision "in each Region of a body of Police of sufficient strength and independence of outlook to deal, for instance, with political 'strong arm groups' ". (*Ibid.*, p.92) In accord with this position, it was the Commission's view that "There should... be one Nigeria Police Force which should serve both Federal and Regional purposes". (*Ibid.*, p.93)

19. Certainly the provisions set out for the protection of Fundamental Human Rights, were the most detailed and extensive of any of the Commission's recommendations. Drawn from the *Geneva Convention on Human Rights of 1954*, these provisions were included in major sections covering: Life and Liberty; Administration of Justice; Social Freedom; Rights Concerning Religion; Discrimination. (*Ibid.*, pp.97-103). It was, however, to be recognised that while this most detailed and elaborate proposal could be viewed as an effective means for establishing that a very high standard of behaviour would be required of the Governing authorities in an Independent Nigeria, still *the truth of the matter was that the minorities submitting evidence had not expressed any strong preference for these Human Rights provisions. The call for the inclusion of Fundamental Human Rights had been made by certain "Christian Bodies"* which had appeared before the Commission; and while Sir Henry and his colleagues indicated that "some

other witnesses... would welcome such provisions in the Constitution", it was clear that *the minorities were far more interested in rather more practical provisions; provisions with "teeth"*. As the Commission, with masterful understatement chose to put it: "Some witnesses... were afraid that (the Human Rights provisions) would not be sufficient". (*Ibid.*, p.97).

20. *Ibid.*

21. See *ibid.*, Chapter 3, pp.13-25.

22. See *ibid.*, pp. 87-88.

23. *London Resumed Conference (September) 1958*, NC (58), 12th Meeting, p. 2 (IRL)

24. *Pilot*, 28 August, 1958.

25. *Ibid.*

26. *West Africa*, 30 August, 1958, p.831.

27. See *ibid.*

28. *Daily Times*, 23 August, 1958.

29. See *Minutes of the Meeting of the Central Executive Committee, held 30 August. 1958, at Osana House, Benin City*, (mimeo.), paragraph 16. (Copy in possession of writer).

30. See *West Africa*, 1 November, 1958, p.1035; also See *West Africa*, issues of 11 and 18 October, *passim*, for details of Conference discussions on Police, and proposals in the *Report of the Fiscal Commission*.

31. *Letter from Eastwood, Whitehall, to Sir Henry Willink, Cambridge, dated 8 October, 1958 at London*, p.1, in "Correspondence File", *op.cit.*

32. See *Memorandum by the NCNC on behalf of The Mid-West State Movement*, NC (58), 65. (IGH).

33. Quoted in *ibid.*, from *Minorities Report*, p.15, para.13.

34. *Ibid.*, quoted from *Minorities Report*, p.19, para.23. Also see p.106, para.20.

35. *Ibid.*

36. *Ibid.*

37. *Ibid.* (Italics added).

38. See *ibid.*

39. These principles were: 1. The wishes of the people of the area should be determined by a plebiscite or referendum; 2. The creation of new states should be consistent with the principles of viability; 3. The component units of the new state should be contiguous; 4. No ethnic group should be split into new states except by the express wishes of a two-thirds majority of the people in the ethnic group determined by a plebiscite. (See *Joint proposals by the NPC, NCNC and Action Group Delegations: The Creation of New States*, being a Statement Submitted to the *1957 London Conference*, June 1957, mimeo.(IGH)). This *All-Party Agreement* which had been reached at the *1957 Conference* was, in effect, the final device employed to forestall the claims of minorities at that Conference. Now at the *1958 London Conference* it remained as a basic device for securing the same objective.

40. *New States: A Memorandum Submitted to the 1958 London Conference by the Action Group Delegation*, NC (58), 22, p.2, mimeo. (IGH).

41. See *ibid.*, pp.3-4.

42. *Ibid.*, p.4.

43. NC (58), *Proceedings of the 12th Meeting*, p.2 (IGH).

44. See *ibid.*, p.4.

45. *Ibid.* (Italics added).

46. *Ibid.*, p.8.

47. *Ibid.*, p.9.

48. *Report by the Resumed Nigeria Constitutional Conference Held in London, September and October 1958*, Cmnd. 569, (London: HMSO, 1958), p.24.

49. *Ibid.*

50. *Ibid.*

51. "Constitution for Minorities", *West Africa*, 25 October, 1958, p.1002.

52. *Ibid.*

53. *Minorities Report. op.cit.*, p.94.

54. NC (58), *Proceedings of the 26th Meeting*, p.9 (IGH).

55. *Ibid.*, p.10.

56. *Ibid.*, p.14.

57. See *Report of the 1958 Conference, op.cit.*, p.26.

58. NC (58) *Proceedings of the 31st Meeting*, p.8 (IGH).

59. *Ibid.*

60. *Ibid.*

61. *Ibid.*, pp.8-9.

62. *Ibid.*, p.11. The Zikist National Vanguard, the militant wing of the NCNC, announced that it accepted the "proposed safeguards for minority areas as an interim measure" only, as the alternative of the moment, to the creation of a Mid-West State. See *Memorandum on the Review of the Nigerian Constitution, Submitted by the Zikist National Vanguard to the London Conference of September 1958*, mimeo. (IGH).

63. *Report of the 1958 London Conference, op.cit.*, p.25.

PART III

AN UNCERTAIN PATH TO AUTONOMY

CHAPTER 11

DARK DAYS IN THE MID-WEST

By the end of the 1958 London Conference, the Mid-West Movement was in a state of virtual collapse. For the mass of Mid-West supporters, the period between November 1958 and the passage of the first Mid-West Bill by the Federal House of Representatives in April 1961, was to be a long and trying one; the abiding faith of Mid-West protagonists in their "cause" was to be sorely tested. However, the Mid-West issue itself was to assume increasing importance in the Nigerian political scene.

Already by mid-1958, and in a political context quite separate from the Minorities Commission, the Mid-West issue assumed a new and more realistic promise in the minds of certain Mid-West NCNC leaders active in the political forums at Lagos and Ibadan. Looking ahead to the Federal Elections of 1959, these leaders envisaged the NCNC emerging as the junior partner in a coalition Government at Lagos dominated by the NPC. With a share of power at the Centre, these men felt it would then be possible to fulfil the lengthy and complex constitutional requirements to bring the Mid-West State into existence.[1]

Nor was this confidence without good grounds. Chief Okotie Eboh, even by this early stage unquestionably the Mid-West's most prominent "son abroad," had in a very short time amassed immense power and influence both at Lagos with the leaders of the NPC, Balewa and Ribadu, and in the councils of the NCNC. Chief Festus, therefore, was in a strong position to assist in securing for the NCNC the role of coalition partner following the Federal Elections, and *to present directly the Mid-West case to the leadership of the NPC as well as to the NEC of his own party.*

Other Mid-West leaders too were gaining in prominence and authority in NCNC councils. Movement Leader Osadebay, an NEC member and NCNC National Legal Adviser, had resumed his post as Leader of the Opposition in the Western House of Assembly following the death of Adelabu in March 1958; Chief Omo-Osagie was not only in close consort with Chief Festus at Lagos, but also was serving as Vice Chairman of the WWC of the NCNC; both Otobo and Amadasun held important posts in the Western Parliamentary Party; and such legislators as Chief Oputa-Otutu of Aboh, Chief Shaka Momodu of Ishan and F.H. Utomi of Ogwashi-Uku determinedly and consistently pressed Mid-West interests in the Debates of the Western House of Assembly. On the basis of these considerations it seemed that Mid West leaders had a plausible case for contending that the NCNC would stand a reasonable chance of securing partnership with the NPC in any post-election coalition Federal Government.[2] Enhanced Mid-West authority in the councils of the NCNC would ensure that the envisaged coalition partners would be compelled to take a long and hard look at the Mid-West issue.

The Action Group, on its part, had launched initiatives in the course of the previous year which seemed further to strengthen these Mid-West prospects. It was no secret that the NPC leadership had bitterly resented Awolowo's forthright support of a comprehensive new states policy both at the hearings of the Minorities Commission and at the *1958 London Conference*. As Enahoro, reflecting on the position and prospects of the Action Group at this time, has put it: "The party's support for the early creation of more regions in the country... widened the gulf between it and... the NPC, which believes in the indivisibility of the North".[3] Adherence to this policy, therefore, was hardly a persuasive qualification for securing any post-election partnership with the NPC. In addition, the Action Group leadership had noted, somewhat ruefully, that the party's pursuit of its new states policy not only had "widened the gulf" between it and the NPC, but also between it and the NCNC. By supporting a comprehensive new states policy—with emphasis on *simultaneous* creation of Middle Belt, COR and Mid-West states—the Action Group had effectively and dangerously isolated itself not only from the NPC but from the NCNC as well. Furthermore in doing this, *it had succeeded in making NCNC prospects as a future junior partner in an NPC-dominated coalition Government look better than ever.*

Even midway through 1958, therefore, it seemed NCNC prospects were good and Mid-West aspirations held growing promise. The Action Group would be hard put to avoid relegation to the Opposition benches after the Federal Elections. Furthermore, *if there was one factor alone which might serve to ensure that both*

NPC and NCNC would follow up on Mid-West demands, it was that a West Region shorn of the Mid-West provinces, would be a West Region deprived of any real ability to challenge an NPC/NCNC Government at the Centre. Such an achievement would go a long way towards safeguarding the Governments of Azikiwe at Enugu and the Sardauna at Kaduna from the undertakings of Action Group "troublemakers". Most important, it would ensure that the territorial jurisdictions of these two Regional Authorities would be retained intact. During the next four and a half years, it was to be the primary task of Chief Festus and his Mid-West colleagues at Ibadan and Lagos, to press relentlessly and with increasing force the suit of the Mid-West; to impress upon the NCNC and NPC leaderships the strength and legitimacy of Mid-West demands; and most of all to ensure that both of these National parties should remain constantly aware of the benefits *to them* which the creation of a Mid-West State would render.

However, while Mid-West Movement leaders envisaged a well-marked path to a triumphant future, there was still one very powerful force in the "Regional present" with which they had to contend, and this was the Action Group. Awolowo and his colleagues recognised clearly that the future of the party—perhaps its very survival—could hinge on its ability to extend and secure its political as well as governmental control over the provinces of the Mid-West. *Action Group thinking was clear enough*: the constitutional settlement agreed to at the *1958 London Conference* provided that a plebiscite in any proposed new state area must be conducted; and that this *plebiscite must record a 60 per cent favourable response of the total registered electors* on the Federal Electoral Roll for the state to be created. Clearly, a *Mid-West over which the Action Group, by one means or another, could secure political control, would be a Mid-West that would rest at the bidding of Awolowo and the Action Group.*

The key to securing this ultimate safeguard against envisaged Centre encroachments lay in the ability of the Action Group to gain political control at the grass-roots level in the Mid-West. This would be a formidable task. The party had been notably unsuccessful in its earlier efforts. And though during the period following the 1955 Local Government elections it had managed to improve its standing in various Mid-West local government councils, its overall presence still fell far short of constituting any serious challenge to NCNC dominance. It was, therefore, a time for vigorous, concerted action by the West Regional Governing party.

THE ACTION GROUP IN THE MID-WEST:
THE POLITICS OF LOCAL CONTROL

The battle for the Mid-West during 1958 and 1959—the period with which this chapter is concerned—was really an assault in which all the advantage lay with the Action Group. As the party in power at Ibadan, Awolowo and his colleagues had a variety of weapons at their disposal, weapons which they were now to put to full use. Since 1951 the Action Group, like its counterpart governing parties in the North and East, had spent much time and effort in devising ways and means of securing its political authority over the territory within its jurisdiction. Legislation had been introduced which vested in the Government party an increasing range of legal powers over certain vital functions and areas of activity, including most notably *local government, chiefs and coercive institutions* in the localities.[4]

By the end of 1957 the roots for this "framework" of control had been securely established. It was now simply a matter of tightening the "steel ring" which this framework created. With the aid of this range of powerful weapons, together with more material and less coercive forms of inducement always available to a governing party,[5] the Action Group set to work extending and intensifying what had now become its very urgent quest for control in the Opposition districts of the Mid-West provinces.

The manner in which this "steel ring" was to be implemented was of extreme importance. If the party's quest for control involved methods which were too overt, too aggressive, it might safely manage to secure extended control in Opposition local councils, but alienate much of the popular support it hoped to attract. Furthermore, if it did not launch its various initiatives at the most auspicious times it might drain valuable resources and hence miss a critical opportunity to gain local advantage. Somehow, the Action Group had to steer a course which would allow it to secure local control, but to do so at minimum cost to what it was hoped would be the party's increasing popularity in the localities.[6] Certainly, this would not be an easy course, yet it was one the party must follow if optimum returns were to be gained.

The Action Group was by no means entering blind into the arena of Mid-West local politics. During the initial (1951-53) period of the party's rule at Ibadan, its leaders had taken only a rather casual interest in the Mid-West districts, much to the frustration and annoyance of such local stalwarts as S.Y. Eke and V.O.E.

Osula. However, as Awolowo and his colleagues began to master the heavy and complex responsibilities of Government and to secure the organisational apparatus of the party, the Action Group by 1954, under the Mid-West leadership of Enahoro, started to take a firm initiative.

In Chapter 6 above, we have seen how during 1954-55 the party launched a powerful assault on the Mid-West heartland of Benin Division. The Action Group had made elaborate preparations for what it hoped would result in a take-over from Omo-Osagie and his Otu Edo/NCNC at the 1955 Local Government elections. The party had, however, badly mis-calculated. Omo-Osagie emerged unscathed, and BTPA/Action Group candidates managed to secure only a few seats in three of the Division's six District Councils. The NCNC retained control of all eight Divisional Councils in the Mid-West provinces.

In the course of the next two years (1955-57), however, Action Groupers were to learn just how effective *post-election* initiatives could be. By the end of 1957 the party had greatly improved its standing in a number of Mid-West local government councils. In Chapter 9 above, we have seen the range of measures— referred to by Movement leaders as "various well-known techniques"[7]—by which this had been achieved. As a result, the Action Group had wrested control in one Divisional Council (Afenmai) from the NCNC, and pulled itself up to a position of equal terms with the NCNC in two others (Urhobo and Ishan).[8] This was an impressive record. All these Action Group gains had been secured in the post-election period. Nor was the party's success to end here.

At the 1958 Local Government elections the Action Group at last achieved a notable triumph.[9] Out of a total of 1,366 Mid-West wards, the Action Group won 612, NCNC 464 and "others" 185.[10] In terms of success at the District and Local Council level, the Action Group was victorious in 26 of 45.[11] Altogether the party had managed to secure control of four—Afenmai, Ishan, Warri and Western Ijaw—of the Mid-West's eight Divisional Councils, the other four—Benin, Asaba, Aboh, Urhobo—going to the NCNC.[12] As one distressed—but foresightful—Mid-West Movement leader put it: a majority of Mid-West electors had, "given their bodies to the governing Action Group party",[13] even if their "souls" remained constant to the Mid-West cause.

TABLE VI[14]

LOCAL GOVERNMENT COUNCIL VICTORIES IN THE MID-WEST, 1958

DIVISION	MAJORITY PARTY	LOCAL AND DISTRICT COUNCIL VICTORIES	
		NCNC	ACTION GROUP
Afenmai	Action Group	1	2
Asaba	NCNC	3	0
Benin	NCNC	4 (1 even)	1
Ishan	Action Group	1	6
Urhobo	NCNC	3	0
Western Ijaw	Action Group	2 (even)	11
Aboh	NCNC	2	0
Warri	Action Group	1	6
	TOTALS	17	26

NOTE: **NCNC** recorded **4** Divisional Victories.
Action Group recorded **4** Divisional Victories.

The Mechanics of Control I: Post-Election Tactics

In the assault it was now to launch on the Mid-West districts, the Action Group was to make full use of post-election measures. The targets were clear enough. Seemingly, without too great difficulty the Action Group could anticipate gaining control of both Aboh and Urhobo Divisional Councils. These objectives could probably be secured with little more than the usual inducements to Independents and a few wavering NCNC supporters. If necessary, control of NCNC councils might be ensured through the device of "injecting" chiefs.[15] On the face of it, however, it appeared that such measures—which, as we have already seen were not popular in the localities—would not be necessary. The Action Group had already secured a level of control in terms of popular electoral support (612 of 1,366 Mid-West wards)[16] which, party leaders believed, would give it adequate strength to resist any Mid-West plebiscite which rivals might seek to implement. So long as the party managed to consolidate the majority control it had gained in the localities, and then extend post-election initiatives of not too disruptive a nature in marginal areas, it would, it seemed, be well protected from any threat which a future plebiscite might constitute.[17]

Post-Election Preliminaries In the post-election initiatives which the Action Group now put into operation, the party encountered little difficulty in securing control of the Divisional Councils in Urhobo and Aboh divisions; both these Councils had emerged from the elections with marginal NCNC majorities. In Aboh, amendment of the Council Instruments of Ukwani and Ndosimili District Councils, enabled the Regional Government to insert an adequate number of chiefs to ensure comfortable Action Group majorities in both—and by June 1958 in Aboh Divisional Council as well. While Mid-West Movement leaders protested bitterly, accusing the Action Group of conspiring to control these councils via "the back door",[18] Government spokesmen expressed astonishment and irritation at such "unfounded" charges.

In justifying the Government's "injection" of chiefs into these Aboh Councils, Chief Enahoro emphasised that the Regional Government was simply taking steps long overdue, which would bring these Council Instruments into line with the statutory provisions set out in the original (1953) *Local Government Law*. The *Law* allowed that traditional members could comprise up to one-third of the total council membership, and so, maintained Enahoro, since the Instrument did not comply with this "vital" provision, the Government had now taken action to correct this situation. Chiefs would now assume "their proper places"[19] in these councils. Indeed, Enahoro went on to say that "if there are other places in the Mid-West, where, in my honest opinion, similar things should be done, I shall not hesitate to recommend it". Such an assurance was hardly likely either to reduce the anxiety of Mid-West Movement leaders, nor enhance the popularity of the Action Group in those localities where such initiatives, it seemed, were now officially in the offing.

In Urhobo Division, "carpet-crossers" secured for the Action Group post-election control in the marginal Western Urhobo and Sapele Urban District Councils. These alterations, supplemented by the removal of an NCNC Chief and replacement by his Action Group son resulted in the Action Group being brought on to even terms with the NCNC in the Urhobo Divisional Council. At this point, however, the party was obstructed in its quest for control by what turned out to be a rather more stubborn obstacle than was at first anticipated.

When the Divisional Council had resumed sittings in May 1958 following the local elections, an NCNC councillor retained the post of Council Chairman. In June 1958, an Amendment to the Local Government Law had been passed. This Amendment, entitled Section 30A, enabled the Minister of Local Government "to appoint a Chairman wherever and whenever, owing to equality of votes, the Council is unable to elect a Chairman in accordance with Section 30 of the Law",[20] and thus appeared to provide the Governing Action Group party with the opportunity to install an "appropriate", i.e. Action Group, Chairman in a number of dead-locked Councils, of which Urhobo Divisional Council was one. In the Urhobo instance this statutory vehicle proved to be inadequate. The NCNC Council Chairman hung grimly to his position; he consistently obstructed the bringing of any motion before Council relating to the proposal of alternative candidates for consideration by the Minister.[21]

In order, therefore, to break the stalemate and force the sitting chairman to comply with this new provision, yet another Amendment to the Local Government Law (Amendment No. 3) was introduced and passed by the Regional House in September 1958. This Amendment made provision "firstly, for the removal of a Chairman of a Council when due notice has been given";[22] and secondly, "to empower the Secretary of the Council to discharge the responsibility of calling a meeting to dispose of that business and to preside at such meeting". This Amendment No. 3 turned out to be adequate to resolve the Urhobo situation. A meeting was held on 26 September, the Council Secretary presided, a vote was held, and despite strenuous objections by NCNC councillors, Action Group members who now constituted a majority returned one of their number as new Chairman of the Urhobo Divisional Council.

The Challenge of Benin   The post-election situation in Benin Division provided the Action Group with a similar challenge. The *Otu Edo*/NCNC had emerged with clear majorities in four of the Division's six District Councils; the BTPA/Action Group had gained victory in only one District Council (Iyekuselu) and had tied with the Otu Edo/NCNC in a second (Akugbe D.C.).[23] While these results as they stood would clearly provide the *Otu Edo*/NCNC with the opportunity to resume control of the Benin Divisional Council (BDC), it was equally apparent that if the BTPA/Action Group forces could secure post-election majorities in Akugbe and one additional District Council, this position would be reversed. With its quota of elected representatives from three District Councils, together with the *Oba*'s "traditional members", the BTPA/Action Group would be able to command a majority in the BDC. From a purely instrumental viewpoint, then, a post-election take-over of the BDC by the Governing Action Group party seemed, on the face of it, to pose no serious problems; control in these vital districts of the Mid-West heartland might be secured with relative ease, and without the kind of fanfare which could seriously damage the party's prospects of turning post-election council control into post-election popular confidence.[24]

In the event, the Action Group's attempt to effect a BDC take-over turned out to be no straight-forward affair. The first indications of *Otu Edo*/NCNC resistance to Action Group designs surfaced following an announcement on 26 May by Alhaji Dauda Adegbenro, Minister of Local Government at Ibadan, that indirect elections (from the six Benin District Councils) to the BDC had been postponed indefinitely. No reason for the postponement was given. Learning of this postponement order, Omo-Osagie gave vent to his suspicions. He rebuked the Minister and accused the Regional Government of employing this postponement as a delaying tactic designed to allow the Regional Governing party adequate time "to buy over successful NCNC councillors in order to form the government of the Divisional Council".[25]

A little more than a week later *Otu Edo*/NCNC supporters were to learn that Omo-Osagie had been only half right in his suspicions. In a statement to the House of Assembly on 4 June, Adegbenro revealed that the *Postponement Order* had far more sinister overtones.[26] In reply to a question by the Benin Central MLA, G.I. Oviasu, the Minister explained that the postponement had been ordered so that the Government might first have time to take the actions necessary to bring the Instruments establishing the six District Councils into line with the provisions of the Local Government Law. This would involve appropriate Amendments to these Instruments to allow for the "full and proper" representation of *traditional* members in Benin's District Councils, and so that "chiefs... [might] have equal rights [with elected members] to stand for election in the Benin Divisional Council".[27] Adegbenro went on to state that the *Oba* of Benin had made certain proposals in relation to the amendment of these Instruments. The Regional Government, he said, had accepted these proposals. Notice of the Government's intention to amend Benin Council Instruments in accord with these proposals would be given "in the Regional Gazette, within a few days time".

The response of the *Otu Edo*/NCNC to these proposed Action Group initiatives was to submit to the West Regional Governor a petition with appended demands and an ultimatum.[28] Two main demands were advanced. The Governor was called on to instruct the *Oba* of Benin "in whom the people of Benin do vote no confidence",[29] to "desist from active party politics"; secondly, the Governor was called on to instruct his Government to "withdraw its intention to inject the so-called traditional members" into the Division's District Councils. These two major demands set out, the *Otu Edo*/NCNC petition went on to issue its ultimatum: if these demands were not met within 14 days, then, it was declared that the *Oba* "should be prepared to face any consequences that may arise therefrom".[30]

This petition, with its enclosed demands and ultimatum, was accompanied in the weeks that followed by agitations and disturbances in Benin City and environs reminiscent of similar scenes in 1948, 1951 and 1955.[31] In the end, however, such tactics had little effect in causing the Regional Government to alter course. The Ministry of Local Government, in response to the first *Otu Edo* demand (which called on the Government to "discipline" the *Oba*) recommended that no action should be taken.[32] In response to the second demand, that "the Governor in Council should *not* amend the Instruments of the several district councils to include traditional members", the only comment made was that when the Governor had reached a decision on this matter then "the petitioners should be informed of that decision".[33]

In due course, the Governor in Council reached his decision. In a letter dated 22 August, 1958, the *Otu Edo* petitioners were informed by the Regional Authorities at Ibadan, that the "Governor in Council has now given approval to the proposed amendments to the Instruments of the district councils in Benin Division...".[34] The letter did not even mention the *Otu Edo*'s first demand.

With Government approval for these appointments secured, events in the Division moved swiftly. By the beginning of September, the newly appointed members had taken their places in their respective District councils. In Akugbe District Council the "injection" of five chiefs provided the Action Group with a comfortable five-man majority (Action Group, 25: NCNC, 20); and in Iyekovia District Council, after prolonged bitter wrangling, a single newly-injected chief allowed the Action Group to secure control. The Action Group now exercised formal control in three of the Division's six District Councils.[35] Indirect elections (to the

Benin Divisional Council) in these District Councils now proceeded. In accord with the Regional Governing party's plan the Action Group, although still in the minority in terms of *elected* members selected, (NCNC, 34: Action Group, 26) nevertheless retained the allegiance of all 19 *traditional* members and thus emerged triumphant in the BDC with a majority of 11 (Action Group, 45: NCNC, 34: Ind. 1) sitting members in the new Council.

By the end of 1958, the Action Group had used its Regional Governing authority to its very considerable immediate advantage. It had now secured majority control in seven of the Mid-West's eight Divisional Councils, a feat achieved in *less than six months*! Asaba Divisional Council remained the sole Council which had not been secured within the party fold. Yet even here the Action Group Organising Secretary, Nduka Eze, regarded by all Mid-Westerners as a very tough and even dangerous man, was using various "well-known techniques" to advertise the benefits of supporting the party in power at Ibadan.[36]

This then completed the first phase in the party's efforts to achieve a political take-over in the Mid-West provinces. With the Federal elections fast approaching, the time had now come to launch the second phase. The tactics to be deployed entailed serious risk.[37] The weapons were to be the *Rates Assessment Committees* and the *Customary Courts*.[38] Neither so far had been much used in any partisan context. This now was dramatically to change.[39] *Coercion of Opposition electors throughout the Mid-West was to commence in earnest.*

The Mechanics of Control II: Coercive Tactics

Instruments of Coercion   The *Rates Assessment Committees* and *Customary Courts*, the "lethal weapons" of the Regional party could bring intense—and, in the instance of the Customary Courts, *coercive*—pressure to bear on citizens coming within the scope of their operations. The Rates Assessment Committees, although appointed by the local rating authority, were subject to confirmation of the area Local Government Adviser, and ultimately to final endorsement of the latter's superior, (to whom he was directly responsible) the Action Group Minister of Local Government. In the localities, these Rates Assessment Committees—manned, not surprisingly, mostly by Action Group loyalists—were to make it very clear, and in direct monetary terms, the advantages of supporting the party in power at Ibadan. As a consequence, it was not surprising, as Mackintosh notes, that there should arise "a general impression that assessments fell more heavily on known opponents of the Action Group",[40] while party supporters and sympathisers might find that their assessment had been "neglected", or, if levied, was well below the appropriate rate level.

For the person taxed with a heavy assessment, there was often no prospect of paying the total rate demand, and it was at this point that the Customary Courts came into play. While there were four levels of Customary Courts, Grades A, B, C and D, the majority of "rates non-payment" cases came before the C or D Grade Courts. These courts, together with most Grade B Courts, in accord with the provisions of the *Customary Courts Law (1957)*, were presided over by Presidents and Vice Presidents—most frequently "recognised chiefs", since elected councillors could not act as judges—appointed by the now notorious *Local Government Service Board* (LGSB). While this manner of appointment did not encourage confidence in the impartiality of these courts, the fact that many chiefs selected as presiding officers were totally inexperienced in modern judicial procedure and even illiterate, did little to improve this image.[41] Furthermore, since it was also expected that the Court judges would "raise enough in fines to pay for their own salaries",[42] this boded ill for Action Group opponents brought before them.

Those duly convicted of tax non-payment or other similar offences were seldom able to escape sizeable fines (up to £50 in Grades C and D, and up to £100 in Grade B courts), or, as became the general rule with "tax-defaulters", a prison term of up to six months (or up to 12 months, if the case happened to be heard in a Grade B Court). There was an established procedure for appeals,[43] but often by the time the appeal action came up for hearing, the appellant had already completed his term of imprisonment. In practice, therefore, the majority of convicted "tax-defaulters" and other opponents of the Action Group convicted on any of a number of minor criminal charges,[44] chose mainly to suffer in silence.[45]

Coercive Reality in the Districts   By March 1959, political conditions had become so intolerable for supporters of the NCNC throughout the West, that Azikiwe and the NCNC hierarchy at Enugu, in consultation with the Mid-West Movement Leader Osadebay and Chief Okotie-Eboh, decided on the formation of a *Legal Defence Committee*.[46] This Committee, under the Chairmanship of Leader Osadebay, (the NCNC National Legal

Adviser) provided lawyers, "one for each Administrative Division, paid by the NCNC, to defend its supporters".[47] While one of these specially appointed NCNC lawyers, Webber Egbe of Warri, maintains that the Legal Defence Committee was effective, and "perhaps most importantly, demonstrated to NCNC supporters that the party was behind them",[48] nevertheless it did little to restrain the Action Group's increasingly oppressive assault in the Mid-West districts.

In Ishan Division, Action Group Minister Enahoro was to come forward as the party's candidate for Ishan East at the forthcoming Federal Elections. Was it mere co-incidence, the NCNC asked, that many of their supporters currently were not only being subjected to the oppressive rigours of the Customary Courts, but to "personal persecution" being carried out by one Chief O.A. Enahoro, father of the candidate (and not a legal practitioner) who had been installed as President of the Grade B Customary Court at Uromi? "Some of the senior Enahoro's decisions", it was said, "were extremely unpopular with certain groups of people in Ishan".[49]

In other areas of the Mid-West, the situation was much the same. Following the issue of an Order-in Council by the Regional Government banning the *"Owegbe* Juju"[50]—a juju (or charm) used by Omo-Osagie and his *Otu Edo*/NCNC colleagues to secure sworn allegiance[51] of party members—it was maintained in Benin that many innocent persons had been unjustly arrested by Nigerian and Local Government police and then punished by the Customary Courts;[52] and that at the level of the Magistrates Court more than 200 Benin Division residents were languishing in prison awaiting trial on charges relating to their association with the *Owegbe* Society.[53] V.I. Amadasun, NCNC Chief Whip in the Western House and a prominent leader of the *Otu Edo* in Benin, declared that the suffering to which *Owegbe* adherents—who happened also to be *Otu Edo*/NCNC supporters—were being subjected in the Courts, was the product of yet another cunning manoeuvre by the governing Action Group party, which viewed the *Owegbe Prohibition Order* as a useful vehicle for extending its oppression and persecution of NCNC supporters in the Mid-West heartland.

In both Asaba and Afenmai Divisions, it seemed the Action Group, by November 1959, had shed any last vestige of restraint and was using the Customary Courts for the "mass oppression" of its NCNC opponents. Following the dissolution of the NCNC-dominated Aniocha District Council on 1 October, 1959, F. H. Utomi, the NCNC MLA from Ogwashi-Uku, stated that "the disgraceful spectacle of 'mass prisoners' going off to jail in lorries became a frequent occurence".[54] In the Etsako District Council area of Afenmai Division, it was reported that during this turbulent period "about 3,000... poor farmers were assessed arbitrarily" at rates "ranging from £3 to £15 against the [standard] rates of £2. 14s. 2d. paid by the supporters of the majority [Action Group] party in Council".[55] Of this number, it was stated that "about 900 actually appealed against their assessments", but in the end only "about 50 of these appeals" were heard at the Magistrates' or High Court level. While approximately 80 per cent of these appeals were successful, the rest of these Etsako "tax-defaulters", it was said, resigned themselves to suffer in silence.

During June and July it was alleged that the Action Group in Warri Division was behaving in an equally oppressive and indiscriminate manner. Mass arrests of NCNC supporters were carried out and charges emanated from such alleged acts as "offences against Itsekiri customary law, ...holding a 'juju' ceremony though they were not priests, wearing coral beads though they were not chiefs, and firing off guns to greet Chief Okotie-Eboh, though only the *Olu* of Warri might be so greeted".[56]

And so the allegations continued. Nor did Action Group leaders make any great efforts to refute them.[57] The NCNC in the West as a whole, but particularly in the Mid-West opposition districts, was under heavy fire. Certainly the party's Legal Defence Committee served as a morale booster to beleaguered NCNC supporters, but its practical effectiveness was little more than minimal. Mid-West NCNC leaders could expose and embarrass the Government party in the course of debates in the House of Assembly; the *Pilot* and the *Defender* could maintain a continuing anti-Action Group press offensive; NCNC Opposition members could warn Action Group leaders of the ominous events which might follow an NPC/NCNC victory at the 1959 Federal Elections. However, when it came down to any really forceful and effective resistance, it was all too obvious that NCNC resources—and certainly in the Mid-West—were inadequate. None the less, while NCNC elements might not, at this stage, be able to meet Action Group force with effective force of their own, there was still one very important weapon which they retained: the ballot box. Looking to the future, Mid-West Movement Leader Osadebay made the following prophecy:

> "When the body is weak, the people say "this Action Group trouble is too much, we cannot bear it anymore. My spirit is in the NCNC

but I have to get my body into the Action Group". But let the Government mark this during the day of the Federal Elections... a ballot paper is given to this gentleman, he has only the Almighty God, the ballot box and himself. *He has not voted for the Action Group*"![58]

HARMONISING THE CAMPAIGN OFFENSIVE: ACTION GROUP RETAINS THE INITIATIVE

These Action Group initiatives in the Mid-West were in fact only a part—if a very significant and vital part—of the total Campaign offensive which the party had launched in these districts. In February 1959, Chief Awolowo processed through the Mid-West on what might be termed a "triumphal tour", visiting each of the seven Divisional Councils where his party now held majority control. In his replies to Addresses of Welcome, he consistently took the opportunity to make it clear that "favourable consideration"[59] would be given to most Council requests, though he was prepared to draw the line in certain instances.[60] And in addition to Awolowo's triumphal tour into newly-captive Mid-West districts, the party's prospects also received a considerable early boost—and the NCNC position a sizeable knock—when on 5 February, James Otobo, the NCNC MLA for Urhobo East and prominent Mid-West Movement leader, who had been long exasperated with the NCNC and had been flirting with the West Regional governing party as far back as 1954,[61] "crossed the carpet" to the Action Group.

"Iniquitous Clause 4"   However, the Action Group campaign was rather more concerned at this stage with sapping the strength of the NCNC Opposition by various local initiatives, than it was with taking positive steps to enhance its position in these areas. Passage of the Government's Amendment No. 4 to the *Local Government Law (1957)* produced outcries of alarm from the NCNC Opposition, and from Mid-West Members in particular.

The Amendment was regarded as another blatant device designed further to undercut NCNC strength and assault the morale of the party's leaders and supporters in the localities. Mid-West leaders took greatest exception to the sections about new provisions applicable to sitting members of councils. This section, referred to as the "iniquitous Clause 4", specified that "any person who sits or votes as an elected member knowing that he was disqualified or his seat had become vacant or having reasonable grounds for so knowing", would be "liable to a penalty of five pounds a day, recoverable by the Attorney General or an elector in the Council area".[62] This relatively harmless looking Clause 4, in fact, meant that Councillors who had been marked by the Council Secretary as being absent for four consecutive meetings (as specified in the *1953 Local Government Law*)—and many NCNC members in the Regional and Federal legislatures fell into this category—should regard themselves as being disqualified. The provision allowing for the penalising of such disqualified members by action of the Attorney-General "or an elector in the Council area", was regarded simply as a device for encouraging Action Group men to sue NCNC councillors.[63]

Mid-West Strongholds Under Attack   There were definite indications also in the early months of 1959 that the Action Group was intent on launching sizeable assaults on the vital Mid-West strongholds of Chiefs Okotie-Eboh and Omo-Osagie. In Benin Division, the Government's Order in Council banning the *Owegbe* Juju, was regarded as a blatant Action Group initiative designed to undermine the fighting strength of Omo-Osagie's formidable *Otu Edo* party machine.[64] In a letter to the West Regional Governor, Omo-Osagie bitterly accused the Action Group Government of victimising the *Otu Edo*/NCNC, claiming that the ban had been implemented on the basis of unproven charges and that it resulted from a promise made by Chief Enahoro in February 1959 to the Action Group's "negligible supporters" in the outlying Council districts of Benin Division, that he (Enahoro) would use his personal influence to see that the Government Order in Council was secured.[65] On the basis of these allegations he demanded that the Government conduct a "public enquiry into the circumstances surrounding the banning of the so-called *Owegbe* Juju, which in fact is a cloak for banning the *Owegbe* Society of the *Otu Edo*, an organisation in alliance with the NCNC".[66] Though pressure from *Otu Edo*/NCNC quarters increased during the March-May 1959 period, the Regional Government continued to hold its ground on the *Owegbe* Juju ban, and to resist all efforts by Opposition members to secure the Public Enquiry they sought. The Prohibition Order, the Government maintained, was justified.

In Warri Division, the Action Group's assault was directed almost solely at the NCNC Federal incumbent, Chief Okotie-Eboh. A Mid-West Movement without Chief Festus to advance its interests in the Councils of the NCNC and at Lagos, would be a

Mid-West Movement no longer formidable. In February the Regional Government had announced the creation of the *Itsekiri Communal Lands Trust*. This body[67] vested in its five (Itsekiri) appointees led by the *Olu* of Warri, the power to regulate the tenure and leasing of lands in Warri Town. This was a hotly contested issue between rival Itsekiri and so-called "non-indigenous"—mainly Urhobo and Ibo—resident elements. Indeed, Post maintains that Itsekiri control of the Lands Trust was regarded by Itsekiris as "final recognition of their ownership of the Division".[68]

Needless to say, Itsekiris were delighted with this Government undertaking. Chief Festus countered with an announcement that the Federal Government had agreed to allocate £80,000 for assisting in the development of Koko Port—the project on which, it will be remembered, the Action Group Government had allegedly reneged. However this act, which directly benefitted Benin River Itsekiris only, did little to offset the probable Itsekiri defections in Warri Town.

The Action Group advanced one further comprehensive and very bold initiative which could have reduced NCNC voting strength in the party's three major strongholds—Benin, Warri and Asaba Divisions—to very dangerous levels. Following the release of the Preliminary List of Electors in March, Revising Officers appointed by the Federal Electoral Commission (a body beyond the reach of Regional Governmental control, it was to be noted) heard objections lodged against names included on the list, together with claims for the inclusion of others. The Action Group, apparently recognising that the surest road to victory in NCNC strongholds might well be by means of ensuring that known Opposition electors would be deprived of their vote, organised a massive objections campaign which focused on Benin, Warri and Asaba Divisions. Indeed, of the total objections for the whole of the Federation (65,655), almost one-half of these (about 33,000) were lodged in these three Mid-West Divisions—Warri alone had over 20,000 objections to a Preliminary List of only about 36,000 names![69]

Yet, for all its exhaustive efforts, only 52 objections were upheld in Warri Division (and not all of these deriving from Action Group complaints), while in Asaba East (3,381 objections), Benin Central (5,194) and Benin West (4,477 objections), only "a few objections" in each of these constituencies were ultimately upheld.[70] This campaign by the Action Group was perhaps the most graphic indicator of the enterprise and deadly earnest with which the party was making its preparations for the election fray.

NCNC "Token Resistance"   Still, the NCNC in the Mid-West was not without some weapons of its own. Already, we have seen that Chief Festus was able to use his special connections with the Federal Government to secure development funds for the Koko Port project.[71] Also, as the NCNC held all ten of the Mid-West Federal seats, the party was in a position to benefit from the customary advantages accruing to the incumbent. Furthermore, in March 1959, the Mid-West NCNC achieved a considerable and long-sought organisational break-through when, after a prolonged session of in-fighting in the Central Working Committee (CWC) of the party, the Mid-West was finally granted a separate Working Committee of its own at Ibadan; it could now shape and pursue its own Mid-West policies without having to submit to the wishes of the NCNC Yoruba element.

Indeed, Movement Leader Osadebay states that he was able to take advantage of this new development, and in his role as National Legal Adviser of the NCNC, "to revise the constitution of the party... to provide for the de facto Regional Status"[72] of the Mid-West "for the purposes of NCNC party organisation". In a memorandum circular sent to all Mid-West NCNC legislators, Mr. R.B.K. Okafor, National Secretary of the NCNC, stated that this decision to create a Mid-West/WC had been made at this time "to prove to the peoples of the Mid-West the strong determination of the NCNC to create a Mid-West State", and "to improve the efficiency of the Party machinery in prosecuting the forthcoming Federal Elections in the Mid-West area".[73] The final step in securing the autonomy of the Mid-West within the organisational structure of the NCNC was taken when on 4 April, 1959, a mass gathering of NCNC legislators, local leaders and party supporters was convened at Benin City, to celebrate the opening of the party's Mid-West Secretariat.

The NCNC in the Mid-West now had a fighting base of its own from which to resist the well-organised and aggressive assaults of the Action Group. And though the NCNC National party appeared destined to persist on a rather *ad hoc* organisational basis, with most of the responsibility for campaign efforts resting on its incumbent members,[74] still it was possible that this approach might, in the end, produce a more favourable electoral response than that secured by the Action Group's "no holds barred" tactics.

The Action Group retained a powerful presence throughout the Mid-West in the final period leading up to the December elections. From 1 September, the party, in launching its full campaign assault, had the grand total of 316 full-time organisers at work in the Mid-West.[75] On 17 September, about a week after the Sixth Annual Congress of the party, Chief Awolowo with a full party entourage commenced his final pre-election tour of the Federation. Towards the end of October he made his appearance in the Mid-West. In the course of local meetings he and his Action Group colleagues re-asserted their commitment to the creation of new states and to a Mid-West state in particular; that the party, if elected, would see that Middle Belt, C.O.R., and Mid-West states were created before 1 October, 1960.[76] Along with extending the usual appeals for electors to recognise the material benefits to be derived from supporting the Regional party in power,[77]

Awolowo provided at least one very vivid reminder for Mid-West dissenters who still chose stubbornly to persist in their political heresy. After speaking in the NCNC-dominated Aniocha District Council on the morning of 1 October, and having stated to the NCNC councillors that he resented certain remarks made in their Address of Welcome, his visit was followed by an announcement from Ibadan in the afternoon that the Council was to be dissolved forthwith. It was to be replaced by a Committee of Management. As earlier noted, it was this Committee of Management which was to inaugurate a campaign of systematic, mass oppression of Opposition NCNC supporters. In Asaba Division, as elsewhere in the Mid-West, Awolowo was as concerned with reminding constituents of the might and muscle of the Regional party in power as he was with stressing its "good intentions".

Clearly, in terms of efforts expended, the Action Group now was in a challenging position in the Mid-West. It had managed to bring a well-organised, well-timed assault to bear and with particular emphasis on the NCNC strongholds of Asaba, Benin and Warri. The party had shown by its deliberate undertakings that stronger, more assertive, even coercive initiatives would best serve to advance its interests. This approach involved obvious risk. Action Groupers, however, calculated these were risks worth taking.

ACTION GROUP'S DAY OF RECKONING:
FEDERAL ELECTION REALITIES

On election day, 12 December, there was a high poll in most Mid-West districts. In Afenmai, Asaba and Benin Divisions, the turnout of Registered Electors was rather more than 80 per cent; in Ishan, the total poll reached the astonishing level of something more than 89 per cent![78] Only in Western Ijaw did the vote fall below 60 per cent of the Division's Registered Electors. To the chagrin of the Action Group, however, the majority of these Mid-West electors did *not* choose to cast their ballots in favour of the Regional party in power.

An Electoral Disaster   After all the calculated effort it had expended in the course of the past two years, Action Group candidates managed to secure victory in *only three of the 15 Mid-West constituencies*: both Ishan seats and one in Afenmai Division. A further bitter disappointment was the fact that the party, for all its concentrated initiatives in the NCNC's three major Mid-West Federal strongholds of Benin, Warri and Asaba, had not even managed to muster a substantial electoral challenge. All three Benin seats—including Omo-Osagie's Benin Central—were won by *Otu Edo*/NCNC candidates with relative ease.

The closest the Action Group came to an NCNC candidate was in Benin West, where the Action Group candidate gained 39.5 per cent of the popular vote against the NCNC candidate's total of 58.6 per cent. In the two Asaba constituencies, NCNC incumbents won equally comfortable victories with margins of approximately 2 : 1 in terms of votes cast. In Warri Division, the Regional Governing party received its greatest setback, in psychological terms at least. Here Chief Okotie-Eboh confounded his Action Group tormentors and the "Rewane clique" which had so persistently harassed him throughout the past 12 months. Chief Festus secured 16,918 votes; his Action Group rival, O.N. Rewane only 10,889.

Thus, the Action Group's overall Mid-West offensive had not only fallen far short of the objectives envisaged, but perhaps of most vital significance, its efforts to dislodge three of the Mid-West Movement's most prominent leaders had failed utterly. Not only had Chiefs Omo-Osagie, Onyia and Okotie-Eboh been returned to their respective seats, but in addition the sizeable votes they had polled could be viewed as a collective *pro*-Mid-West State mandate.

This Mid-West result was very distressing to Action Groupers, nor did the failure of the party's bid for National power lessen anxieties. Within the Federation as a whole, the Action Group had managed to secure only 75 seats in all, while the NCNC/NEPU alliance had returned 89 candidates and the NPC 148—only 9 seats short of an overall majority. Although it did appear during the frenetic negotiations which took place during the few days (14-18 December) following the elections, that the Action Group might manage to secure the position of junior partner in either an NPC or NCNC Government coalition at Lagos,[79] the announcement on 20 December that the NPC in partnership with the NCNC would form the Federal Government brought Action Group aspirations to an abrupt end. Chief Awolowo and his party colleagues were now to occupy the Opposition benches in the Federal House of Representatives.

Altogether, the Action Group found itself in a most perilous position, and not just in the Mid-West. In the course of the past two years, Mid-West leaders had repeatedly declared that when the NCNC, victorious in the Mid-West, formed a coalition Government with the NPC at Lagos, the necessary steps would be taken to ensure that a Mid-West State would be created—whether the Action Group liked it or not. Furthermore, NCNC leaders had not hesitated to hint that the new Federal Government might make use of the *Emergency Powers* conferred on it by the provisions of the Independence Constitution to bring Action Group rule in the West to a dramatic end. It was, therefore, hardly a settling prospect to Action Groupers that Movement leaders and the NCNC had now secured the base from which they could make good on their threats.

Glimmers of Hope   Yet, there were other factors to be borne in mind, factors which suggested that the Action Group position—at least in relation to the Mid-West State issue—was not quite so fraught with danger as at first it appeared. For one thing, although the Action Group had won only three Mid-West seats, this represented a 300 per cent improvement over the party's Mid-West performance at the 1954 Federal Elections! Furthermore, on closer examination of the voting figures it became apparent that with only a slight alteration in Action Group fortunes the party might easily have emerged with six of the 15 Mid-West seats. In three constituencies the contest had been very close. In Afenmai North West, Urhobo East, and Western Ijaw, Action Group candidates would have required only another 4 to 5 per cent of votes cast to overtake their NCNC rivals. Had the Regional Governing party been able to secure the allegiance of Independents—one Independent ran in each of these three marginal constituencies— Action Group victories would have been assured. Lastly, and certainly not least, Action Groupers could draw re-assurance from the fact that in only five Mid-West constituencies had the NCNC secured more than 60 per cent of the popular vote—the highest total, 69 per cent, being recorded in Omo-Osagie's Benin Central, while in two of these five constituencies, Benin West and Warri, the NCNC vote amounted to only 61.5 per cent and 60.2 per cent respectively.

It was, therefore, clear that *so long as the Action Group could continue to ensure that the NCNC would be unable to secure more than 60 per cent support from registered voters in the Mid-West, then its chances of preventing the success of any NCNC-inspired Mid-West Referendum were good.* While there was always the chance that Mid-Westerners might behave differently if provided with the opportunity for a free vote—which a Mid-West Referendum would afford them—still there was reason to believe that with continued diligent efforts Action Groupers could hope at least to reduce the imminence of this threat. It was to be remembered that the Action Group did not oppose the *idea* of the creation of a Mid-West State, so long as this was undertaken in concert with simultaneous action to create COR and Middle Belt states. What the Action Group opposed and feared was the prospect of *unilateral* action by the NPC/NCNC Centre Government, to create a Mid-West state *alone.*

As Nigeria moved into its celebratory year of National Independence, Movement supporters could at least feel that in the battle for the Mid-West, the fighting-odds had been somewhat evened up. Reduced to simplest terms, Movement prospects for victory now rested on the ability of their leaders to persuade the Centre Government to take appropriate—and hopefully, swift— action. On the other hand, the chances of the Action Group prevailing, and in the end mustering an adequate anti-NCNC vote to frustrate Movement ambitions, rested on the party's ability to prevent any unilaterally imposed Mid-West Referendum from securing a 60 per cent "Yes vote". It was to be within the context of these basic Movement and Action Group objectives, that the second and decisive stage in the "Battle for the Mid-West" was now to be waged.

References

1. The key to this "new and more realistic promise" in relation to the Mid-West issue, was to be found in the statement of Chief Okotie-Eboh at a meeting of the Movement Executive that "What is paramount... in the event of no success at the (1958 London) Conference... is that we should work harder than ever... to get the NCNC to rule the Federation after Independence, and then we shall have our own state easily". (See *Minutes of the Meeting of the Central Executive Committee, held 30 August, 1958, at Osana House, Benin City, op.cit.*)

2. In May 1958, the NCNC leader Dr. Azikiwe went to the North to confer with the Sardauna of Sokoto. Chief Enahoro suggests that "it may have been at this meeting that an understanding was reached in broad terms for the NCNC and NPC to work together, if neither was in a position to control the Federal Government" following completion of the 1959 Federal Elections. (See Enahoro, *Fugitive Offender, op. cit.*, p.163). Certainly, such an interpretation would seem to explain why Mid-West Movement leaders were able in June, 1958 (See *Western House of Assembly Debates*, 5 June, 1958, col. 695), and August 1958 (See *Minutes of the Central Executive Committee of the Mid-West State Movement, held at Benin City, 30 August 1958, op.cit.*) to express such confidence in their potential ability to secure governmental partnership with the NPC following the 1959 Federal Elections. It was to be noted also that in the course of these June and August utterances, Mid-West leaders made it clear not only that an NPC/NCNC coalition Federal Government would deliver the Mid-West State, but also that they might "consider using the same Action Group methods" to humble Awolowo and his colleagues at Ibadan. In an obvious reference to the *Emergency Powers* which would then be held by the Federal Government, Action Groupers were further warned that they should remember that "the use of the army... is not a Regional subject". (*Western House of Assembly Debates, op. cit.*, col. 695).

3. Enahoro, *Fugitive Offender, op.cit.*, p.162.

4. For a useful summary of these legislative and other weapons employed by the ruling Action Group in Western Nigeria, see section entitled "Methods of the AG" in Mackintosh, *Nigerian Government and Politics, op.cit.*, pp.430-437; also, *ibid.*, pp.509-515. Also see Emmet U. Mittlebeeler, "Legal Controls over Local Government in the Western State of Nigeria", *The Quarterly Journal of Administration*, Vol.5, No.2, (January, 1971).

5. In commenting on the consolidation of Regional single-party rule in Nigeria, Sklar states that it is difficult to exaggerate the

contribution of Regional "powers over local government and chieftaincy, including the power to recognise and depose chiefs and the power to regulate the participation of traditional authorities in local government councils". These powers, together with Regional control over an extensive system of "commercial patronage", he maintains, were the building blocks upon which Action Group interests were advanced. (See Sklar, *Nigerian Political Parties*, *op. cit.*, pp.500-501).

6. Ja' Isuman, who had crossed over to the Action Group in December 1957, and was a prominent member of the party's Mid-West leadership, rising to the post of Principal Organising Secretary (Mid-West) in 1960, contends that the non-coercive approach was a difficult one to counsel. Isuman points out that many of the Mid-West local Action Group leaders were individuals who had deep grievances against the NCNC and leaders like Nduka Eze, "a very hot fellow", in Asaba; or who, like O.N. Rewane and the Itsekiri members of his clique in Warri, had profound fears about the Mid-West issue. In general, the party had always attracted the more aggressive and militant persons, and to this amalgam in the Mid-West were added disaffected and disgruntled elements. (See, Interview with Isuman, Int. VII, p.61).

7. *Case for a Mid-West State*, *op. cit.*, p.10.

8. See, *ibid.*, pp.10-11.

9. These Local Government elections were held at the following times:

Western Ijaw and Asaba Divisions	12 April, 1958
Aboh Division	19 April, 1958
Asaba Division (Aniocha District)	3 May, 1958
Ishan, Warri and Urhobo Divisions	10 May, 1958
Warri and Benin Divisions	17 May, 1958
Afenmai Division	7 June, 1958

For further details see *Report on Local Government Elections in the Western Region of Nigeria. 1958*, Sessional Paper, No.7(1958), Appendix A, p.5, (INA).

10. See *Report on 1958 Local Government Elections...,op. cit.* These figures are extracted from *Appendix C: Regional Summary of the Report*.

11. See *Table VI*, p.249.

12. *Report on Local Government Elections...*, *op.cit.*, Appendices B and C.

13. Otobo, Int.VII, p.1.

14. See, *ibid.*, Appendix B.

15. See n.5, above, this chapter.

16. This figure is, however, a little misleading. Action Groupers had secured victory in only 258 contested wards. The balance it had

won in *unopposed* elections. A large number of these, it was alleged, had been won as a result of partial actions by Council Secretaries who were generally acknowledged by NCNC Opposition elements to be the local administrative instruments of Action Group political designs, and who at these 1958 local elections had served as Electoral Officers. The most outstanding allegation in this context occurred in Akugbe District Council, Benin Division. After the District Council Secretary/Electoral Officer had dis-qualified 18 NCNC candidates on the grounds that their nominations were invalid, the Action Group, securing unopposed victories in these 18 seats, together with contested victories in two further seats, managed to gain a total of 20 seats. This brought it level with the NCNC which had won 20 contested seats to the Akugbe Council. (See comments of Local Government Adviser for Benin Division, in issue of *Daily Times* 3 June, 1959; also observations by the Mid-West leader Otobo on the issue of "invalid nominations", in *Debates of the Western House of Assembly*, 5 June, 1958, cols.690-91).

17. The question of which way Mid-Westerners would vote at a Referendum on the Mid-West State issue was the source of much anxiety to Action Group leaders. After the 1958 Local Government elections, the general view endorsed by Awolowo, was that the party could expect to secure majority control at any such Referendum; that is, that a 60 per cent "Yes vote" would *not* be gained. Even as late as August 1962, this continued to be the official party view.

18. *Pilot*, 6 June, 1958.

19. *Debates of the Western House of Assembly*, 4 June, 1958, col.673.

20. *Debates of the Western House of Assembly*, 5 June, 1958, col.689.

21. See *Defender*, 10 July and 13 August, 1958.

22. Debates of the *Western House of Assembly*, 2 September, 1958, cols. 766-767.

23. For details of Benin Divisional election returns see, Sklar, *Nigerian Political Parties*, *op.cit.* p.241.

24. Sklar provides a lucid account of the party's ultimately successful effort to secure control of the BDC in September, 1958. See "Benin: A Study in the Mechanics of Chieftaincy Control", in *ibid.*, pp.238-42.

25. *Pilot*, 27 May, 1958.

26. See *Debates of the Western House of Assembly*, 4 June, 1958, cols. 671-673.

27. *Ibid.*, col. 672.

28. See, petition submitted to the Governor of the West Region, entitled, *No Confidence Motion at Mass Meeting*, dated 13 June, 1958 (Copy in possession of writer).

29. The foundation for this claim derived from a "no confidence vote" secured at a meeting of the *Otu Edo*/NCNC-controlled Benin City District Council, held 23 June, 1958. (See copy of *Motion of No Confidence in Oba of Benin*, BNA/Vol/120 (BCA).). Also Iyekovia District Council passed a "no confidence" motion against the *Oba* on 15 June, 1958. (See *Pilot*, 26 June, 1958).

30. Additional details of *Otu Edo*/NCNC allegations in relation to the *Oba*'s proposals on the "injection" of chiefs into the Division's District Councils are set out in a memo entitled *A Resolution by the People of Benin Rejecting Injection of Traditional Members into Benin Councils*; the memo was attached to the petition of 13 June submitted, by *Otu Edo*/NCNC to the Governor of the West Region. (See BNA/Vol/120, *op. cit.*).

31. See *Pilot*, 28 and 30 July, 1958.

32. See *Memorandum from Parliamentary Assistant (Political) to Minister of Local Government*, dated 8 August, 1958, at Ibadan. (Copy in possession of the writer).

33. *Ibid.*

34. *Letter from Permanent Secretary, Ministry of Local Government Ibadan to the Secretary-General, Otu Edo Secretariat, Benin City*, dated 22 August ,1958. (Copy in possession of the writer).

35. For a detailed portrayal of the effect of these "Chiefs injections" on Action Group and *Otu Edo*/NCNC numerical strengths in these six District Councils and in the Benin Divisional Council between May and 16 September, 1958, see Sklar, *Nigerian Political Parties, op.cit.*, Table I, p. 241.

36. See *Pilot*, 6 June, 1958; see also *Debates of the Western House of Assembly*, 4 June, 1958, Cols.673-78.

37. Interview with Ja' Isuman, Int. VII, pp.61-62

38. In 1957, the powers of these Customary Courts, which derived from an initial jurisdiction over land, inheritance and family matters, were extended to include a range of minor criminal matters. This development, together with the authority of the *Local Government Service Board* (LGSB) (which, as we have already seen in the last three chapters, was regarded with a good deal of suspicion by Mid-West opponents of the Action Group) to confirm appointments to the C and D Grade and most B Grade Courts, served considerably to heighten the anxiety of Mid-West Opposition members.

39. *Ibid.*

40. *Nigerian Government and Politics, op. cit.*, p.432.

41. Only Grade A Courts and specified Grade B Courts were presided over by qualified legal practitioners; these being appointed by the Judicial Service Commission. However, Mackintosh notes that

even by 1962 "of some eighty Grade B courts, only ten had lawyers as presidents". (*Nigerian Government and Politics, op.cit.* p.433).

42. *Ibid*.

43. "Appeals were to the Customary Court of Appeal", presided over by a Grade A Court judge, "or to the Magistrate's Court and hence to the High Court and the Federal Supreme Court". (Post, *Nigerian Federal Election of 1959, op.cit.*, p. 289). Since these (Grade A) Customary Courts of Appeal ,were very few (thus resulting in an enormous bulk of "appeals pending" at this level), appeals were often better directed to the Magistrate's Court, and then, as necessary, on to the High Court; though even at the High Court level, congestion was considerable. (See *Debates of the Western House of Assembly*, 15 April, 1959, cols.65-68 for comments on Court congestion, and proposal for the establishment of a "roving Customary Court of Appeal").

44. Perhaps the most common charge of this nature brought against "offenders" in the Mid-West during the 1959-62 period was "contempt of court". This charge was particularly favoured when the accused made the fatal mistake of openly expressing his outrage in the course of Customary Court hearings (*See* Int.III, p.19 and pp.74-75). In these two interviews informants spoke of the separate contempt charges brought against them. In the first instance, B.U. Ellams, NCNC Opposition Leader in the Etsako District Council, stated that when he objected strongly to the initial tax-default charge brought against him, the contempt charge was simply added to it. In the second instance, Webber Egbe, an NCNC lawyer who defended cases brought against his party's supporters in Warri Division, stated that he was brought to Court on a contempt charge following a verbal dispute with the prominent Warri Action Group leader, O.N. Rewane. The rather bizarre aspect of this action was that this dispute did not even take place in court but during an Inquiry being conducted in March 1959 by the Warri Divisional Council. Other charges frequently brought included: disorderly conduct; behaviour likely to cause a breach of the peace; leading or participating in a procession without a permit; possession of a firearm without a permit; and an array of charges arising from the very fruitful ground of Local Council Ordinance (housing and sanitation) infringements.

45. See, *A Welcome Address by Members of the Opposition. Etsako District Council, Presented to the Commissioner for Mid-West Affairs. Hon. B.M. Uzorka, on his Maiden Visit to Etsako, 24 July, 1962,* (Benin City: Abayomi Printing Works, 1962) (pamphlet), p.6 (INA).

46. See Osadebay, unpublished *mss., op.cit.*, p.305. Osadebay also notes that prior to the formation of the Legal Defence Committee, the NCNC on an *ad hoc* basis "paid lawyers to defend supporters of the party in the Mid-West, in cases inspired by their political opponents, and also paid court fines for them".

47. *Ibid.* Osadebay remained Chairman of the Legal Defence Committee until 1960, when he handed over the Chairmanship to Mr. J.O.W. Izuora, Barrister-at-Law, so that he could "devote more time to other commitments in the party".

48. Egbe, Int.III, p.19. In outlining the tactics employed by Committee lawyers, Egbe pointed out that since most of the cases with which they were concerned were heard in the Grade C and D Customary Courts where legal representation of the accused was *not* permitted, an indirect approach had to be adopted. This involved securing a High Court writ against the Customary Court involved (on the basis of alleged "political bias", "false accusation" etc.) and an order that the particular case or cases be transferred to the Magistrates Court, or directly to the High Court. Egbe maintains that he and other Committee lawyers had considerable success with this tactic.

49. Post, *Nigerian Federal Elections of 1959, op. cit.*, p.289.

50. See "Western Region Legal Notice No. 137 of 1959" in the *West Regional Gazette*, No.14 of 19 March, 1959. This Order-in-Council followed an initial Resolution passed by the BDC on 25 November, 1958, banning the *Owegbe* Juju in Benin Division.

51. For details of *Owegbe* Juju, see *Report of the Commission Appointed to Enquire into the Owegbe Cult*, (Benin City: MOI, 1966), p.103.

52. See *Debates of the Western House of Assembly*, 27 May, 1959, col.865.

53. *Ibid.*, col.866.

54. W.G. Odiase, "Field Administration and Local Government in Mid-West Nigeria Considered as Aspects of Political Development", (unpublished *mss.* 1972), Chapter 6, p.14.

55. *A Welcome Address by Etsako District Council...* , *op.cit.*, p.6.

56. Post, *Nigerian Federal Elections of 1959, op.cit.*, p.289.

57. In July 1959, the Action Group made some attempt to show that it was prepared to take action against Customary Courts, where it could be satisfactorily proved that such Courts had been used for political purposes. On 4 July, Chief F.R.A. Williams, West Regional Minister of Justice and Attorney-General, announced that "eighteen members of these courts had been dismissed". (Post, *ibid.*, p.290). This action, however, appeared to do little to improve the credibility of the Customary Courts in the Region. In fact, NCNC leaders used these dismissals to reinforce their contentions that these Courts were now acknowledged even by the Action Group leadership to be the political vehicles of the Regional party in power.

58. *Western House of Assembly Debates*, 13 April, 1959, col.63. (Italics added).

59. *Defender*, 4 March, 1959.

60. See *ibid.*

61. See pp.118-20 above.

62. *Debates of the Western House of Assembly*, 30 April, 1959, cols.463-470. (Italics added).

63. *Ibid.*, col.465

64. Strenuous efforts were made by *Otu Edo*/NCNC members to persuade the Government to revoke its *Prohibition Order on the Owegbe Juju*. (Detailed arguments advanced by Otu Edo/NCNC members are set out in a number of letters and memos included in Appendices 17-21, of the *Owegbe Report, op.cit.*, pp.137-143). These arguments did not reduce the impression that the *Owegbe* was harmful. Still it was difficult to see that it constituted any more of a threat to public safety than that other *non-national* "Juju", the *Ogboni*, the juju by which most BTPA/Action Group leaders had for many years been sworn into the rival *Reformed Ogboni Fraternity*. (See *Debates of the House of Assembly*, 27 May, 1959, col.863).

65. See *Owegbe Report, op.cit.*, Appendix 19, pp.139-140.

66. *Ibid.*, p.140.

67. See, Post, *The Nigerian Federal Elections of 1959, op.cit.*, p.414.

68. *Ibid.*

69. See *ibid.*, p.216.

70. See *ibid.*, pp.216-18. For further details on objections see *Report of the Nigeria Federal Elections, December, 1959*, (Lagos: Government Printer, 1960), pp.6-7.

71. The Koko Port project which was started in January 1959, was officially opened in June 1959. (See Post, *op.cit.*, p.420).

72. Osadebay (unpublished *mss.*), *op.cit.*, pp.301-302.

73. *NCNC: Mid-West Working Committee*, memo circular dated 16 March, 1959, at Yaba (Ref. No. NC/HG, 188/1.). (Copy in possession of writer).

74. NCNC party organisation, despite certain modifications designed to tighten it up and improve its efficiency, "remained fragmentary... in the West, and Mid-West during this pre-election period. (See Sklar, *Nigerian Political Parties, op.cit.*, p.394).

75. See Post, *op. cit.*, p.143.

76. These Mid-West and "new states" commitments were set out in the twelfth point of the Action Group's, *14-Point Programme*, which had been released on 4 June, 1959 by Chief Awolowo. (Copy in possession of writer).

77. One of the Action Group's most spectacular gestures during the final days before the elections was made at Benin City. On 7 November, 1959, at a gala gathering, Chief Tony Enahoro in his capacity as Minister of Home and Mid-West Affairs laid the cornerstone for the Mid-West Secretariat; the building which was to become the headquarters for the Mid-West Advisory Council and its administrative staff. (*See* Interview with Chief Lawal-Osula, Int.V, p.11). In fact, work on the Secretariat never started. In July 1972, the writer discovered the elaborately engraved stone lying face down at the rear of the site where the Secretariat was to be built. This site is now the location of Palm House on the Sapele Road.

78. These figures and others used in this section (unless otherwise specified) are taken from *Appendix D: Registration and Results*, in Post, *The Nigerian Federal Elections of 1959, op.cit.*

79. An account of the Action Group's whirlwind manoeuvres during this critical 14-18 December period is detailed by Post in, "The National Council of Nigeria and the Cameroons: The Decision of December 1959", in Mackintosh, *Nigerian Government and Politics, op. cit.*, pp.424-26.

CHAPTER 12

THE MID-WEST AT THE CROSS-ROADS

The first few months of Federal rule during 1960 was a period of great anxiety for both Movement supporters and the Action Group. Mid-West supporters were well aware that if everything went the way they hoped, this second stage in the Battle for the Mid-West could be brief; that the Action Group Government in the West could be suspended; and with an "Emergency Administration" in the West controlled by *Federally-appointed* officers and party politics banned, all the constitutional requirements, *including* the 60 per cent "Yes vote" could be engineered with relative ease. Action Group leaders, for their part, fully recognised this threat. Under such circumstances, the party's "statistical victory" and its claim of adequate voting strength to forestall any NCNC-inspired Mid-West referendum would count for nothing. It was a critical juncture. Everything depended on the actions of the Federal Government.

Certain new developments at Lagos now appeared further to enhance Movement prospects. Foremost amongst these was the fact that Chief Okotie-Eboh had emerged from the post-election scramble for Government offices as an immensely powerful figure. He now occupied a position which placed him second only to Prime Minister Balewa. Not only had he retained his post as Minister of Finance, but also he had been selected to serve as Leader of the Parliamentary Party. This latter post was a vital one, and particularly so for Mid-West interests. As Leader of the Parliamentary Party, *Chief Festus would have much influence over the nature and substance of Government policy. Also, as Chairman of the Business Committee of the House, he could exercise equal influence over which motions — including relevant Mid-West legislation — would appear on the Order Paper.*

Equally encouraging to Movement supporters was the departure of the "chameleonic" Azikiwe from active politics at Lagos. As the Sardauna had insisted the post of Prime Minister must go to one of his "lieutenants," Azikiwe had been stranded politically—there was no other office in the Federal Government which accorded to his own estimate of an appropriate status. He therefore decided to resign his seat in the House of Representatives and accept appointment as President of the Nigerian Senate—a position of eminence but little direct political power. Azikiwe had finally been politically "caged". Mid-West protagonists were delighted. Chief Festus could now more easily start the machinery to bring home the Mid-West State.[1]

With Chief Okotie-Eboh "in", so to speak, and Azikiwe "out" at Lagos, and indeed with the NCNC now operating under a new President, Dr. Michael Okpara, who had succeeded Azikiwe also as Premier of the East Region Government, Mid-West prospects were bright with new promise. *And there was one final, crucial factor. It was commonly believed that the Sardauna had been prevailed upon not to oppose creation of a Mid-West State.* Consistently, the Sardauna had publicly stated that he opposed creation of *any* new states. It had, however, been rumoured that the Sardauna— following a June 1958 meeting with NCNC representatives, including Chiefs Festus, Osadebay and Omo-Osagie—was *privately* prepared to make creation of the Mid-West an *exception* to his rule, and that this had been written into the NPC/NCNC post-election pact.[2] Given these encouraging considerations Mid-West supporters felt they could hardly fail in their quest.

By the beginning of May 1960, however, grey clouds of doubt once again were gathering. The single most devastating blow to Movement expectations was delivered by Chief Okotie-Eboh himself. Chief Festus, rather than using his position to advance Mid-West interests in the House of Representatives, had been silent at its January Inaugural meeting—a silence which continued during its second meeting in April and May. And though at least one Mid-West Member in the Federal House, Chief Oweh, threatened he would oppose the National Independence Motion on the grounds that "the people of the Mid-West... would not support the country's Independence *unti*l a Mid-West State was created",[3] when the motion was debated there was again silence. On only two occasions was the new states issue brought to the attention of the House; and on both—to the acute embarrassment of Mid-West Members—it was Chief Awolowo, the new Leader of the Opposition, who took the initiative.[4]

However, it was not only Chief Festus who fell short of Movement expectations. The Sardauna's position had been seriously mis-judged. During a final round of meetings with the British authorities at London where the finishing touches were being applied to the Independence Constitution, the Sardauna with characteristic bluntness announced that "the question of more states and the adjustment of our boundaries is already closed".[5] And as if to make a total mockery of Movement reasoning and aspirations, Okpara, who also was in attendance at the London talks, stated that the NCNC had decided to endorse a policy of "Provincialism" for Nigeria which envisaged creation of 23 Provinces within the Federation—Benin and Delta Provinces being two.[6]

By mid-May 1960, any lingering hopes of a swift and successful resolution of the Mid-West issue had been shattered. Indeed, if these most recent statements by NPC and NCNC leaders represented the long-term view of the Centre Government, then it seemed possible the Mid-West issue had not simply been once again shelved, but this time terminally discarded.

ACTION GROUP RESUMES THE INITIATIVE

The failure of Mid-West expectations during the early months of 1960 afforded the Action Group new and fruitful grounds on which to extend its quest for support. Hollow promises, Federal Government inaction, NPC resistance and the NCNC's retreat from the Mid-West issue, the alleged insincere and self-seeking behaviour of Mid-West NCNC politicians; all these provided promising opportunities. And there was an added incentive. Regional elections were due in the West before September.

New Minorities Policy   The Action Group chose this moment to advance a re-vamped —from that produced for the *1958 Constitutional Conference*—pro-Mid-West case of its own. It was simple, persuasive and designed to show it was *only* the Action Group which could be expected to deliver the Mid-West—indeed that such an outcome was assured because it was in the *political interest* of the Action Group to ensure that these new states (COR, Middle Belt and Mid-West) were in fact created.

The party's Principal Organising Secretary in the Mid-West, Ja' Isuman, pointed out that any hope of the Action Group gaining Federal power, rested on its ability to secure the confidence and support of electors in Nigeria's minority areas.[7] With their support—72 seats in the Middle Belt, 24 from the COR area, 15 from the Mid-West—together with 47 seats from the Yoruba West, the Action Group would be in a position to command an overall majority of 169 seats, 12 more than the 157 seats required for an absolute majority.[8] Once in Office the Party could then take the needed steps to bring these three new states into existence.

The *insurance* for these minorities that the Action Group would actually carry out its commitment resided, Isuman stressed, in the simple fact that without the continued support of its minorities allies the party would soon be deprived of its majority, and without its majority it would not last long in Federal Office.

But first things first. A display of Mid-West commitment at the forthcoming West Regional elections would help convince the party that its new policy position on Nigeria's major-minorities was the right one, and indeed deserving of support.

Movement Mounts A Challenge   This Action Group initiative triggered alarms in NCNC and Movement quarters—and was not to pass unchallenged. Awolowo became a particular target. In a sharp challenge to his party's "new states" policy a *Pilot* editorial asked bluntly, "If Chief Awolowo honestly believes in the creation of more states",[9] why did he and his party cling so tenaciously to Regionalism? "Why did he launch the slogan 'West for Westerners' "? The editorial went on to point out that the Action Group leader expected "other Regional Governments to willingly assent" to proposals which would result in the re-adjustment of *their* territorial boundaries, while the Action Group Government in the West "stood rigidly by 'what we have we keep'."

The whole of this "New States" policy, it maintained, was little more than an "elaborate political ruse". Until the party demonstrated that it was prepared to meet the established (1955) West Regional Government-endorsed Movement demand for the creation of a Mid-West State, and cease its temporising through adhering to such "sabotage devices" as the Mid West Advisory Council, no serious consideration should be given to the Action Group's "ardent advocacy" of new states.[10]

In July (1960) the Movement was provided with a massive—and timely—propaganda coup when the *Oba* of Benin announced his resignation as Minister of State in the Action Group Government.[11] Since joining the party in 1955 as Minister-Without-Portfolio, the *Oba* had been subjected to a number of attacks which ruffled his dignity; he had been excluded from consultation on many vital Mid-West matters; and above all the Action Group *still* had not fulfilled its part of their 1955 bargain—

that is, to create a Mid-West state. The end finally came when the *Oba* failed to secure appointment as new President of the House of Chiefs. On 7 July, the *Oni* of Ife succeeded Sir John Rankine as Governor of the West; and on the same day, by an overwhelming vote of 33-8, another Yoruba, the *Alake* of Abeokuta, was elected President of the House of Chiefs.[12]

Attacking the "Yoruba Groupers" for overlooking *Oba* Akenzua, Omo-Osagie pointed out how in pre-British days, the *Oba* of Benin was the only monarch with the title of *Oba* and that it was only in recent years since the advent to power of the Action Group that this title had come to be used in "designating *any* head chief of *any* place".[13] Omo-Osagie called on Mid-Westerners to take close note of this shabby treatment meted out to their *Oba*: "Despite his unflagging support of the Action Group, this has been his reward—relegation to the background".

It was nevertheless to be noted that while Omo-Osagie welcomed the defection of the *Oba*—insofar as it represented a serious blow to Action Group prestige in the Mid-West area—this was the extent to which he was prepared to applaud. Referring to a recent statement in which the *Oba* had called on all Mid-Westerners to resist "the forces... which were threatening the people of the area",[14] Omo-Osagie, clearly mindful of *Oba* Akenzua's cunning intrigues of earlier years, maintained that this appeal had come too late. The *Oba*, he declared, "has offended his people and the Mid-West State to the point of unforgiveness". And just to ensure that Mid-Westerners should fully recall his earlier "treachery" to the Mid-West cause, Omo-Osagie accused the *Oba* of "veiled opposition to the creation of a Mid-West State; mal-administration with regard to building plots in Benin; and reversing the verdict of the electors at the 1958 Local Government elections, through supporting the injection of traditional chiefs into councils to the prejudice of the NCNC".[15]

Thus, while it was clear that news of the *Oba's* defection from the Action Group was warmly welcomed—and indeed that his presence as traditional *spiritual* leader was unquestioned—there were limits. The *Oba* should leave Movement *politics* to its Deputy Leader and his colleagues.

Mid-West Mandate for the Action Group   In early July, Premier Akintola announced the dissolution of the House. General elections, he stated, would be conducted on 8 August, 1960. In the intervening period between the dissolution of the House of

Assembly and the date set for the poll, there was little time for the contesting parties to do much more than emphasise the positions they had already advanced.

NCNC Movement leaders received some assistance from the National and Eastern branches of the party. Dr. Okpara and a team of prominent NCNC politicians made a rush tour with Mid-West NCNC leaders through the Mid-West districts; and Okpara himself diplomatically offered his congratulations to the *Oba* on the latter's "decision to quit the sinking boat of the Action Group,... which was not only wise, but timely".[16] The Mid-West NCNC also expressed outrage over alleged foul play. M.A. Deke, an Afenmai NCNC leader, told how "the Action Group had taken him into the Customary Court 21 times without just cause";[17] in Asaba, Movement Leader Osadebay expressed concern over alleged efforts being made by the Action Group "to remove presiding electoral officers already appointed, and to appoint instead known supporters of the Action Group"[18]; in many Opposition districts there were repeated allegations of Action Group thuggery. For the rest, the contesting parties contented themselves with exchanging mutual recriminations and extending the now customary Mid-West electoral promises.

On 8 August, following this whirlwind mini-campaign, the Regional elections were conducted. The Action Group emerged triumphant. Within the Region as a whole, the Action Group won 78 of the 124 seats, while the NCNC gained 34, the *Mabolaje* 10 and Independents two—though both Independents declared immediately for the Action Group. For the Action Group, the most important outcome of the election was the size of the majority it had secured. This should enable the party to retain comfortable overall control in the Western House.

As for the Action Group's showing in the Mid West districts; this was impressive. It secured victories in Asaba (1), Urhobo (2), Ishan (4), Warri (1), Western Ijaw (2) and Afenmai (4); even in Benin Division the Action Group managed finally to secure a seat when its candidate Ben Edo-Osagie defeated his *Otu Edo*/NCNC rival by the narrow margin of 681 votes. In Ishan West Central, the Action Group had another very close call when M.O. Ijie, formerly employed as a steward by Prince Shaka Momodu, gained victory over his eminent, powerful and now enraged former master, by only 61 votes! Altogether, the party had registered a great improvement over its previous Mid-West showing at the Regional Elections of May 1956: at that time the Action Group had won only 4 of 20 Mid-West seats; now at these August 1960 elections, the party had secured the impressive total of 15 out of 30—50 per cent of the Mid-West seats.[19]

The Action Group had gained nearly 46 per cent of the popular vote in the Mid-West—although this figure was not quite so impressive when it was recognised that there had been a relatively low turnout of voters; only 45 per cent of the total number of registered electors on the Regional Roll.[20] Still, the meaning of these Mid-West voting figures was clear enough: the *Action Group had now virtually ensured that any NCNC-inspired Mid-West referendum could not hope to secure the requisite 60 per cent "Yes vote."* No Movement initiative on the Mid-West issue, it seemed, could achieve a successful result without the support of the Governing party in the West.

Indeed, so long as the Federal Government continued to forego use of its *Emergency Powers*, it now lay within the authority of the Action Group to use the Mid-West issue—albeit its own truncated version—to its own political advantage and to set its *own* timetable and conditions for creating the Mid-West state. Chiefs Awolowo and Akintola had made it clear that any set date for such an initiative would now almost certainly have to wait on the outcome of the *next* Federal Elections. If at that time (1964), the Action Group could manage to gain office—with, of course, the electoral assistance of Nigeria's major minorities—then there was every likelihood that the Mid-West State, along with the COR and Middle Belt states, would soon be created.

Rewards and Controls   With the Regional Elections safely behind it, the Action Group now set forth to consolidate its control in the Mid-West districts. While there was little indication that the party was prepared to modify its harsher tactics, it did now commence to honour its political promises. The first act of demonstrable beneficence by the Akintola Government was to appoint seven Mid-Westerners to Cabinet posts.[21] Nor were these token appointments; three involved heavy responsibilities. S.O. Ighodaro—who had been acting in the dual capacity of Minister of Justice and Minister of Mid-West Affairs since the departure of Chiefs Williams and Enahoro for the Western House of Chiefs and the Federal House respectively—now had his load reduced to more manageable proportions. Ighodaro retained the portfolio of Minister of Justice and Attorney-General, while the post of Minister of Mid-West Affairs now went to his Mid-West colleague,

James Otobo. The third Mid-Westerner to be appointed to a major Cabinet post was K.S.Y. Momoh, the fiery Action Group leader from Auchi in Afenmai Division who was selected to serve as Minister of Labour. The remaining four Cabinet posts went to C.I. Akere, of Ishan who was appointed Minister of State in the Ministry of Agriculture and Natural Resources; Chief Ekwejunor Etchie, of Warri, Minister of State, (Trade and Industry); Olatunji Oye, Minister of State (Education); and E. Anuku, of Asaba, Minister of State (Economic Planning).

In addition to these appointments, the Regional Government during September and October 1960, announced its intention to proceed with a number of "development projects" promised for the Mid West. Work was to be completed on the second and final phase of the Ishan Water Supply Scheme; the road between Benin City and Ekpoma in Ishan was to be re-constructed and certain sections tarred, as was the road between Benin City and Abudu; in Warri Town work on the new buildings for Hussey College was already well-advanced; and in the former Mid-West Movement stronghold of Asaba, the new Western Ibo Minister of State (Economic Planning), Mr. Anuku, announced that water engineers had already completed a survey prior to implementing a "£370,000 water supply scheme for the Division".[22] These projects were only a few of the many which the Regional Government now committed itself to completing in a number of former Mid-West Opposition districts.

While Akintola and his colleagues seemed bent on demonstrating Action Group beneficence through this new flood of allocations, party leaders also turned their attentions to securing the party's interests in other contexts. Threats of NCNC unilateral action to create a Mid-West State had not gone unheeded. At the Seventh Annual Congress of the party in September 1960 and at meetings of the Federal Executive Council which preceded it, Action Group leaders sought to arrive at a plan whereby party interests might be secured in the event of an attempt by the Federal Government to dissolve the West Regional Authority.

The Action Group Government—for reasons stated above— was not unduly anxious about the possibility of an NCNC-inspired Centre initiative to gain the creation of a Mid West state *via* a Referendum. If, however, the Federal Government should undertake first to dissolve the West Regional Government, then Action Groupers were well aware that the party would be bereft of any powers to prevent it (the Federal Government) taking whatever initiative it desired in relation to the Mid-West—quite apart from other actions which might threaten the very existence of the party itself.

Consequently, at these September meetings of Action Group leaders it was decided that a "Tactical Committee" should be set up; that it should be left to this "Tactical Committee... to decide on ways and means of protecting the Action Group base in the Western Region and of circumventing any plans by the Federal Government to assail democracy or the rule of law in Nigeria".[23] The names of these Committee members were not revealed, but the Committee's functions, even though unspecified, were clear: the Committee, it was stated, should be put in charge of party tactics, "mature tactics... altered to suit the times"; and in the event that "the worst should happen... it should plan what action to take".[24]

A final decision taken at the Annual Congress had greatest immediate significance for Mid-West elements. It was agreed that "the *party's constitution would be amended to provide for six Regional Conferences and Executives*—the North, the Middle Belt, the East, COR, the West, *the Mid-West*".[25] Effectively, therefore, *so far as the Action Group was now concerned, the Mid-West—for purposes of party organisation and structure—was regarded as a Region already in existence.*

Movement Under Pressure—Again!   Viewed from even the most optimistic perspective, the Movement was clearly once again in a most sorry condition. Nor was it just the improved position and renewed confidence of the Action Group which was responsible for this state of affairs. Developments at Lagos, and in the forums of the NCNC at Ibadan and Enugu had gone a very long way towards deflating any remaining NCNC/Movement aspirations. Indeed, in the remaining months of 1960, the Movement was to become the target of a series of devastating body blows delivered by none other than its ostensible "allies" and "champions."

At Lagos, of course, it was already clear that the Federal Government was reluctant—and the NPC flatly opposed—to endorse any initiative which might bring the Movement closer to its objective. Nor was this demoralisation eased when, by the end of November it became evident that all the threats and warnings aggressively voiced by Chiefs Okotie-Eboh, Oweh and other Movement leaders had been exercises in rhetoric only. There was no sign that the rumoured separate Mid-West political party was in the offing; Leader Osadebay's confident statements that a Mid-West

Motion would be introduced into the Federal House before the end of October, had fallen flat; furthermore there was no indication that Chief Okotie-Eboh was prepared to act on his earlier threats and to resign his posts in the Federal Government and the NCNC.

In the West Region itself, the Movement and the NCNC suffered further serious and demoralising reverses. A.M.F. Agbaje, the powerful and influential leader of the Ibadan *Mabolaje* party, defected to the Action Group. As for the *Mabolaje* party itself, it had broken with the NCNC and was now in alliance with the NPC. The defection of Agbaje and the loss to the NCNC in the West of the *Mabolaje*'s ten seats in the House of Assembly meant that the Action Group's majority looked to be more than ever unassailable. The NCNC Opposition was now reduced to an impoverished level. The Action Group commanded 80 and the NCNC only 34 seats when the House of Assembly convened for its inaugural sitting on 28th September, 1960.

While Movement supporters could be somewhat cheered by the fact that their Leader Osadebay had been returned as Leader of the Opposition in the Western House—even though he had had to fight hard to secure his re-selection[26]—this minor boost to sagging Movement morale turned out to be brief. On 17 November, 1960, Osadebay "after some weeks of deep reflection" and in what he maintains was an effort to "save myself and the NCNC future embarrassment",[27] resigned his seat in the House to succeed Dr. Azikiwe—who, the day before had taken office as Governor-General—as President of the Nigerian Senate.[28]

With Osadebay as Leader of the Opposition in the West, and as perhaps the most respected Mid-West and NCNC spokesman in Nigerian politics, the Mid-West Movement had possessed an influential champion. However, with their Leader now departed—and not just as Opposition Leader, but as a sitting Member also—and with his place taken by the ex-Action Grouper Fani-Kayode, the man who had advanced so successfully the Action Group case before the Minorities Commission, Movement supporters could no longer expect that the House of Assembly would serve as an even half-effective forum within which to advance their interests. It had been an oft-expressed contention of Action Groupers like the outspoken Ja' Isuman that the NCNC/West was essentially the vehicle of Yoruba rather than Mid-West Opposition elements.[29] Now, with the resignation of Osadebay and the assumption of his office by the "Yoruba newcomer" Fani-Kayode, it seemed that these Action Group contentions had been borne out.

CONSOLIDATING THE FRAMEWORK OF CONTROL

The fact that the Movement and the NCNC in the Mid-West were demoralised and disorganised made the Action Group's further efforts to secure its position a relatively straight forward task. The party set to work with a will, making use of all the weapons at its command—both coercive and non-coercive.

The Customary Courts and Tax Assessment Committees were still very much in business and their activities generated new outcries and *alarums* from harassed NCNC'ers—though in Etsako in Afenmai Division, the number of prosecutions brought by the Action Group-controlled District Council against "tax-defaulters" fell from an alleged high of 3,000 during 1959-60, to about 2,500 during 1960-61.[30] And while the Regional Governing party appeared to have abandoned, for the time being, its "dissolution tactics",[31] Mid-West and other NCNC Opposition members continued to rain abuse on the Action Group Government for its alleged persisting efforts to pack Tax Assessment Committees and judicial panels of the Customary Courts with party supporters.

The Action Group repeatedly stated that these seemingly unending new appointments were required in order to ensure that men of "unimpeachable character" should hold these positions of public trust. But exasperated NCNC'ers continued to ask *why* these new appointments, these men of "unimpeachable character", happened *always* to be Action Group supporters? Referring to recent appointments to the Tax Assessment Committee of Aniocha District Council, at this time operating under the guidance of a government-appointed Management Committee, F.H. Utomi declared that he and his colleagues had found that these new appointees, ostensibly of "unimpeachable character", in fact incl-uded "gaol-birds, ex-convicts, etc."[32]

With the "injection of chiefs" into local councils going on apace;[33] and with appointments to Local Loans Boards and the allocation of local loans continuing—allegedly—to go to party supporters, the Action Group seemed comfortably to be achieving its objectives. There were only two notable additions to the party's instruments of control and inducement. Each served as a sobering reminder of its remarkable ingenuity, steely commitment and determined application.

Additional Controls and Inducements   The first of these was to be found in a rather curious Amendment to the *Local Government Law* which was introduced by Local Government Minister Adegbenro, in March 1961. In addition to extending the Government's powers of appointment to local councils, which Opposition members contended was being done simply because "The Minister of Local Government is now tired of dissolving Councils for unjustifiable reasons",[34] the Amendment provided that *women, in order that they should secure a more representative position in the respective governments of their home districts, should be appointed to local councils.* Once again, the NCNC Opposition seized on this provision. It was pointed out that "We... are not opposed to women sitting in the councils *per se*, but to the obnoxious word 'nomination'. Women in the West Region have voted and can be voted for".[35] Putting Opposition criticisms more bluntly, F. H. Utomi alleged that "this Government, despite its 'subtleness', has come with this plan to inject women through nominations into Councils which, by the Grace of God, will still be controlled by the NCNC".[36]

The second tactical innovation had more far-reaching implications. Amongst papers laid on the Table of the House when it first met on 28 September, 1960, was one in which the Regional Government proposed the creation of a Mid-West Minority Area.[37] On the face of it, the Government's proposal appeared to offer nothing very different from what had existed previously in the form of the Mid-West Advisory Council. Like its predecessor, the proposed Mid-West Minority Council was to be "mainly advisory"[38] and was to continue under the chairmanship of the Minister of Mid-West Affairs, now James Otobo. Indeed, there seemed to be a good deal of truth in Movement allegations that the proposed Minority Council might serve as little more than a vehicle to reward Action Group "good boys" in the Mid-West.[39]

Closer examination, however, revealed that the proposed Minority Council represented something rather more than its predecessor. For one thing, rather than a selected list of appointees, its membership was to comprise *all* Mid-West legislators—that is, *all* Mid-West Members sitting in the Western House of Assembly and House of Chiefs, together with members representing the Mid-West in the House of Representatives and the Nigerian Senate at Lagos. All these persons, irrespective of party, were automatically entitled to membership in the Minority Council.[40]

Furthermore, it was specified that while the Council would remain for the time being an advisory body, in future "certain executive powers" would be exercised by the Minister of Mid-West Affairs, "on the advice of the Mid-West Minority Council".[41] These powers, declared Premier Akintola, were to extend over "certain aspects of Chieftaincy matters, Local Government affairs and Customary Land Tenure in the Mid-West area".[42]

Finally, in setting out the executive machinery by and through which the Minority Council was to function, it became evident that the Government was intent on ensuring that the Council would be afforded the maximum opportunity of penetrating the Mid-West districts. Under the guidance of the Minister of Mid-West Affairs and the Minority Council, a "Mid-West Circle", comprising officers of "appropriate seniority" representing "each of the major arms of Government activity in the Mid-West",[43] was to decide on the implementation of proposals received from the "local office of Mid-West Affairs in Benin". The Benin office, it was stated, was to serve as the main avenue for channelling local demands and approved Government plans submitted by its various administrative and executive officers in the Mid-West localities, to appropriate departments of Government at Ibadan.

Outlining more specific responsibilities, it was stipulated that the executive authority of the Mid-West Affairs Minister and the Minority Council would extend over "policy matters initiated at the Headquarters of the various ministries at Ibadan". Such policy matters, it was stressed, must be cleared with the Ministry of Mid-West Affairs "insofar as they affect the Mid-West",[44] and the Ministry's supervisory powers would include responsibility for "Government projects and plans for... development", the appointment of members of Public Boards and Corporations; and "the manner of application of any loans to be issued by the Finance Corporation in the Mid-West area".[45] In addition, and of great significance to Mid-West Movement supporters, the Council's scope of operations was to be limited to the *Action Group's concept of the Mid-West area — i.e., Benin and Delta provinces less Warri Division and the Northern Edo district of Akoko Edo* (conveniently renamed *Akoko-Eko* in the Government's proposal, to signify Action Group contentions of the area's greater cultural and linguistic proximity to Yorubaland than to Benin).

With the creation of the Mid-West Minority Area and its Minority Council the Action Group had formulated a comprehensive and potentially very advantageous initiative. In a very real sense it symbolised the Regional Government's untiring ingenuity and iron-willed determination to ensure that whatever plots the NCNC and Federal Government might hatch, Action Group prospects of retaining the Mid-West within the party's political embrace would remain good. It had been made clear that as the Minority Council progressively demonstrated it was able and willing to collaborate "in getting Government decisions to be understood and accepted"[46] by the Mid-West people, then so also would the authority of the Council and its autonomy be increased.

Indeed, in concept at least, it could be said that in a micro-context, the Akintola Government was now doing for the Mid-West what the British Authorities not so long ago had done for the West Region itself: it was establishing guidelines towards an eventual "responsible"—and needless to say, Action Group-dominant Self-Governing Mid-West. The Mid-West Minority Council provided for all essential Governmental and legislative machinery in the "embryo" state, complete with its "Premier Apparent", Mid-West Affairs Minister James Otobo, a fact fully appreciated by the Minister himself.[47] By early 1961, Action Group prospects in the Mid-West had never looked better.

TOWARDS THE FIRST FEDERAL MID-WEST MOTION

In November 1960 there were renewed political rumblings in the NCNC camp at Lagos. Once again, rumours were abroad that a Motion calling for the creation of a Mid-West State would be tabled "very soon" in the Federal House. Accustomed to NCNC posturing, the Action Group had dismissed these rumours as yet further exercises in empty rhetoric. Chief Odebiyi, declared that if the rumoured Motion "comes to the Federal House, I can speak for the Action Group Opposition in the Federal House, that they will *support* it".[48] In a scornful final gesture to "NCNC dissemblers" he was even prepared to state openly that "the sooner this is done, the better, so that the whole people of the Mid-West will know their true friends".[49]

By February 1961, this rumour of an NCNC Motion appeared to be gaining in strength. It was "reliably reported" that Chief Festus, through the mediation of Alhaji Ribadu and Prime Minister Balewa, had finally secured the Sardauna's support for the introduction of a Mid-West Motion—and a Mid-West Motion *only*! Still, no formal statement from the NCNC was forthcoming. Nor did Action Groupers show any apparent concern. At the Action Group's

Mid-West Regional Conference held 28 February, 1961 at Agbor, Leader Awolowo re-affirmed that his party "would continue to press for the creation of Mid-West, Middle Belt and COR States within the Federation";[50] furthermore the Conference passed a motion supporting the creation of a Mid-West Region. No mention, however, was made of the rumoured Motion.

The first indication that the rumours might be serious came during a debate in the Federal House on 23 March, 1961. A few days earlier, the Mid-West NCNC had taken strong exception to the fact that both Warri Division and Akoko-Eko had been deleted from the Mid-West Minority Area as gazetted by the Regional Government.[51] In the Federal House debate Chief Festus rounded hard on Awolowo. He accused the Action Group Leader of trying to excise these Benin and Delta districts from the Mid-West area. Chief Festus expressed outrage over the excision of Warri Division. He was, he maintained, "the only one competent to speak for Warri Division; anyone else was an imposter".[52] The people of Warri Division, were not opposed to inclusion in a Mid-West State, and he declared, they certainly had no desire to be transferred to Ondo Province, as was being currently rumoured. After a further lengthy attack on the Action Group Leader for what he termed Awolowo's "inconsistent and duplicitous" behaviour in relation to the Mid-West issue, *Chief Festus ended his harangue by declaring flatly that a Motion was soon to be brought forward in the Federal House and that "whether the Opposition liked it or not... the Mid-West State will be created".*[53]

Unruffled by this vigorous assault by his old antagonist, Awolowo's reply to Chief Festus was cool and coherent.[54] Awolowo stated that his party supported the creation of more states, but that these states *must be created together*. The Mid-West State, he declared, "would not be created in isolation". He stated that his party considered the 1955 Mid-West Bill no longer to be binding, as the country was then under Colonial rule. However, the Action Group Government in the West, he maintained, had made every possible provision for Mid-Westerners, in keeping with the recommendations of the Minorities Commission, and within the limits set out by the West Region Constitution. Awolowo ended his reply to Chief Festus on a warning note of his own. He stated that he and his colleagues welcomed the opportunity for the creation of a Mid-West State, and that a Mid-West Motion brought before the Federal House would have their support. However, if the Federal Government sought to create a Mid-West State without at the same time creating COR and Middle. Belt States, then, he would "call on his supporters to vote 'No'", at the subsequent Mid-West Referendum.

A little more than a week following this encounter between Chiefs Okotie-Eboh and Awolowo, a Mid-West Motion—to include *all districts of both Benin and Delta Provinces*—was moved in the Federal House on 4 April, 1961. It appeared to come as a surprise to no one, except perhaps to Movement supporters in the Mid-West. In keeping with his earlier promise, Awolowo and his Action Group colleagues—after an attempt to secure an Amendment to provide for the creation of *three* new states (COR and Middle Belt, as well as Mid-West)—obligingly gave the Mid-West Motion their full support. After a Division on the Amendment, which was defeated by a vote of 205-51, the main Motion was put and unanimously passed.[55]

With breath-taking sudden-ness, the creation of a Mid-West State was very much back on the political and constitutional agenda. Within just 12 months, prospects which had appeared terminally bleak were now bright with new promise. After the initial shock of dis-belief had passed, the joy of Movement supporters was unconfined. Could momentum this time be maintained?

———————————————

References

1. See Ja' Isuman, *Facts about the Mid-West State, op.cit.*, p.63.

2. For interpretative accounts of the June 1958 meeting see, Post, in Mackintosh, *Nigerian Government and Politics, op.cit.*, pp.421-22, and Enahoro, *Fugitive Offender, op. cit.*, p.163.

3. Isuman, *Facts About the Mid-West State, op.cit.*, p.78.

4. See *Debates of the House of Representatives*, Lagos, 7 April, 1960, col.812.

5. *Daily Times*, 9 May, 1960.

6. See *Pilot*, 6 May, 1960.

7. Details of Isuman's arguments in support of the Action Group position are to be found in his *Case for a Mid-West State, op.cit.*, pp.55-70.

8. See *ibid.*, p.66.

9. *Pilot*, 31 May, 1960.

10. See, *ibid.*

11. See *Pilot*, 11 July, 1960.

12. See *Pilot*, 8 July, 1960.

13. *Ibid.*

14. *Daily Times*, 6 July, 1960.

15. *Pilot*, 8 July, 1960.

16. *Pilot*, 5 August, 1960.

17. *Ibid.*

18. *Pilot*, 6 August, 1960.

19. See Pilot, 10 August, 1960, for details of Mid-West results at the West Regional elections.

20. See *Daily Times*, 18 August, 1960.

21. See *Daily Times*, 16 August, 1960.

22. For details of local allocations, see *Daily Express*, 25 October, 1960.

23. Enahoro, *Fugitive Offender, op.cit.*, p.170.

24. *Ibid.*

25. *Ibid.*

26. Osadebay maintains that when the time came for members of the NCNC Parliamentary Party in the West to select a new Leader following the August 1960 Regional Elections, "Yoruba members... again tried to take away [from me] the leadership of the Opposition". (Osadebay, unpublished *mss., op.cit.*, p.311). He points out that "This time they wanted the post for Mr. Fani-Kayode, a Yoruba lawyer and politician who had left the Action Group and crossed to the NCNC not long before the 1960 General Elections in the Western Region". Osadebay goes on to say that with the support of a number of NCNC members who felt "it would be grossly unfair to replace me with a newcomer...", he put his case direct to the CWC of the NCNC, then meeting at Lagos. He "warned the CWC that if the drama of 1956 over the Leadership of the West Opposition was repeated"—when Osadebay had been replaced by Alhaji Adelabu—he would himself "take a most dramatic step". This tactic, says Osadebay, worked. At the Parliamentary Party meeting of the NCNC held subsequently at Ibadan, he was for the third time elected Leader of the Opposition in the Western House.

27. *Ibid.*, p.312.

28. See *Profile on Chief D. C. Osadebay*, by F.O. Konwea, (Benin City, M. O. I., n.d.).

29. See Isuman, *Facts About the Mid-West State, op. cit.*, pp.41-43.

30. See *A Welcome Address by The Etsako District Council...*, *op.cit.*, p.6.

31. The writer was able to discover only one council dissolution during this October 1960-April, 1961 period. This involved the Iyekoriomwon District Council, in Benin Division, which was dissolved on 4 February, 1961, on the instructions of Local Government Minister Adegbenro. (See *Pilot*, 5 February, 1961).

32. *Debates of the Western House of Assembly*, 12 April, 1961, col.573.

33. In an interview with the writer, James Otobo stated that early in 1961, as the increasingly powerful Minister of Mid-West Affairs, he approved the recognition of *over 80 chiefs in Urhobo Division, and that of this number approximately 30 were later "injected" into local councils in the Division.* (See Otobo, Int. VII, p.5).

34. *Debates of the Western House of Assembly*, 29 March, 1961, col.204.

35. *Ibid.*

36 *Ibid.*, cols.205-206.

37. See *Proposals for the Creation of a Minority Area for the Mid-West Area of the Western Region, and the Establishment of a Mid-West Minority Council*, Sessional Paper No. 14 (1960), (Ibadan: Government Printer, 1960), pp.4.

38. *Ibid.*, p.3.

39. See *Pilot*, 14 June, 1960.

40. See *Proposals for... a Minority Area...*, *op.cit.*, p. 2.

41. *Debates of the Western House of Assembly*, 28 September, 1960, col.11.

42. *Ibid.*

43. *Proposals for... a Minority Area...*, *op.cit.*, p.3.

44. *Ibid.*

45. *Ibid.*

46. *Ibid.*

47. Otobo states that when he first took over as Mid-West Affairs Minister in August 1960, he was serving largely as a "Public Relations man" for Mid-Westerners, visiting different ministries and "lobbying for particular projects", consulting with Mid-West legislators of both parties, and dealing with local problems brought to him by Mid-West Action Group party organisers. By the beginning of 1961, however, he notes that in accordance with the extensive provisions laid out in the *Proposal for... a Minority Area*, his powers were considerably increased, to the point where he was regarded as "Mini-Premier of the Mid-West". (See interview with Otobo, Int. VII, pp.2-6).

48. *Debates of the Western House of Assembly*, 23 November, 1960,

col.143.

49. *Ibid.*

50. *Pilot*, 2 March, 1961.

51. See *Pilot*, 19 March, 1961.

52. *Pilot*, 24 March, 1961.

53. *Ibid.*

54. See *ibid.*

55. See *Federal Parliament Debates*, 4 April, 1961, col.802. In conducting a simple voice vote on the main motion, the Speaker had committed a costly technical error. As the Federal Constitution provided that this amending motion had to be passed by a two-thirds majority of all (312) sitting members, it was essential that a full count of those in favour be taken. As this was not done, and since it was later maintained that many members had left the Chamber after voting on the Action Group Amendment, this initial Mid-West Motion had to be nullified. A second Mid-West Motion was introduced and then passed, without technical faults on 24 March, 1962.

CHAPTER 13

BATTLE FOR THE MID-WEST

Mid-West Movement supporters were delighted and relieved. The Mid-West Motion represented a vital milestone thankfully passed. Yet it was a far from convincing piece of legislation. Clearly, the Federal Government was determined to retain maximum distance. The Mid-West Motion was a *Private Member's* and *not* a *Government Motion*; and in the Speech from the Throne, delivered by Governor-General Azikiwe only a week before, no mention of the Mid-West issue had been made.[1] Furthermore, it said little for the commitment of Mid-West NCNC Members that a *non* Mid-Westerner and *non*-Movement member—and what was worse, an "alien Yoruba" NCNC back-bencher (Ogunsanya)—should have brought the Motion before the House!

It seemed that the Federal Government was seeking to emulate the West Regional Government when in 1955 it had secured passage of the Mid-West Bill. The only difference was that the Federal Government had taken scrupulous care that the Mid-West Motion would stand clearly as a *Private Member's Motion*,[2] so that should problems arise, it could not be held accountable. Indeed, it seemed there might be more than a grain of truth in Awolowo's observation that the Federal Government, now considering its obligation to Mid-Westerners to have been met, might allow the Mid-West issue to fade back into obscurity.[3]

While this guarded stance assumed by the Federal Government and Mid-West NCNC leaders did nothing to inspire confidence, it was also to be remembered that this Motion had been passed in open defiance of the Action Group Opposition.[4] Chiefs Awolowo, Enahoro and their Opposition colleagues had made it clear that if the Federal Government gave support to a Mid-West Motion *alone* then the Action Group would resist. Awolowo had warned that should the time come for a Mid-West Referendum, he would instruct his party's supporters in the Mid-West districts to vote "No". This was a serious warning, for it was now generally accepted that—given the party's success at the 1960 West Regional elections—the fate of the Mid-West at a Referendum would hinge on the votes of Action Groupers.

Still, Movement protagonists could take satisfaction from the fact that the Mid-West Motion had been passed and the vital first constitutional hurdle therefore cleared. This provided a much-needed boost to Mid-West morale. As one Mid-Westerner, Senator M.G. Ejaife, observed in the course of the subsequent Senate debate on—and successful passage of[5]—the Mid-West Motion:

> "I am always worried each time I come to Lagos about this Motion not being on the Order Paper. Then I began to doubt whether or not our leaders and the Federal Government were not going to let us down. ... You can then imagine my joy [even though the Motion was not mentioned in the Speech from the Throne], imagine my happiness when I was told that it was not only going to be debated but that it was going to be passed in this House".[6]

As Mid-West supporters prepared to regenerate their crusade, there was room for renewed confidence. The task which confronted them remained formidable. Still, if Movement leaders were able to devise effective measures for meeting the Action Group challenge, while securing more active and committed support from their NCNC allies and the Federal Government, then *de facto* creation of the new state might prove a less daunting challenge than it appeared.

MOVEMENT OFFENSIVE STRATEGIES

Initial Sparring   Movement/NCNC leaders first made a concerted and uncharacteristically amicable effort to persuade the Action Group into coming to terms.[7] A co-operative response in supporting the Movement's concept of a pan-Mid-West construct, it was stressed, would ensure minimum damage to the Action Group position in the Mid-West provinces and elsewhere, when the new state was implemented. The Action Group, however, was not in a responsive mood. Party spokesman, Afenmai's Kessington Momoh, declared that before any agreement on co-operation could be achieved, "all participant elements should know in advance" what they were agreeing to.[8] "We are not going to sign a blank cheque", he asserted. "We are ready to co-operate to the fullest, provided we are not going to sign our own death warrants".

Having failed in its conciliatory approach, the Movement/NCNC now reverted to more customary tactics. Chief

Festus on an extensive May tour of the Mid-West districts, launched bitter attacks on the "alien Yorubas" and their "obstructive Action Group".[9] In Benin and Asaba, Chiefs Omo-Osagie and Osadebay occupied themselves with similar exercises designed to whip up anti-Action Group sentiment.[10] Amongst the range of measures being employed at this time by the Movement/NCNC, it was alleged by an infuriated Premier Akintola that residents in the Mid-West localities were being instructed by touring NCNC teams "to ignore Customary Court summonses and rates payment notices".[11] Since passage of the Federal Mid-West Motion, Mid-Westerners, he maintained, were being told to ignore these matters, "since very shortly, with the creation of the Mid-West State, the authority of the West Regional Government in these districts" would be at an end.

Not amused by these latest and overtly hostile initiatives, the party released a document entitled "A Nine Point Programme". This stipulated the terms which the Movement/NCNC must first meet to secure the full support of the Action Group for the creation of a Mid-West State. The response of Osadebay and his Mid-West NCNC colleagues was to issue an equally uncompromising "Nine Point Reply", a document refuting the Action Group's terms while re-asserting in forceful terms the Movement/NCNC position.[12]

No sooner had the Movement launched its "Reply" salvo, than it found itself under attack from unexpected "friendly" quarters. The NCNC National Party, called on Osadebay and other Mid-West NCNC leaders "to stop making any further statements on the proposed Mid-West State".[13] The Action Group, it was maintained, "is busily engaged in looking for excuses to back out from their commitment to create the new state". In seeming justification for its action the NCNC National party stated: "We do appreciate that without the co-operation of the Action Group, it will be extremely difficult to ensure that *60 per cent. of the total registered voters vote for the state*". In order to achieve this objective, the NCNC was "not only prepared to negotiate with all concerned, but to make necessary sacrifices to ensure the creation of the new Region".[14] It called on its Mid-West supporters and leaders, to avoid "indiscreet words or actions".

This statement by the NCNC Mother party, was a clear and quite categorical rebuff to Mid-West NCNC leaders. In effect, the NCNC National party appeared to agree with the position taken by the Action Group : that there could be *no unilateral NCNC creation of a Mid-West State*; that Movement leaders must be prepared to negotiate; and furthermore, that the Action Group's conditions must be given serious consideration, with a view to eventual acceptance (or at least substantial compromise) if the Mid-West was to be created.

Mid-West leaders did not take kindly to this advice. In fact, already the Movement/NCNC leadership had started a new and aggressive strategy which sought to employ far more drastic measures.

Tougher Tactics   On 23 May, 1961, Chief Oweh, the Federal Member for Urhobo Division and Secretary of the Mid-West Working Committee of the NCNC, called on the Federal Government "to intervene in the Mid-West to prevent a breakdown of Law and Order".[15] Oweh, recently returned from a two-week tour of the Mid-West, told a Press conference that an explosive situation now existed, a situation arising largely from the iniquities of the system of Tax Assessment: "Tax Assessment has been converted to the machinery of oppression, victimisation, oppression and cruelty to opponents of the Action Group". The provisions of the 1960 Regional Tax Law, he declared, were being "flagrantly violated", and the Divisional Appeal Committees, manned in the main by leaders of the Action Group, were using their position "to victimise and take reprisals against their political opponents".[16]

Aggrieved tax-payers, Oweh stated, were not given a fair hearing. Notices to attend the Committees were not served on them, and as a result their appeals were "invariably struck off without justification". Furthermore, in some of those cases which did reach the Committees, the rate originally assessed was often raised by "50 to 100 per cent". Finally, Oweh stated that perhaps the worst aspect was that the Committees made it "impossible for appellants [mostly NCNC supporters] to lodge appeals with the High Court by instructing their secretaries not to accept appeal notices". As a result of this "oppressive and discriminatory" behaviour declared Oweh,

> "The situation has reached a pitch where there could be an out-break of violence in the area of the Mid-West any time from now. Tax-payers who are members of the NCNC now feel that they have been driven to the wall. The Action Group rulers of the Mid-West have charged the magazine which may now explode at the slightest provocation".[17]

During July and early August, Mid-West NCNC leaders stepped up the pressure. Further alleged Action Group abuses were exposed. Tactics included making life for Chief Awolowo and his Action Group hierarchy as anxious and uncertain as possible. At the Ondo Provincial Conference of the NCNC, held 28-30 June, a Motion was adopted calling on the Prime Minister "to institute an inquiry into Chief Awolowo's recent Mission to Ghana, and other Action Group missions abroad since 1959".[18] Since returning from his visit to Nkrumah, it was maintained that Awolowo had been making "increasingly alarming" attacks on the Federal Government, and that these attacks were quite unwarranted and in fact constituted "high treason".

Chief Olu Akinfosile, Federal Minister of Communications asserted that Awolowo's "alarming statements" in the Lagos House were in keeping with his party's tyrannous behaviour in the West, where "local government councils... have been turned into weapons of political oppression against Action Group opponents".[19] Indeed, Akinfosile maintained, there were reliable rumours that this situation would soon further deteriorate as it was believed that "plans were being hatched by the Action Group to embolden supporters to use acts of hooliganism to secure an overall victory... in the forthcoming Local Government elections".

In Aboh Division, Chief Oputa-Otutu maintained that the Action Group had launched a "new wave of terror". At a Lagos Press conference, Oputa-Otutu produced 30 criminal summonses which, he said, had been served on various NCNC members in his home District Council area, Ukwani. One of these had been issued for "building a kitchen without obtaining an approved plan", while another was for "displaying garri—meant for sale—on a bare floor".[20] Oputa-Otutu stated that "hundreds of such summonses are served on a people, the majority of whom are stark illiterates in the rural areas"; many had "already been imprisoned with hard labour or fined heavily in Customary Courts". If immediate steps, were not taken by the authorities to curb these "excesses of Action Group agents in the Mid-West", then, he warned, there was bound to be serious trouble.

Omo-Osagie, adding fuel to NCNC fires, declared that "prospective NCNC candidates for the forthcoming Local Government elections", were being, "maliciously prosecuted and jailed" in many Mid-West areas, "in order to make it possible for Action Group opponents to be returned unopposed".[21] An NCNC prospective candidate, he stated, had been murdered by Action Group thugs at Auchi in Afenmai Division, when he tried to file his nomination papers. Nor was this the only instance of alleged killings by Action Group hooligans. Omo-Osagie appealed to the Federal Authorities to take immediate steps in order to avoid what was otherwise bound to be an "explosive reaction".

Mid-West "In Crisis"   Following these damning allegations—allegations which Action Groupers made little effort to refute—Mid-West NCNC leaders sought to bring the "Crisis in the Mid-West" to a head. In a telegram to the NCNC National President, Okpara, at this time in London on East Regional Government business, Chief Festus stated that the political situation in the West had reached "crisis proportions". He called on Okpara to "return home immediately".[22] In his telegram, Chief Festus stated that he had just returned from the Mid-West, and "while there, received delegations from all parts asking me to request your return; that on your return you should summon an early meeting of the National Executive Committee".[23] On a concluding note of alarm, Chief Festus stated that he had been told that it was imperative the party decide "whether supporters be allowed to perish by unconstitutional use of governmental machinery at hands of Action Group"!

On his return to Nigeria, and with the crisis in the Mid West rapidly coming to a head, Okpara presided over an Emergency Meeting of the NCNC NEC which was attended also by "political refugees from Action Group persecution in the West".[24] In his initial statements following the Lagos NEC Meeting, the NCNC National President was evasive on Mid-West/NCNC demands for a Federal Declaration of Emergency in the West; nor was he prepared to endorse an "eye for an eye" approach to Action Group tormentors—there were "not enough Action Groupers in the East to victimise", he quipped.

By the time he had completed a brief tour of affected West and Mid-West districts, however, Okpara, recognising the gravity of the situation, now called on NCNC'ers "From now onwards... to fight back oppression wherever it exists. There is a limit to human endurance, and if the Action Group wants to run a dictatorship, don't give them a chance,... give them an eye for an eye".[25] In a further heartening message for Mid-Westerners, Okpara confirmed that the Mid-West Motion which had earlier been passed by the East Regional legislature, would "soon be passed by the North".

In the violent disorders which now engulfed many districts of the Mid-West during the last week of August and the first two weeks of September 1961, there was to be found no particular pattern to cascading events. It could really only be said that Dr.

Okpara's call for retaliation had been taken literally. Obviously, the Mid-West NCNC was very much interested in establishing sufficient grounds for claiming a "breakdown of law and order" in the West, and certainly, it sought fully to exploit this incendiary situation. The extent to which the Mid-West Crisis was the product of careful NCNC staging,[26] or simply the result of increasingly oppressive Action Group behaviour was not easy to assess.

Following a particularly ugly outbreak of violence in Ishan on 29 August,[27] the Mid-West NCNC once again sought to press the Federal Government to take "remedial" action in order to prevent the breakdown of law and order in the West. U.O. Ayeni, the NCNC Federal Member for Afenmai, introduced a Motion, subsequently tabled, which stressed "That this House views with concern the grave state of law and order in Western Nigeria, and desires the Federal Government to look into this and report to the House".[28] On the same day, the Prime Minister, responding to increasingly anxious appeals by both NCNC and Action Group leaders, convened a meeting of the Police Council to discuss the situation.

The following day, Balewa issued a statement in which he outlined the facts of the West and Mid-West "crisis" as he had been informed of them. The situation, he stated, had grown to serious proportions. Increased police support would be sent into trouble spots. The Prime Minister however, gave no indication that he was prepared to endorse the NCNC call for a Declaration of Emergency in the West. While the situation was indeed grave, it was, he said, one which at present called for Police action only.

The "Crisis" Escalates   This refusal by the Prime Minister to invoke the Federal Government's Emergency Powers was followed closely by a new spate of violent outbreaks in a number of Mid-West districts. In these instances, it was clear that NCNC supporters were largely responsible for fomenting the trouble, though once again it was difficult to estimate to what extent these outbreaks were in fact the result of Action Group provocation. On 2 September, at Idowa Irrua, it was reported that "an armed gang with dane guns and matchets raided the house of an Action Group Councillor, and also the house of the Customary Court Judge during the night".[29] In the resulting battle between occupants of these houses and the raiders, it was reported that "five persons with gunshot and matchet wounds have been admitted to hospitals at Agbor and Uromi". One of those receiving gunshot wounds was said to be none other than Prince Shaka Momodu, leader of the much feared NCNC "shock troops".[30]

Two days later another violent outbreak occurred in the precincts of the Customary Court at Asaba. Ignoring the advice of Nigeria Police present in Court, that he should not pronounce judgement in a case involving an NCNC supporter, Judge Ogbolu, the presiding court officer had gone on to pass sentence. A violent disturbance immediately followed. Things only quietened down after the Police, with assistance from "a half unit of Nigeria Police stationed at Sapele", and "The Provincial Police officer from Benin", under a hail of "stones, bottles and sticks" drove the angry crowd back to Cable Point, with the additional help of 24 smoke grenades. Ring-leaders organising the violence were arrested and "two demonstrators were admitted into hospital".[31]

While the Action Group made determined attempts to play down the apparent seriousness of the situation in the Mid-West, the NCNC under the guidance of Osadebay and Okpara launched one last effort to secure the support of the Federal Government in declaring a State of Emergency in the West. On 11 September, Okpara and Osadebay flew to Kaduna where they held what were termed "routine consultations" with the Sardauna. Unofficially, however, it was well known that the NCNC leaders had two things in mind, and these were: passage of the Federal Mid-West Motion through the Northern Legislature; and the issue of the alleged "breakdown of law and order" in the West.

The talks with the Sardauna did not last long, and though no official *communique* was released it was understood that the Sardauna had given the NCNC leaders an undertaking that the "Northern House of Assembly would pass the Mid-West Motion".[32] On the second matter, however, it was reported that the Sardauna had maintained "the same stand as the Prime Minister": that the persecution of political opponents by the Action Group, deplorable as it might be, "does not amount to a breakdown of law and order", which would necessitate the Federal Government exercising its constitutional powers.[33]

STALEMATE POLITICS IN THE MID-WEST

Conflict and Brinkmanship   Immediately following the failure of the NCNC's "crisis talks" with the Sardauna at Kaduna, the West Premier, Chief Akintola, in an address to the Benin City Council, launched a blistering attack aimed almost solely at the

NCNC President, Dr. Okpara. Since Okpara had become the Leader of the NCNC, he declared,

> "...the party has committed suicide in the North [by rejecting Middle Belt demands, and antagonising its NPC Centre partner]. It has died a natural death in the West. It has degenerated into a mere tribal cult in the East. In the Federal territory of Lagos it has dwindled into a small pocket of place seekers and favour hunters and glorified sycophants more loyal to the NPC than their own party".[34]

A number of Mid-West Action Group MLA's hastened to their home areas to address local branch meetings—though tours, in the first instance, omitted those trouble spots where Action Group/NCNC feelings were still running high. At a meeting of the Akoko Edo District Branch of the Action Group held at Ososo, relief and thanks were expressed over the recent statements by Chiefs Akintola and Awolowo. The meeting also called on the Regional Government to take "immediate action... to ensure that Akoko-Edo District is merged with Ondo Province, and made a separate Division".[35]

At Bomadi, in Western Ijaw Division, Mr. A. Atie, Parliamentary Secretary to the West Regional Minister of Local Government, presided over a conference attended by Ijaws not only from Western Ijaw, but also from Port Harcourt and as far away as Ghana. The Conference, declaring that the categorical position set out by Action Group leaders had been timely, moved an "unanimous vote of confidence in the Action Group Government of Western Nigeria".[36] Ijaws, it was stated, wanted a state of their own. The Conference called on the Regional Government to recognise Ijaws' claim to a separate state, and to ensure that Western Ijaw Division would be *excluded* from any future Mid-West State.

At Asaba, a local branch meeting of the Action Group declared that "the NPC/NCNC has made the creation of the Mid-West State a personal property".[37] This, it was stated, was a "foolish and spiteful" action, for without acceptance of the conditions laid down by Chief Awolowo, "Asaba Action Groupers", like Action Groupers throughout the Mid-West, would vote "No" at the referendum.

Finally, at Benin, the sole Action Group MLA elected from the Division, Ben Edo-Osagie advanced his party's position in a rather different and understandably more cautious manner. While re-asserting his party's support for the creation of a Mid-West State, Osagie declared that the Action Group was "irrevocably committed to this sacred task, because it was the only party which demanded that certain safeguards for minorities should be written into the Nigerian Constitution".[38]

In the face of this new and confident Action Group onslaught, the Movement/NCNC maintained its pace and poise. In reply to Leader Awolowo's earlier statement, the NCNC observed that the Action Group Leader was once again behaving in a most "hypocritical and inconsistent" manner. Chief Awolowo, it was pointed out, had solemnly pledged the support of his party to the creation of a Mid-West State. It was observed that the Action Group had not only voted in favour of the Federal Mid-West Motion, but in addition had "urged the Federal Government to ensure that the State was created not later than 31 March, 1962".[39] Now, however, Leader Awolowo and his colleagues had reversed their stand and were threatening to oppose creation of a Mid-West state. This demonstrated that the Western Mother party was merely "using the issue and that of other states to win support in the areas concerned". The NCNC declared that "it had no quarrel with the demand of Chief Awolowo for an All-Party Meeting" to discuss the relevant issues, "but, like the Prime Minister", the NCNC felt that such a meeting "should await passage of the [Federal] Mid-West Motion in the Western Legislature".

The Movement/NCNC also complained bitterly about the "harsh and arbitrary" treatment which, it alleged, its supporters still were receiving at the hands of the governing party's agencies in the Mid-West localities. In Ishan, where inter-party violence was again on the increase, following dissolution of all eight of the Division's newly-elected councils by decree of the Minister of Local Government on 3 November, 1961, "NCNC victims" put their case to *West Africa*'s "Matchet's' diarist in the following terms:

> "Orders have gone from Ibadan that discrimination of every kind is to be used against NCNC people, particularly in the Customary Courts backed by the local authority police; that all elections are to be rigged, and that it is generally to be made plain that it is dangerous to oppose the Action Group. Now there is added to these usual forms of intimidation, the invasion of paid thugs who... beat up prominent NCNC people, burn their houses and damage their vehicles".[40]

It seemed there was little to be gained by these now predictable assaults on the Action Group's alleged partisan use of governmental agencies, and "strong arm" tactics—indeed, NCNC'ers might have something to lose, as exemplified in the rejoinders of Akoko-Edo Action Groupers.[41] There was, however, some solace for Movement protagonists in certain developments well beyond the bounds of the Mid-West.

Constitutional Progress and Political Developments   In the North Region, the Federal Mid-West Motion was passed by the Regional Legislature at Kaduna on 30 September.[42] The vote in support of the Mid-West Motion was unanimous, and while the Sardauna was careful to stress that his Government was content to lend its "whole-hearted" backing to the Motion, because the Mid-West demand had proven "popular, practicable and had been endorsed by the Regional Government in the West"—through the 1955 Mid-West Bill—he emphasised, that the Mid-West case was an "isolated instance", and that the Middle Belt "demand for the creation of a state had, on the contrary, only been supported by a misguided minority". Geographical conditions as well as ethnic grouping, he stated, "do not favour the creation of such a state".[43]

With passage of the Mid-West Motion by the Northern Legislature, the first major constitutional hurdle—i.e., that of securing the required backing from the Federal Parliament, and a *majority* of the Regional Legislatures, (the Eastern Legislature having passed the Mid-West Motion at an Emergency Session called in mid-June) had been cleared. Constitutionally, the Mid-West issue was making progress.

At Lagos also, sporadic developments served to re-build optimism amongst Movement protagonists. Since passage of the Federal Mid-West Motion in April 1961, the NCNC and the Federal Government had successfully been creating apprehension in the Action Group camp by a series of threats to the safety of the West under the existing federal Constitution. Mid-West NCNC leaders had warned Action Groupers that unless they "came to terms", revisions in the Constitution might be effected which would make creation of the Mid-West a "certainty". The Prime Minister had refused to give Awolowo any assurance on the issue of which Governmental Authority would be responsible for the administration of the remaining West Regional territory following a Mid-West creation; and, of course, Action Groupers had been living under the continual fear that Mid-West and NCNC leaders might finally break through the reservations of the Sardauna and the NPC, and secure consent for a Declaration of Emergency in the West by the Federal Government. All these lurking threats to the security of the Action Group position in the West—and by extended implication throughout the Federation—had become facts of life with which the party had had to live.

Pressure from Without and Within   Within the Mid-West, however, Action Group abuse and subversive manoeuvrings continued. Furthermore, intra-Movement dissent had again become serious. In Ukwani District of Aboh Division, formerly an NCNC stronghold, local residents were having second thoughts on the Mid-West issue, thoughts which had clearly been influenced by Action Group propaganda. Barth Oji, in an article in the *Echo*, indicated that Ukwanis were in a position to gain very little from the creation of a Mid-West State.[44] Referring to rumours which were causing considerable embarrassment to Movement/NCNC leaders, Oji declared:

> "We have heard of the promises given to Akenzua of Benin [that he has been proposed] as Governor-Elect of the new state; that Benin will be a suitable capital town; that, in addition a Mid-West university will be sited there... [and all this] despite the fact the Binis do not compare, on a population basis, with the Urhobos and we Western Ibos.... We, as a Majority group [seem to be] taking delight in signing a blank cheque with a Controlling minority group... which cares less about our affairs".[45]

Oji went on to review the NCNC record in Ukwani District: "No scholarship, no water supply, in fact, Nothing! And here are some disgruntled politicians who want to lead us into a lifeless state, with a view to achieving their own ends". In concluding, Oji stated that he could see no reason for "collaborating any longer in the hue and cry for a Mid-West State" when, for Ukwanis, a Mid-West State offered nothing more than the opportunity "to catch a few crumbs from the Master's Table".

During the whole of the October-December period, rumblings of dissent accompanied by revelations acutely embarrassing and potentially very damaging to the Movement, continued. A no-nonsense report in the *Echo* summed up growing non-Bini reservations about the Mid-West issue. Chief J. A. Ayomanor of Sapele put the essence of the dissenters' position very simply:

> "How can the Mid-West leaders from Benin Province alone imagine that we of the Delta Province will surrender the posts of Governorship, Premiership and the Headquarters to be situated at Benin when the Delta Province has a say in the affairs of the new Region"?[46]

Chief Ayomanor went on to make an "urgent appeal" to the *Oba* of Benin and the *Orodje* of Okpe "to summon a meeting of all natural rulers, *Obas* and recognised chiefs in their respective Provinces" to discuss the Mid-West issue. Furthermore, naming no names, he warned that "if the Mid-West State is to be a reality", then "Mid-Westerners who had already accepted certain offices" in the proposed state, "should immediately refute publications made in both National and Local newspapers about their 'back-door' plans".[47]

By the end of 1961, it was obvious that much of the internal dissent in what remained of the much-patched Movement front was being fomented, directly or indirectly by the Action Group. *Yet it was equally clear that growing reservations of non Bini (and non-Benin Province) elements had their origins in the fundamental suspicions and distrust with which the Mid-West's "disparate ethnic elements" had always regarded one another. Furthermore, it was perhaps inevitable that these normally latent divisions should emerge, as they had in times past, when Movement fortunes appeared to be showing promise.*

The Okpara Offensive   Towards the end of January 1962, reports confirmed that Okpara and the NCNC, apparently still intent on securing a Federal Declaration of Emergency in the West, were preparing an assault on the Mid-West which, it was said, would make the disturbances of 1961 seem "as child's play".[48] A top-ranking NCNC columnist had "unconsciously let the cat out of the bag",[49] when he had reported in the *Pilot* of 31 January, that:

> "Dr. Okpara does not believe in defensive battles. I can, therefore, foresee an all-out offensive with himself in the front line in the Mid-West area where he has sworn to smoke out Action Group inhabitants. Dr. Okpara is assembling his vehicles, guns and bullets at Enugu, ready for the coming holocaust in the Mid West, with special attention to Ishan".

The substance of this report was confirmed by a Police Intelligence Report in which it was stated that the "NCNC at an Executive Meeting held in Port Harcourt" had voted "the sum of £20,000 for the purpose,... of arming thugs and sending them to the Mid-West to smash the Action Group organisation" and to create conditions of breakdown of law and order "in anticipation of the Mid-West referendum".[50]

This general threat to the security of the Action Group and to its presence in the Mid-West area, was further supplemented by rumours that serious divisions had opened in the party leadership. These rumours were confirmed when at the party's Annual Congress held at Jos (1-8 February), the long-simmering conflict between Leader Awolowo and Deputy-Leader Akintola broke into the open. For Movement protagonists, of course, this was good news indeed.

It soon became apparent, however, that neither the Action Group's internal problems, nor the renewed threat of an NCNC-backed violent offensive would seriously challenge the party's poise and confidence in the Mid-West provinces. Drawing on experience gained during the 1961 "Mid-West Crisis", the Action Group, under the guidance of Enahoro, Chairman of the party's Mid West Region Executive Committee, was able to carry out defensive preparations to fend off any NCNC initiatives, should Okpara and his assault team attempt to fulfil their threats.

Following consultations with Leader Awolowo and senior party officials before and after the Jos Conference, it was agreed that, amongst other measures, "party stewards should again be dispatched to the Mid-West from Ibadan"; that special guards and joint patrols for isolated villages and wards should be arranged; that party leaders in the Mid-West area should be given "personal protection by party stewards as in 1961".[51] Should Okpara's NCNC "shock troops" seek to create a disturbance in the Mid-West, Enahoro and his Action Groupers—thanks to advance warning— were at least prepared to meet force with force. Indeed, shortly after the NCNC's assault plans for the Mid-West became public knowledge, it was rumoured that Okpara, angered and embarrassed by "unauthorised disclosures" had, for the time being, called off the whole operation.[52]

First Signs of Accommodation   Action Group determination to retain its now well-established position in the Mid-West remained unaltered. Perhaps the most graphic indicator of the party's confidence and stability in the Mid-West was that during early February there emerged the first serious indications that the Movement/NCNC might now consider coming to terms.

Mid-West Affairs Minister Otobo received from Movement Leader Osadebay a letter in which Osadebay, asserting that he had "the mandate of my party", stated that, "I think it is time for your party and ours to enter into conversation as to the creation of the Mid-West Region".[53] After further exchanges between Osadebay and Otobo, it was finally agreed that party delegations from their respective Mid-West Regional Executive bodies should meet at Ikeja on 21 February.

Certain decisions were reached at this meeting. These included:

"a. That both parties support in principle the creation.

b. That a top-level meeting be arranged to discuss and reach agreement on the subjects listed by the Action Group delegation.

c. That... any agreement reached [at such a future top level meeting] would be embodied in the Mid-West Constitution Act, and that the Action Group would not be expected to co-operate further unless and until agreement had been reached.

d. That neither party should say nor do anything which might prejudice or mar these negotiations, and the Minister of Mid-West Affairs gave an undertaking to look into any complaints made to him by NCNC leaders and supporters in the Mid-West".[54]

Clearly, the Action Group had achieved an important break-through. The points agreed to at this meeting showed that the Movement/NCNC finally was prepared to recognise that the Action Group's "Mid-West conditions" must be met, or there would be no Action Group co-operation. With continued careful negotiation it now seemed possible that the Mid-West might be created under the terms of a joint Action Group/NCNC pact. As a final point at this February meeting, it was further agreed that a second "All-Party" meeting should be held on 7 April—this date later being brought forward to 18 March.

By early March, therefore, it seemed that Action Group tenacity and determination in the Mid-West were finally starting to pay off. The Movement/NCNC had reached the point where it now appeared to accept that for the requisite 60 per cent Referendum "Yes vote" to be achieved, Action Group co operation must be secured. However, having reached this new pinnacle of promise, things started suddenly and dramatically to go wrong for the Action Group.

MOVEMENT PROSPECTS RENEWED

The first hint that new difficulties were starting to loom for the Action Group in relation to the Mid-West issue came on 16 March when it began to appear from unofficial sources that the 18 March meeting would not be held.[55] Relating events that followed in the next two days, Otobo stated that "on the 18th, no NCNC delegation turned up"; nor, he added, "was any explanation made to us. All that we were told on the evening of the 19th was that certain Motions and Bills connected with the Mid-West issue would be taken up in the Federal Parliament".[56]

Three days later stunned Action Groupers learned that Osadebay and his Movement/NCNC colleagues had, for once, been true to their word. On 22 March, the Prime Minister himself introduced a *second* Mid-West Motion into the Federal House, explaining that this second Motion was required due to the rejection of the April 1961 Motion on the grounds of a technical error, no count having been taken at the time of passage of the first Mid-West Motion.[57] Awolowo and his Federal Action Group colleagues angered and alarmed, and clearly caught off guard—"we did not see the text of the Motion until this morning"[58]—indignantly sought, and were granted permission, to set forward an Amendment to the Motion.

The Amendment simply set out the conditions which the Action Group had earlier stipulated: 1. That the area of the stipulated Mid-West State should be Benin and Delta Provinces, *less* Akoko-Edo District, Warri and Western Ijaw Divisions; 2. That the "remaining part of Western Nigeria shall continue to be a Region under the Constitution; 3. That a "prior agreement shall be reached between the major political parties in the area of the new Region" on certain proposals advanced already by the Action Group, and that "such agreement shall be embodied in the Act of Parliament establishing the new Region".[59]

Finally, as a new finishing touch to Action Group demands, Leader Awolowo made the creation of not just the Mid-West, but in all, *eleven new states*, a condition which the Federal Government must be prepared to meet before his party would be willing to give its support to the Motion before the House.

After a Debate lasting nearly two days, and during which all the usual arguments and allegations were produced by Opposition and Government spokesmen, a vote was taken on the Action Group Amendment; it was rejected. The substantive Motion then put to the vote was passed with a substantial majority, 214-49.

Following passage of this Second Mid-West Motion, two further pieces of legislation bearing on the Mid-West issue were passed through the Federal House in rapid succession. The first, the Mid-West Referendum Bill, which set out specific provisions bearing on the conduct of a Mid-West Referendum, cleared the House on 30 March; the second, the Parliamentary Bill endorsing the creation of the *NCNC concept* of a Mid-West State to *include*

Akoko Edo, Warri and Western Ijaw Divisions, was passed by the Federal House and Senate on 17 and 18 April, respectively.[60]

Events favouring the Movement/NCNC were now moving with unprecedented pace. Once again, the "Battle for the Mid-West" had swung in favour of Mid-West protagonists, and in an incredibly swift and spectacular fashion. The whirlwind passage of this Federal legislation now meant that *only the Mid-West Referendum remained as a major constitutional hurdle still to be surmounted.* And yet, while Movement prospects continued to thrive in this aura of renewed expectations, the Action Group remained unimpressed. As Awolowo observed in the course of the debate on the second Federal Mid-West Motion, "It is possible that after the passing of this Motion, everybody will just go to sleep".[61]

The Action Group leadership managed to convey apparent scant regard for this flurry of Federal Mid-West legislation. However, should the Federal Government attempt to support the Mid-West State creation without first accommodating to Action Group "conditions", the position of the party was made quite clear. Not only would Action Group supporters be instructed to vote "No" at the Mid-West Referendum, but the party now threatened to block the Mid-West issue through yet another avenue. During the debate in the Western House on the Akintola Motion calling for the House of Assembly to reject the second Federal Mid-West Motion, the Premier hinted openly that if the Federal Government pressed ahead with its intention to pass the Mid-West Bill, without first meeting the Action Group's specified conditions, then the West Regional Government would bring the Mid-West Bill before the Courts. In a fine display of stubborn confidence, Akintola declared, "whether they [the NCNC] like it or not, the constitutional power to hold this Region intact is on *this* [the Action Group] side. Let their legal advisers tell them the truth", he warned, for, "unless we give our blessing to the proposed state it will be an impossibility".[62]

Action Group Takes to the Courts   For some time, Movement leaders, and perhaps most notably Omo-Osagie, had been maintaining that it was the Action Group's intent "to take us to court over this issue of the Mid-West".[63] In the midst of heated debate on the second Mid-West Motion in the Federal House, Omo-Osagie alleged that the Action Group had been boasting everywhere that "they, the Action Group, own the courts" [64] since Yorubas were the predominant ethnic element in the courts, and particularly at the Supreme Court level. In keeping with these notions, the

Movement Deputy-Leader maintained that the Action Group had expressed an arrogant confidence that any action brought by the West Regional Government against the "NCNC-inspired" Mid-West Bill would inevitably meet with success. It was even stated by E.A. Mordi, the Federal Member for Asaba East, that the Action Group in order to ensure an outcome in their favour had pursued this tactic to the point where certain trusted Action Groupers had been "delegated to go and meet all the Yoruba-born Judges" who would be "likely to have a part to play".[65]

During subsequent debates on the Mid-West Motion in the Federal and Regional House, the Action Group had little to say in reply to Omo-Osagie's allegations—though in the Eastern House, Opposition Leader, S.G. Ikoku, declared that it was known that the Prime Minister's Motion in the House of Representatives was "invalid on two grounds", grounds which he then failed to specify.[66] However, following passage of the Mid-West Bill on 17 April, the party swung into action. On 18 April, it was reported from Ibadan, that the Regional Minister of Justice, S.O. Ighodaro had filed two suits at Lagos High Court contesting the validity of the Federal Mid-West legislation.[67] The Prime Minister and Federal Government were named as defendants in the first action; the East Regional Government and the Federal Government as defendants in the second.

Each of these suits hinged on a legal technicality which Action Groupers were confident would be upheld by a Supreme Court decision. The first suit—that brought against Balewa and the Federal Government—was based on the Action Group statement that the definition of "majority" as employed in Section 4, Sub-section 3 of the Constitution (the Section specifying requirements to be met in creating a new Region), had been "wrongly interpreted" and "wrongly applied" by the Federal Government.

It was the Regional Government's case that under the provisions of the *Nigeria (Constitution) Order in Council of 12 September 1960*—the statutory instrument which still stood as the *de jure* Federal Constitution—the required support for a new state proposal from a "majority" of the Regions, meant, technically, the support of *three of the four Regions then (in 1960) existing—the fourth Region being the Southern Cameroons*. As no alteration had been made to this section of the Constitution following the subsequent departure of the Southern Cameroons from the Nigerian Federation in 1961, it was the West Government's contention that the existing (1960) definition of "majority" still stood. On this narrow ground the Action Group Government argued that the Federal Mid-West Bill was" null and void"; that since the Mid-West Motion had not secured "majority" approval—that is, approval of three Regional legislatures (the third Region, the West, having not only rejected the Federal Motion, but in fact passed a "contrary Motion" of its own)—it must be rejected.[68]

The second suit was based on the "purely legal grounds" that the Eastern House of Assembly which had approved the Federal Mid-West Motion, "was elected according to rules laid down by the Governor and not by the Eastern House, as required by the Constitution".[69] The Action Group Government stated that the resolution passed by the Eastern Legislature approving the Federal Mid-West Motion should therefore be nullified, and hence, once again that the Supreme Court should act to invalidate the Federal Mid-West Bill.

To these two actions, two further suits against the Federal Government were later added. The *Olu* of Warri and Chief Reece Edukugho filed separate suits challenging the terms of the Federal Mid-West Bill which called for the inclusion of Warri Division in the proposed Mid-West State, and at the same time challenging the authority of the Federal Government to enact the Mid-West Bill.[70]

Movement Regains the Offensive   During this period, Movement/NCNC forces once again moved onto the offensive in the Mid-West districts. Various local organisations and "mushroom parties" which sprung up overnight, prepared for what was now referred to as "the Referendum Campaign". From distant localities in the other Regions campaign teams were sent home for what they were assured would be the final stage in the "Battle for the Mid-West".[71] At Ibadan, the local branch of the Mid-West Movement announced that it had "declared political war on the Action Group Government in the West".[72] It called on all Mid-Westerners in the West Regional Government "to stop being stooges and resign their offices forthwith". A rally attended by over 6,000 Mid-West citizens resident in Ibadan called on the Prime Minister and his Federal Government to "stand firm against reactionary activities of the Action Group".[73]

With the tempo of Movement/NCNC activity accelerating sharply, a two-day "All-Party Mid-West Conference" was convened at Benin City on 5 and 6 May.[74] The Conference was well-attended by Mid-West Movement leaders; Action Group delegates were conspicuous by their absence. The only "semi-official" Action Group delegate present was none other than the irrepressible Ja' Isuman.[75] The failure of the Action Group to send a full delegation resulted, apparently, from the strength of feeling expressed by "political fanatics who refused to attend the Conference" on grounds of "conscience".[76]

The Conference managed to get through a lengthy agenda. After hearing from the *Oba* of Benin, who had resumed his position as figurehead, non-party leader of the Mid-West cause, and who piously warned "against the introduction of party politics into the Mid-West issue",[77] and following the appointment of Senator Dahlton Asemota of Benin as Chairman, the Conference moved on to deliberate on a number of matters. Chief Okotie-Eboh enumerated "Nine Points" which set out in specific terms what "the creation of the new state would mean" to Mid-Westerners. The Conference also resolved to "set up five special committees to formulate plans for the proposed Mid-West Region".[78] These included:

> "A Finance and General Purposes Committee; a Constitutional and Legal Committee; a Civil Service Committee to plan the set-up of Ministries in the Mid-West-Region; a Delimitation Committee; a Minority Protection Committee, to ensure just provision for all ethnic groups in the Mid West".[79]

Finally, before the Conference adjourned, it was decided that a Mid-West United Front Committee should be formed. The Committee (UFC), to be chaired by Senator Asemota, was to have as its members "at least one representative" from each of the main ethnic elements in the Mid-West. Its main task was to consider "proposals already submitted by various personalities and organisations on how best to overcome differences of the various political factions and parties in the Mid-West".

OPENING THE FINAL DOOR...?

In the midst of this renewed and sharply rising political activity in the Mid-West, and in the face of growing Movement/NCNC momentum and confidence, Chief Awolowo took the fatal step. This was, in the course of five agonising days, to lead directly to the political demise of himself, most of those party leaders who had remained loyal to him since the debacle at the Jos Congress, and the Action Group itself as a party of power and influence in the Federal and West Regional governmental contexts. At the same time his action was to open the road to what Movement leaders had long maintained would be the "easy" creation of the Mid-West State.

It is not the intention of the writer to comment in detail on the "Action Group Crisis of May 1962"; this has been done by others elsewhere.[80] Suffice to say that on 20 May, at Ibadan, Awolowo convened a meeting of West, Mid-West and Federal Executive Committees, together with members of the party's West and Federal Parliamentary Councils. At this meeting, Premier Akintola was "found guilty" on charges of "maladministration, disloyalty and anti-party activities".[81] When the Western Premier (Akintola) then refused to resign quietly from office, it was eventually resolved that he should be replaced as Premier by Alhaji Dauda Adegbenro, Minister of Local Government—or, as he was more commonly known in the Mid-West districts, "Minister of Terror". It was further resolved that the office of Deputy Leader of the Party, at this time an office also occupied by Chief Akintola, should be abolished.

Akintola, on his part, chose simply to dis-regard the resolutions passed at the Ibadan meeting. Though there was not much he could do about his deposition from the post of Deputy Leader, Akintola made it clear he would resist any effort to remove him from the post of Premier. Even when the Parliamentary Council in the West, by a vote of 66 out of an Action Group bloc of 84 Members, "formally" dismissed Akintola and endorsed Adegbenro as his replacement, Akintola baulked. He refused to comply with the request of the party or its Parliamentary Council and finally even the instructions of the Governor, on the grounds of his claim that he still retained the support of a majority of supporters in the House of Assembly.

On 25 May, the day of destiny for the Action Group arrived. The House of Assembly was convened and Chief Akintola was given the opportunity to test his claim that he could muster a majority of Members to support him. The infamous events which followed the abortive meetings of the House on this day are now set large in the pages of Nigerian political history. Twice an attempt was made to conduct an orderly meeting of the House; and twice violence and general disorder broke out in the Chamber. On the afternoon of 25 May, following the second and final outbreak of violence, the doors of the Parliament buildings were locked. They would not be re-opened for another six months—and certainly it would be a very different political world upon which they would open then.

The Federal Government now moved into action. Troops and armoured vehicles were sent to Ibadan. On 29 May, the Federal Authorities, ignoring pleas made by a delegation of *Obas* and Chiefs who begged "for time so that Westerners could settle matters among themselves",[82] passed a Motion in the Federal House declaring that a *State of Emergency* existed in the West.

Parliament then went on to approve what Enahoro states were "thirteen sets of legislation of the most draconian character", to meet a situation which "after all, [was a fracas] confined solely to the Chamber of the Western Legislature".[83] Under these provisions an Administrator, Dr. M.A. Majekodunmi was appointed by the Federal Government. Majekodunmi's authority under the Emergency Powers Regulations was extensive, and his decisions on most matters of any significance, final. He was empowered:

> "... to nominate commissioners [ministers], make all necessary orders, and amalgamate and command the Local Authority and Nigeria Police Forces. The Governor, Premier, Ministers, President of the Senate [in this instance, President of the House of Chiefs], Speaker of the House, and the Superintendent-General of Local Government Police were relieved of their posts. The Administrator was given powers to imprison anyone spreading misleading reports, to prohibit public processions and meetings, to detain or restrict any person in the interests of public order and to search premises without a warrant".[84]

Mid-West protagonists welcomed these events with unbridled enthusiasm. As Movement supporters celebrated, local Action Group leaders and supporters who had escaped initial "detainment" and "restriction" orders, had now to move sharply to escape the wrath of their NCNC antagonists.[85] The display of this local "enthusiasm" in the Mid-West districts, was, however, relatively brief. By the end of the first week of June, Majekodunmi and his Emergency Administration, which included three leading Mid-Westerners,[86] appeared to have the situation in the Mid-West and elsewhere well under control. The West, including the Mid-West, was now to settle down to six months under the control of Majekodunmi and his Administration.

Movement leaders, in spite of everything, could now look back on the past 14 months with some measure of satisfaction. As a result of their unrelenting efforts, four pieces of Mid-West legislation, the 1961 and 1962 Mid-West Motions, the Referendum Bill and the Mid-West Bill, had been passed through the Federal Parliament—and few would deny that in the decision of the Prime

Minister and the Federal Government to declare a State of Emergency in the West, Chief Festus, alias "Alhaji Warri", had played a vital, if not determining role. But encouraging as these "battle triumphs" were, the "war" was not yet won. Despite the Emergency restrictions now in place, the Action Group still posed a threat; the Federal Government could change its mind; and internally there was the vital matter of maintaining a unified Mid-West front.

It was a time for steady nerves, careful negotiations and continued pressure.

————————————————

References

1. See *Federal Parliament Debates*, 4 April, 1961, col.791.

2. Though Chief Awolowo, then Premier of the West, stated that the Regional Government adopted "no official attitude whatsoever" towards the 1955 Mid-West Motion, Opposition NCNC Members were later able to maintain that the Mid-West Bill was a *Government Bill*, and hence that the Awolowo Government had a binding commitment to create a Mid-West State. NCNC opponents based their case on the technically minor point that the 1955 Mid-West Motion had been seconded by a member of the Regional Government, one J.G. Ako, who then held the minor post of Minister of State in the Ministry of Public Health. (See *Debates of the Western House of Assembly*, 14 June, 1955, cols.58-59).

3. See *Federal Parliament Debates*, 4 April, 1961, cols.791-92.

4. Prime Minister Balewa, it should be noted, indicated that he had been deeply offended when Awolowo had suggested in the course of the debate on the Mid-West Motion that the Federal Government was simply "going through the motions" of support. In reply to the Opposition Leader, Balewa declared that Awolowo was simply "afraid that the Federal Government will sit on the Motion as he sat on it". (*Federal Parliament Debates*, 4 April, 1961, col. 792). This, however, said Balewa, would not be the case. Following passage through the Federal House and Senate, "we will push[the Mid-West Motion] on to the.Regional legislatures... and I hope they will pass it". The Prime Minister, however, would not stipulate a timetable for the clearance of these hurdles. Neither he nor any other Government leader was prepared to accede to the Action Group demand that the Mid-West State be created "before or by the 31st. March, 1962".

5. It was to be noted that the Senate President and Movement Leader Osadebay, carried out all the required procedures strictly in accord with the constitutional provisions. This included a hand vote

rather than a voice vote, an error by the House Speaker which was to result in the nullification of the 1961 Federal Motion. Osadebay, ensured that the hands were counted, the names listed: the vote in favour of the Motion was unanimous; 37 for, with seven absentees. (See, *Senate Debates*, 26 April, 1961, cols.498-500).

6. *Ibid.*, col.496.

7. See *Pilot*, 1 and 3 May, 1961, for reports on statements issued by Chief Okotie-Eboh and the NCNC Western Ijaw MLA, Atohengbe.

8. See *Echo*, 7 May, 1961.

9. *Champion*, 13 May, 1961.

10. See *Echo*, 24 May, 1961.

11. *Ibid.* For earlier similar complaints by Akintola, see *Debates of the Western House of Assembly*, 12 April, 1961, cols.577-78.

12. See A.A. Osaghae, "Struggle for a Mid-West State", unpublished *mss.* (Benin City: n.d.). pp.41-2.

13. *Daily Times*, 29 May, 1961.

14. *Ibid.*

15. *Pilot*, 24 May, 1961.

16. *Ibid.*

17. *Ibid.*

18. *Pilot*, 1 July 1961.

19. *Ibid.*

20. *Pilot*, 14 July, 1961.

21. *Pilot*, 17 July, 1961.

22. *Pilot*, 18 August, 1961.

23. *Ibid.*

24. *Pilot*, 25 August, 1961.

25. *Pilot*, 28 August, 1961.

26. There was evidence that in Ishan, the NCNC under the local leadership of Prince Shaka Momodu and Chief G. E. Odiase at Irrua, took deliberate steps to manufacture a crisis in the Irrua-Ewu area and indeed throughout the Division. W.G. Odiase, in his unpublished *mss.* (*op.cit.*, Ch.6. pp.16-18) states that "what the NCNC in Ishan termed 'Operation D,' was the implementation of their veiled threat to resort to violence, to attack local leaders of the Action Group and create a situation where it would *appear* that law and order had broken down in the Mid-Western area".

27. See *Pilot*, 30 August, 1961. A report from the Irrua Branch of the NCNC declared that the "people of Ishan are against the wall. There is great fear of an explosion". This situation, it was stated, had reached its present level when Ishan NCNC supporters had strongly objected to the Action Group's "injection" of 13 Traditional Members into the Irrua-Ewu District Council. By this act, the NCNC which had won 23 of 38 seats against the Action Group's 15, was relegated to the minority in Council. (see *Ibid.*)

28. *Pilot*, 30 August, 1961.

29. *Daily Times*, 6 September, 1961.

30. *Pilot*, 5 September, 1961.

31. *Daily Times*, 6 September, 1961.

32. *Daily Times*, 12 September, 1961.

33. *Ibid.*

34. *Express*, 13 September, 1961.

35. *Echo*, 29 September, 1961.

36. *Echo*, 3 October, 1961.

37. *Echo*, 12 October, 1961.

38. *Morning Post*, 12 October, 1961.

39. *Pilot*, 29 September, 1961.

40. *West Africa*, 11 November, 1961, p.123. In the same article, equal coverage was given to Action Group assertions about the Ishan "crisis". The official position of the Regional Government, it was stated, was that there had been "much abuse of power by individual supporters of the Government... but that redress is available. The NCNC, according to the Action Group have grossly exaggerated these abuses, and after the (August 1961) Local Council elections violently intimidated Councillors to 'cross the floor' (to the NCNC)—which many did". It was because of this "violent confusion", the *West Africa* columnist reported, that the Minister of Local Government had decided that the Councils must be dissolved. J. A. G. (Johnny) McCall, "an [ex-British Colonial Officer] Administrative Officer with long Mid-West experience" (Odiase [unpublished *mss.*], Ch.6, p.20) was appointed as Sole Administrator for the Division.

41. Action Groupers were quick to reply to NCNC contentions of "tyranny and oppression". What violence there had been in the area, it was alleged, had been the result of NCNC "incitements". (See interview with S.U. Unuekhai, Int.III, pp.63-65).

42. See *Sunday Post*, 1 October, 1961.

43. *Ibid.*

44. See *Echo*, 16 October, 1961.

45. *Ibid.*

46. *Echo*, 9 December, 1961.

47. *Ibid.*

48. Enahoro, *Fugitive Offender, op.cit.*, p.181.

49. *Debates of the Western House of Assembly*, 13 April, 1961, col.743.

50. Enahoro, *Fugitive Offender, op.cit.*, p.180.

51. *Ibid.*, pp.181-83.

52. See *Debates of the Western house of Assembly*, 13 April, 1962, col.744.

53. Letter from Osadebay, as Chairman, NCNC Mid-West Working Committee, to Otobo, dated 8 February, 1962 at Lagos, quoted in *Debates of the Western House of Assembly*, 13 April, 1962, col.708.

54. *Ibid.*, col.709 (Italics added).

55. See *Ibid.*

56. *Ibid.*

57. See *Federal Parliament Debates*, 22 March, 1962, col.26.

58. *Ibid.*, col.40.

59. *Ibid.*, cols.26-27.

60. To satisfy constitutional provisions, the second Federal Mid-West Motion had been sent to the Regions, where it received the required majority support from the North and East legislatures. The West Regional Government, however, ignoring the substantive Federal Motion, passed a contrary Motion introduced by Premier Akintola. This Motion rejected the Prime Minister's Mid-West Motion. The Mid-West Motion was passed by the Eastern Legislature on 4 April, and by the Northern Legislature on 5 April, 1962. (See *Pilot*, 6 April, 1962). The West Regional Government's "contrary Motion" was passed by the Western Legislature on 13, April, 1962. (See, *Daily Times*, 14 April, 1962).

61. *Federal Parliament Debates*, 23 March, 1962, col.104.

62. *Debates of the Western House of Assembly*, 13 April, 1962, cols.749-50.

63. *Federal Parliament Debates*, 22 March, 1962, col.60.

64. *Ibid.*

65. *Federal Parliament Debates*, 17 April, 1962, col.1885.

66. See *Pilot*, 6 April, 1962.

67. See *Pilot*, 18 April, 1962.

68. For details see issues of the *Pilot*, for 18 April and 14 May, 1962; see also Mackintosh, *Nigerian Government and Politics, op.cit.*, p.58.

69. Mackintosh, *ibid.*, p.59. In providing further detailed explanation, Mackintosh goes on to point out that: "Section 15 (1) of the Fifth Schedule to the Constitution reads: 'Every constituency established under Section 14 of the Constitution shall return to the House of Assembly one Member who shall be directly elected in such manner as may be prescribed by the legislature of the Region'. In fact, the Eastern (and Northern) Region had simply passed an enabling act allowing the Governor of the Region to make the necessary electoral rules".

70. See *Pilot*, 28 April, 1962. See also *Debates of the Western House of Assembly*, 13 April, 1962, cols.733-36., and *Debates of Western House of Chiefs*, 13 April, 1962, cols.100-105.

71. See *Pilot*, 25 April, 1962; also Osaghae, unpublished *mss., op.cit.* pp.45-46.

72. *Pilot*, 30 April, 1962.

73. *Ibid*.

74. See *Pilot*, 7 May, 1962.

75. Isuman states that two other Action Groupers attending the All-Party Conference—though in no official party capacity—were Chief J.E. Odiete, and Chief D.O. Ehanire of Benin City. (Isuman, *You and the Mid-West Plebiscite: What You Must Know*, [Lagos: Ribway Printers, 1963], p.40) Isuman fails to add that Senator Dahlton Asemota, Chairman of the Mid-West Minority Council, and reputed to be an "Action Group good boy", also attended the Conference, and in fact was appointed its Chairman, as well as Chairman of the Mid-West United Front Committee, which was formed before the Conference finally adjourned on 6 May. (See Osaghae *mss., op.cit.*, pp.58-60).

76. *Pilot*, 14 May, 1962. Indeed, shortly after completion of the All-Party Conference, Isuman was disciplined by the Mid-West Regional Executive Committee of the Action Group. The Committee called for Isuman's suspension from the party. It was held that he had failed to heed a "boycott note withdrawing a goodwill message" which the Mid-West Action Group Administrative Secretary, R.N. Ikpo, "had sent to the Conference on behalf of the Action Group". (Osaghae *mss. op. cit.*, p.58). Isuman maintained that he attended the All-Party Conference because the Action Group's initial "goodwill message" had in fact committed the Action Group to attend the Conference. On appeal to Leader Awolowo, the demand of the Executive Committee for Isuman's

suspension was turned down. (Isuman, *You and the Mid-West*

Plebiscite:.... op.cit., p.40).

77. Osaghae *mss., op. cit.*, p.59.

78. *Ibid.*

79. *Ibid.*

80. See particularly, Enahoro, *Fugitive Offender, op.cit.*, pp.185-91; also Mackintosh, "The Action Group: The Crisis of 1962 and its Aftermath", in his *Nigerian Government and Politics, op. cit.*, particularly pp.447-50.

81. Enahoro, *Fugitive Offender, op. cit.*, p.185.

82. Mackintosh, *Nigerian Government and Politics, op.cit.*, p.450.

83. Enahoro, *Fugitive Offender, op.cit.*, p.189.

84. Mackintosh, *op.cit.*, p.450. For details of *Emergency Powers Regulations*, see *Federation of Nigeria Official Gazette, supplement to No. 38*, Vol.49, 29 May, 1962.

85. See *Pilot*, 15 June, 1962.

86. These three were: Webber Egbe, a leading NCNC'er from Warri who regarded himself as the "political god-son" of Chief Okotie-Eboh, appointed Commissioner for Justice; Chief T.E. Salubi, an Urhobo with known NCNC leanings, appointed Commissioner for Education; and Mark Uzorka, a Western Ibo whose political leanings at this time the writer was not able to determine, (but who later, during the March-July, 1963 pre-Referendum period, campaigned strongly in the Asaba area on the Movement/ NCNC platform) Commissioner for Mid-West Affairs.

CHAPTER 14

HOW THE MID-WEST WAS WON

It was the confident belief of Movement/NCNC supporters and many of their leaders that the Mid-West Referendum would be held, perhaps even before the end of June.[1] Even the embattled Action Group Leader Awolowo, at this time (the beginning of June) under restriction at Ibadan, was convinced that the Federal Government would press home its advantage, and that the Mid-West Referendum was imminent.[2] Accordingly, he gave instructions to Enahoro (at this time *en route* to Uromi in compliance with the restriction order served on him) to make appropriate preparations. The Leader, as during the 1961 "Mid-West Crisis", approved arrangements for the dispatch of "party stewards" to the Mid-West from Ibadan; furthermore he endorsed the appointment of organising secretaries and field secretaries in the Ishan area where, Enahoro lamented, the "Action Group was now at its weakest-ever strength vis-a-vis the NCNC".[3]

THE EMERGENCY ADMINISTRATION:
FEARS AND UNCERTAINTY

Court Actions — Unfinished Business   Towards the end of June, however, it became apparent that the Referendum was not imminent after all. The first indications that the Federal Authorities might not be so eager to bring the Mid-West issue to a swift resolution surfaced when Dr. Majekodunmi appeared to be having a change of heart on one of the two Mid-West suits which had been filed by the Akintola Government in May. In early June, 1962, Majekodunmi had instructed his Solicitor-General, D.A.R. Alexander, to ask the Lagos High Court that the West Government's first suit, which challenged the validity of the Motion passed by the East Regional Legislature in support of the Federal Mid-West Motion, might be withdrawn.

Majekodunmi stated simply that he felt, under the circumstances, it was undesirable "in the interests of unity and goodwill" to pursue a course which would bring the two Regional Governments into conflict.[4] Nor, he added diplomatically, did he think it was his place as "Administrator of Western Nigeria to question the legality of another Regional Government".[5] Regarding the second suit, which challenged the authority of the Federal Government to pass the Mid-West Bill, Alexander was instructed to file a "notice of discontinuance", which, if successful, might mean that this suit too would be abandoned.

At this point, about 8 June, Movement/NCNC protagonists were content with these undertakings by the West Region Administrator. On 24 June, however, the day that these two actions came before the courts, Movement/NCNC supporters were startled by a sudden and rather dramatic turn of events.

There was no trouble with the first action. This suit was withdrawn and costs of 20 guineas were awarded to the defendants, the East Regional and Federal Governments. When, however, the second action was brought forward, and counsel for the West Regional Government then asked that it also should be withdrawn, in view of the "notice of discontinuance" which had earlier been filed, the court did not comply with this request. A seven-day adjournment was ordered, to allow further "consideration to be given to this matter".[6]

This adjournment and the apparent failure of the Western Administration to have this second suit abandoned created uproar in the Movement/NCNC camp. Why had the courts baulked on this second suit? No explanations were forthcoming from Chief Justice Ademola and his colleagues. To Movement protagonists, hypersensitive and acutely suspicious of the Federal Authorities, the implications of this situation were ominous. On 30 June, Movement/NCNC fears turned to fury when it was learned that it was Majekodunmi himself who was causing the "obstruction", having "sworn to an affidavit in which he withdrew the original (5 June) notice of discontinuance".[7] This could lead to a long delay in holding the Referendum, even rejection of the Mid-West Bill. Was this simply a move to ensure that the Mid-West issue would be shelved yet again?

Fortunately, before Movement/NCNC anxieties could produce serious problems for the Administrator, the issue raised by the second suit was resolved—but not as the result of a concession by Majekodunmi. On 2 July, Webber Egbe asked the court for a further adjournment so that "certain other papers could be filed".[8] Egbe, Commissioner for Justice in the Emergency Administration and a seasoned Mid-West NCNC leader who regarded himself as the "political son" of Chief Festus, was replacing the Federal Government's Senior Crown Counsel Adebiyi (who had represented the West Government in bringing forward its action on the second suit at the 24 June Lagos High Court proceedings). The reply of Chief Justice Ademola, who apparently had had quite enough of Majekodunmi's manoeuvrings, was to reject Egbe's application for adjournment and to dismiss the West Government's second suit. Ademola's parting words to Egbe were: "If you intend to come back, file it [the suit] again, and if you don't, that is your business"![9]

Restraint and Impartiality   While Movement/NCNC supporters were relieved by this welcome turn of events in the Lagos High Court, a date for the Referendum had still not been set. Time was passing. Once again Movement/NCNC supporters began to feel restless and suspicious. Was the Federal Government up to something; and this time in collusion with its Emergency Administrator in the West? Movement/NCNC leaders had counted on securing an early date for the Referendum and then to strike fast. Had the Referendum been held in June or early July, 1962, they were confident the required "Yes" vote might have been secured with relative ease. But now, this opportunity had been lost.

Movement/NCNC'ers also had been looking forward to a purge of major (Action Group) Government agencies. Such retributive activities were considered by the formerly "oppressed NCNC'ers" not only to be their just due, but a useful preparation for the Referendum. Little by little, however, Movement supporters were disappointed, and now increasingly frustrated and enraged by what they came to regard as the Administrator's inexcusable caution and impartiality.

One of the Administrator's "obstructive" acts which most infuriated Movement leaders, was his refusal to permit a wholesale purge of the Customary Courts. This was not to say that a little house-cleaning was not permitted. The Administrator issued a decree that all judges Sin Grade B Courts must be legal practitioners.[10] The effect of this order was that about 70 of the 80 Grade B Court judges in the West were sacked. Certainly, this afforded Movement/NCNC supporters some satisfaction, for at least 18 Grade B Court presidents in the Mid-West were summarily dismissed. Indeed, the Commissioner of Justice, in the Emergency

Administration, the redoubtable Mid-West NCNC leader, Webber Egbe, must have gained some measure of personal satisfaction in executing this order. For one of the judges to be dismissed was Chief U.E. Onuwaje, the Action Group judge before whom he had appeared on a "trumped up" charge in 1959.[11] However, while these Grade B Court sackings were welcome, the hundreds of Grades C and D Court judges, the functionaries who had most frequently been the principal instruments of Action Group harassment, remained in place.[12]

Movement/NCNC'ers were exasperated also by the frustratingly correct behaviour of the Administrator in relation to the Local Government Police Forces, the agencies of Action Group oppression which had stirred up almost as much hatred in the hearts of Mid-Westerners as the Customary Courts. Under the Federal Emergency Powers Regulations, the only Regional Government Officer to be suspended was the Superintendent General of Local Government Police Forces. For the rest, the Federal Regulations specified that "all forces established under the Local Government Police Law of the Region... shall be deemed part of the Nigeria Police Force".[13] Thus, with the Administrator adhering totally to the Federal Regulations this meant that all Local Authority Police Officers in the Mid-West, as well as in other West Regional localities, now remained beyond the reach of vengeful Movement/NCNC'ers.

The final area of major frustration to Movement/NCNC elements, was that relating to Local Government Councils. Though there were wide-spread indications that local NCNC'ers in the Mid-West were pressing the Emergency Administration and Mid-West Affairs Commissioner, Uzorka, to dissolve Action Group Councils and Management Committees, and particularly in the trouble spots of Ishan and Afenmai,[14] there was little response. The only Mid-West appeal on which Majekodunmi took immediate action (in July) was that relating to the Warri Urban District Council. In this instance he called for the dismissal of the Action Group Management Committee and for the restriction of the elected council, *a council which had an NCNC majority.*

Nor did the slights to Movement/NCNC'ers end here. Even in small matters there were more affronts. One which seemed most directly to add insult to injury was the decision of the Administrator to appoint as advisers to his Administration—to represent the views of Benin and Delta Provinces respectively—the *Oba* of Benin and the "Action Group lackey", Erejuwa II, *Olu* of Warri![15]

What all these acts—but mostly inactions—made clear was that Movement/NCNC'ers had been granted token concessions only. The real and thoroughgoing assault which they had fully expected the Emergency Administration either to endorse or at least to turn a blind eye to, they had not been permitted to mount. For Movement warriors who felt they had won the Battle for the Mid-West, the pickings had been lean.

With Movement/NCNC elements held—if not exactly put—in their place, and with the new United People's Party (UPP)[16] and Action Group elements showing marked signs of recovery, Mid-Westerners were subjected to their most shattering disappointment yet in what had become three months of cumulative frustration. The Prime Minister announced on 13 August that the *Mid-West Referendum would not be held until after 1 January, 1963, the date set for the termination of the Period of Emergency in the West.*

All along, Movement leaders had been confident they would be permitted to hold the Referendum *sometime* during the Period of Emergency; that they would be given a loose rein to enable them to ensure acquisition of the required "Yes" vote. However, the delay which they now faced, together with the prospect of dealing with an Akintola/UPP Government in the West, made it clear that they could end up nowhere! Once again, therefore, it was apparent that the Mid-West creation could involve a serious contest.

Querying the Prime Minister's statement on the Referendum date, Ja' Isuman asked why "a State of Emergency in the *Western* Region" should prevent "the creation of the *Mid-West* Region when there is no trouble in the Mid-West at all"?[17] Saying what most Movement and other Mid-West leaders were thinking, Isuman contended that "the Federal Government ought to have done more to relieve the anxiety" of Mid-Westerners "as they were naturally suspicious of any movement that could be calculated to mean anything".[18] Isuman's observations brought hurried disclaimers from Federal officials who explained that the Prime Minister's action was prompted by the advice of Federal Law Officers who had pointed out that "nothing involving the casting of votes during the period of Emergency in the West"[19] should be permitted. It was, however, clear that Isuman had yet again spoken clearly and without artifice, expressing the fears and doubts of Mid-Westerners.

The Politics of All-Party Unity

The Benin Conference   With Mid-Westerners in a state of some bewilderment and apprehension over the future of the Mid-West issue, Movement leaders chose this moment to launch a timely initiative. Under the patronage of the *Oba* of Benin who once again was considered an acceptable "front" man by Movement leaders, an *All-Party Round Table Conference* was convened at the *Oba*'s Palace, Benin City, on 9 September, 1962.

Other than in name, the Conference bore little resemblance to an "All-Party" affair. The Mid-West leaders attending the Conference were almost all of Movement/NCNC persuasion, and most of these were of Bini, Western Ibo or Benin Province origins. Two marginal Action Groupers, Chief Odiete and the redoubtable Ja' Isuman (who for some time had been stirring the wrath of his more hard-line Action Group colleagues because of his increased leanings in the Movement direction) together with the former Chairman of the Mid-West Advisory Council, Senator Dahlton Asemota, (out of his job since the take-over of the Emergency Administration), were in attendance. But None of the Action Group (Awolowo-loyal) Mid-West leaders—including such prominent personalities as K.S.Y. Momoh, Olatunji Oye, O.N. Rewane, Chief Edukugho or even the fiery Nduka Eze—put in a showing. As for representatives from the newly-formed UPP, the sole delegate scheduled to attend, James Otobo, withdrew at the last moment. Finally—though a Mid-West Branch of the NPC had been formally inaugurated in July, 1962[20]—no NPC delegate attended the Benin gathering.[21]

For dubious and apprehensive Mid-Westerners, the Conference provided much re-assurance.[22] Only Chief Omo-Osagie had the temerity to suggest that the Referendum could still be "a very high hurdle for Mid-West leaders and their followers to jump",[23] although the two marginal Action Groupers, Isuman and Odiete, added further polite *caveats*. For the rest, it seemed the Conference was in the form of a celebratory Mid-West "family reunion" pervaded by an aura of expectation and self-congratulation. As Omo-Osagie, rising to the occasion, put it, "What first struck me when I entered the conference hall was the beauty—the personality of the people of the Mid-West, a beauty which I have never seen in any gathering of the Yoruba West".[24]

Before concluding, the Conference agreed to send "messages of gratitude" to the Prime Minister, the Sardauna, and Premier Okpara. More important, the setting up of a Mid-West Planning Committee, with a recommended slate of officers under the chairmanship of Senator Asemota, was approved.[25] Before adjourning, Mid-West Affairs Commissioner Mark Uzorka offered Mid-West leaders his support and encouragement, and Ja' Isuman, who was now to put his considerable energies and skills as both politician and publicist to full use in his new post as Chairman of the Plebiscite Committee, issued his own reminder to Conference delegates.

The different Committees and those who had been appointed to them, Isuman declared, had been selected also for the purpose of forming "the nuclei of campaign teams in their respective divisions". He pointed out it would now be "the duty of these divisional teams to prepare the list of places in their respective areas that they wished the Central Regional Campaign Team to visit". The co-operation of divisional teams would be essential also for "locating the most suitable spots for polling stations".[26]

Certainly, this *Round Table All-Party Conference* constituted a convincing declaration of Movement intent. In the Conference's decisions and declarations, there was something for everyone. For Movement supporters there was the reassurance that the time-table for the conduct of the Referendum—at least according to the contentions of Omo-Osagie—had been set. For non-Movement/NCNC elements resident in areas like Akoko-Edo, Warri and Western Ijaw, the setting up of special committees to deal with issues of particular concern to them, such as Minorities Protection and Delimitation, provided encouragement that if the peoples of these areas must compromise, then at least they would have an opportunity to secure favourable terms. Finally, it seemed that the creation of the Mid-West Planning Committee, with automatic membership for every Mid-West legislator, regardless of political affiliation, could well serve as a most effective lure to the more apprehensive Action Group and UPP leaders.

And yet, while *general* assurances had been liberally dispensed to Conference delegates, *no specific or written promises* had been made. No commitment, for instance, had been given about the proposed *composition* of the envisaged Mid-West Interim Administration. Nor had any of the vital *provisions* to be written into the *future Mid-West Constitution*—provisions which had understandably been causing some disquiet in non-Movement areas—been given even passing consideration. As for the plebiscite "time-table" which had been outlined by Omo-Osagie, this also had to be accepted at his word. In any general sense, therefore, the Conference had been a very important public relations exercise. Its practical effects, however, would only be revealed by future events.

The Mid-West issue now faded temporarily from view as all eyes focused on the spectacular revelations emanating from Lagos and Ibadan. This was the period of Chief Awolowo's ordeal. The young nation was first rocked by the disclosures of the *Coker Commission* which revealed extensive findings of "impropriety" against the Action Group Leader during the time of his incumbency as Premier of the West.[27] Then with the *Coker Commission* continuing its Inquiry, the Prime Minister generated further alarm when he announced on the eve of Nigeria's second anniversary of Independence, that Police had uncovered a plot to overthrow the Federal Government by force. The *coup d'etat*, it was alleged , had been planned for 22 September, 1962; it was further alleged that Awolowo together with certain other named Action Groupers— including the Mid-West's Tony Enahoro—had been the principal figures behind the planned *coup*. By the end of October, the so-called "Treason Trial" was under way. It was to last nine months.

In the welter and turmoil of these ongoing events, the only overt indication that the Mid-West Planning Committee was attempting to move ahead with its commitments was revealed when on 5 November, a Press release announced that a Mid-West delegation had met the Prime Minister at Lagos.[28] In keeping with Omo-Osagie's promise, a group of Planning Committee members asked that Balewa now set a date for the Mid-West Referendum.[29] The response of the Prime Minister to this Planning Committee request was, however, not revealed; nor indeed was anything further heard from Omo-Osagie or other Planning Committee officers about a Referendum date. For the time being, the matter was allowed to drop from public sight.

Planning Committee Progress   Events in relation to the Mid-West issue began to pick up pace when on 21 January, 1963, it was announced by the Federal Government that Barrister Gabriel E. Longe, a native of Afenmai Division, had been appointed to serve as Mid-West Referendum Supervisor.[30] On receipt of this news Mid-West leaders at Lagos and Ibadan hurried back to Benin where a Special Meeting of the Mid-West Planning Committee was held on 24 January.

Following this Special Meeting, the leaders dispersed, many visiting their home districts in company with members of their respective Divisional Campaign Teams which were under the energetic guidance of Plebiscite Committee Chairman, Isuman, before again departing the Mid-West to attend to their respective duties. Longe himself was not long in settling into his new work Soon after his appointment,[31] he announced the appointment of Divisional Referendum Officers and their respective Assistant Divisional Referendum Officers.[32] Things once again were on the move in the Mid-West.

And yet, despite this renewed rise in Mid-West expectations, strengthened by fresh assertions of confidence by Mid-West Planning Committee members that the Prime Minister was fulfilling his end of the bargain, any significant progress towards the securing of All-Party unity seemed still to be lagging. Chief Akintola and his new UPP regime now installed in Office at Ibadan appeared to believe that silence on the Mid-West issue was—for the time being—the best policy. As for the Action Group and the newly emergent MPC (Mid-West Peoples Congress);[33] it seemed that these Mid-West "minority parties" also preferred to remain silent. There was little to indicate that Mid-West minority parties were now any closer to a "co-operative posture" on the Mid-West issue than they had been in September 1962.

On 26 January, 1963, only two days after the most recent Mid-West Planning Committee meeting, the Action Group, breaking dramatically from its previous non-committal stance, shattered any immediate prospects for the enhancement of Mid-West All-Party unity when K.S.Y. Momoh, Chairman of the Action Group Mid-West Regional Executive Committee, announced that his party had "decided to oppose the creation of a Mid-West Region".[34] This would mean that recognition of and co-operation with the Mid-West Planning Committee would continue to be withheld. Momoh announced also that it had been decided by the Mid-West Regional Executive Committee that the party's erstwhile Principal Organising Secretary in the Mid-West, Alhaji Ja' Isuman, should be immediately expelled from the Action Group for "persisting anti-party activities".

Neither Movement/NCNC elements, nor their ally in the Mid-West cause, the now ex-Action Group leader Isuman, demonstrated any noticeable concern at these developments.

Planning Committee Campaign Teams were busy in the Mid-West districts. Isuman went about his duties as Plebiscite Committee Chairman as energetically as ever. Isuman also found time to indulge in one of his most favoured pastimes, pamphleteering—and this time, in support of the Mid-West issue and its Movement/NCNC leaders about whom, in earlier publications, he had been less than complimentary.[35]

The various subordinate bodies of the Mid-West Planning Committee moved ahead with Referendum preparations, apparently undeterred by the lack of co-operation of UPP and Action Group elements. Then, quite suddenly, at the beginning of March, 1963, things started swiftly to develop.

It was rumoured that on 23 February, certain Mid-West Action Groupers and Movement/NCNC'ers had met in secret and that these particular—and un-named—Action Groupers were prepared to pledge their support for the creation of a Mid-West state.[36] No formal public statement to confirm this rumoured pact was released.

On 9 March, however, at a meeting of the Mid-West Planning Committee held to complete final preparations for the first major Referendum Campaign Tour, the Chairman of the Mid-West Regional Executive Committee of the Action Group, K.S.Y. Momoh was *in attendance*. Furthermore, he was accompanied by two other prominent Mid-West Action Groupers who, up to this point, had also been standing aloof from the Planning Committee: C. E. Akere of Ishan and Olatunji Oye of Akoko Edo.[37] Added to this encouraging news, there were unconfirmed reports that the MPC leader, Apostle Edokpolor, and a UPP representative were also in attendance at the 9 March meeting.[38]

The only remaining major Mid-West political leader who refused to enter the circle of Planning Committee co-operation—with the exception of members of the Itsekiri "Rewane Clique"[39]—was the UPP Minister of Health, James Otobo, the sole Mid-Westerner to cross successfully from ministerial office under the Action Group administration to ministerial office under the new UPP regime. He had at no time given any indication that he was prepared to throw in his hand with the Movement/NCNC-dominated Planning Committee; nor in the current situation had he relaxed this position.

The Parties on Tour   Exploiting to the full this new spirit of fellowship and co-operation, on the day following the Planning

Committee meeting, "the *Oba* and his retinue of chiefs" headed by the Iyase,[40] leaders of the "Otu Edo/NCNC, Action Group, UPP and MPC parties"—less the recalcitrant Otobo—commenced a week-long tour which "took them to all the important towns in the Mid-West".[41] During this tour, as in the BDPP campaigns of former years, it was the *Oba*, now a seasoned platform orator, who conveyed the main message—"A Mid-West For All"—and who, once again, was responsible for drawing large crowds to the meetings *en route*.

Things, however, had changed for the Mid-West Movement since the "bad old days" of 1953-54, and there was perhaps no more graphic indication of this change than in the words of the set address which the *Oba* now repeated, with minor variations, at these tour gatherings. Indicative of the confidence which Movement leaders now felt, the *Oba* no longer sought gently to solicit the support of Mid Westerners in the localities, but rather now chose to lecture and admonish residents to vote "Yes".

> "The part all people are expected to play is to vote YES by putting their ballot papers in the YES ballot boxes... the WHITE ballot boxes.
> ...Enemies are going about secretly, telling some voters to abstain, or... not to drop ballot papers into WHITE boxes... because the WHITE boxes, according to these enemies, are for... collecting votes in order to restore the white man's rule.
> [In fact, however] the WHITE ballot boxes are for the collection Of votes in order to be free from Black Imperialism within the Federation of Nigeria".[42]

If by this point in his address, those in attendance had not been adequately impressed with the necessity of voting "Yes", the Oba's concluding words now drove home the urgency of the matter with fearful finality:

> "Whoever does not drop his or her ballot paper into the WHITE ballot box... will be condemned by future generations. Even those who die before the plebiscite takes place will be condemned in the Other World, if they die with the bad intention of voting against or persuading people to vote against the creation of a Mid-West Region"![43]

This was strong medicine from the *Oba*. It smacked not a little of the familiar flamboyant style of Plebiscite Committee Chairman, Isuman. However, whatever the source of this forceful and fiery language in his address, the *Oba*, clearly intent on exploiting to the full his authority as religious as well as traditional political figurehead, left no room for doubt in the minds of any of his audience: to vote against the Mid-West, to abstain, even to harbour thoughts of malice towards the Mid-West issue, would be to risk peril in both this world and the next! In view of the deeply-held traditional religious beliefs retained by residents of most Mid-West districts, it would be a brave, even foolhardy, person who would now choose consciously to obstruct the success of the Referendum vote!

Though considerable campaign momentum and Action Group co-operation on the Mid-West issue was being generated, still no date for the proposed referendum had been set. Up to April, 1963, the only action taken by the Federal Government in relation to the Mid-West issue had been to appoint Barrister Longe to the post of Referendum Supervisor.

This failure of Movement leaders to secure a set date for the referendum caused renewed apprehensions amongst Mid-West supporters about the actual intent of the Federal Authorities in relation to the Mid-West issue. To this source of fundamental fear and uncertainty was added, in mid-April 1963, another of very threatening implications.

The Price of Co-operation On 23 April, the Mid-West UPP Minister James Otobo, breaking his prolonged silence on the Mid-West issue, declared that the proposed Referendum should be "postponed indefinitely".[44] In an address to the House of Assembly, he stated that the Referendum should be deferred to allow for "certain issues" that might "guide the future of the proposed state" to be discussed; that to this end talks between the Mid-West NCNC, and "the UPP, Action Group and MPC minority parties in the area", should be arranged as soon as possible.

The cause of greatest alarm to Mid-West supporters about Otobo's declaration, was that he was speaking not just for himself, but apparently for his UPP colleagues and other minority parties, including the Action Group and the MPC. Indeed, making quite clear the import of his message, Otobo warned that "Any attempt to steam-roll the Mid-West State might lead to a situation which could spell the doom of the proposed state"!

This declaration and warning by Otobo created immediate and great alarm in the Movement/NCNC camp. Had not the co-operation of the Action Group, the MPC and the majority of the Mid-West UPP leadership been already virtually secured? This was reported to be the understanding which had emerged from the Planning Committee meeting of 9 March. And had not these Mid-

West minority party leaders then taken part in the *Oba's* subsequent "Mid-West for All" campaign Tour? What then was the cause of this seemingly sudden about-face?

The actual reasons for this dramatic reversal in form by these minority parties were not revealed. However, it is probably safe to assume that the matter of *ministerial allocations* in the envisaged Mid-West Interim Administration had still not been settled to the satisfaction of the minority parties; hence the need for Otobo as the representative of these elements to make the position clear to Movement leaders: No satisfactory terms, no support at the Referendum. Certainly, the message got through to the Movement/NCNC.

On 12 May, 1963, a meeting of Movement/NCNC leaders and leaders of the Mid-West minority parties, Action Group, MPC and UPP, was convened at short notice at the Prime Minister's Onikan residence, Lagos.[45] At this meeting it was reported that the minority party leaders managed to extort the concession that "all political parties should be kept informed by Supervisor Longe of all arrangements" being made to carry out the Referendum.

Still, however, no satisfactory settlement was reached on those "certain issues" to which Otobo had referred in his 23 April speech. The Lagos meeting was, therefore, adjourned, and the leaders attending agreed to re-assemble on 20 May at Benin City.

When the meeting was re-convened on 20 May at Edo College, Benin City, Mid-West minority party leaders found to their alarm and anger that Movement/NCNC leaders had called a *full-scale* meeting of the Mid-West Planning Committee—a total of 80 persons, all claiming to be members of the Planning Committee were in attendance! In the chair was a stranger to many non-Bini minority party leaders, Morgan Agbontaen, a Benin rubber and timber magnate and former Chairman—albeit during the period of Action Group control—of the Benin Divisional Council. Agbontaen was elected by the meeting to succeed Senator Dahlton Asemota, who had died suddenly on 2 May, 1963.

Faced with this intimidating and avidly pro-Movement/NCNC assemblage, the Mid-West minority party leaders baulked. They demanded that the meeting be restricted to those leaders, and only those, who had been in attendance at the Prime Minister's meeting the week before. When Chairman Agbontaen gave no indication of acknowledging their demand, minority party delegates, led by Otobo, Momoh and Edokpolor, stormed out and proceeded to the Benin V.I.P. Rest House. There they held a closed meeting of their own, "the details of which were not officially released, but were open secrets"[46]

It soon became apparent that this latest bold manoeuvre by the Mid-West minority party leaders had had the desired effect on dominant Movement/NCNC elements. On 30 May, Movement Leader Osadebay issued a statement in which it was clear that at long last, after nearly three years of procrastination and political manoeuvring, the Movement/NCNC had decided to come to terms with rival party elements in the Mid-West. *Practically all the points raised in Osadebay's statement related to the proposed composition of the envisaged Mid-West Interim Administration.*

First, it was pointed out by Osadebay, that the "Interim Government in the Mid-West" could take one of three forms:

"1. The Interim Government should consist only of a number of Commissioners at the head of whom is an Administrator.

2. There should be an Interim Government of Commissioners consisting of all the recent Ministers of Mid-West origin in the Western Region Government plus a few more legislators... whose services are required in the Interim Cabinet of the Mid-West Region. All the Members of the House of Chiefs and House of Assembly will then together form a joint Advisory Council to advise the Interim Government.

3. Under this scheme all Mid-West Members of the House of Chiefs should move from Ibadan to the Mid-West and constitute the Mid-West House of Chiefs. All the Mid-West Members of the House of Assembly, and the present Ministers of Mid-West origin in the Western Region will go on to the Mid-West as Ministers or Commissioners, in order to bring in some [other] personalities... whose services are required in the Interim Government of the Mid-West Region".[47]

The second section of Osadebay's statement set out what were clearly the vital conditions for appeasing the minority party elements. Here, the Movement Leader went on to declare categorically:

"Every Division in the Mid-West must be given a seat in the Cabinet... That we are committed to creating two more Divisions, Isoko [the home area of Otobo] in the Delta Province and Akoko-Edo [the home area of Olatunji Oye] in Benin Province... That altogether there should be a Cabinet of fifteen consisting of one Administrator, one seat for each of the [ten] divisions... [Seats for] two chiefs from the Delta Province [plus two others "whose services would be required" by the Interim Administration]. [48]

Osadebay did add that in relation to the proposed Cabinet composition the Prime Minister must endorse the structure and selections proposed to him—"All we can do is to make the suggestions which the Prime Minister may or may not adopt". Still, it was apparent that Osadebay's conditions and assurances, this time, were sufficient to resolve the fears and reservations of the Mid-West minority party leaders. Indeed, from this time on, and up to the date on which the Referendum was finally held (13 July, 1963), no more open opposition to the Mid-West State was heard from any quarter in the Mid-West.[49]

Countdown to the Referendum   The remaining six weeks before the anticipated Referendum were now given over to what Osadebay states was "the biggest and most thorough campaign for votes ever undertaken in Nigeria".[50] Movement/NCNC leaders and their Planning Committee associates, apparently privy at least to the date on which the Federal Government was to announce the July Referendum day, [51] set out a comprehensive Campaign strategy.

The first phase in this final, and now almost totally Mid West NCNC assault[52] on the Mid-West districts, was put into motion when on 5 June, Osadebay in his role (officially and formally) as Leader of the Mid-West Movement set out on a lengthy tour with a number of leading Movement personalities.[53] Moving like clockwork through Ishan, Afenmai and Benin Divisions, Osadebay and his Movement entourage, completing their tour of Benin Province, arrived at Benin City on 14 June. Benin was in a positive flurry of Movement activity caused by the official announcement three days earlier (12 June) that the date for the Mid-West Referendum had been set for Saturday, 13 July, 1963.[54]

Osadebay and his Movement entourage now pressed on with their tour into the districts of the rather less receptive Delta Province. This second phase of Osadebay's tour, although meeting with enthusiastic receptions arranged by the respective Divisional Leaders, was a whirlwind affair as it lasted only five days (20-25 June). Still the Movement Team managed to visit centres in Aboh, Urhobo, Warri and even Western Ijaw Divisions.

A brief lull followed the completion of Leader Osadebay's triumphal Movement tour. During this time the Divisional Teams busied themselves in their respective territories following up on the Movement Leader's appeal that citizens in all localities should be educated to recognise that a "Yes" vote was expected of them and that any thought of a "No" vote or abstention was unacceptable. On 1 July, with less than two weeks remaining until voting day, the NCNC President and East Regional Premier, Dr. Okpara launched the second and final Referendum Campaign assault in the Mid-West districts. No longer attempting even to pay lip-service to all-party participation, as had been the case in the earlier Movement tour by Leader Osadebay, this final all-out Campaign tour was an unabashedly NCNC affair.[55]

During this final period before Referendum Day, the formal *front* of All-Party support for the Mid-West creation was retained intact[56]—albeit that breakdown in this unaccustomed harmony seemed constantly imminent. But as polling day drew closer Movement/NCNC leaders made an increasing number of allegations against Action Group and UPP elements. They stated that these minority parties were in fact informally obstructing Movement efforts. The former Mid-West Affairs Commissioner in the West Emergency Administration, Mark Uzorka, alleged that "at Asaba, the Action Group was conducting a house-to-house campaign against the creation of a Mid-West State".[57] He further declared that "two prominent Asaba Action Group members were directing their supporters to collect their ballot papers" and to deliver them to the party's Divisional Headquarters.

Premier Akintola and his UPP also came under sharp attack. Leader Osadebay accused Akintola of giving support to "certain people who are currently campaigning against the creation of the Mid-West Region".[58] Indeed, Osadebay stated that information had reached him which indicated that "some people who openly campaigned for the new state during the day" were then returning "in the night to campaign against it". Akintola had also angered Movement leaders when he called for the placing of UPP observers at Referendum Counting Stations.[59]

Plebiscite Committee Chairman, Isuman, assailed the Western Premier for casting doubt "on the honesty and efficiency of those constitutionally charged with the duty of counting votes". In lending support to Isuman's attack, the NCNC President Okpara stated—though rather lamely—that if the West Regional Government was sincere about the creation of the Mid-West State, then "there is no need for it to plant observers at the counting stations".[60]

Okpara, during his NCNC Referendum Tour, had also given vent to misgivings over reports of anti-Mid-West activity in the Delta, when at Burutu he alleged that there were "certain people" going about the creek areas of Warri and Western Ijaw divisions in motor boats, "preaching that there would be no Mid-West State". Okpara called on Burutu residents to ignore these men, whom, he explained, were "messengers of slavery".[61]

THE PEOPLE DECIDE

13 July, the day of reckoning for Mid-Westerners, finally dawned. Leader Osadebay, looking back on this historic day, states that he and his colleagues were, on the one hand, confident about the prospects for a Referendum victory:

> "The results of elections in Benin and Delta Provinces since 1951 had shown that whoever and whatever the NCNC supported in the Mid-West would win. The Mid West was a veritable stronghold of the NCNC and we were sure that the Mid-West Referendum would go the way of all other polls in Benin and Delta Provinces".[62]

Yet, on the other hand, Osadebay was all too aware that despite the existence of formal All-Party support, "the forces of reaction, particularly in Western Nigeria, had sworn to see that the Mid-West was *not* created".[63] Indeed, the Action Group, he alleges, "its members and leaders alike... organised opposition and planned failure for the Referendum". And, of course, the point was that "forces of reaction" in the West needed only *marginal* support at the polls to ensure that the requisite 60 per cent "Yes" vote would *not* be secured and hence that the Mid-West issue would fail.

Mid-West protagonists needed a "Yes" vote of at least 60 per cent (or about 390,000) of an electorate of about 640,000[64] to secure the Mid-West state. While Movement protagonists could draw some measure of confidence from the fact of past NCNC successes in the Mid-West, still it was to be recognised that each of these triumphs had been based on marginal victories at the polls. *In no instance since the first general elections of 1951, had the NCNC secured a total vote in excess of 60 per cent of Registered Electors* in the Mid-West.

At the 1959 Federal Elections, Mid-Westerners ran up their largest total voting turnout to date when 515,410 electors, or about 78 per cent, of the Mid-West's Registered Voters actually cast ballots. Yet even in this instance only about 46 per cent of those balloting had cast their votes for Movement/NCNC candidates, the remaining 32 per cent opting for Action Group and other intra-Mid-West opposition candidates. In the August 1960 West Regional elections, with an average Regional turnout of 71.3 per cent of Registered Electors, the Movement/NCNC had managed to secure the votes of only about one-half of these electors, or 36 per cent of Registered Electors voting in the Mid-West; the remaining 35.3 per cent again went to Action Group and other intra-Mid-West opposition elements. It was therefore apparent that *acquisition of the requisite 60 per cent "Yes" vote was not a foregone conclusion.*

The Referendum Question to which voters were to answer "Yes" or "No" was lengthy and complex. It was unsuitable for the majority of electors who were, of course, illiterate. Still, it was obvious that the outcome of the polling would rest less on the ability of electors to read the Referendum Question, than on their willingness to carry out the oft-repeated and explicit Movement/NCNC instructions to put their ballot papers in the White, or "Yes", Ballot Box.[65] The Referendum Question was:

"Do you agree that the Mid-Western Region Act, 1962, shall have effect so as to secure that Benin Province including Akoko Edo District in the Afenmai Division, and Delta Province including Warri Division and Warri Urban Township area shall be included in the Mid-West Region"?[66]

The first reports coming in from the polls were encouraging for Mid-West protagonists. Voting turnouts were said to be strong in most districts. Also, voting was reported largely to have gone off peacefully. Although trouble had been anticipated in a number of the stronger anti-NCNC areas, the only reported disturbances occurred in Benin and Asaba Divisions where voters had been excluded from certain polling stations.[67]

By Tuesday, 16 July, the first unofficial confirmation of the impending triumph of Mid-West protagonists was revealed in a report from the office of Referendum Supervisor Longe. In this report, it was announced that with "22 of the 30 polling areas" having submitted full returns, the requisite 60 per cent "Yes" vote had already been obtained. Returns from these areas, it was declared, had shown that 395,000 electors, nearly 6,000 more than the number required to satisfy the 60 per cent minimum, had cast "Yes" votes.[68]

On Thursday, 18 July, Supervisor Longe released final and official figures on the Referendum outcome.[69] These figures demonstrated that Movement/NCNC protagonists had not only secured an overwhelming victory at the polls, but had been able to realise their two most important objectives *en route*: these were, first, a massive turnout of about 90 per cent of all those registered as electors; and second, a negligible "No" vote, as only slightly more than one per cent of voters dared to place their ballots in the Black box.

TABLE VII

RESULTS OF THE MID-WEST REFERENDUM: A DIVISIONAL BREAKDOWN[70]

DIVISIONS	*TOTAL OF REGISTERED ELECTORS*	*TOTAL OF "YES" VOTES*	*TOTAL OF "NO" VOTES*
Aboh	39,483	33,072	722
Afenmai	90,795	76,998	1,260
Asaba	74,445	68,637	365
Benin	143,247	130,562	2,081
Ishan	83,098	73,088	563
Urhobo	160,227	150,382	273
Warri	39,742	30,703	1,377
Western Ijaw	22,913	15,635	577
TOTALS	653,950*	579,077	7,218

Percentage of total Registered Electors who cast "Yes" Votes, = *88.5 per cent*

* The total of 650,130 given in official papers, is incorrect. As a result, the official 89.07 per cent "Yes" vote figure, when corrected, is reduced to 88.55 per cent.

Clearly, this monumental "Yes" vote of 88.55 per cent of all Registered Electors obliterated any lingering doubts about the creation of a Mid-West State. This vote ensured the new state would become a reality. It also indicated that any efforts of minority opposition elements to influence voting had been abortive. It had been anticipated by Osadebay and Movement leaders, that an affirmative vote could be undercut by sizeable "No" votes—or as a last resort, abstentions in Western Ijaw, Ishan and Afenmai divisions, the major areas of established dissent.

In fact, Benin Division recorded the largest total of "No" votes (2,081). As for the recognised opposition areas; perhaps the biggest surprise came in Ishan where not only was there a near 90 per cent turnout of registered electors, but of these only 563 cast "No" votes. Even bearing in mind the close attention that Prince Shaka Momodu and his "Shock Troops" were paying to activities at Ishan polling stations, this total seemed incredibly low.

It is difficult to believe that this truly overwhelming Referendum success, was due solely to the appeal which the Mid-West issue had for electors in both pro and anti Movement/NCNC areas. Movement/NCNC organisers and polling agents kept a very close watch at all Referendum Polling Stations. In an NCNC Circular addressed to "Campaign leaders" it was pointed out that a total of 3,930 party "polling agents"—approximately two to each of the 1841 polling stations—were to serve the party's interests on Referendum Day.[71]

Furthermore, these agents were to be assisted in their duties by members and leaders of the powerful and much-feared *Owegbe* Society. Indeed following the Referendum *Owegbe* members received the plaudits of Movement leaders for their "contribution" to its success.[72] How *Owegbe* members contributed to the Referendum success, is not stated. However, it has already been established that *Owegbe* methods could be both direct and effective.

These factors, together with the alleged strategic placing of the white and black ballot boxes—often behind a canvas screen which did not reach ground level[73]—must have contributed to the willingness of voters to place their ballot papers in the white, or "Yes" boxes. Furthermore, it is difficult to believe that the Federally appointed Presiding Officers—all but a few of them Mid-Westerners—did not perhaps take their duties as Mid-West patriots more seriously than their obligations as returning officers when it came to compiling results at the counting houses.[74]

However, whatever the methods employed, the result of the Referendum was clear enough. It showed that Movement leaders and their supporters had secured their long-sought goal, and in spectacular fashion. They had been able, in terms of voting numbers, to demonstrate that it was they who were truly masters of the Mid-West.

References

1. See *Daily Times*, 3 June, 1962, and *Pilot*, 2 June, 1962.

2. See Enahoro, *Fugitive Offender, op.cit.*, p.192. On his way to Uromi (his home town in Ishan), Enahoro, on 1 June, visited Leader Awolowo at Ibadan. Awolowo and Enahoro were convinced that the Mid-West Referendum would shortly be held for, since the *Mid-West Region Act* had been gazetted (this had been done on the eve of the fateful 25th of May), there was now nothing to stop the Federal Government from completing its unfinished business in the Mid-West.

3. Ibid.

4 See *Express*, 7 June, and 25 June, 1962.

5. *Tribune*, 7 June, 1962.

6. *Express*, 25 June, 1962.

7. *Express*, 3 July, 1962; see also *Express*, 2 July, 1962.

8. *Express*, 3 July, 1962.

9. *Ibid.*

10. See *Express*, 27 June, 1962.

11. See above p.229, n.44.

12. The Local Government Service Board (LGSB) was responsible for handling any matters relating either to appointment or dismissal of Customary Court judges. Since the LGSB had been suspended at the outset of the Emergency Administration, there was no appropriate authorised body to attend to the detailed procedural matters raised by dismissal appeals, had the Administrator wished these appeals to be heard.

13. *Federation of Nigeria Official Gazette*, Vol.49, No.38, L.N. No. 54 of 1962; see also *Express*, 25 July, 1962 for comments by the Administrator on the integration move.

14. See, *Express*, 29 June, 1962, for allegations of Ishan NCNC attempts at Local Government take-overs in the Division.

15. See *Pilot*, 16 July, 1962.

16. The UPP was the party inaugurated in August 1962 under the leadership of Akintola. Its support came from the anti-Awolowo faction in the Action Group. Very quickly, the UPP grew to prominence.

17. *Minutes of Round-Table Conference of Mid-West Political Leaders, held at the Oba of Benin's Palace, Benin City, 9 September, 1962,* (mimeo.), p.21. (Copy in possession of the writer).

18. *Ibid.*

19. *Ibid.*, p.22.

20. See *Express*, 16 July, 1962. In one of its initial Press releases, the Mid-West NPC made certain embarrassing allegations, including statements that "top Mid-West NCNC members... were already in possession of NPC party cards,... a fact that has been kept from the Nigerian public"; also that at an Ibadan meeting held on 14 July, NCNC leaders had discussed "ways of thwarting NPC plans to establish itself in the Mid-West".

21. Shortly after the *Benin All-Party Conference*, the Mid-West People's Congress (MPC), in mid-September 1962, formally endorsed by the *Sardauna* as the Northern party's ally in the Mid-West, made its appearance on the Nigerian political scene under the leadership of John (the "Apostle") Edokpolor. Edokpolor, a new-comer to politics, brought a rather novel brand of political evangelism to the Mid-West. Head of the 6,000-strong Church of the Lord and an established rubber trader, he claimed he had been "drawn into politics during the disturbances in Ishan Division in mid 1961".(K.W.J. Post and M. Vickers, *Structure and Conflict in Nigeria 1960-66*, (London: Heinemann, 1973) p.92). Shocked by these events, he stated that he had sought a "God-fearing" party. After flirting first with the Action Group, "in mid-1962, he swung to the NPC, attracted by the *Sardauna* of Sokoto who—he held—was not out to make money and was charitable and God-fearing". (*Ibid.* p.93) In a letter from the *Sardauna* to Edokpolor dated 23 September, 1962, the "Apostle", was granted permission to form the MPC.

22. Even the setting up of the Mid-West Planning Committee at the end of the Conference was a mere formality. All those selected to serve on the Committee, with the exception of Asemota, were either leading Movement/NCNC officers or had led discussion on specific areas of activity for which as Committee members, they were to be responsible.

23. *Minutes of Round Table Conference of Mid-West Political Leaders..., op. cit.*, p.7

24. *Ibid.*, p.8.

25. The Mid-West Planning Committee, conforming to the specifications earlier outlined by the *Oba* in his comments about a proposed "general working committee" with a "fairly large" number of representatives, was indeed, formidable in size. In addition to specified executive officers, automatic membership on the Planning Committee was extended to all Mid-West Members in both the West Regional and Federal Legislatures. Total Planning Committee membership, therefore, numbered about 75 persons! At one meet-

ing of the Planning Committee on 20 May, 1963, a total of 80 members were in attendance! (See Osaghae *mss., op.cit.*, p.91).

In addition to Chairman Asemota, those selected to serve on the executive of the Planning Committee included: General Secretary, E.B. Edun-Fregene; Assistant-Secretary, J.A.E. Oki; Treasurer, Dr. Xto Okojie; Political Adviser, Chief Okotie-Eboh; Mid-West Movement Leader, Chief Osadebay; Mid-West Movement Deputy Leader, Chief Omo-Osagie. Chairmen of the respective sub-committees were: Constitution/Legal Committee, O. Chukura; Finance Committee, Chief A.Y. Eke; Delimitation Committee, Chief Obasuyi; Minority Committee, Chief Odiete; Plebiscite Committee, Ja' Isuman; and Civil Service Committee, Chief J.I.G. Onyia. (See Osaghae *mss.*, p.85)

26. *Ibid.*

27. Shortly after the Interim Administration went into operation, a Commission of Inquiry headed by Mr. Justice Coker, was appointed to investigate allegations of corruption in six public corporations in the West. For details, see *Report of the Coker Commission of Inquiry into the Affairs of Certain Statutory Corporations in Western Nigeria: 1962*, (Lagos: MOI, 1963).

28. See Isuman. *You and the Mid-West Plebiscite ...*, *op.cit.*, p.41

29. See Isuman, *ibid.*, and Okoh, *Men and Matters...*, *op.cit.*, p.57.

30. See *Daily Times*, 22 January, 1963; and Okoh, *Men and Matters...*, *op.cit.*, p .57.

31. See Okoh, *op. cit.*, p. 25.

32. The Divisional Referendum Officers appointed, were; Aboh, G. Olokee; Asaba, F.E.O. Nwajei; Afenmai, A. Aitalegbe; Benin, D.N. Oronsaye; Ishan, A. A. Ordia; Urhobo, S. W. Anauche; Warri, F.O. Moore; Western Ijaw, O.Dobrim. A total of 31 Assistant Divisional Referendum Officers were also appointed by Supervisor Longe. (See *Ibid.*, p.26).

33. See n. 21 above, for origins of the MPC.

34. Isuman, *You and the Mid-West Plebiscite...*, *op.cit.*, p.42.

35. To do justice to the bombastic, but courageous Ja', it should be pointed out that his encomiums on the likes of Chiefs Festus, Omo-Osagie and Osadebay did not represent a total reversal of his earlier bitter denunciations of these Mid-West/NCNC leaders. In his most recent pamphlet, *You and the Mid-West Plebiscite...*, *op.cit.*, p.5,) his words in "praise" of these eminent politicians could be taken either way.

36. Okoh, *Men and Matters...*, *op.cit.*, p.57.

37. See Isuman, *You and the Mid-West Plebiscite...*, *op. cit.*, p. 42.

38. See Osaghae *mss., op.cit.*, p.45.

39. Both Rewanes at this time were under a cloud. They had good reason to be apprehensive. Alfred Rewane, as a Director of the "infamous" National Investment and Properties Company (NIPC) which was alleged to have served as the main conduit for channelling more than £4m. to the Action Group, had come in for strong criticism from the *Coker Commission*. He had also, during this period, served not only as Chairman of the Western Region Production Development Board, but in addition as Political Secretary to Awolowo himself when the latter had occupied the post of Premier of the West. (See Sklar, *Nigerian Political Parties, op. cit.*, pp.457-58). Alfred's senior brother, barrister O.N. Rewane, was a whole-hearted supporter and contributor to the Action Group's "swing to the left". He was in close consort with other Action Group radicals including S.G. Ikoku who had been named as a "principal leader" in the alleged *coup* plot. Like Ikoku he had visited Ghana often and, as early as 1958, had lectured as a guest of the Nkrumah regime. He therefore had good reason to fear developments at the *Treason Trial* (See Sklar, *ibid.*, pp. 273-75).

40. The appointment of Omo-Osagie to this vacant title had been confirmed by the Emergency Administration in July, 1962.

41. Osaghae *mss., op.cit.*, p.45.

42. *Ibid.*, pp. 86-88; these excerpts are taken from the full text of a speech given by *Oba* of Benin at Agbor, 12 March, 1963.

43. *Loc.cit.*

44. *Pilot*, 26 April, 1963.

45. See Osaghae *mss., op.cit.*, p.91.

46. *Ibid.*

47. *Ibid.*, p.92.

48. *Ibid.*

49. See *ibid.*

50. Osadebay, "We Built a Nation", (unpublished *mss., op.cit.*, p.429.

51. If Osadebay did not have advance information by the beginning of June on the precise date set for the Referendum along with the date on which the Federal Authorities were prepared to make this news public, then, the Movement Leader and his colleagues possessed a gift for uncannily accurate prediction! By 1 June, and probably before this date, Movement/NCNC and Planning Committee leaders had made detailed arrangements for the six-week period running up to mid-July. These arrangements included

meetings and rallies timed in such a way as to secure maximum advantage for the Mid-West campaign from the Federal Government's announcement of the Referendum date.

52. While formally the Mid-West Planning Committee was responsible for the overall orchestration of the Referendum campaign, from the beginning of June it was apparent that the participation of minority party elements—Action Group, MPC and UPP —was token only. It was the Movement/NCNC which provided the leadership, organisation, finance and personnel for this final drive for "Yes" votes. In addition, the Mid-West NCNC received extensive backing from the NCNC President, the party's National Secretariat (which was moved from Lagos to Benin City for the duration of the Referendum campaign) and an assortment of top ranking extra-Mid-West NCNC National leaders. (See Osadebay, unpublished *mss.*, *op.cit.*, p.430). It was, he stressed, impossible to minimise or deny the importance the role of these Eastern elements "in making the existence of the Mid-West Region possible". (*Ibid.*).

53. These included: Chiefs Oweh, Salubi, Erhiajakpor, Mr. Uzorka (the former Commissioner for Mid-West Affairs in the West Emergency Administration), Chief Odiase; also Women's Wing (of the Mid-West Movement) leaders Madam Sarah Elabor and Mrs. Arinze. (See *Ibid.*, p.424).

54. See *Federation of Nigeria Official Gazette (Extra-ordinary), of 12 June, 1963*, Vol. 50, No. 38, G.N. No. 1172.

55. NCNC National leaders who served as interim Divisional Team Leaders in the Mid-West, included: Asaba, Dr. G.C. Mbanugo; Afenmai, T.O.S. Benson; Benin, Omo-Osagie; Ishan, R.A. Fani-Kayode; Aboh, R.A. Akinyemi; Urhobo, Dr. K.O. Mbadiwe; Warri, Chief Okotie-Eboh; Western Ijaw, Chief Akinfosile. (See, Okoh, *Men and Matters...*, *op.cit.*, pp.36-39). It was to be noted that for this NCNC Tour, most of the local (non-interim) Mid-West Divisional Team Leaders, were simply demoted to the rank of Deputy-Leader in their respective Divisional Teams.

56. By the beginning of the second week in July, statements of formal support had been received even from the formerly die-hard anti Mid-West Itsekiri leader, the *Olu* of Warri (See *Pilot*, 8 July, 1963). Also on 28 June, Premier Akintola announced that the UPP campaign *in support* of the Mid-West region would commence—though there was subsequently no indication that it did so. (See *Pilot*, 2 July, 1963). As for the Action Group, the Mid-West Branch of the party under Momoh had earlier given its formal undertaking, at least "not to oppose" the Mid-West issue; Edokpolor had given a similar undertaking on behalf of the MPC. On 10 July, Chief Awolowo, from his prison cell in Lagos, released a statement on behalf of the National Action Group party, calling on all Action Groupers in the Mid-West to vote "Yes" at the Referendum. (See, *Pilot*, 11 July, 1963).

57. *Pilot*, 8 July, 1963.

58. *Pilot*, 11 July, 1963.

59. *Ibid.*

60. *Pilot*, 12 July, 1963.

61. *Pilot*, 11 July, 1963.

62. Osadebay *mss., op. cit.*, p.431.

63. *Ibid.*, p.429.

64. As earlier explained, the Electoral Roll compiled for the Federal Elections of 1959 was employed for the Mid-West Referendum. This Electoral Roll showed that a total of 650,130 persons in the Divisions of Benin and Delta Provinces had been registered to vote at the Federal Elections of 1959. (For details of these registration figures, broken down by Federal Constituency—15 of them—see Post, *The Nigerian Federal Elections of 1959, op.cit.*, Appendix D; and *Guide to the Parliament of the Federation*, (Lagos: MOI, 1961)). Allowing for deaths and departures of registered electors since 1959, Plebiscite Committee Chairman, Isuman estimated that the total number of electors remaining was approximately 640,000. (See Isuman, *You and the Mid-West Plebiscite...*, *op. cit.*, pp.32-33). It was, of course, to be remembered, that Mid-Westerners newly qualified to vote since 1959, were *not* included on the Mid-West Referendum Rolls.

65. Chief Omo-Osagie maintained that use of the White ballot boxes for "Yes" votes and Black boxes for "No" votes had a material effect in ensuring a successful outcome at the Referendum. The use of white and black not only allowed for simple identification of the "Yes" and "No" ballot boxes, but played on basic African superstitions: fear of black—the colour symbolising the powers of darkness—; and on the other hand the promise of "good things", which the colour white is thought to represent. Thus, in the outlying districts of the Mid-West in particular, Omo-Osagie maintained that the African's approbation of the colour white, had the effect of "immeasurably strengthening" the "Yes" vote. (See interview with Omo-Osagie, Int.I, p.6).

66. *Mid-West Referendum 1963*, (mimeo.), handout (1 page), circulated under the authority of *Referendum Supervisor*, Longe. (Copy in possession of writer.)

67. See *West Africa*, 20 July, 1963, p.815.

68. See *West Africa, ibid.*, also see issues of the *Pilot* and *Daily Times* for 16 July, 1963.

69. See Table VII, below p.298, for detailed results of the Referendum.

70. **Source**: *Results of the Mid-West Referendum, 1963* (Circular mimeo., released by Referendum Supervisor Longe), dated 18 July, 1963. (Copy in possession of writer.).

71. See NCNC Circular, *Mid-West Plebiscite: Directives to Campaign Leaders*, dated 2 July, 1963. (Copy in possession of writer.)

72. *Owegbe Report, op.cit.*, p.78.

73. See Rewane, Int.VI, p.16.

74. See interviews with Otobo, Int.VII, p.12; and. Rewane Int.VI, p.16.

CHAPTER 15

TO A SELF-GOVERNING MID-WEST REGION

With the Referendum now complete, Mid-Westerners had but one last formal requirement to fulfil. The Nigerian Federal Constitution provided that before any new Region should become self-governing, it must first complete a six month period of "probation" under a Federally-appointed Interim Administration. If at the end of this period the Federal Authorities were satisfied with the performance of the Interim Administration—run by an Administrative Council of appointees from the proposed new Region—elections for a fully self-governing Region would be allowed to take place.

THE INTERIM ADMINISTRATION

A Bill providing for the establishment of an Interim Administration in the Mid-West was passed by the Federal Parliament on 7-8 August, 1963.[1] This Bill, the *Mid-West (Transitional Provisions) Bill*, called for the establishment of an Administrative Council, comprising an Administrator, three Deputy Administrators and a number of Commissioners, each to be assigned certain portfolios. The Bill also specified that all existing laws of Western Nigeria would continue to apply—that was to say that "all local authorities, customary courts, and other public bodies within the area of the new Region" would continue to perform their respective functions until other arrangements were made.[2] The only exception was the West Regional High Court. Its jurisdiction was to be replaced by that of the High Court at Lagos.

In order that the new Region should not be stripped of assets built up in the area during the period of Ibadan rule, Clause 7 (Transfer of Public Property), provided that "Any immovable property and any chattels that were in the Mid-West at the time of the take-over"[3] would automatically become the property of the Mid-West Region. And in an effort to assist the infant Region financially, Clause 8 (Financial Provisions) specified that "a fund to be known as the Mid-West Regional Administration Fund" was to be established under the control of the Federal Government. Clause 8 provided that "There shall be paid or credited to the Fund, such sums of monies provided by Parliament, as Parliament may, from time to time, decide".

The actual powers with which the Administrative Council was to be vested, were set out in Clause 3 (The Power to Make Laws) and Clause 4 (Transfer of Functions of Certain Western Regional Authorities). Under Clause 3, though subject to restraints set out in Clause 2 (Continuance of Existing Laws) and Clause 5 (Continuance of Powers of Local Authorities, etc.), it was specified that the Administrative Council

> "...may, by order published in the Gazette of the Federation, make Laws for the peace, order and good government of the Region; and power to make laws conferred by this section shall extend to any matter whether or not the matter is included in the Legislative Lists within the meaning of the Constitution of the Federation".[5]

After passage of this *Mid-West (Transitional Provisions) Bill*, and, on the next day (8 August), the *Constitution of Western Nigeria (Amendment) Bill*, signifying "its consent to the Constitution of Western Nigeria (Second Amendment) Law, 1963, having effect",[6] the Federal Parliament had completed its legal tasks for setting the Interim Administration into operation. On 12 August, Governor-General Azikiwe completed the final act in the Federal Government's undertaking when he announced the names of those who had been appointed to the Administrative Council (See **Table VIII** below. p.309). A quick perusal of the list served to confirm that Osadebay—appointed Administrator—had fulfilled his promise to the Prime Minister.

The Council was admirably balanced, in terms of political parties and ethnic groups. The NCNC enjoyed no majority advantage: eight members of the Council were NCNC'ers, and eight owed allegiance to Mid-West Minority parties (See **Table VIII (a)** below, p.311). Nor was there any indication that the Movement Leader had been less resolute in his commitment to "ethnic equity". A Divisional breakdown of the Interim Council showed that all major Mid-West ethnic elements had been given representation (See **Table VIII (b)** below, p311).

TABLE VIII

MID-WEST ADMINISTRATIVE COUNCIL

***APPOINTEES TO THE MID-WEST "INTERIM ADMINISTRATION"
BY THE FEDERAL GOVERNMENT***

ADMINISTRATOR: D.C. Osadebay.
Depy-Administrator, Local Government: Chief H.Omo-Osagie.
Depy-Administrator, Chieftaincy Affairs: Chief S.J. Mariere.
Depy-Administrator, Finance and Economic Development: James Otobo.

COMMISSIONERS

Rev. Edeki, *Commissioner for Health*
Dr. Christopher ("Xto") Okojie, *Commissioner for Works & Transport*
Webber Egbe, *Commissioner for Justice*
Chief Oputa-Otutu, *Commissioner for Education*
F.H. Utomi, *Commissioner for Information*
N. Ezonbodor, *Commissioner for Lands and Housing*
B.I.G. Ewah, *Commissioner for Internal Affairs*
Apostle John Edokpolor, *Commissioner for Trade and Industry*
Mr. K. S. Y. Momoh, *Commissioner for Agriculture & Natural Resources*
Chief J.D. Ojobolo, *Commissioner for Labour and Social Welfare*
Albert Okojie, *Commissioner without Portfolio*
J. O. Oye, *Commissioner without Portfolio*

Osadebay stressed that in designing the provisional appointments list, scrupulous care had been taken to ensure "First, that each Division had one seat at least; then that each political party in a Division"[8] had one seat. It was for the latter reason, he maintained, that Ishan, with a smaller population than Benin, had three members in the Council: "In Ishan Division there were three strong personalities, each leading a political party in the Division".[9] Furthermore, his home Division of Asaba was represented only by Utomi—"As Administrator, I did not represent any Division"—and that the Mid-West heartland of Benin Division was represented only by Omo-Osagie and Apostle Edokpolor. Finally, Osadebay pointed out that the appointment of Otobo and Oye to posts in the Interim Council was largely to show that citizens of Isoko and Akoko-Edo were to be recognised, as promised, separately and in their own right; that these appointments might serve as a tangible indication of Movement/NCNC intentions to create separate Isoko and Akoko-Edo Divisions at the earliest available opportunity.

Administrator Osadebay, his Deputies and Commissioners flew from Lagos to arrive at Benin City on 17 August. At Benin, Mid-Westerners had turned out in strength to welcome them.[10] At a mass rally Osadebay wasted little time in setting out the Interim Council's programme. In announcing what he termed "his Government's Blueprint for Development", Osadebay declared that the priorities were clearly set. These included, "good roads, good water supply, a sound educational system and industrialisation to provide jobs for the unemployed".[11] He stated that there would be "such establishments as a Tourist Corporation, Road Development Corporation and Sports Commission". The Primary education system, he declared, "would be overhauled and improved to ensure a solid educational foundation".[12] He stated that prospects for industrial development were promising, with "a number of overseas industrialists... anxious to set up new industries in the Region.[13]

Osadebay went on to assure Natural Rulers they had nothing to fear in his administration. "We have not come to destroy", he declared "We have come to build, ...to secure, to protect and maintain the sacred institution of chieftaincy".[14] He stated also that "arrangements were well in hand" for setting up a Mid-West Advisory Council where Mid-Westerners who had ceased to be Members of the House of Chiefs and House of Assembly" at Ibadan would be absorbed. This he felt would enable former Members of the West Regional Legislature "to receive their salaries to which they were hitherto entitled" as Legislators at Ibadan.[15]

Administrator Osadebay now sought to convey to Mid-Westerners the magnitude of the task facing them all. Stressing first the challenge of establishing the roots of an effective administration, he observed that:

"I am awe-stricken when I contemplate the enormous task which I and my colleagues are called upon to do. We are called upon to set up a Government where there is no Government, and to establish a Civil Service and other organs of modern administration where there are none. There are no public buildings for the headquarters of the new administration and no quarters for the staff. We are not taking over from anyone on the spot. In short we are sent to a thick forest with the instructions to produce a plantation. We do not know what money we have. We do not know what tools we have and we do not know whether we will have to use a hoe or a tractor. The odds facing us are great".[16]

Nor did Osadebay shy away from giving equal emphasis to the perennial and divisive dangers of ethnic rivalry.

"We know that we have been chosen to cater for the happiness and well-being of the two million people in the Mid-West. Their interest is paramount. Diverse tongues, clans and ethnic groups live in the Mid-West. We who have been chosen to rule have a sacred duty to be fair and just and turn away from prejudice and partial affection. We are called upon to love and serve the common man, whatever his tribe or clan. ...I will not flinch from this duty and I know that I can count on the support of any colleague".[17]

The very large question mark which remained was obvious

TABLE VIII (a)

MID-WEST ADMINISTRATIVE COUNCIL: COMPOSITION BY POLITICAL PARTY

NCNC (8 Appointees) —	Osadebay, Omo-Osagie, Okojie, Oputa-Otutu, Utomi, Ezonbodor, Egbe, Mariere.
UPP (4 Appointees) —	Otobo, Edeki, Ewah, Ojobolo
MPC (2 Appointees) —	Apostle Edokpolor, Albert Okojie

TABLE VIII(b)

MID-WEST ADMINISTRATIVE COUNCIL: COMPOSITION BY ETHNIC GROUP

Benin Division, Omo-Osagie, Edokpolor.
Urhobo Division[7] Mariere, Otobo.
Asaba Division, Utomi.
Ishan Division, Xto Okojie, Ewah, Albert Okojie.
Afenmai Division, Edeki, Momoh, Oye.
Aboh Division, Oputa-Otutu.
Western Ijaw Division, Ezonbodor, Ujobolo.
Warri Division, Egbe.

enough: would this declaration of "Administrative intent" by Leader Osadebay, and the finely balanced government structure which he had painstakingly shaped, suffice to see Mid-Westerners through this precarious Interim period? Would the general esteem in which Leader Osadebay was held at local and national level prove adequate to ensure successful completion of the Interim Administration's term of office? This "probation period" clearly would be no mere formality; no "virtual prelude to NCNC rule" in the Mid-West, as the party's detractors were not slow to point out.

The enormity of the administrative undertaking with which the Interim Government was faced was soon recognised. Physical facilities, as Leader Osadebay had already noted, were practically non-existent. Most Commissioners had to "make do" with rented private accommodation which doubled as office space. Even the Administrator, it was pointed out, had no office of his own.[18] All the new ministries were badly handicapped also by an absence of relevant files, documents and other requisite reference materials.

The gravity of the situation was exacerbated by the sudden decision of the Akintola Government to implement a series of "Mass Transfer" orders, whereby Civil Servants and other West Regional Government employees of Mid-West origin were instructed to return to the Mid-West. Under these "Mass Transfers" which commenced in earnest during the fourth week of July, 1963, Mid-Westerners were informed, often on less than 24 hours' notice, that their employment under the West Regional Authority was at an end, and that they should return to the Mid-West to assist in the administration of the new Region.[19]

By mid-August, Osadebay and his Administration were faced with an inundation of over 600 Mid-Westerners formerly on the payroll of the Akintola Government. These numbers grew to include not only Civil Servants and staff formerly employed in Ibadan departments and field offices, but also those who held positions in the West Regional Authority's Statutory Corporations and Boards. Teachers of Mid-West origins were also affected, and, of course, the Mid-West's 60-odd legislators were no longer on the Ibadan payroll following Federal confirmation of the West Regional Government's Bill providing for disqualification of Mid-West legislators from both the West's House of Chiefs and House of Assembly.

A Delicate Ethno-Political Balance

Despite considerable pressures the Interim Council, by mid September, was at least showing itself equal to the vital task of containing any outbreak of overt hostilities between Leader Osadebay and Omo-Osagie and their respective rival factions. Relations between these two Mid-West NCNC factions, as we have seen throughout this study, had never been cordial. In the current situation, there were rumours that Omo-Osagie once again was feeling displeased; that he was far from satisfied with his position and that of the Edo ethnic element within the ruling Interim Council.[20]

Still, if there was any truth to these rumours, the important thing was that Omo-Osagie refrained from voicing his grievances publicly, and hence did not threaten the formal unity and rather tenuous stability of the Council. Although there is good reason to believe that there was a more compelling reason for Omo-Osagie being amenable to "keeping the peace" during this initial period,[21] still, the Interim Council was proving itself capable of containing these dominant rival elements and of serving as an avenue for attempting some reconciliation of their respective and closely guarded interests.

Ethnic and Political Equity   The "equity formula" which had been employed by Leader Osadebay in setting up his Interim Council, seemed to be serving its purpose. The formal unity of varied ethnic and political elements which it secured was now to some extent being transformed into operational unity, even in respect to the powerful Bini and Western Ibo rival factions. However, this was not to say that the composition of the Council met with universal approval. On 14 August, only two days after appointments to the Council had been announced, the Action Group Leader in the West, Alhaji Adegbenro declared that the Osadebay "equity formula" had fallen far short of providing just representation for his party's following in the Mid-West.

Laying the blame at the door of the NPC and the Federal Government rather than on Osadebay, he alleged that Action Group representation in the Council had suffered; party representatives (Oye and Momoh) occupied only two of the 16 posts in the Interim Government, because the NPC was doing "all it could to bolster its UPP allies in the West" together with "its MPC satellite in the Mid-West".[22] Although these two parties were, he said, virtually unknown to the electorate of the Mid-West, each had been allocated two seats in the Administrative Council. This unjust allocation, which, he maintained, was obviously undertaken to discriminate against the Action Group, made it "patently clear that the NPC is now... [seeking] to extend its influence to areas where it has not as a party made efforts to manoeuvre itself into the hearts of the people".[23]

Leader Osadebay's espoused principle of "ethnic equity" also came in for a certain amount of criticism. J.M. Agindotan, an active Mid-West crusader in earlier years, put the case of disgruntled majority group elements. In a Press statement released at Benin, Agindotan urged Leader Osadebay to recall

> "...the principles and understanding on which the creation of the Mid-West Region... was fought for and won: 'That it shall be a welfare state where no Division or tribe shall dominate the other irrespective of size or population' ".[24]

Agindotan declared that he did not think the correct interpretation of these principles was that "the minority group should now hold the majority group to ransom where such majority group has no champion".[25] Yet, he asserted, "this is exactly what I think is happening now when one takes a look at the appointment of the people to run the Interim Government of the new Region".

In getting down to cases, Agindotan asked why it was that the less populous Divisions of Ishan and Afenmai should have three Commissioners each "whereas Urhobo and Benin, the two largest Divisions, have less"? This, he alleged, could be viewed as part of a plan intentionally designed to "reward carpet-crossers" while meting out punishment to "loyal and steadfast' Movement NCNC supporters. Referring specifically to the Western Urhobo area, "the largest parliamentary constituency in the Mid-West, and including Sapele, the largest cosmopolitan township [in terms of ethnic mix] in the new Region"—and an area where a head-on collision between NPC and NCNC National parties contesting a Federal by-election was soon to create immense and critical problems for Osadebay and his Administration—Agindotan declared that it was quite unacceptable that this area should have been left without representation in Osadebay's Interim Council.

In apparent response to Mid-West majority group critics and to Agindotan's pointed reference to Urhobo West, Leader Osadebay proceeded to make one minor but important modification to his Council. On 27 August, he announced the appointment of Chief P.K. Tabiowo, formerly Minister of Mid-West Affairs in the

Akintola Government, to the post of Commissioner for Establishment.[26] The appointment of Tabiowo served not only to meet, at least partially, the criticisms of Urhobo and majority group leaders, but in addition, with the inclusion of Tabiowo—a Movement/NCNC leader—the NCNC as a party was now in majority control (9 : 8) of the Interim Council, an advantage which might well prove its worth in the future. On the completion of this modification, overt criticisms by party and ethnic elements subsided.

By the end of September 1963, it seemed that Osadebay and his Commissioners were making a passably successful effort to cope. As for the Interim Council itself, it appeared that the intricate ethnic and political "equity formula" had created a Council which was showing itself capable of bearing the strain exerted by the Mid-West's complex of indigenous elements. Having reached this position, however, certain new and threatening developments quite suddenly started to emerge during the month of October, developments which were to challenge sharply the leadership of Osadebay and indeed bring his Interim Government to the very brink of breakdown.

"Interim" Unity Threat: Urhobo-West By-Election   These ominous developments for Mid-West protagonists stemmed mainly from the decision of the Federal Government to conduct a by-election in the Federal constituency of Western Urhobo. This by-election set for 12 October, had been called to fill the seat vacated by the Movement/NCNC incumbent Chief Oweh who recently had been appointed as Nigeria's Ambassador to Guinea.

On the face of it, this by-election appeared to raise little in the way of serious problems. Certainly the constituency of Western Urhobo had always been a contentious one. Traditionally there existed sharp rivalry; but this was not so much between competing parties, as between rival factions within the NCNC. At past Regional and Federal elections, bitter in-fighting over who was to be selected as the NCNC candidate had taken place between the one main local faction, led by Messrs. Rerri, Okumagba and Akpore, and the other dominated by supporters of Chief Okotie-Eboh.

With the exception of the 1960 Regional elections, it had on every other occasion been the Okotie-Eboh (NCNC-Festus) faction which had succeeded in securing the nomination for the candidate its leaders had put forward. Although on each occasion Rerri and his NCNC-Pure[27] colleagues vented their bitterness against Chief

Festus and the personal influence which, they alleged, he had brought to bear in order to secure the nomination for his chosen candidate,[28] factional differences had eventually been patched over. As a result NCNC candidates had consistently been returned. Indeed, the NCNC had come to regard Western Urhobo as a "safe" seat for the party.[29]

In the current by-election, these customary divisions were once again revealed over the issue of which faction's candidate should be given the party nomination. Rerri and his NCNC-Pure colleagues maintained that A.E.K. Ukeuku had been nominated by the Executive Committee of the Western Urhobo NCNC, a body under the control of Rerri and his NCNC-Pure colleagues, to stand as the party's candidate. They were, however, resisted in their efforts by the NCNC-Festus faction. This rival group maintained that its candidate, Sunday J. Odjie, was the legitimate nominee. The NCNC-Festus faction stated that the nomination had in fact been "reserved" for Odjie.

It was pointed out that at each of the past two general elections—the 1959 Federal and 1960 West Regional—there had been a "line-up" of candidates for the nomination.[30] In 1959, Rerri the Western Urhobo Executive Committee's choice, had been persuaded to step down in favour of the incumbent Chief Oweh, on the understanding that he would be "first in line" for the party nomination at the next general election. In keeping with this promise, Rerri eight months later received the party nomination as Western Urhobo candidate at the 1960 West Regional elections. In this election, it was Odjie who had contested the nomination, and like Rerri in 1959, it was held that Odjie had been "persuaded to wait his turn". Thus, the NCNC-Festus argument went, Odjie, in keeping with the promise given him in 1960, had established "prior right" to the nomination and hence deserved selection as the Western Urhobo NCNC candidate.

The dispute between the rival factions became heated, and in due course was referred to higher party authorities. Finally, after a party Inquiry held under the "impartial" auspices of the East Regional Branch of the party, and subsequent deliberations by the NCNC/CWC at Lagos and the Mid-West/WC at Benin, Odjie's claim to the Western Urhobo NCNC nomination was confirmed. It was at this point, however, that the custom established in the course of past nominations contests broke down. Rerri and his NCNC-Pure colleagues made it clear that they were not prepared to accept the nomination of Odjie, and as an act of protest against the "Almighty

Alhaji Warri",[31] they announced they would back their candidate Ukueku to run under the opposition banner of the MPC. This was the first serious indication that the NCNC could be running into grave trouble in Western Urhobo.

Mid-West NCNC anxieties were further heightened by the announcement on 5 October, just one week before the by-election, that the Mid-West minority parties, MPC, UPP and Action Group, had agreed to join forces in a new merger party entitled the Mid-West Democratic Front (MDF).[32] "With the formation of the MDF", it was declared, "the three [Minority] parties in the Mid-West no longer exist". Alarm in the Mid-West NCNC camp spread when soon after this announcement it was learned that the MDF had been formed with the blessing and support of the Sardauna of Sokoto, and that an NPC Federal Minister had been dispatched to the Mid-West to supervise the MDF campaign in Western Urhobo.[33]

By the time the by-election was due to be held, it had become apparent that an NCNC victory was by no means assured. Furthermore, it had become equally clear that the by-election was no longer a "local Mid-West affair", but rather was an event which suddenly and dramatically had taken on national significance. During the past year, the NPC had been moving progressively further away from its NCNC partner in the Federal government. Following the demise of the Action Group, relations between Akintola and the UPP, and the Sardauna and the NPC had grown increasingly cordial. The NCNC National party had become increasingly uneasy about these developments. This anxiety had increased sharply when on 2 July 1963, the NCNC in the West went into alliance with the UPP and the rump of the Action Group.

The NCNC Central Working Committee was quick to denounce the pact, but this denunciation had little impact. While in a joint UPP/NCNC statement it was announced that the Action Group would be dropped from the alliance, it was made clear that the NCNC would stay. Thus, so far as the NCNC National party leadership was concerned, this action in the West was but another indication of the NPC's covert attempts to undercut the NCNC National party position, this time by using Chief Akintola, the Sardauna's new ally at Ibadan, to emasculate by absorption, the NCNC's Western branch party.[34]

In the context of these ongoing developments, the Urhobo West by-election had been transformed into what was now regarded as a preliminary test of strength between Nigeria's two dominant political parties, the NCNC and the NPC—the Federal elections of 1964 were fast approaching. If the NCNC could retain the seat, perhaps with an impressive majority, then it could claim that the NPC had no place in Southern politics. On the other hand, if the MDF candidate should win, then the NPC would have established impressive grounds for pressing on hard with its "Operation South".[35]

The result of the by-election was received with disbelief and amazement by all parties throughout the Federation. Ukueku, the MDF candidate, emerged as victor. He polled a total 16,559 votes as against the 14,667 cast for his NCNC rival Odjie[35], a narrow majority of 1,892 which, following a recount, was trimmed to only 702 votes. Still, Ukueku had won. Hearty congratulations were forthcoming from the Sardauna at Kaduna, and in the MDF camp there was jubilation.

Urhobo West—Grave Implications   The immediate reaction of NCNC leaders was one of shock and anger.[37]A new political party (the MDF) which had been in existence for only one week—albeit with NPC logistical support—had wrested the hitherto "safe" Western Urhobo seat from the grasp of the NCNC!

In an initial effort to find a scapegoat for this "humiliating turn of events", NCNC National leaders lost little time in placing the blame for the party's failure at the door of "Almighty Alhaji Warri", Chief Festus. In a *Pilot* editorial, it was declared that the NPC should "give credit where credit is due", and that accordingly they owed "thanks for their success [in Western Urhobo] to the blundering leadership of 'Alhaji Festus Warri,' who has made himself so powerful he can hold the party to ransom".[38] The NCNC, the editorial went on, "knew it was in trouble" in Western Urhobo, and by the time election day had arrived, "the only issue in doubt was whether the MDF would win by a land-slide or by a hair's breadth".

As for the behaviour of the embittered NCNC-Pure loyalists Rerri and Okumagba, the *Pilot* appeared to be in full sympathy with their decision to withhold the support of their backers from Chief Festus' candidate, Odjie—"Rerri and Okumagba had made it clear they were out to spite Alhaji Warri, if only to clip his absolute dominance in party affairs". What had happened in Western Urhobo, the editorial maintained, was simply "a repeat of the 1956 blunder when the NCNC lost two [Warri Division] seats [at the Regional Elections], because one man, Chief Festus must have his way". The NCNC, it was asserted, "could not have been shamed in its own bastion, were the Urhobo branch of the party given a free hand to select a popular candidate."

However, not content to vent its grievances at Chief Festus alone, the *Pilot* editorial chose this moment to extend its assault and to launch an equally bitter attack against the "arbitrary influence" of the NCNC-Festus faction in the Mid-West in general. Because of "bad generalship", it was alleged that the NCNC had lost Western Urhobo; but this, it was felt might well be simply the tip of the iceberg, the beginning of the end for the party in the Mid-West:

> "The same story will be repeated in many other constituencies, and particularly in the Edo area, unless the party takes action now to end the absolute rule of its all-powerful field commanders. Chief H. Omo-Osagie is in the same class as Alhaji Warri. The NCNC as a party has no say in the areas over which it holds sway. The party is being blackmailed to swing to the wishes of these two men who are by no means indispensable. If they are not curbed now, the future is loaded with disaster"![39]

Such blanket condemnations could have only a negative effect on Leader Osadebay and his valiant efforts to retain the exceedingly precarious balance not only between NCNC and Mid-West opposition party elements, but also between the rival NCNC-Pure and NCNC-Otu Edo factions in his Interim Council. The party's NCNC-Pure National leaders now proceeded to step up its bitter attack on Chief Festus and his faction. On 19 October, it was reported that NCNC-Pure elements in Benin Division had charged that the loss of the NCNC in Urhobo West had not only been the result of "certain Machiavellian manoeuvres" by Chief Festus in collusion with his *Otu Edo* colleague Omo-Osagie, but that in fact the MDF was now "reserving leadership posts" for Chiefs Festus and Omo-Osagie.[40]

Following this theme, F.U. Anyiam, the NCNC National Publicity Secretary, declared that the defeat which the NCNC had suffered in Western Urhobo was the product of a "carefully calculated design, and the beginning of a long chain of treachery to ruin the NCNC as a political force not only in the Mid-West" but within the Federation as a whole. Expanding on these very thinly veiled allegations against Chiefs Festus, Osagie and their NCNC-Festus colleagues, Anyiam declared,

> "When we pointed out the danger of some NCNC leaders having membership cards of two parties, and warned that this practice

could be dangerous..., our warning was not heeded... by the party. Now the truth of our prophecy has been driven home.... Western Urhobo is just the start of a plan which has been systematically hatched with the set purpose of exterminating the NCNC as a force, and drawing what remains of the party into Opposition in the Federal Parliament. ...This is no secret, because some leaders of certain political parties are alleged to be boasting that the days of the NCNC in the Federal Coalition Government are numbered".[42]

Finally, in an attempt to bring pressure on Chief Festus and his colleagues from rather different quarters, Anyiam, in an article entitled "If I were the Prime Minister of Nigeria", maintained that as he saw it, there were

> "One or two members of Balewa's Cabinet who seem to feel that they are greater than Nigeria itself. ...They know everything under the sun, and the interest of the Republic is a secondary matter to them.
> If I were the Prime Minister, I would not hesitate to remove any minister who thinks he can with impunity insult the nation. After all, it does not need any degree holder to be a Minister of State, like Okotie-Eboh. The destiny of Nigeria should not be trifled with and any Minister who thinks he is too big for Nigeria is better advised to return to his former trade".[43]

This bitter and prolonged assault made by Anyiam in conjunction with his NCNC-Pure colleagues in the National leadership of the party, left little doubt about the suspicion and hostility with which Chief Festus and his own band of NCNC loyalists were regarded by the more orthodox party elements. It could be said that Anyiam had done a service to the party by bringing out into the open long-simmering grievances against the Federal Finance Minister. Still, in speaking the "truth" in this forthright fashion, Anyiam had done no favours to Leader Osadebay and his Interim Council.

With the formation of the MDF, Osadebay's "equity formula" had suffered one serious set-back; but now Anyiam's "truthful" allegations had dealt the Interim Council a second and far more grievous blow. To a very large extent, the survival of Osadebay's Administrative Council through the Interim Period depended on the co-operation —if not mutual trust—of the NCNC-Pure and NCNC-Otu Edo factions. Through his vehement assaults, however, Anyiam had driven a sizeable wedge between these rival Mid-West NCNC elements. Within Benin Division itself, the leader of the Benin NCNC-Pure-Otu Edo faction, G.I. Oviasu had taken full advantage of the assaults made by NCNC-Pure National leaders to attempt to foment direct agitation against Omo-Osagie both within the NCNC-Otu-Edo party and within the broader context of the Mid-West NCNC.[44] As a result of this ill-timed and ill-advised assault on Chiefs Festus and Omo-Osagie, the survival of Leader Osadebay and his Interim Government was now in serious jeopardy.

CRISIS AND BRINKMANSHIP IN THE MID-WEST

From this point on, Leader Osadebay's Interim Government operated in an aura of suspicion and heightened mistrust. Its stability became so tenuous that its continued existence was in doubt. The MDF leaders, with the Western Urhobo electoral triumph to their credit and the backing of their powerful NPC ally, were brimming with confidence, and behaved in an increasingly obstructive manner. As for Omo-Osagie and his NCNC/*Otu Edo* leaders, they were, from this point on, clearly on their guard against any actions which might strengthen the position of Osadebay and his NCNC-Pure colleagues. In essence, the remaining period of Provisional Rule in the Mid-West turned into a grim battle for survival.

Constitutional Traumas   The troubles of the besieged Administrator Osadebay finally reached crisis proportions in mid-December over matters arising from the Delimitation of Constituencies for the prospective Mid-West Regional Elections. Early in November, an "Instrument proposing a constitution for the Mid-West"—and which had been agreed upon by the Interim Council—had been forwarded to the Federal Attorney-General, Dr. T.O. Elias, at Lagos.[45] However, by mid-December this consensus on the proposed constitution appeared to evaporate over the issues raised by the demarcating of new constituencies,[46] minorities safeguards and the allocation of seats by Administrative Division. The precise details of this squabble amongst the Interim Council's members are not known to the writer, but it is the contention of Leader Osadebay that, "But for [the intervention] of the Prime Minister on this occasion, the Cabinet would have broken up". [47]

According to Osadebay's account of the crisis, when the political parties in the Mid-West failed to arrive at any agreement on the issues in dispute, the whole Interim Cabinet flew to Lagos to submit their dispute to the Prime Minister in person. The MDF leaders, apparently confident that they would receive the backing of the NPC leader, now their formal ally, pushed their arguments with arrogant forcefulness. They were, however, both annoyed and astonished when they found their tactics gained no support from the Prime Minister who in the end, it was said, told Osadebay and his colleagues "to go somewhere" and resolve their differences if they wanted to retain their new Region.[48] The efforts made by Osadebay to secure a satisfactory settlement were, however, to no avail.

> "When the time given to us was up, I and my NCNC colleagues went to see Sir Abubakar and he informed us that our other [MDF] colleagues had left for the Mid-West saying that there could be no agreement reached between them and us".[49]

At this impasse, Osadebay states that the Prime Minister came to his aid:

> "Sir Abubakar, after listening to me, acted like the great man he was. He decided to support the contention of the NCNC and we went back to Benin City. Our [MDF] colleagues were disappointed. They had expected Sir Abubakar to support them, right or wrong. But Sir Abubakar did not".[50]

With Leader Osadebay thus struggling to retain some semblance of order with both the Mid-West NCNC and the Interim Government, while at the same time holding the obstructive MDF leaders at bay, preparations for the still unconfirmed inaugural Mid-West Regional elections were going forward apace. These preparations hardly eased the immense strain under which the Interim Government was already operating. Once again, as in the Urhobo West by-election, both the NCNC and NPC National parties pursued their respective interests with relentless force; they seemed quite oblivious to the devastating political repercussions which their active involvement in the Mid-West was bound to produce.

Party Mergers and Political Conflict   On 30 November, it was announced that the NCNC National party had decided to go into alliance with Acting-Leader Adegbenro and his National Action Group party remnant.[51] The immediate impact of this announcement was to throw the Mid-West NCNC back into renewed turmoil and bitter intra-party antagonism. Chief Festus and his NCNC-Festus/NCNC-Otu-Edo colleagues were furious. The "regular organs of the party", they maintained, had not been informed of the "arrangements being made for the alliance";[52] this decision on a party merger, they bitterly complained, had been made solely by NCNC-Pure elements, including Osadebay, in the National leadership. Chief Festus thus dismissed the NCNC/Action Group merger plan as "a marriage of convenience". His NCNC-Pure rivals, however, maintained that the proposed alliance was "absolutely necessary and has to be accomplished in the interests of the people in the Mid-West and the greater interests of the 'progressive' elements in the nation".[53]

To this profoundly unsettling development in Mid-West NCNC politics, another of equal gravity was added when, on the very day that the NCNC/Action Group proposed merger was announced, it was reported that the UPP, going behind the back of its MDF allies, had entered into a pact with the Mid-West NCNC at the beginning of November. At the time that this pact had initially been made, the participant parties had agreed that their alliance should be kept secret at least until 30 November, 1963.[54] This "secret", however, was now out. And while this new revelation caused considerable embarrassment to the NCNC National party,[55] still in the context of Mid-West NCNC-Pure manoeuvrings, the aims of the NCNC-Pure Leader Osadebay were all too obvious.

For some time, Osadebay had been expressing interest in creating a single party in place of the existing plethora of "splinter parties" and political factions in the Mid-West;[56] he felt that this would greatly facilitate the creation of stable Government in the Region. Clearly, an alliance which would effectively bring the Action Group and UPP elements into alliance with the NCNC in the Mid-West would take Osadebay a very considerable distance towards his objective. At the same time, it would weaken the NCNC-Festus/NCNC-Otu Edo factions within the Mid-West NCNC. Rumours now started to circulate that Chiefs Okotie-Eboh and Omo-Osagie were once again giving serious consideration to forming a Mid-West Political Party, a party in alliance with "Alhaji Warri's" NPC affiliate.[57]

While these undertakings by NCNC-Pure elements in the National, Mid-West and West branches of the party once again enhanced the conditions of political brinkmanship in the Mid-West, the NPC also was making its presence felt. On 24 November, MDF leaders had met with the Sardauna at Kaduna. At this meeting they had "signed an agreement to work together" as the official Mid-West ally of the NPC at the forthcoming inaugural Mid-West Regional elections.[58] Apparently spurred by the success of the MDF in Western Urhobo, the NPC now opted to extend its efforts in the

Mid-West area. Alhaji Ahman Galadiman Pategi, General Secretary of the NPC was assigned the task of organising the MDF campaign. He was assisted by a sizeable contingent of NPC party organisers imported for the occasion, a fleet of NPC vans and cars, along with considerable funds made available to him for purposes of advertising the MDF position[59] and, presumably, for inducing support by more customary methods.

THE FINAL LAP

Under these precarious circumstances, the Mid-West approached its final "day of judgement" when the Federal Authorities would pronounce their decision on Osadebay's Interim Government, and hence whether the anticipated February 1964 inaugural Mid-West Regional elections would be held. Viewed from any relatively objective viewpoint, it seemed that the prospects of the Mid-West actually "passing" its probation, were slim indeed.

In the course of the Interim Period, domestic politics in the Mid-West area had reverted to conditions of sharp rivalry between and amongst traditional factions now operating in some instances behind new covers. These enormous stresses had been exacerbated by the direct involvement and callous meddling of Nigeria's National parties—most notably the NPC and the NCNC—in the politics of the infant Region. As for the Administrative Programme of the new Region, there was little to indicate that anything more than modest beginnings had so far been achieved.

Despite these decidedly gloomy prospects, however, Mid-West protagonists during the first week of January 1964, heard the news they had so long awaited: *the Mid-West Interim Administration had "passed" its probation*; inaugural Mid-West Regional Elections would take place *before* 8 February, 1964, the date on which the six-month tenure of the Interim Administration was scheduled to come to an end.[60]

Certainly, in general terms, it could not be disputed that Movement leaders and their supporters as a result of their efforts over the past 15 years had not earned the right to a Self-Governing Mid-West Region. It could only be said, however, that their success in passing the Interim probation had rested as much on the respect with which Leader Osadebay was regarded by the Prime Minister, as on the efforts of Mid-West protagonists themselves. Mid-Westerners once again could be thankful that they had two such respected and influential leaders as Leader Osadebay and Chief Okotie-Eboh at Lagos.

With the final half of the "Battle for the Mid-West" now won, it remained only to be decided at the Regional Elections, set for 3 February, which party and which political personalities would form the Government of the new Region. Although it was difficult to believe that the NCNC under Leader Osadebay as Premier could actually, at this stage, have the fruits of office snatched from them, there were obstacles to be overcome. The Mid-West NCNC, as we have seen, was by no means united; indeed it seemed that a break-away by the NCNC-festus/NCNC-Otu Edo faction could not even at this late date be entirely ruled out. As for the MDF, though its actual strength and unity were in doubt following the hiving off of many of its Action Group and UPP supporters during the political shuffles and re-shuffles of December 1963, nevertheless, it had retained the active support of the NPC and hence its challenge could not be ignored.

The Action Group Acting-Leader Adegbenro also announced that the Western party would be taking a full part in the election. He declared that Action Group candidates would stand in all 65 Mid-West constituencies and that the party "expects to win at least 45 seats".[61] It was, therefore, apparent that if the NCNC hoped to secure the victory which Osadebay and his colleagues clearly felt they deserved, they would have to work for it. Indeed, as a *West Africa* "correspondent" reviewing Mid-West electoral preliminaries put it: "For the first time for some time in an African election, the result is genuinely in doubt".[62]

Campaign Pledges and Problems   The campaigns which the various parties now set into motion were short but intense. The MDF, playing on the support it had from the NPC, advanced a comprehensive electoral assault throughout the Mid-West. Drawing on the elevated views of political participation which its Northern patron was currently espousing, it was said that the MDF, while prosecuting the campaign with vigour, was not prepared to lower itself to "vitriolics and vulgarism".[63] MDF leaders concentrated their efforts in the Urhobo areas where the NCNC had experienced its recent grave problems, and also in Ishan.

In Urhobo Division, the MDF, behind the leadership of the ex-NCNC'er, Chief T.A. Salubi, launched what was rather aptly titled, "Operation NO NCNC". By the use of this tactic, the MDF hoped to exploit current antipathies between Urhobos and the NCNC. In Ishan, having secured the consent of Chief Okotako Enahoro the erstwhile B Grade Customary Court President in

Ishan and father of Chief Tony Enahoro, to stand as MDF candidate, the party in its campaign sought to trade on the "magic" of the Enahoro name. Although problems arose, as the Action Group was also making full play on the Enahoro name, the MDF maintained staunchly that it spoke for both father and son, and that it was "not aware there is any political divergence between Chief Tony Enahoro and his father".[64]

The Action Group continued to express confidence in its prospects. It was reported to have fielded a 100-man campaign team, which played on its social-democratic ideology and against what it maintained was the malevolent influence of NPC "feudalism" and the NCNC's "tribal fascists". There were few material indications, however, that the party's quest for votes was really as comprehensive or intense as its leaders sought to convey. Of all the competing parties, it seemed to be only the NCNC which was establishing a campaign performance which measured up to its campaign propaganda.

As at the time of the July Referendum Campaign, the NCNC National and Eastern Branches of the party made ample resources of personnel and finance available to their Mid-West compatriots. Leader Osadebay, Chief Festus, Chief Omo-Osagie, were joined by the NCNC President Okpara, Dr. Mbadiwe, Chief T.O.S. Benson and other prominent NCNC personalities with their sizeable entourages. The tours which they conducted ensured a full and penetrating coverage of all Mid-West districts. In acknowledgement of the comprehensive and relentless nature of the NCNC's undertaking, the party's Mid-West campaign was nick-named "Operation Caterpillar"—like the Caterpillar tractor, "taking all before it".

De-limitation and Electoral Fears   Though the NCNC conducted the most aggressive campaign, perhaps the clearest indication of its lurking fears was revealed by the reservations expressed by some of its NCNC-Pure leaders over certain provisions bearing directly on the elections. When the provisions of the Mid-West Constitution had been debated in the Federal House on 8 January, 1964, Mid-West NCNC Members had hotly contested two main points.[65] The first related to the total number of seats to be allocated to the Mid-West House of Assembly. The original number agreed on in the proposed Mid-West Constitution had been 68.

The De-limitation Commission which had been appointed in December, 1963 by the Federal Government to delimit the Mid-

West Constituencies, recommended that the total should be lowered to 65; and this alteration apparently had taken place *without* consultation with Mid-West NCNC leaders. Hence when the Mid-West Constitution Bill was presented in the Federal House by the Prime Minister, it was 65 and not 68 seats that were proposed for the Mid-West House of Assembly. Mid-West NCNC Members complained loudly about the lack of consultation; furthermore they alleged that the "adjustment" to 65 had first been made by the Delimitation Commission and then confirmed by the Federal Government solely as a concession to MDF demands that the total number of seats in the House of Assembly should not exceed 62.[66] As a final insult to the Mid-West NCNC, it was declared that in carrying out the downward adjustment of seats, it had been from "safe" NCNC areas only, Aboh and Asaba, that the three seats had been excised.[67]

The second point which had raised the ire of Mid-West NCNC Federal Members, was the provision in the Mid-West Constitution that called for the creation of four "Special Areas". These "Special Areas" comprised the "minority ethnic areas" of Warri (Itsekiri), Western Ijaw (Ijaw), Akoko-Edo (Edo-speaking Yoruba) and Isoko. Each had been allocated proportionately more seats *per* head of population than the Mid-West's "non-Special Areas". Furthermore, the Mid-West Constitution (Bill) provided that candidates must come from each of the respective specified "Special Area" ethnic groups; this latter provision being included largely as a concession to the insistent demands of Chief Okotie-Eboh who, (with a sharp eye to his own best political interests) had taken it upon himself to ensure that Itsekiris might enjoy the greatest protection possible under the terms of the new Constitution.

Chief Opia, the Aboh M.P. and Ezekiel Mordi, the M.P. for Asaba, contended that these special "safeguards" written into the Constitution, in fact, meant that the minority elements were to be placed yet again in the rather extra-ordinary position of being able to "hold the majority elements to ransom". How, they demanded, did the Federal Authorities find a basis for justifying the allocation of four seats to Warri Division, with a population of only 54,000, while Aboh Division with more than twice the number of residents (126,000) was to be granted only four seats also?

While Warri Division provided the most obvious target for these angry complaints by Mid-West NCNC leaders, they pointed also to the inequity in relation to Isoko Division (70,000 and 4 seats), and Western Ijaw Division (80,000 and 4 seats). Aboh, a solid area of NCNC support, had, they felt been hard done by. Furthermore, they maintained that the adjustments which had been made to "protect" the Mid-West's ethnic minorities, in reality represented concessions to the MDF. In each of the "Special Areas", Warri, Isoko, Akoko-Edo, and Western Ijaw, it was pointed out that over-representation would operate in the favour of MDF and Action Group elements.

The *Mid-West Constitution (Bill)* was in due course, and after some difficulty, passed by the Federal House and two days later (10 January) by the Nigerian Senate. Mid-West NCNC Members, supported by a number of their colleagues, had made it clear that the controversial "safeguard" provisions put them and their party at a considerable dis-advantage to their political opponents in the four "Special Areas" of the Mid-West—a dis-advantage they were not prepared to accept without a fight. The NCNC in the Mid-West, they were obviously convinced, was by no means assured of a "safe" victory. They appeared to believe that every seat would count, and hence that the inequities which they felt existed in the minorities "safeguards" provisions should be corrected.

Certainly, it was through no lack of effort on their part that the amendments sought were not made. Indeed, looking for a scapegoat on whom to vent their grievances in relation to these "unsatisfactory provisions" the NCNC directed its hostility against Sir Kofo Abayomi, the Chairman of the Federal Electoral Commission, (the body which had been responsible for what NCNC'ers regarded as a most disappointing and discriminatory delimitation) denouncing him as the "disrespectful toying tool of the NPC".[68]

The other major issue arose when the party again came "up against the Electoral Commission, [and this time] over the question of electoral officers".[69] Following a series of sharp attacks by Leader Osadebay against the Commission Secretary Obeya, alleging that "he was departing from all known acceptable or tolerable conduct" in appointing his own electoral officers, the NCNC obtained a judgement from Mr. Justice Thomas in Benin, restraining the Commission from appointing electoral officers.[70] Finally after a number of urgent meetings at Lagos between NCNC Mid-West leaders and the Prime Minister, a compromise was reached whereby it was agreed that the Electoral Commission and the Mid-West Interim Administration should share the appointment of electoral officers to preside at the 3 February elections, on a 50-50 basis.

Violence and Rhetoric   In the final week preceding the elections, campaigning by competing parties assumed a familiar form. There were several violent outbreaks; most of these occurring in Urhobo and Ishan Divisions where the MDF was mounting its strongest challenge. The MDF Leader, Otobo, making allegations reminiscent of NCNC contentions in June-July of 1961, claimed that the new Region was "on the verge of civil disorder, ...and unprecedented rioting".[71] The NCNC, he claimed, was importing thugs from Eastern Nigeria; that these thugs were destroying and burning property belonging to MDF candidates and supporters "sometimes under the nose of the Nigeria police". In Ishan Chief Enahoro Sr., was narrowly missed by an assassin's bullet. At Ugboka (Benin Division), Agbor, and Isoko there were reports that MDF candidates and supporters had been harassed and assaulted by NCNC stalwarts.[72] Even the eminent O.N. Rewane, on his return journey to Warri after making an MDF election broadcast at Benin, had been attacked by "12 NCNC thugs" with matchets. He had only escaped by making a hurried exit into the nearby bush. A similar assault had been carried out against A.T. Rerri, now Urhobo Divisional Secretary for the MDF, and candidate for Urhobo West II constituency.

Counter-allegations by the Mid-West NCNC, however, suggested that these sporadic violent incidents were not totally one-sided. There were reports of MDF assaults on NCNC campaign teams in the Ughelli and Oleh areas of Urhobo Division.[73] Further, it was alleged that MDF thugs had precipitated clashes with rival NCNC'ers in a number of areas; and again, particularly within Ishan and Urhobo divisions.[74] Regarding MDF allegations of a "Law and Order Breakdown" in the Mid West, NCNC leaders dismissed these claims as being merely a crude device to get the election postponed, and a new MDF-dominant Interim Administration installed. With the MDF in control, the NCNC statement declared, the NPC would be invited in; and with their help, the new (MDF) Administrator and his colleagues would have the opportunity to "rig" elections after the Period of Emergency should be revoked. The NCNC statement concluded that supporters should be vigilant and ready "to meet any emergencies".[75]

It was, then, under what were reverting to normal Nigerian electoral conditions, that the Mid-West moved on to the eve of its 3 February inaugural election. On 1 February, 1,400 Nigeria Police were sent from Lagos to the Mid-West "for the purpose of keeping the peace".[76] Violent incidents, however, persisted; the MDF continuing to maintain that the area was on the verge of a "breakdown of Law and Order"; the NCNC dismissing these allegations and denouncing what they (the NCNC) regarded as the MDF's "evil ulterior motives".

With only a few days remaining before the election, both parties turned briefly from their campaigns of mutual harassment to substantive issues. On its part, the MDF repeated its promise that Tony Enahoro would be released and made Premier if the party was voted into office. The NCNC, in a 12-page manifesto released only 4 days before the election, promised *participation for Mid-Westerners in the Region's new* **oil wealth** *which was about to be realised*; and that Mid-Westerners would secure participation in and maximum benefit from the glass and textile industries which were to be established in the new Region.[77]

If there was one question that remained, it was that of whether the MDF, by its allegations and assertions, had managed successfully to undermine sufficient NCNC support in the Mid-West districts that prior NCNC dominance might at least be reduced to marginal proportions. It was an obvious risk to have openly-stated support from the NPC patron (to the MDF) party; yet NPC resources and their well-publicised denunciations of (Eastern) NCNC manoeuvrings in the Mid-West[78] could provide the margin of support needed to ensure a truly effective electoral challenge.

THE ELECTION RESULT:
A QUALIFIED MOVEMENT/NCNC TRIUMPH

MDF—A Formidable Challenge   When, finally, on 3 February, the election was held, the final result showed that the MDF had indeed mounted an impressive challenge, at least in terms of votes cast. The NCNC had little difficulty in securing an overwhelming overall victory, gaining 54 seats to the MDF's 11.[79] But on a total vote which ranged from a high of 86.7 per cent of registered voters in Aboh Division, to 54.3 per cent in Isoko, the MDF managed to secure a minimum of 40 per cent of votes cast in four divisions. These were: Afenmai, 41.4 per cent; Ishan, 40.7; Isoko 43.5; and Urhobo, 45.7.[80] Even in the NCNC-dominant

TABLE IX

RESULTS OF THE INAUGURAL 1964 MID-WEST REGIONAL ELECTIONS

Administrative Division	Total of Registered Electors	NCNC: % of Total Votes Cast		MDF: % of Total Votes Cast		AG: % of Total Votes Cast		Total Votes Cast: As % of Total Registered Electors		No. of Seats Won NCNC	No. of Seats Won MDF
ABOH	39,483	21,764	63.3	12,592	36.7	—	—	34,289	86.7		
AFENMAI	90,795	37,434	55.1	28,159	41.4	2,400	3.5	67,993	74.8	4	0
ASABA	74,445	37,039	71.7	14,618	28.3	—	—	51,657	69.3	8	2
BENIN	143,247	65,459	65.6	33,669	33.6	873	0.8	100,001	69.8	8	0
ISHAN	83,098	35,841	54.1	26,312	40.7	4,081	5.2	66,234	79.7	13	0
ISOKO	34,853	10,547	55.7	8,239	43.6	147	0.7	18,933	54.3	6	2
URHOBO*	125,374	27,988	51.6	24,818	45.8	1,419	2.6	54,225	43.3	3	1
WARRI[1]	39,742	5,542	46.3	2,030	16.8	4,447	36.9	12,019	30.2	7	3
WESTERN IJAW[2]	22,913	—	—	—	—	—	—	—	—		
TOTAL	653,950									54	11

Notes: * Published Figures on votes cast for 7 of 10 constituencies only.
1. Published Figures on votes cast for 2 of 4 constituencies only.

Source: "Mid-West Election Score-card", *Daily Times*, 5 February, 1964; also supplementary results reported in *Daily Times* and *Pilot*, issues of 6—11 February, 1964. No Official Report of the election was published.

divisions of Aboh and Benin, it was to be noted that the MDF still managed to gain 33.7 and 33.6 per cent respectively of the votes cast—the former on the basis of a very high poll (86.7 per cent of registered voters); and the latter on a surprisingly low poll of 69.8 per cent in Omo-Osagie's Benin constituencies.

As expected, the MDF made its strongest showing in Urhobo Division, securing 3 of 10 seats. In Ishan the party won 2 of 8 seats; in Afenmai, 2 of 8; in Western Ijaw, 2 of 4; and in Warri and Isoko Divisions 1 of 4 seats respectively. However, detailed results revealed how close the MDF had come to sizeably increasing its number of victories. Had not the Action Group (which, in the end, fielded only 21 candidates) split the anti-NCNC vote, the MDF might have emerged with another 6 seats; these taking the party total to 17.   These seats would almost certainly have been secured in: Urhobo Division (2); Ishan, Akoko Edo, Warri and Benin Divisions, 1 each. Furthermore, it was apparent that with only a marginal shift of 100-500 votes in constituencies where there was no third party contesting, the MDF might easily have taken an additional 10 seats from the NCNC.

Thus, in terms of the actual voting result secured, the MDF had effected a very creditable challenge. And, in terms of seats secured, the party might in straight two-party contests and with marginally greater effort and good fortune have ended up with a minimum of 27 seats. A 38 (NCNC), 27 (MDF) composition in the new Mid-West House of Assembly might have ensured not only an effective Opposition, but a Government which then might have been held to much closer account—something which might have usefully averted the conditions of crisis, largely created by continuing fierce intra-NCNC party rivalry, which were to persist unabated to the first coup in January 1966.

NCNC/Movement—Victors and Victims   Nevertheless, it was the NCNC which had in fact won the election. Each of the major NCNC Movement leaders had emerged triumphant, although in a few instances the contests had been very close. As expected Chief Omo-Osagie, on a 5,568 NCNC vote, secured a 3 : 1 majority over his MDF rival G.E. Uyigue. In Asaba Urban, Chief Osadebay, on a low vote of 2,820, still managed to gain an 1,801 (3 : 1) vote majority. Chief F.H. Utomi, of Ogwashi-Uku, on the strength of a 5,187 NCNC vote, gained a 3,723 (5 : 1) triumph over the MDF candidate B.A. Olue. Olue's challenge, however, was no doubt considerably weakened by his arrest on the eve of the election (2

February) on charges of being in possession of a quantity of arms, drugs and hospital equipment.[81] He was released in time to vote. Dr. Xto Okojie, on a vote of 4,884, devastated his Ishan East MDF rival who managed to poll only 472 votes; while Prince Shaka Momodu, Dr. Okojie's Irrua neighbour, managed a comfortable 3 : 1 victory margin. In Afenmai, recent returnee, John Umolu, formerly a Regional Commissioner in Eastern Nigeria, secured a 3 : 1 victory margin as did another returnee, Chief O.I. Dafe, of Aboh, former Chairman of Nigeria Airways.

Not every NCNC Movement leader, however, had been so fortunate. In Warri Urban, Webber Egbe, Commissioner for Justice in the Interim Administration, with a poll of 4,039 managed to defeat his Action Group contender, R.T. Nkune by only 200 votes. In Afenmai North East I, the NCNC margin was only 9 votes. Here A.O. Brimah managed to oust, former MDF Interim Administration Commissioner, K.S.Y. Momoh, with a poll of 4,159 to the enraged Momoh's 4,150. For two other NCNC Movement leaders, the election brought embarrassment and humiliation. B.I.G. Ewah, polled only 2,980 votes against 3,792 polled by his Ishan MDF rival Albert Okojie; while in Urhobo Central II, P.K. Tabiowo was narrowly defeated by one S.O. Pela, an MDF virtual unknown.[82]

Ethno-Political Equity in Practice   The election over, leader Osadebay wasted little time in announcing on 7 February, the appointment of a 19-man cabinet.[83] It was immediately apparent from its composition that Osadebay had kept to his "ethnic equity" formula.

The only ethnic element left without ministerial representation was Western Ijaw. Here, N.A. Ezonbodor, the only established Ijaw NCNC'er had been defeated by his MDF rival A.F. Atie. For the rest, each ethnic group and division was represented by at least one minister. Where favouritism showed, however, was perhaps predictably in the actual number of ministerial allocations to respective groups, and in the political (factional) loyalties of the individuals concerned. Five ministerial posts went to Western Ibos; four to Binis; 4 to Urhobos; 3 to Northern Edos; 1 to Itsekiris and 2 to Ishans.[84]

Furthermore, it was to be noted that of the 5 Western Ibo allocations three of these were to key portfolios: Chief Osadebay, Premier; Chief Dafe, Finance; and Chief Utomi, Education. And not only did these key ministers possess common ethnic association; in addition each retained allegiance to the (Eastern NCNC-oriented)

TABLE X

MID-WEST REGIONAL GOVERNMENT
INAUGURAL 19-MAN CABINET
Appointed 7 February, 1963

Premier   Chief Osadebay *(Ibo)*

Minister of Education	*Chief Utomi* (Ibo)
Minister of Finance	*Chief Dafe* (Ibo) & *G.I. Oviasu* (Bini)
Minister of Justice........................	*Webber Egbe* (Itsekiri)
Minister of Agriculture &Natural Resources................	*V.I. Amadasun* (Bini)
Minister of Health	*J. Igbrude* (Isoko/Urhobo)
Minister of Internal Affairs	*Prince Shaka Momodu* (Ishan)
Minister of Lands & Housing	*E.S. Ukonga* (Northern Edo)
Minister of Economic Planning &Development	*Chief O. Oweh* (Urhobo); to be appointed a "Special Member" on his return from Guinea, where he was at this time Nigerian Ambassador.
Minister of Trade &Industry	*J.A. Ororho* (Urhobo)
Minister of Labour & Social Welfare	*E.O. Imafidon* (Bini)
Minister of Information	*Rev. I. Edeki* (Northern Edo)
Minister of Establishment	*John Umolu* (Northern Edo)
Minister of Local Government &Chieftaincy Affairs	*Chief H. Omo-Osagie* (Bini)
Minister of State	*Enosegbe II*, Onogie of Ewohimi (Ishan)
Minister Without Portfolio	*Obi of Agbor* (Ibo)
Speaker	*P.K. Tabiowo* (Urhobo)— Special Member
Government Chief Whip	*A. Opia* (Ibo)

NCNC-Pure faction in the Mid-West. The one Bini to share in these key appointments was Gabriel Oviasu who was selected to share the Finance portfolio with Chief Dafe. It was, perhaps, not surprising that Oviasu too belonged to the NCNC-Pure faction.

While the powerful Omo-Osagie was not pleased to have been overlooked in what he regarded as his rightful claim to the Premiership, still he was not without an important power-base in the new government. As Minister of Local Government and Chieftaincy Affairs, he would have ample scope to make his own form of contribution—a contribution which was soon to become apparent.[85] The *Oba* of Benin too was gravely distressed not to have been selected as Governor of the new Region. Chief Samuel Mariere, an Urhobo was allocated this post.[86] Still, on 13 February, it was announced that the *Oba* had accepted the post of President of the Mid-West House of Chiefs, a post later confirmed by his election to this office at the first meeting of the House on 4 March.[87]

This, then, was the shape of politics with which the new Region now set out on its self-governing path. Movement/NCNC candidates had managed, electorally, to realise their claim to the leadership of the new Region. With an overwhelming majority in the House of Assembly, the NCNC had a strong base from which to press forward the ambitious development policies to which it was committed. Chief Osadebay had been largely instrumental in these final, extremely complex and delicate undertakings, in "winning the war" for the Mid-West. He was now faced with what promised to be the rather more daunting task of "securing the peace". With Chief Omo-Osagie and the *Oba* of Benin, deeply affronted by the seeming Western Ibo/NCNC-Pure orientation of the new Mid-West government; and with MDF and other internal political and ethnic factions far from content with their share in the emergent political system, the task of the new Premier and his administration, was not to be an easy one.

In the self-governing period prior to the end of Civil Political Rule in January 1966, the stability and order of the new Region was to be under constant stress. Given the complex internal ethnic and political composition of the Mid-West, it could be said that this was perhaps inevitable. Still, in view of all that had been proclaimed by Mid-West protagonists over the past 15 years, it was now at least a "domestic" conflict.

References

1. See *Federal Parliament Debates*, 7 August, 1963, cols.2751-2789; also *Senate Debates*, 8 August, 1963, cols.682-739.

2. See *Pilot*, 8 August, 1963.

3. *Federal Parliament Debates*, 7 August, 1963, col.2785.

4. *Ibid.*, col.2787.

5. *Ibid.*, col.2782.

6. *Federal Parliament Debates*, 8 August, 1963, col.2810. The Amendment to the Constitution of Western Nigeria referred to here, was one which provided for the "disqualification of legislators of Mid-West origin" from the Western Region House of Assembly and House of Chiefs. This West Regional Amendment had been "steam rolled into law" by a unanimous vote in the Ibadan House of Assembly, on 5 August.   (See *Pilot*, 6 August, 1963). With the passage of this (Amendment) Law, 30 Members of the House of Assembly and 28 Members of the House of Chiefs ceased to be West Regional legislators.

7. The Urhobo contingent, was later strengthened by the addition of Chief P.K. Tabiowo, former Minister of Mid-West Affairs in the Akintola Government at Ibadan. Tabiowo, who was appointed Commissioner of Establishment on 27 August, 1963, also raised the NCNC representation in the Administrative Council to a (9 : 8) majority. (See *Pilot*, 28 August, 1963).

8. Osadebay *mss., op. cit.*, p.439.

9. *Ibid.*

10. Okoh, *Men and Matters..., op.cit.*, p.52.

11. *Planting the Vineyard: Six months of Interim Administration in Mid-Western Nigeria*, (Benin City: MOI, 1964), p.7.

12. *Ibid.*

13. Plans were already well advanced for the siting and construction of glass, cement and textile industries. At this time Osadebay, Chief Okotie-Eboh and Omo-Osagie were deeply involved in negotiations with representatives of two separate Expatriate firms competing for the above contracts. (See *Report of the Tribunal of Inquiry into the Assets of Public Officers in the Mid-Western State of Nigeria*, Vol. 2, (Benin City: MOI, 1969), p.19).

14. *Planting the Vineyard...* , *op. cit.*, p.7.

15. See Okoh, *Men and Matters...* , *op. cit.*, p.52.

16. Osadebay *mss. op. cit.*, p.441-42.

17. *Ibid.*, p.442.

18. *Planting the Vineyard...* , *op. cit.*, p.14.

19. See *Pilot*, 3 and 4 August, 1963.

20. In a letter to his *Owegbe* "captains" and *Otu Edo* leaders, following the inaugural I did-Mid-West Regional elections of 3 February, 1964, Omo-Osagie made it clear that he had fully expected that he and not Osadebay, would be appointed to the post of Administrator in the Mid-West Interim Government:

    > "Chief Okotie-Eboh promised to make me the Administrator through the help of the Prime Minister; and Leaders of the NCNC agreed to this because of the part the *Otu Edo* had played. [However] when we achieved the 60 per cent. vote to create the Interim Administration, I was surprisingly thrown to the post of Deputy-Administrator, and [hence] was placed in a position where I could not help anybody".

    (See *Owegbe Report, op. cit.*, Appendix 24, pp.144-45).

21. At about this time, Omo-Osagie, in collusion with Osadebay and Chief Festus, was on the point of completing a "deal" with foreign industrialists. In the course of the next year this deal was to enrich by approximately £300,000, each of these Movement-NCNC leaders at the expense of the Mid-West tax-payer. See *Report of the Tribunal of Inquiry into the Assets of Public Officers in the Mid-West State*, (Benin City: MOI, 1969), Vol.2, pp.16-18 and 51-54.

22. *Pilot*, 14 August, 1963.

23. *Ibid.*

24. *Pilot*, 27 August, 1963.

25. *Ibid.*

26. See *Pilot*, 28 August, 1963.

27. See n.29 below, for definition of "NCNC-Pure".

28. For details of Rerri's earlier battles in quest of the NCNC nomination in Urhobo Division, preceding the 1954 and 1959 Federal Elections, see Post, *The Nigerian Federal Election of 1959*, op. cit., pp.251-52.

29. During this period, the NCNC in the Mid-West broke into a number of identifiable factions. In order that the activities of these factions may be more easily traced, they will be given separate names in the text. Defined in terms of membership, they are as follows:

    1. An "NCNC-Pure" member, was one adhering to the policy and leadership of the National branch of the party. In the Mid-

West, Chief Osadebay was leader of the NCNC-Pure.

2. An "NCNC-Festus" member was one who supported the faction led by Chief Okotie-Eboh within the Mid-West and larger national party and governmental contexts. Chief Omo-Osagie was Chief Festus' deputy in this faction.

3. An "NCNC-Otu Edo" member, was a Mid-West (normally Bini) NCNC'er who followed the leadership of Omo-Osagie.

4. An "NCNC-Pure-Otu Edo" member was one who followed the breakaway Otu-Edo faction led by the Bini NCNC-Pure leader, G.I. Oviasu.

30. See *Pilot*, 22 October, 1963.

31. *Ibid.*

32. *Pilot*, 7 October, 1963.

33. See Post and Vickers, *op. cit.*, p.93.

34. See *ibid.*, p. 89.

35. *Daily Times*, 18 January, 1964. *Alhaji* Galadiman Pategi, General Secretary of the NPC, used this term when outlining the NPC's expressed intent to extend the party's activities into the East and West Regional strongholds of its southern rivals.

36. See *Pilot*, 14 October, 1963.

37. See *Daily Times*, 15 October, 1963.

38. *Pilot*, 15 October, 1963.

39. *Ibid.*

40. See *Pilot*, 19 October, 1963.

41. See *ibid.*

42. *Ibid.*

43. *Pilot*, 29 October, 1963.

44. See *Pilot*, 19 October, 1963; also See *Pilot*, 3 and 11 October, 1963.

45. See *Pilot*, 3 November, 1963.

46. See Osadebay *mss., op. cit.*, p.449.

47. *Ibid.*

48. See *ibid.*, p.450.

49. *Ibid.*

50. *Ibid.*

51. See *Pilot*, 1 December, 1963.

52. M. Vickers, "Nigerian Federal Election of 1964-65: A Study of

Politics and Electoral Process in Modern Nigeria", M.A. Thesis, (Ottawa: Carleton University, 1966), p.36.

53. *Daily Express*, 2 December, 1963.

54. See Vickers, "Nigerian Federal Election of 1964-65...", *op. cit.*, pp.34-35.

55. See Post and Vickers, *op. cit.*, p.95.

56. See *West Africa*, 14 December, 1963, p.1414; also *Pilot*, 4 December, 1963.

57. It was often maintained by Chief Festus' NCNC-Pure rivals and assorted other political foes, that because of his close relationship with the Prime Minister and other NPC leaders at Lagos, Chief Festus was as much, and perhaps more a member of the NPC, than he was a member of the NCNC. Hence the appellation, "Alhaji Warri".

58. See *West Africa*, 14 December, 1963, p.1414.

59. O.N. Rewane, the former Warri Action Group leader, now turned MDF, maintained that the MDF position was disseminated "more by radio than by printing". This, of course, was a costly undertaking, but apparently NPC funds made this direct approach to the Mid-West populace feasible. (From notes of an interview with O.N. Rewane, conducted by David Abernethy of Stanford University, U.S.A.; the interview was conducted at Warri in January, 1964. Copies of these interview notes are in the possession of the writer).

60. See *Federal Parliament Debates*, 8 January, 1964, cols.3191-92.

61. *West Africa*, 18 January, 1964, p.62.

62. *West Africa*, 1 February, 1964, p.119.

63. *Ibid.*

64. *Ibid.*

65. See *Federal Parliament Debates*, 8 January, 1964, cols.3191-3220.

66. See *Ibid.*, cols.3194-95. For details of the MDF demand for a maximum of 62 seats in the House of Assembly, see *Pilot*, 24 December, 1963.

67. See *Federal Parliamentary Debates, ibid.*

68. *West Africa*, 1 February, 1964.

69. *Ibid.*

70. See *ibid.*

71. *Daily Times*, 28 January, 1964.

72. See *ibid.*

73. See *Daily Times*, 23 January, 1964.

74. See *Daily Times*, 25 January, 1964.

75. *Ibid.*

76. *Daily Times*, 2 February, 1964.

77. See *Daily Times*, 31 January, 1964. (Emphasis added).

78. See *Daily Times*, 1 February, 1964.

79. See "Mid-West Election Scorecard", *Daily Times*, 15 February, 1964. See **TABLE IX** below.

80. It should be noted that due to lack of complete returns, the figure of 45.7 per cent for Urhobo, might in fact have been lower if detailed returns for all of the division's constituencies had been available. Similarly, had returns for Western Ijaw been available, it is probable that a fifth Division would have been shown to have exceeded a total vote of 40 per cent. It is rather surprising that *no Official Report* on the results of this inaugural Mid-West election was ever published. Detailed results given in the *Daily Times'* "Mid-West Election Scorecard", were extensive; but, as **TABLE IX**, shows, these were incomplete.

81. See *Daily Times*, 4 February, 1964.

82. For details of election returns, see "Mid-West Election Scorecard", *Daily Times, op. cit.*

83. See *Pilot*, 8 February, 1964.

84. See *ibid.*

85. See *Pilot*, 11 March, 1964. Opposition leader Otobo expressed grave reservations about selection procedures and qualification for appointment of Chiefs set out in a Bill presented by Omo-Osagie. It would, he said, lead to "partisan political abuse".

86. See *West Africa*, 15 February, 1964, p.179.

87. See *Daily Times*, 10 March, 1964.

PART IV

CONCLUSIONS

CHAPTER 16

MID-WEST EXPERIENCE
IN RETROSPECT

At the outset of their activities in 1948, Mid-West protagonists felt that attainment of a separate state should pose no serious problem. Both of the country's leading Nationalists at that time, Nnamdi Azikiwe and Obafemi Awolowo had expressed firm support "in principle" for the creation of new states. The British Colonial Authorities, still in a receptive mood after the re-structuring of the *Richards Constitution* (1946) could well be expected to extend sympathy to any pro-Mid-West demands advanced at the forthcoming (1950) *Constitutional Conference*. Finally, ready support had been forthcoming to the *Oba*'s preliminary (1948) soundings even from proto-Yoruba areas like Warri Division. In the minds of Movement leaders, therefore, creation of a Mid-West State seemed a straight-forward affair.

By the end of the (1950) *Constitutional Conference*, however, Mid-West and other minorities elements had been brought to an abrupt realisation that there could be no swift and easy path to the creation of a Mid-West state, nor new states in general. Azikiwe and Awolowo showed no interest in translating their "in principle" support, into practical backing. The British Colonial Authorities, while giving Mid-West elements full opportunity to express their views through the extensive consultations preceding the Conference, then proceeded in their actions to demonstrate that it was the 3-Region structure they were intent on consolidating. As for the multiple internal ethno-linguistic units resident within the Mid-West provinces; these made very clear, with the exception of Bini and certain Edo groups, that they had no desire to see the creation of a Central (or Mid-West) state within which they would be incorporated.

This was the basic framework of reality within which Mid-West protagonists were to be constrained to operate throughout the duration of their subsequent 13-year struggle. Certainly, in the face of these formidable obstacles, we have seen their quest was not an easy one. Yet gradually the Movement was able effectively to advance the Mid-West issue; to reduce opposition and gain support from external political and governmental elements; to create and maintain adequate internal consensus and electoral support. It was the combined effect of these attainments which served progressively to elevate the Mid-West issue, and to move it closer to its ultimate fulfilment.

STRUCTURE, PROCESS AND POLITICAL INITIATIVES

In any retrospective assessment due credit must first be given to the favourable *structural conditions* (that is, the legal-constitutional and cultural-institutional conditions) under which the Movement was enabled to act. These structural conditions were of fundamental importance in facilitating the advance of the Mid-West issue. While Nigeria's Westminster parliamentary institutions provided Mid-West protagonists with the basic freedom of activity to articulate and press their demands, it was the evolving federal structure which made available to them the multiple avenues through which this pressure could effectively be brought to bear. These basic structural conditions afforded Mid-West protagonists ample provision of that "most valuable of political resources",[1] *access.*

But for this general "structural conduciveness"[2] and the opportunities it afforded to be used to greatest effect, equally, or at least adequately favourable structural conditions needed to be operative *internally*. Here it was that *traditional* institutions of the Mid-West polity, although of a narrow, more specific nature, were duly found to possess the requisite supportive properties.

These favourable *external*, and more limited *internal* structural conditions were vital to the prospects for advancement of the Mid-West issue. But favourable structural conditions, in themselves, afford no advantage. They can only be as supportive as the will and ability of the leadership which seeks to exploit them. Here again the Movement was most fortunate. It possessed a *"composite leadership"* (that is a leadership few in number, and operative largely individually rather than collectively within separate internal and external political contexts) capable of taking full advantage of available structural opportunities. This composite leadership will here be referred to as *"external leadership"* (that operative within *extra*-Mid-West contexts) and *"internal leadership"* (that operative within the Mid-West itself).

Turning first to the Movement's external leadership, it was apparent that it was this leadership element which was able to use general (federal/parliamentary) structural conditions to greatest advantage. By gradually extending Mid-West initiatives within the federal structure as it evolved, it was able to construct what might be termed a "reinforcement matrix of support" (See **FIGURE I** below).

Direct access to West Regional institutions formalised by the constitutional provisions of 1951 (MW—>W), further complemented by direct access to the the new federal institutions

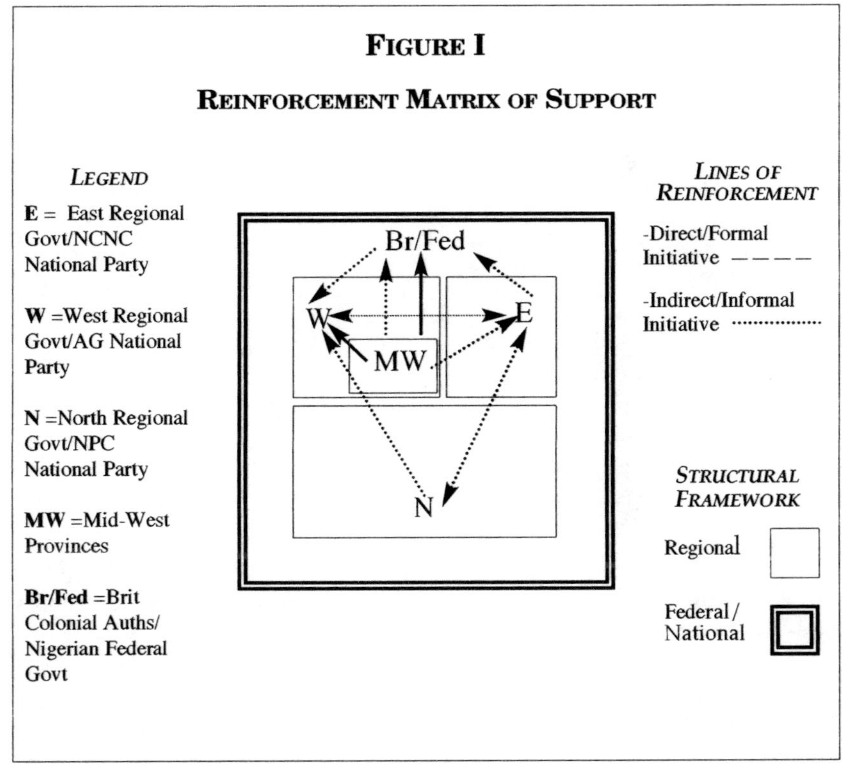

inaugurated in 1954 (MW—>F); these access opportunities provided the Movement's external leaders with the fundamental institutional base from which to extend direct and formal influence.

Phases of Development

Yet while these formal institutional opportunities were of vital underlying importance, in fact, they constituted only the starting point, the common base from which Mid-West leaders commenced their more ambitious external undertakings. These were pursued through *informal* (party structures and inter-personal relationships) and indeed formal institutions in the East and North regions, to which they had only *indirect* access. Broadly speaking these combined (direct/formal and indirect/informal) initiatives, moved through 3 phases; each phase seeing a gradual extension of the Mid-West issue

First Phase   During the *first phase (1950-53)*, Mid-West protagonists made use of newly-acquired direct access to legislative institutions at the West Regional level to articulate the Mid-West issue in both the House of Assembly and House of Chiefs (MW—>W). However, other important structural opportunities were both available and duly exploited. As a result of the early and close association of Mid-West leaders with the NCNC National party, (MW—>E) the Mid-West issue received consistent (party) policy support; this being reflected in National party statements, and in the articulation of West Regional (NCNC) Branch initiatives and commitments at Ibadan (E—>W).

In principle, of course, the NCNC was also committed to support of the Mid-West issue at the Central or National level of government. In fact, however, as shown in Chapters 3 and 4, it received scant attention. Indeed it was largely the failure of the NCNC to pursue supportive action within the Legislative Council at Lagos and at the *1953 Constitutional Conference* which led the *Oba* of Benin and Chief Omo-Osagie to proceed with their independent pro-Mid-West BDPP initiative in September 1953.

Second Phase   In the early part of the *second phase (1954-59)* direct pressure by Mid-West protagonists continued to be concentrated on the West Regional Authority (MW—>W). Largely, as a result of this pressure reinforced by the East Regional Branch of the NCNC, the NCNC Parliamentary Party at Ibadan together with the BDPP and Action Group-oriented *Oba* of Benin, the Action Group was forced to grant its first major concession. The *Mid-West Bill* was passed through the Western House of Assembly in June 1955. By 1957, however, Mid-West external leaders were devoting greater efforts to initiatives at the Federal level.

In the period leading up to the deferred *(London) Constitutional Conference of 1956* (finally held in June 1957), the Mid-West issue was articulated and reinforced in the Federal legislature. Furthermore, the increasing prominence of both Chiefs Festus and Osadebay in the National Executive Committee (NEC) of the NCNC (MW—>E) ensured increased party support for the Mid-West issue at both federal and West regional levels (E—>F; E—>W). Indeed, even before the 1957 Conference was convened adequate cumulative pressure had been generated by Mid-West protagonists in concert with their NCNC allies that the West Regional Government was prepared to make its second major concession, the creation of a Ministry of Mid-West Affairs, and a Mid-West Advisory Council.

When the *1957 Constitutional Conference* was duly held, clear evidence was available that the Mid-West's external leaders had also made significant progress with their NCNC allies (MW—>E). For the first time, the NCNC indicated it was prepared to give effective practical backing to the Mid-West issue. Not only did Azikiwe fight hard in an unsuccessful attempt to secure first place on the Conference Agenda for the Mid-West issue; but on behalf of the National Branch of the party he then argued a strong case in support of the Mid-West issue. In fact, it was a measure of the influence which leading Mid-West NCNC politicians had built within the party that what amounted to a three-pronged NCNC assault was launched at the Conference. This offensive comprised Azikiwe's National Branch initiative; Alhaji Adelabu's submission on behalf of the West Regional Branch of the party; and the comprehensive "Case for a Mid-West State" presentation put forward by the Movement itself.

Thus, while Osadebay and Otobo (the two official Mid-West delegates) expressed bitter disappointment in having to return to Nigeria—and to dismayed and angry supporters—without the Mid-West State, in fact, the Mid-West issue had made significant progress by the end of the *1957 Constitutional Conference*. For from its position in the first phase, when both the Action Group and the NCNC had expressed "in principle" support, both now had been influenced to the point of rendering effective practical backing. The reluctant and cautious British Authorities too, had been forced to recognise the strength of the Mid-West and minorities case (E/MW—>Br). The creation of the *Minorities Commission* was representative of their realisation that these issues could no longer be evaded. Finally, the NPC, as a majority participant at the

Conference, had been brought to an awareness of the particular circumstances of the Mid-West claim to which the party now began to recognise that support might safely be given (MW/E—>N) This reassurance to the Sardauna and the NPC was, of course, provided by the NCNC/Movement rationale, that by rendering support to the Mid-West claim, the NPC was merely co-operating in the fulfilment of the (West Regional) *1955 Mid-West Bill.*

The remaining two years of the second phase (1957-59) saw inconsistent yet continuing reinforcement of the Mid-West issue upon the NCNC and NPC National parties (MW—>E/N). In 1959, the NEC of the NCNC announced that it was now prepared to regard the Mid-West as a state "already in existence". Accordingly, it split the Mid-West NCNC from the Western Branch of the party—something which had been long-sought by Osadebay and his Mid-West colleagues, and long resisted by Yoruba NCNC'ers— thus inaugurating a Mid-West Regional Branch. Far more significant, though less dramatic, following private meetings with the Sardauna in late 1958, it was confidently rumoured that due to the "special conditions" surrounding the Mid-West case, the NPC might be prepared to give support to—*and only to*—the Mid-West issue (MW/E—>N).

As a result of Movement efforts in the *external* political environment, therefore, the Mid-West issue, prior to the Federal Elections of 1959, had gained gradually greater practical support from its NCNC ally, and gradually extended accommodations from its Action Group opponents. Even the NPC was prepared to consider "exclusive support". With the advent of Independence and the departure of the British Authorities, the final significant institutional restraints would be removed. The opportunity of utilising influence built within the structures of "multiple reinforcement" to bring further and perhaps determining pressure to bear on the respective controlling majority party and governmental authorities, would be available.

Third Phase   During the *third and final phase* there followed merely a further strengthening of the Mid-West issue within the context of this now fully evolved reinforcement "matrix of support". Increasing mutual interest between the new federal government NPC/NCNC coalition partners resulted in reinforced awareness, support and finally active commitment not only by the Federal Authority itself, (E/N—>F; F—>W) but separately by both North and East Regional Governments (N<—>E). The passage of the *1961 Federal Mid-West Bill*, was duly followed by the requisite supplementary Bills passed through the North and East legislatures.

Optimum cumulative pressure upon the Action Group and the West Regional Government it controlled resulted in: the concession of a separate Mid-West Regional Branch of the party; a much-strengthened Mid-West Minority Council complete with its own "mini-Premier"; a range of material concessions (mostly to Action Group-Loyal Mid-West districts); and the appointment of a number of Mid-Westerners to various Government, state corporation and agency offices (MW—>W/F; E<—>F; E<—>N; N<—> F; N/E/F—>W).

Indeed, by the end of 1960, due to the effect of this reinforced influence, Action Group accommodations had brought the Mid-West Movement to the pen-ultimate stage of its quest. Short of consenting to the cession of full Regional autonomy the Action Group could go no further. It was the political self-interest of the federal coalition parties combined with persisting pressure—exerted most notably by Chiefs Festus and Osadebay—which now ensured adequate momentum to bring the Mid-West issue through a still-remaining period of uncertain allied support (1961-62), and on to the successful referendum of 1963.

Tradition and Modernity—Leaders and Parties

The impact of *external initiatives* was greatly enhanced due simply to the fact that the Movement was following a developmental path parallel to that of the National polity as a whole; and that the Federation which emanated was restricted to three Regions. Its "parallel" development with evolving institutions of the National polity allowed a progressive growth within its own evolving resource capabilities. Furthermore, in that Mid-West protagonists were able to press their interests within the relatively comfortable confines of a three-Region structure, this ensured that excessive strain was not placed on these resources. In a larger more diverse federation (say the 50 states of the United States of America, 10 provinces of Canada, or indeed the 36 states of Nigeria today) it is doubtful that either the leadership resources or the degree of common interest generated within the three-Region structure would have been adequate to ensure effective operation of the critical reinforcement function.

Finally, insofar as *external* leadership effected increasing influence in the final phase of Movement activity (1960-63), opportunities for this influence were, rather paradoxically, enhanced by the *minority or "marginal" ethnic status* of these Mid-West leaders amongst their majority allies.[3] Between the Ibo-dominant NCNC and Hausa/Fulani-dominant NPC there persisted a continuing high level of suspicion and distrust. Given this condition, it can well be appreciated the importance of Chief Festus, and to some extent Chiefs Osadebay, Omo-Osagie and Oweh, as *broker or mediating elements* between the federal coalition partners. Increased use of Chief Festus, the Movement's leading "practical man of action",[4] to negotiate a range of inter-party interests—by 1961, his political influence was considered to be second only to that of Prime Minister Balewa[5]—could only enhance his opportunities and those of his Mid-West NCNC federal colleagues for advancing Mid-West prospects. These were opportunities of which, after a rather disquieting silence during 1960, they duly took full advantage.

In terms of favourable *internal* structural conditions, it first seemed that such conditions might in fact not be available. As shown in Chapter 3, the outcome of the *1950 Constitutional Conference*—in particular the preparatory Benin and Delta Provincial Conferences—made clear that there existed little consensus in relation to any pan-Mid-West construct. Indeed, it seemed that any appeal to common cultural/historical identity would, in fact reinforce a divergence rather than an integration of intra-Mid-West ethno-linguistic elements. By 1953, however, and with the creation of the BDPP, it became apparent that *internal traditional institutions* could prove structurally conducive and allow the access—albeit narrow and specific—and the influence which might serve to advance internally the Mid-West issue.

The Oba and Omo-Osagie   These structural prospects first became apparent in the course of campaign tours following the formation of the BDPP. These tours made clear that existing traditional institutions could and did offer considerable promise for facilitating local penetration; that they could afford the requisite mediating support to draw internal Mid-West backing into modern participant political structures. Briefly, the utility and effectiveness of these institutions was manifest more specifically in the "identitive assets"[6], the *symbolic influence* of the Mid-West overlord, the *Oba* of Benin. More than any other factor, it was this traditional symbolic status of the *Oba* which ensured not only access to, but vital articulative influence within the Mid-West districts. Even within opposition proto-Yoruba areas in Delta Province and the northern reaches of Benin Province, it was the symbolic influence of the *Oba*, the traditional respect in which he was held, which afforded BDPP politicians access, and their organisers subsequent opportunities for recruitment.

What was perhaps most significant about the contribution made by the *Oba* during the first and to some extent the third phase of Movement activity was that it was basically *"syncretistic"*[7] in nature. *It quickly became apparent that in addition to his (traditional) symbolic influence, the Oba was both willing and able to perform an effective (modern) political role.* Nowhere was this capability more clearly demonstrated than in his vigorous—though largely covert—actions during 1953-55 aimed at neutralising the leadership and political control of Omo-Osagie. Of course, the *Oba* had been well-versed in the tactics of non-traditional politics. His experiences, going back to the "Great Water Rate Agitation" of 1938 had afforded him ample experience in dealing with the Colonial Authorities and the indigenous new elite. Still, it was questionable whether he would or could effectively involve himself in the rapidly evolving modern politics of Nigeria.

In keeping with the pattern of leadership in Nationalist movements of the time it seemed likely that Omo-Osagie, as the leading "agitator/organisational"[8] figure would emerge as the Movement's "charismatic" champion. Certainly, Omo-Osagie possessed many qualities normally attributed to charismatic leaders;[9] and there was little question that he regarded himself as such. However, by the end of the 1954 BDPP tours, it was clear that Omo-Osagie's charisma did not extend beyond the districts of his fellow Binis, or at most, beyond Edo boundaries. Insofar as the Movement had an accepted Leader, this was the *Oba*. As for Omo-Osagie, as frustrating and personally humiliating as this was to him, nevertheless his position (internally) was now to be limited to that of an organisational functionary—albeit the most powerful functionary—under the over-arching syncretistic leadership of the *Oba*.

So it was that essentially the *symbolic and identitive properties of traditional structures relating to the office of Oba secured for the Movement a rather narrow but nevertheless effective access to Mid-West districts.* The Movement, behind the organisational skills of Omo-Osagie made effective use of this access to penetrate the Mid-West localities, to articulate an evolving ideology, and to secure the recruitment of an initial and basic membership. As for the BDPP, the primary organisational agency through which the Movement operated during this important first phase of internal activity, it may in retrospect be seen to have had a questionable impact.

The BDPP and Mid-West Movement   On the one hand, it is clear that the BDPP did briefly perform useful functions during the 1953-55 period. It raised internal awareness through articulation and reinforcement of the Mid-West ideology; it facilitated recruitment and active commitment to the Mid-West cause. And certainly, its important mediating role should not be overlooked. The BDPP afforded the *Oba* the political "cover" under which he effected his 1954-55 transfer of allegiance to the Action Group. Although at the time regarded as treachery, it can be recognised that this timely shift was of the greatest importance to the Mid-West cause. It was the pledge of the *Oba* together with the support of other prominent Mid-West leaders brought over to the Action Group under cover of the BDPP, which contributed significantly to Awolowo's willingness to pass the fateful—for the Action Group—(1955) *Mid-West Bill*. Furthermore during this early period the BDPP also performed an effective internal brokerage function by providing through its collective leadership an agency for securing a measure of reconciliation between and amongst the leaders of member ethno-linguistic elements.

By the same token, however, the creation of the BDPP as a political party, rather than a movement, resulted in the immediate dis-affection of the Western Ibo element. Other incorporated elements too, as shown in chapter 5, expressed strong reservations about the pre-dominance of Bini elements in BDPP executive ranks and activity. But more than anything else it quickly became apparent that the BDPP *qua* "independent mass party"[10] as initially conceived by Omo-Osagie was far too optimistic and ambitious. Within a short time it became clear that the BDPP was more a "caucus"[11] of NCNC legislators and notables than it was a "mass party". Indeed, by mid-1954 it had already fallen into what Sartori terms the "hegemonic party situation"[12]—that is one where the minority party (BDPP) is permitted to exist, but only as the satellite of the patron or majority party (NCNC). Its independence was shown to be a fiction in the mind of Omo-Osagie.

Thus, the BDPP served as a mediating institution both promoting internal integration, and yet creating a measure of reinforced differentiation. This was to be, perhaps inevitably, a pronounced characteristic of Movement activity in later years. Certainly the Mid-West State Movement (post-1956) under its "caucus" leadership was to become an important agency for reciprocal exchange, largely between the NCNC and internal Mid-West leadership—and both for internal and external reinforcement of Mid-West interests. To this end, it served as an effective guide to the formulation of the most advantageous policy acts from multiple options[13] and as Despres has put it, to link local concerns with broader institutions and "wider spheres of... [political] activity".[14]

But still the internal integrative effect of these attainments was ambiguous. On the one hand, the BDPP and later the Mid-West State Movement, ensured a reinforcement of ideological unity. By consistent stress on varied emotive and cognitive appeals[15] Mid-West citizens were made aware of the separateness of their collective identity from "Alien Yorubas"; of the economic benefits which could accrue to them; and of the need for a separate, autonomous Region to secure, protect and consolidate their interests. But in more fundamental and practical terms, the resurgence of "disparate demands" in the final phase of Movement activity, and ultimately, the need for Chief Osadebay's "ethnic equity" formula[16] to achieve a satisfactory measure of internal pan-Mid-West integration must raise serious doubts about the penetration and effectiveness of this ideological thrust.

Nevertheless, whatever the actual effectiveness of the BDPP and its successor the Mid-West State Movement in achieving substantive internal integration, these bodies did manage to secure and support those initiatives requisite to maintain adequate consensus amongst Mid-West peoples and their leaders. Consistent legislative and electoral support was thereby assured. Although the BDPP was regarded as a failure at the time (1955), it is in retrospect, possible to recognise that an extended life and activity by such an envisaged "independent Mass party" was not only unrealistic but unnecessary.[17] A succession of Regional, Federal and local government elections, along with continuing NCNC interest reinforced and safeguarded by Mid-West leaders prominent in the party hierarchy, ensured the adequacy of continuing internal awareness and support.

Altogether, then, it was these favourable structural conditions and this composite leadership which served to build and maintain the momentum of the Mid-West issue, and to ensure the requisite internal and external support for it. *Internally*, narrow access afforded by traditional institutions and the syncretistic leadership of the *Oba* provided an unlikely but effective over-arching integrative framework. It was within this framework that the requisite practical initiatives under the guidance of Omo-Osagie and Osadebay were undertaken. These initiatives were supported and reinforced by the limited, to some extent counter-productive, but nevertheless important assistance of the BDPP and the Mid-West State Movement.

Externally, it was, of course, initiatives extended through and reinforced by federal-parliamentary institutions which ensured the progressive advance of the Mid-West issue in Nigeria's party, legislative and governmental forums. And here it was not merely a matter of pressure exerted through formal institutions to which Mid-West legislators had direct access. It was the ingenuity and persisting effort of the Movement's external leaders in exploiting opportunities afforded by indirect access and informal influence which noticeably enhanced the cumulative impact of their collective efforts.

Self-Interest & Incrementalism

There were, of course, external factors, quite separate from Movement initiatives which proved supportive to the Mid-West issue. Most obvious amongst these was, firstly, the desire of the 1960 Federal Authorities to shatter the political threat posed by the federal Opposition challenger Awolowo and his Action Group. The excising of the Mid-West provinces from the West Region was seen as a useful means to this end; hence the willingness of the Federal Government finally to accede to Mid-West pressure and permit introduction of the 1961 Mid-West Bill. Secondly, and more basically, the consistent concern both of the NCNC and the Action Group with regional and national electoral support, ensured that the Mid-West issue was given continued exposure: the more persistent the internal thrust and external pressure by Movement leaders, the greater the support (and concessions) extended by these national parties, and the greater the visibility and political legitimacy of the Mid-West issue.

Yet, while these external factors made important contributions to the overall advance of the Mid-West issue, the limit of these contributions should be stressed. Certainly, the electoral interest of NCNC and Action Group ensured an increasing prominence for the Mid-West issue; and direct political self-interest had much to do with the Federal Government's willingness to allow introduction of the *1961 Mid-West Bill*. However, it will be recalled that the *Mid-West Bill* was passed *not* on a Government, but on a Private Member's Motion; further, following passage of the *1961 Bill* (and a subsequent *1962 Bill*, which corrected a procedural fault), there was a noticeable reluctance of the Federal Authorities to proceed with further requisite measures. Indeed, following the demise of the Action Group in mid-1962, and with links growing between the new UPP regime and the NPC, there really remained no urgency about the issue. It could even be said that the Northern party now had a very strong incentive for jettisoning the NCNC-promoted Mid-West issue once and for all.

There seemed, therefore, every reason to believe that the federal coalition parties, if left to their own devices, would simply let the Mid-west issue lapse in much the way the NCNC had let it lapse on frequent occasions in the past. It was here that the Movement's external leadership once again proved its worth. What ensured the final grudging support of the governing federal parties was the forceful and persistent advocacy of Chiefs Festus, Osadebay and their colleagues—albeit an advocacy which, sadly, was later shown to be not totally motivated by public interest.[18]

Insofar as there is any additional general factor which afforded basic support to the Mid-West Movement, this might be said simply to have been that of *"incrementalism"*. By generating, gradually elaborating and consolidating internal awareness and active commitment; and equally, by similarly, if with greater ideological restraint, advancing the Mid-West case in West Regional and then federal political contexts, the acceptance of the Mid-West issue as a regional and then gradually as a National issue was secured and strengthened. It was thus as a result of patient and persisting efforts *intra-constitutionally* advanced that, for instance, vital NPC support at Lagos and Kaduna was ultimately secured.

Whether a more forceful, possibly *extra-constitutional* approach might have more swiftly advanced Mid-West interests is extremely doubtful. Not only have we seen that the Movement was limited in its resources; but from what was indicated of Action Group "politics of control"—particularly in Chapter 11—any such initiatives might well have ensured suppression and an abrupt end to the Mid-West quest. Whether by accident or design, therefore, it was this incremental approach which served vitally to enhance Mid-West prospects of success.

It must be asked, however, whether even allowing for the positive and supportive roles of political, constitutional and traditional structures; of composite leadership; of the limited but significant contribution of Movement organisational structures; of the more prominent contribution of ideology; whether collectively all of these are adequate to account for the ultimate success of the Mid-West Movement? It was Chief Osadebay who declared that "without Chief Festus, there would have been no Mid-West State",[19] at least at this (1963) juncture. It was the immense influence and authority of Chief Festus exerted through legislative, constitutional, party and inter-personal contexts; it was his consummate skill as, almost certainly Nigeria's pre-eminent political broker, which would seem to have been primarily responsible for translating evolved Mid-West prospects into the political reality of a separate state.

MID-WEST EXPERIENCE AND NIGERIAN POLITICS

Moving away from the immediate substantive and instrumental context of the Mid-West experience, and to its meaning within the overall setting of Nigerian politics before and immediately after Independence, it would seem, in general terms, that this study has revealed nothing that is not already well recognised. The intransigence of the British Authorities in relation to the "new states" and Mid-West issues; the evasiveness of the NCNC and Azikiwe on the Mid-West issue when it came down to practical support; the rationale of the Action Group position and its unrelenting determination to oppose the "unilateral" creation of a Mid-West state without the simultaneous creation of COR and Middle Belt states; the unrelenting opposition of the Sardauna, and hence his NPC, to the creation of new states in general; all these basic facts of Nigerian political life are well known.

In relation to these basic facts, however, where it may be suggested that this study has made a modest contribution is in the comprehensive empirical affirmation which it has provided for these facts. We have, for instance, been able to see under what particular circumstances the Sardauna, at the *1958 London Conference*, was prepared to endorse the proposal for the inclusion of "new states" provisions in the Independence Constitution, and how in 1961 he was willing to endorse the Mid-West demand for a separate state; each of these critical undertakings followed out only on the basis of what he felt could be assured safeguards to protect the sacrosanct territorial integrity of the Northern Region. Similarly, this study has documented in considerable detail, the incredible range of ruses and varied measures of political evasion employed by the NCNC to retain the loyalty of its Mid-West satellite area. The portrait of the NCNC which emerges would seem to be one which all too strongly confirms the observation of Tony Enahoro, when he stigmatised the party as being the instrument of the "chameleonic politics" of Azikiwe.

As for the British Colonial Authorities, the account of events preceding, during and after the Mid-West hearings of the *Minorities Commission* has shed little favourable light on their activities at this critical juncture. Indeed, as indicated in Chapter 10, the feelings of bitterly disappointed minorities protagonists that the *Minorities Report* was a "cowardly document" would seem to have been something of an understatement. In effect, the *Minorities Commission* provided yet another instance of "rule by the Royal Commission";[20] an elaborate device to de-fuse a potentially explosive situation; one which in this instance allowed the British Authorities to evade the real issues, defer the problem, and by so doing pass it neatly on to the future National Independence Government.

Action Group—Expose and Testament

In relation to the Action Group, this study may, on the one hand, be regarded as a detailed *expose* of the party's unrelenting opposition to the Mid-West issue; a collective and unsavoury revelation of the harsh and often dubious measures deployed to get Mid-West protagonists to come to terms. Yet, on the other hand, this study stands equally as an impressive testament to the party's quite extra-ordinary ingenuity, to its discipline and sheer nerve in devising and carrying out its policies of Mid-West containment. Indeed, this present work has certainly confirmed Sklar's contention that the Action Group was by far "the best organised, ...and most efficiently run political party in Nigeria". It is to a brief consideration of the Action Group's activities within the Mid-West context that it is worth turning here.

We have seen how the Action Group, starting from negligible beginnings in an overtly hostile political environment managed through cunningly devised and largely covert initiatives, to construct a position as early as 1955 from which to challenge for control in the "Bini Heartland" of Benin Division. This position, had it been secured, would have provided an excellent base from which to challenge for political control throughout the whole of the Mid-West. However when this challenge failed we have seen how the party, far from being discouraged, then simply made increasing use of the variety of "weapons" available to it as the Governing party in the West Region.

The party used amenity and other benefit allocations to enlist political support in the Mid-West districts; and as its Mid-West offensive moved relentlessly forward these non-coercive initiatives were increasingly supplemented by measures of a more coercive nature. Still, even when during the 1958-61 period the Minister of Local Government, Adegbenro, known locally in the Mid-West as the "Minister of Terror", was making full use of the Tax Assessment Committees, the Customary Courts and Local Government Police Forces, to bring maximum pressure on Mid-West dissenters, these initiatives were being harmonised with a variety of conciliatory measures.

New appointments, and greater benefit allocations; the creation of the Ministry of Mid-West Affairs, and the appointment of an "Advisory Council"; these conciliatory actions, and many more, were undertaken by the Action Group in the period leading up to 1960. The result of the 1960 West Regional Elections was an impressive indication that these harmonised tactics of the party were achieving the desired effect. The Action Group emerged from these elections with 50 per cent of the Mid-West seats—a 30 per cent improvement over its showing at the 1956 West elections.

During the 1960-63 period, the Action Group, under growing pressure, retained its nerve and discipline, and adhered to its established policy of an essentially harmonised strategy. It has been shown that with the evolution of the ominous (for the Action Group) events of 1961 and 1962, the party made more extensive efforts to secure Mid-West support—efforts impressively manifest through the increased powers and responsibilities allocated to the "Mid-West mini-Premier" Otobo.

In addition, its strategies ensured firstly that in the event of a Declaration of Emergency in the West, it might be able to combat any swift effort by Mid-West NCNC'ers, to gain unilateral support for the creation of a Mid-West State; and secondly, should the worst come to the worst (in the form of a Mid-West Referendum), that it might ensure the required 60 per cent figure of all registered electors in the Mid-West provinces, would *not* be attained. Indeed, the success of this Action Group strategy was clearly manifest in the very considerable residual fears of Leader Osadebay and his colleagues that the Action Group remnant in the Mid-West and Mid-West UPP supporters might through opposition or abstention ensure the failure of the Mid-West quest at the July referendum.

While the Action Group emerges from this study as the "villain of the piece", nevertheless its consummate skill in undertaking its "villainy" has to be recognised. This study has provided extensive proof that the Action Group was a party very much "in possession of itself". It employed its weapons within a harmonised strategy which only on occasion used excessive coercion. In terms of the party's commitment to its own objectives and the instrumental expertise which it demonstrated in seeking these objectives, the Action Group's failure to contain the Mid-West issue cannot be attributed to any weakness in its organisation and strategies, nor to any inadequacy in its discipline or efficiency. Indeed when compared, *qua* party, with the hesitant, ill-disciplined, dis-organised and dis-united approach of the NCNC to its various political responsibilities, the Action Group clearly emerges from this study with a most creditable image.

One-Party Dominance—Ingenuity and Discipline

In at least one additional major respect, this study has confirmed yet another and vital, if well-recognised, basic fact of Nigerian political life: the trend towards "one-party dominant" rule in the West Region. The "one-party dominant" theme runs throughout this study. It also provides a comprehensive account of the gradual emergence of the Action Group to a "one-party dominant" position, at least in the Mid-West provinces of the Western Region. It confirms and expands on tendencies which by the early 1960's had been commented on by Mackintosh, Bretton, Sklar and Post, amongst others.

There is no need for further comment here on the emergent "one-party dominant" theme, at least in relation to the policies and instrumental techniques through which it took form. However, some comment seems appropriate in relation to this study's particular interpretation of the "one-party dominant" theme—an interpretation which is generally in keeping with that emerging from the works of Sklar, Post and Mackintosh, but very much at variance with the analysis and interpretation provided by Bretton.

Bretton has made it clear in his published works that he regards the movement towards "one-party dominant" rule to have been part and parcel of an established general trend towards the emergence of "machine politics" and "authoritarian rule" in the new states of Africa.[21] Bretton maintained that in Nigeria's Regions, the controlling parties evolved into "political machines"—that is "unofficial organisations in the hands of the bosses and their followers"[23]—and that as another writer has put it, these "personal tribal machines",[24] operating with an increasing range of authoritarian techniques, existed "almost exclusively to stay in power", and to this end their main concern was "to offer rewards and bribes" to anyone who could keep them in power. According to this definition of "machine politics", office is the party's sole reason for existence, and with office comes the corollary: "the opportunity for enrichment at public expense".[25]

Certainly, in the terms of the above definition, it is apparent that Awolowo and his Action Group provided ample demonstrations of both these tendencies. Without having to refer to the more celebrated revelations of the *Coker Commission*,[26] or of the *Lloyd Report*[27], this study has made it quite clear that the party was prepared to deploy an extensive range of coercive measures normally associated with the operation of "authoritarian regimes"; and, indeed, that Awolowo was frequently prepared to dispense a variety of rewards to build and secure his personal position and that of his party.

Yet it is one thing to indicate that these tendencies were present, as has been clearly demonstrated in this study. It is, however, quite different to declare, as Bretton does, that these tendencies were not only dominant, but that they constituted the *sole fundamental and determining factors in the conduct of politics under the vigilant supervision of Nigeria's Regional "personal-tribal machines"*. It would seem that Bretton, by concentrating attention on the "players and processes" of power politics, virtually ignores the impact of a range of additional vital elements, each of which had an important part to play in shaping both the conduct of politics and the environment within which they operated. As Robert Mortimer, addressing his remarks to just this pre-occupation in Bretton's analysis, has noted:

> "One need not deny the linkage of politics and economics to attribute independent analytic significance to political ideas and forces. Certainly the "game" of power, [as Bretton stresses] may oft be nasty and brutish, as we have long known, but it is in fact a more complex game embracing cultural, sociological and ethical matters, as well as economic factors".[28]

Within this broader framework of analysis suggested by Mortimer, we can see, in the context of the Mid-West experience, that the "players and processes" of power politics recede somewhat in their significance. This more balanced perspective enables us to recognise that "cultural, sociological and ethical" factors, amongst others, were of considerable importance in shaping the conduct of politics in the West Region under the guidance of Awolowo. In viewing the Mid-West experience within this broader analytical perspective we can see that in the operations of the Action Group—in relation to the Mid-West at least—there was a great deal more flexibility, compromise and democratic process operative than Bretton's interpretations would allow. In fact, these factors in any cumulative sense, counter-acted the more rigid and authoritarian tendencies suggested by Bretton's concept of "machine politics".

When considered in the context of Nigerian political reality, the highly emotive and pejorative concepts of "machine politics" and "authoritarian rule" would thus seem to have little real meaning. Indeed, while it would be unwise to press the point too far, still, even allowing for the restraining effect of Nigeria's federal parliamentary institutions, the Action Group actually behaved in a most moderate manner. Given the conditions of something approaching a Hobbesian free-for-all, which were—and still are—the conditions operative in many African states, Mid-West protagonists had escaped rather lightly.

MID-WEST EXPERIENCE AND AFRICAN MINORITY POLITICS

Favourable Structures and Composite Leadership

In considering the Mid-West experience in instrumental terms, within the broader context of African minority politics, a few points would seem worthy of emphasis. Certainly, this study has made clear the *value of favourable structural conditions. Internally,* such conditions, albeit narrow, specific and relating mainly to traditional institutions, can provide the foundations necessary for securing requisite intra-group support. Within the broader *external* context of minority activity such conditions can afford important opportunities not only for *direct, but perhaps most significantly indirect access and influence.* In particular, it is this indirect access which may allow the claimant minority to secure practical, possibly determining support from external allies.

Yet, while favourable structural conditions can afford valuable political supports, it has also been indicated that a properly balanced *composite leadership* incorporating both internal and external "intellectual", "agitator" and "bureaucratic" elements;[29] such a leadership acting under far less supportive conditions might well be expected to generate adequate thrust to ensure requisite initiatives. Where the *will and commitment* of leadership is available, even severely restrictive structures, such as those under which the Mid-West Movement often operated within the West Region, may be found to possess a measure of flexibility and support not immediately apparent. Furthermore, insofar as the claimant minority comprises a single sub-national ethnic element—or in the Mid-West instance, a number of ethnic sub-groups responsive to the unifying influence of traditional symbolic factors—then a *single traditional "syncretistic" leader* may fulfil the requisite internal functions of issue articulation, support aggregation and popular mobilisation, or at least serve as the primary enabling instrument to these ends.

It is perhaps worth noting that the *absence* of *an aspirant "charismatic" leader could be an advantage.* Such a leader may only challenge and possibly undermine the authority and integrative influence of the "syncretistic" traditional leader; he may alienate internal movement and allied party leaders operating in determining external political contexts. Indeed, such an aspirant charismat may merely cause the controlling authorities to invoke increasingly oppressive measures of social and political control;[30] measures which in fact may bring the Movement to a sudden and costly demise.

Much more valuable to the successful advancement of the minority cause after the initial phase of internal mobilisation may be the orthodox (in movement theory) *"second generation" bureaucratic/administrative leaders*[31] *who serve to advance an essentially cognitive and "participant"*[32] *case in external political fora.* It is this latter type of leader—and if one of these should be of the extra-ordinary capability of Chief Festus, it will help—acting within the context of an incrementalist strategy who may, with persisting effort, exploit the available organisational base and ideology, and hence secure those opportunities needed progressively to elevate the issue and approach the minority objective.

Autonomy and Devolution—Benefits and Costs

While these instrumental considerations may bear close relevance to the (intra-constitutional) operations of process in African ethnic minority politics—and perhaps to a larger minority context than this—there is a far more crucial issue which this study as a whole raises. This is the question of the validity of sub-national autonomy to the overall attainment, maintenance and consolidation of national (or macro-state) stability, integration and peace.

The position advanced by modern theorists of devolution is, of course, that the granting of appropriate concessions to "legitimate" claimant sub-national groups can only strengthen and stabilise the national unit; reinforce its effective integration.[33] In the view of Victor Olorunsola, such accommodatory policies are the only preventive against the imminence of massive political breakdown.[34] Dominant assimilationist regimes, fearful for their survival are, he maintains, their own worst enemies. Harsh, oppressive policies may only reinforce rather than remedy or forestall minority problems.

Autonomy and Legitimacy   What insights, then, has this Mid-West study provided? Was the Movement, first of all, a "legitimate" claimant body? Did it accurately and fully represent the views of all Mid-West peoples? In terms of popular electoral response, the 1963 Referendum could be regarded as the clearest indication of the legitimacy of the Mid-West State Movement. Furthermore, the consistent return of pro-Mid-West candidates at a succession of elections might be seen as impressive reinforcement for this view. At a more basic level, the capacity of the *Oba* and traditional symbolic/identitive structures to generate a unified, supportive response to the Mid-West issue certainly served to enhance the internal legitimacy of the Movement.

Yet, at the same time, it has also been shown that despite favourable response to ideological and leadership initiatives, fundamental internal ethnic divisions persisted. This was early demonstrated in the course of the *1950-51 Constitutional Conference* proceedings; at the time of the creation of the BDPP in 1953; and perhaps most forcefully during the *Minorities Commission* hearings. In this last instance Itsekiri, Western Ijaw, certain Ishan and Northern Edo elements made very clear their reasons for wishing to be excluded from any pan-Mid-West construct.

In this sense, then, the Mid-West Movement might be said *not* to have been a legitimate claimant group; rather that it was, as Chief Prest and others maintained, simply the vehicle for certain Bini, Edo-speaking and allied politicians securing their own political advancement. Indeed, taken to the extreme, and bearing in mind what was revealed by the *(1965) Assets Inquiry,*[35] it could be said that the Movement was, in fact, merely the institutional body through which certain Mid-West politicians—in this instance Chiefs Festus, Omo-Osagie, Osadebay and Okojie—corruptly pursued their respective material self-interests, and at the cost of the integrity and financial well-being of the state they were so ardently promoting.[36]

Autonomy and Stability   Now, secondly, did the Mid-West creation, and the lengthy process towards its creation, serve to strengthen and stabilise the Nigerian national unit? Did these serve to reinforce its integration? Certainly, Chief Osadebay's (1963) "ethnic equity" formula suggested an effective method whereby the "co-operative integration" of sub-group ethno-linguistic elements could be secured. Furthermore, it could arguably be maintained that it was the success of the Mid West experiment which at least partially contributed to the 1967 decision of the Federal Authorities to implement their 12-state devolutionary initiative.[37]

At a more basic level, however, it is clear that the Movement and the Mid-West issue, very sizeably contributed to the re-awakening and reinforcement of internal divisions within the Mid-West districts. Indeed, just as the advent of Nationalism, contrary to the expectations of most development theorists,[38] tended to strengthen divisions between and amongst majority cultural sections, so at the sub-national Mid-West level, it has been demonstrated that similar cleavages quickly started to emerge. What was perhaps most noticeable about these cleavages was the extent and depth of their penetration; the marked tendency for latent sub-group divisions to become prominent; and further for these divisions to become increasingly pronounced the closer the Movement came to its goal.

At the lowest level, within the Western Ibo ethnic community, we have seen how as early as 1953-54, cleavages between Ukwani, Agbor and Asaba clans emerged. Conflicts long resolved within existing structures could no longer be contained. Co-operation and relative stability gave way to suspicion, hostility and increasingly unstable intra(Western Ibo) group relations. Similar marked divisions were to develop within the Itsekiri community (between urban Warri, and outlying clans), within the Ishan community (particularly between Irrua and Uromi clans), in Ivbiosakon (between Ora and Okpe elements) and in Afenmai (between Auchi and Uzairue elements). At a higher level, between the dominant Mid-West sub-groups, common participation in the Movement and within the NCNC served at least to retain an over-arching commitment adequate to reinforce the pan-Mid-West ideology.

But with the approach of the Mid-West state in the post-1960 period, common ideological commitment foundered on issues of a more immediate and pragmatic nature. In the end, (1962), it was only on the basis of specific benefit allocations to separate groups that a united front adequate to meet the electoral challenge of the 1963 Referendum was secured.[39]

Autonomy and Disintegration   In terms of relations between majority parties at the National level, it is clear that the Mid-West issue had a considerable disintegrative effect. Indeed, insofar as the Federal Authorities deployed the Mid-West issue (in the post-1960 period) as a weapon against Awolowo and the (Federal) Opposition Action Group, it could be said that the Mid-West issue was a primary underlying factor contributing to the eventual breakdown of West Regional government in June 1962. Had Awolowo and the Action Group not been openly threatened with unilateral action on the Mid-West issue by Chief Festus, Movement leaders, and implicitly by the Federal Authorities, immediate Action Group anxieties would certainly not have been so great. The result of this could well have been party policies and initiatives which would have adhered to more moderate and intra-constitutional lines, rather than reinforcing what was seen as the need for extreme policies of "defensive radicalism"[40] and extra-constitutional initiatives.

Finally, and perhaps most sadly, it could be said that the "booty politics"[41] engaged in by the "corporate profiteers",[42] Chiefs Festus, Omo-Osagie and Osadebay, served to reinforce those very ethics and practices which already by 1963 were seriously undermining the order and stability of the national polity. Insofar as corruption, nepotism, etc., were considered to be primary motivating causes for the eventual breakdown of Civil Political Rule in 1966—and indeed today continue to threaten Nigeria's stability under its Military Authority[43]—it is clear that Movement leaders made their due contribution.

Altogether, then, while the Movement demonstrated a considerable instrumental capability in the course of its activity, and ultimately was successful in its quest, one might reasonably ask "at what cost" this success was secured? If conceding to the politics of sub-national autonomy means the re-awakening and reinforcement of internal cleavages and conflicts; the critical exacerbation of relations between ethnically-based national parties; and the reinforcement of "booty politics", can it all be worth it? And, in the end, as the British Colonial Authorities argued at the *Minorities Commission* hearings, may not the new autonomous construct be as "artificial" as the incorporate entity from which autonomy was initially sought?

AUTONOMY OR ASSIMILATION?: A MEASURED JUDGEMENT

Theorists of political devolution may, of course, be correct about the demonstrated dangers of nationalist regimes which render strong support to assimilationist policies. Such policies which are shaped to what these theorists regard as a monolithic and inflexible concept of national integration and nation-building[44] may indeed be counter-productive to the objectives of peace, order and stability they seek. Such regimes might well be better off to concede extensive measures of internal autonomy to claimant elements. Similarly, it may well be that the "parochial imperative"[45] is not only pronounced, but permanent.[46] Perhaps contrary to what Marxists, development, most integration and nation-building theorists tell us, the demands of ethnic minority particularism may *not* be assimilated into the homogeneous national cultures envisaged;[47] they may *not* just die away. Vertical structures, may be both more flexible and persistent[48] than structural-functionalists of Parsonian persuasion would have us believe.[49]

Furthermore, insofar as the politics of sub-national autonomy may produce multiple internal conflicts, it may be that such conflicts are not so profound or lasting as they appear.[50] It may be that they merely represent continuing, if accentuated alterations in inter-ethnic relations, or simply inevitable phases in the evolutionary dialectic towards new and ultimately more stable socio-cultural and political forms.[51] In view of these possibilities, it may be justifiable for Ronen to declare that political systems should be made to fit people, *not* the other way round,[52] and hence that autonomy solutions afford the logical and legitimate answer. All this may be quite plausible, in theory. In practice, however, it would seem that such theory may not always accord so well with the realities subsumed within ethnic minority movements.

Insofar as there is any lesson to be taken from the Mid-West experience, it may be that sheer instrumental capability proves neither the legitimacy of a Movement's claim, nor the integrative potential of its activity. Each minority claim must be judged on its particular merits; the apparent reality of its legitimacy carefully assessed. As assimilation theorists have long appreciated, the threat to established, let alone fragile developmental systems posed by sub-national autonomy claims can be severe. Certainly, the disintegrative potential—intra-group (regional) as well as intra-national—of such claims should never be under-estimated. Thus there is an obvious and legitimate need for governing authorities to proceed with considerable caution.

Yet, the existing realities of contemporary African politics must be recognised. It is a fact that the majority of Africa's national polities operate with harshly assimilationist regimes. At the same time, minority ethnic claimant groups continue aggressively to press their demands. Certainly, the parochial, for the foreseeable future, will persist. As Ali Mazrui points out, the demands arising from ethnic particularism are clearly destined to continue into the 21st century[53]—and some might say for many centuries to come.

The *survival of these regimes thus depends not only on confronting internal minority/parochial issues, but on making significant progress towards resolving these issues*. Hence, insofar as assimilationist regimes are able to retain their nerve; to grow in awareness of the superficially simple but basically highly complex particularistic demands of claimant minorities; to develop the crucial infra-structural capabilities with which to cope with existing minority demands and new claims as these should arise; then given such evolved conditions—or some approximation to them—it is possible to envisage the emergence of satisfactory mutual accommodations.

Indeed, regardless of future political/ideological direction; and regardless also of the form which crucial plans for Africa's economic development may take, *there remains a strong case that such plans can only succeed on the basis of a prior or parallel development of more flexible political structures capable of accommodating heterogeneous intra-state ethnic populations*. This is something which present day Marxist-oriented academic planners, no less than development theorists of the pre and early post-Independence eras, seem in some danger of overlooking.[54]

It must always be borne in mind that *while it is the minority/particularistic group which presses the demand, it is from the dominant or governing authority that the accommodatory initiative must come*. Thus, while the nature of minority pressure, as indicated in this study, may have a significant effect on the nature of majority response, nevertheless, it is with the majority authority that the responsibility rests for ensuring that this response is a constructive one.[55] Where a devolutionary policy is regarded to be requisite or desirable, it is possible that time and satisfactory evidence may in future justify the cession of full sub-national autonomy to a growing number of claimant groups. But as Ronen emphasises, other well-known and less radical forms of devolutionary concession are available.[56]

In this sense, the nature and level of autonomy concession secured by Mid-West protagonists should perhaps not be regarded as the optimum—or, in view of obvious shortcomings, even desirable—model. Though hardly contributing to the popularity of existing regimes amongst their minorities peoples, *it may well be that long-term national and sub-national interests will often be far better served by varied concessions of a far more limited and diffuse nature.*

References

1. M.N. Hagopian, Regimes, Movements and Ideologies, (London and New York: Longman's, 1978), p.361.

2. Neil J. Smelser, *Theory of Collective Behaviour*, (New York: The Free Press, 1962), p.14.

3. In this context "marginal" may be defined as "a concept employed to designate persons who occupy a peripheral role between any two (or more) differentiated but largely exclusive institutions or cultural complexes". David O. Arnold (ed.), *The Sociology of Sub-Cultures*, (Berkeley: Glendessary Press, 1970), p.88.

4. Eric Hoffer, *The True Believer*, (New York: Mentor Books, 1958), p. 120.

5. Osadebay, unpublished *mss.*, *op.cit.*, p.423.

6. "Broad acceptance of established relationships as 'legitimate' provides the basis of the identitive assets possessed by traditional leaders". Such persons are thus regarded as "both best suited and fated to lead". Monte Palmer, *Dilemmas of Political Development* (Chicago: Peacock Publishers, 1973), p.31. In general terms, such identitive assets, relating to common factors of history, culture and kinship, may be said to be based upon "symbolic ties with tradition and the supernatural", p.32.

7. In his "The Political Survival of Traditional Leadership", *Journal of Modern African Studies*, Vol.6, No.2 (1960), p.183, Norman Miller defines as "syncretistic", a leadership pattern "which is a reconciliation of the opposing forces of traditionalism and modernism. The result is a form of leadership which is neither modern nor traditional, but an incorporation of both".

8. In the literature of Social movements, leadership is normally seen to fall broadly into three separate classes or categories: the leadership of "the intellectual", of "the agitator". and of "the organiser/administrator". See Lewis M. Killian, "Social Movements" in R.E.L. Faris (ed.), *Handbook of Modern Sociology*, (Chicago: Rand-McNally, 1964), pp.440-43. In certain rare inst-ances—Lenin and Castro are two examples—a leader may perform dominant roles within all of these categories. It could be argued that this was true also of Omo-Osagie. Certainly, he merits inclusion within the two categories of "agitator" and "organiser/administrator".

9. See Max Weber, *The Theory of Social and Economic Organisation*, (New York: MacMillan, 1947), p.328, for the classic definition of charismatic leadership: "...resting on devotion to the specific and exceptional sanctity, heroism or exemplary character of an individual person, and of the normative patterns or order revealed or ordained by him".

10. See Maurice Duverger, *Political Parties*, (New York: Wiley, 1963), p.35.

11. Duverger outlines his concept of "caucus"—a gathering of the party's parliamentary contingent—in the course of developing his concept of "cadre" party. *Ibid.*, pp.40-52.

12. See Giovanni Sartori, "The Typology of Party Systems: Proposals for Improvement", in E. Allardt and S. Rokkan (eds.) *Mass Politics*, (New York: The Free Press, 1970), p.327.

13. See R.C. Macridis (ed.), *Political Parties: Contemporary Trends and Ideas*, (New York: Harper, 1967), p.17.

14. Leo Despres, *Cultural Pluralism and Nationalist Politics in British Guiana*, (Chicago: Rand-McNally, 1967), p.23.

15. Following early, near-exclusive emphasis on emotive appeals, the cognitive content in the evolving Mid-West ideology gained increasing emphasis in the post-1955 period. This increased cognitive emphasis was perhaps most fully demonstrated in the Movement's memorandum, *Case for a Mid-West State, op.cit.*, submitted to the *1957 London Conference on the Nigerian Constitution*.

16. See above p.336, n.7; also p.289, n.38.

17. In his "Party and Mass Organisation", in *Communism in Italy and France*, eds., S. Farrow and D. Blackmer, (Princeton: University Press, 1975), p.537, George Ross stresses the comprehensive support which dominant patron parties, always in search of extended electoral backing, are willing to render to even the most narrowly based of client elements.

18. See *Report of the Assets Tribunal...*, Vol.2, *op.cit.*

19. Osadebay, unpublished *mss., op.cit.*, p.434.

20. J. Murray-Brown, *Kenyatta*, (London: Allen and Unwin, 1972), p.212.

21. Sklar, *Nigerian Political Parties*, *op. cit.*, p.422.

22. Bretton makes specific use of his concept of "machine politics", in his *The Rise and Fall of Kwame Nkrumah* (London: Pall Mall Press, 1967), pp.5-6. In his earlier *Power and Stability in Nigeria, op.cit.*, and his later *Power and Politics in Africa*, (Chicago: Aldine, 1973), he adheres to interpretations which make clear his pre-occupation with the dynamics of "personal rule" and power abuse—that is to say, elements central to his concepts of "machine politics" and "authoritarian rule".

23. Quoted in Bretton, *Rise and Fall of Kwame Nkrumah, op. cit.*, p.6, from Maurice Duverger, *Political Parties, op. cit.*, p.147.

24. Edward Feit, "Military Coups and Political Development", *World Politics*, Vol.20, No.2, (January, 1968), p.184.

25. *Ibid.*

26. See *Report of the Commission of Inquiry into the Affairs of Certain Statutory Corporations in Western Nigeria*, Four Vols., (Lagos: Federal Printing Office, 1962).

27. See R.D. Lloyd, *Report of A Commission of Inquiry into Disturbances at Oyo*, (Ibadan: MOI, 1955).

28. Robert Mortimer, "Politics and Greed", a review article of Bretton's, *Power and Politics in Africa, op.cit.*, in *African Studies Review*, Vol.XVI, No.3 (December, 1973), p.462.

29. See Killian, "Social Movements", *op.cit.*, pp.440-43.

30. See Smelser, *Theory of Collective Behaviour*, op.cit., p.17.

31. See Killian, *op. cit.*, p.442. Indeed, Shils points out that the failure of a movement to produce or secure the services of such "second generation" leaders, can quickly lead to its failure. See E.A. Shils, "Authoritarianism: Right and Left" in R. Christie and M. Jahoda (eds.), *Studies in the Scope and Method of the Authoritarian Personality*, (Glencoe: The Free Press, 1954), pp.24-29.

32. See Hagopian, *Regimes, Movements and Ideologies*, op.cit., p.266.

33. See particularly, Cynthia H. Enloe, *Ethnic Conflict and Political Development*, (Boston: Little-Brown, 1973); and "Beyond Modernisation: The Implications for Underdeveloped Nations", *Journal of Developing Areas*, Vol.3, No.3, (April, 1969), pp. 313-18. Also, see Stephanie G. Newman, (ed.), *Small States and Segmented Societies, op.cit.*, particularly her introductory chapter "Integration: Conceptual Tool or Jargon?"; Marguerita Ross Barnett, *The Politics of Cultural Nationalism in South India*, (Princeton: Princeton University Press, 1976), *passim*; Walker Connor, "Nation-Building or Nation-Destroying?", *World Politics*,

Vol.24 (April, 1972), pp.318-342; Dov Ronen, *The Quest for Self-Determination, op.cit., passim*; P. Van den Berghe, *The Ethnic Dimension, op.cit., passim*.

34. See, Olorunsola, *The Politics of Cultural Sub-Nationalism in Africa, op.cit.*, p.xiv-xv.

35. See *Report of the Assets Tribunal...*, Vol.2, *op.cit.*

36. Here, it could be said that the Mid-West State Movement accorded very closely to Bretton's concept of "political machine". (see above p.337, n.21).

37. See B.J.O. Dudley, *Instability and Political Order: Politics and Crisis in Nigeria*, (Ibadan: Ibadan University Press, 1973), p.230.

38. For useful critiques of development theory and the alleged inadequacy of the assumptions upon which it was constructed, see Newman, *Small States and Segmented Societies, op. cit.*, pp.1-43; Harvey Glickman, "Dialogues on the Theory of African Political Development", (Parts. I and II), *Africa Report* (May, 1967), pp.38-39, and (June, 1967), pp.31-32; and Claude Ake, *The Theory of Political Development: Social Science as Imperialism, op. cit., passim*.

39. See above, pp.370-71.

40. Claude Ake, *Revolutionary Pressures in Africa*, (London: Zed Press, 1978), p.91.

41. *Ibid*, p.80.

42. Frantz Fanon, *The Wretched of the Earth*, (Harmondsworth: Penguin, 1967), p.134.

43. See Anthony Kirk-Greene and Douglas Rimmer, *Nigeria Since 1970*, (London: Hodder and Stoughton, 1981), pp.153 ff.

44. Newman reminds us that these terms themselves are misnomers, "...terms such as 'national identity', 'nationalism' and 'nation building' have taken on fixed meanings in the vocabulary of social sciences. To be precise, these terms should be referred to as 'state identity', 'statism' or 'state-building'", Newman, *Small States and Segmented Societies, op. cit.*, p.2).

45. See L.C. Bucheitt, *Secession: The Legitimacy of Self-Determination*, (New Haven: Yale University Press, 1978), p.2.

46. *Ibid*. See also Enloe, *Ethnic Politics and Political Development, op.cit.*, p.268.

47. For assimilationist arguments of "traditional" (American social science) development theory, see particularly, Leonard Binder, "National Integration and Political Development", *American Political Science Review*, Vol.LVIII (September, 1964), pp.622-663; Myron Weiner, "Political Integration and Political Development", *Annals of the American Academy of Political and Social Sciences*,

Vol.358 (March, 1965), pp.52-64; Claude Ake, "Political Integration and Political Stability", *World Politics*, Vol.XIX, No.3 (April, 1967), pp. 486-499, and *A Theory of Political Integration*, (Homewood, Ill.: The Dorsey Press, 1967); Karl Deutsch, "Communication Theory and Political Integration", and "Transaction Flows as Indicators of Political Cohesion", in Philip E. Jacob and J. V. Toscano, (eds.), *The Integration of Political Communities*, (Philadelphia: Lippincott, 1964), pp.46-97.

For assimilationist arguments of modern Marxist-oriented development theory, see particularly, P.C.W. Gutkind and I. Wallerstein (eds.), *The Political Economy of Contemporary Africa*, (London: Sage, 1977); P.C.W. Gutkind, Robin Cohen and Jean Copans (eds.), *African Labour History*, (London: Sage, 1979); Richard Sandbrook and Robin Cohen, *The Development of an African Working Class*, (London: Longmans, 1975); Robin Cohen, *et al*, *Peasants and Proletarians: The Struggles of Third World Workers* (London: Hutchinson, 1979); Claude Ake, *Revolutionary Pressures in Africa, op.cit.*; T.M. Shaw, "From Dependence to Self-Reliance: Africa's Prospects for the Next Twenty Years", *International Journal*, Vol. XXXV (Summer, 1980), pp.821-44

48. See Harold R. Isaacs, *Idols of the Tribe: Group Identity and Political Change*, (New York: Harper and Row, 1975), p.41; and Enloe, *Ethnic Conflict and Political Development, op.cit.*, pp.267-68. Also see Leo A. Despres (ed.), *Ethnicity and Resource Competition in Plural Societies*, (The Hague: Mouton, 1975), particularly chapters by Onigu Otite, "Resource Competition and Inter-Ethnic Relations in Nigeria", and Elliot E. Skinner, "Competition within Ethnic Systems in Africa".

49. See Robert Gamer, *The Developing Nations* (Boston: Allyn and Bacon, 1976), p.369; S.N. Eisenstadt, "Breakdowns in Modernisation',' *Economic Development and Cultural Change*, Vol.12. (July, 1964), pp.345-67; Rajni Kothari, "Tradition and Modernity Re-Visited", *Government and Opposition*, Vol. 3 (Summer, 1968), p.273-93; Ali Mazrui, *The African Condition: A Political Diagnosis*, (London: Heinemann, 1980), p.93.

50. See Max Gluckman, *Custom and Conflict in Africa*, (Glencoe: The Free Press, 1964), pp.1-4.

51. See Basil Davidson and A. Bronda, *Crossroads in Africa*, (Nottingham: Russell Press, 1980), p.86.

52. See Ronen *The Quest for Self-Determination, op.cit.*, p.20.

53. See Mazrui, *The African Condition, op.cit.*, p.93.

54. Indeed, rather than diminishing ethnic identities, Robert Melson sees Marxist-Socialist developmental systems producing popular insecurity which in turn will serve only to strengthen these identities. (See Melson's review of Gutkind and Wallerstein's, *The Political Economy of Contemporary Africa, op.cit.*, in *American*

Political Science Review, Vol.72 (September, 1978), p.1104). See also, Arnold Hughes, "The Nation-State in Black Africa", in Leonard Tivey (ed.), *The Nation State: The Formation of Modern Politics*, (Oxford: Martin Robertson, 1981), pp.122-147 for a most useful overview which seeks to put the problems of contemporary ethno-pluralism into a meaningful "statist" and "nationalist" perspective.

55. See Robert Bierstedt, "The Sociology of Majorities", *American Sociological Review*, XIII, (December, 1948), p.709.

56. See Ronen, *The Quest for Self-Determination, op. cit.*, p.22.

BIBLIOGRAPHY

*GENERAL LISTING OF MATERIALS
CONSULTED FOR THIS STUDY*

PART I: PUBLISHED MATERIALS

*BOOKS AND PAMPHLETS**

Aitalegbe, R.M. *Profile: Oba Akenzua II, CMG*. Benin City: MOI, 1964.

Ajisafe, A.K. *Laws and Customs of the Benin People*. Lagos: Kash and Klare Bookshop, 1946.

Ake, Claude. A Theory of Political Integtration. Homewood, Ill.: Dorsey Press, 1967.

— *Revolutionary Pressures in Africa*. London: Zed Press, 1978.

— *Social Science as Imperialism: The Theory of Political Development*. Ibadan: University Press, 1979.

Alagoa, E.J. *A History of The Niger Delta*. Ibadan: University Press, 1972.

Aluko, S.A. *The Problems of Self-Government for Nigeria: A Critical Analysis*. Devon: Stockwell, 1955.

Anene, J.C. *Southern Nigeria in Transition, 1885-1906*. Cambridge: University Press, 1966.

Arnold, David O.(ed.) *The Sociology of Sub-Cultures*. Berkeley: Glendessary Press, 1970.

Avbenake, J.C. *Memorandum on Rubber Development Programmes*. (Prepared and submitted to the Federal Ministry of Agriculture and Natural Resources, in connection with the Six Year Development Plan). Sapele: Oluyemi Printing Works, n.d.

Awolowo, Obafemi. *Path To Nigerian Freedom*. London: Faber, 1947.

Awolowo, Obafemi. *Forward to a New Nigeria*. Speeches at the Nigerian Constitutional Conference and Other Occasions. London: 1957.

Awolowo, Obafemi. *Awo: The Autobiography of Chief Obafemi Awolowo*. Cambridge: University Press, 1961.

Azikiwe, Nnamdi. *Zik: Selection from the Speeches of Nnamdi Azikiwe*, edited by Philip Harris. Cambridge: University Press, 1961.

Azikiwe, Nnamdi. *Political Blueprint for Nigeria*. Lagos: Africa Book Company, 1943.

— *After Three Years of Stewardship*. (An Address). Enugu: 1957.

— *The Development of Political Parties in Nigeria*. London: 1957

Barnett, Marguerite Ross. *The Politics of Cultural Nationalism in Southern India*. Princeton: University Press, 1976.

Bradbury, R.E. *The Benin Kingdom*. London: International Affairs Institute, 1957.

Bretton, H.L. *Power and Stability in Nigeria*. New York: Praeger, 1962.

— *The Rise and Fall of Kwame Nkrumah*. London: Pall Mall, 1967.

— *Power and Politics in Africa*. Chicago: Aldine Press, 1973.

Buchanan. K.M and Pugh J.C. *Land and Peoples in Nigeria*. London: University of London Press (revised ed.), 1958.

Bucheitt, L.C. *Secession: The Legitimacy of Self-Determination*. New Haven: Yale University Press, 1978.

Coleman, J.S. *Nigeria: Background to Nationalism*. Los Angeles: University of California Press, 1955.

Cohen, Robin, et al. *Peasants and Proletarians: The Struggles of Third World Workers*. London: Hutchinson, 1979.

Cowan, L.G. *Local Government in West Africa*. New York: Columbia University Press, 1958.

Davidson, Basil and Ademola A. (eds.) The New West Africa. London: Allen and Unwin, 1953.

Davidson, Basil and Bronda, A. *Crossroads in Africa*. Nottingham: Russell Press, 1980.

Despres, Leo A. *Ethnicity and Resource Competition in Plural Societies*. The Hague: Mouton, 1975.

— *Cultural Pluralism and Nationalist Politics in British Guiana*. Chicago: Rand-McNally, 1967.

Dike, K.O. *Trade and Politics in the Niger Delta, 1830-1885*. Oxford: Clarendon Press, 1956.

Dofny, J and Akiwowo, A. (eds.) *National and Ethnic Movements*. London: Sage, 1980.

Dudley, B.J.O. *Instability and Political Order: Politics and Crisis in Nigeria*. Ibadan: University Press, 1973.

Duverger, Maurice. *Political Parties*. New York: Wiley, 1963.

Egharevba, Jacob. *A Short History of Benin*. Ibadan: University Press, 1960.

Elias, T.O. *Federation vs. Confederation and the Nigerian Federation*. Port of Spain Trinidad: Government Printer, 1960.

Emerson, R.E. *Self-Determination Revisited in the Era of De-Colonisation*. Occasional Papers on International Affairs, No.9, December 1964. Cambridge: Harvard University Press, 1964.

Enahoro, E.A. *Fugitive Offender: The Story of a Political Prisoner*. London: Cassell, 1965.

Enloe, Cynthia H. *Ethnic Conflict and Political Development*. Boston: Little, Brown, 1973.

Ezera, Kalu. *Constitutional Developments in Nigeria*. Cambridge: University Press, 1960.

Fanon, Frantz. *The Wretched of the Earth*. Harmondsworth: Penguin, 1967.

Forde, D. and Kaberry, P. (eds.) West African Kingdoms in the Nineteenth Century. Oxford: University Press, 1967.

Gamer, Robert. *The Developing Nations*. Boston: Allyn and Bacon, 1976.

Gluckman, Max. *Custom and Conflict in Africa*. Glencoe: The Free Press, 1964.

Gutkind, P.C.W., Cohen, Robin and Copans, Jean (eds.) *African Labour History*. London: Sage, 1979.

Gutkind, P.C.W. and Wallerstein, I. (eds.) *The Political Economy of Contemporary Africa*. London: Sage, 1977.

Gwam, L.C. *Inventory of Administrative Records Assembled from Benin Province*. Ibadan: National Archives, 1961.

Hagopian, M.N. *Regimes, Movements and Ideologies*. London and New York: Longman's, 1978.

Harris, Philip. *Local Government in Southern Nigeria*. Cambridge: University Press, 1957.

Hodgkin, Thomas. *Nationalism in Colonial Africa*. London: Muller, 1956.

Hodgkin, Thomas (ed.) *Nigeria Perspectives: An Historical Anthology*. London: Oxford University Press, 1960.

Hoffer, Eric. *The True Believer*. New York: Mentor Books, 1958.

Hubbard, J.W. *The Sobo of the Niger Delta*. Zaria: Gaskiya Corporation, 1952.

Ikime, Obaro. *Merchant Prince of the Niger Delta*. London: Hutchinson, 1968.

— *Niger Delta Rivalry: Itsekiri-Urhobo Relations and European Enterprise, 1884-1936*. Ibadan History Series.

Imoukhede, F.A. *Chief Omo-Osagie*. (Printed Circular). Benin City: MOI, n.d.

Isaacs, Harold R. *Idols of the Tribes Group Identity and Political Change*. New York: Harper and Row, 1975.

Isuman, J.U. *Need for More States in Nigeria with some Submissions for a Mid-West State*. Sapele: 1957.

— *Facts About the Mid-West State*. Lagos: Amalgamated Press, 1960.

— *You and the Mid-West Plebiscite: What You Must Know*. Lagos: Ribway Printers, 1963.

Kirk-Greene, A.H.M. and Rimmer, Douglas. *Nigeria Since 1970*. London: Hodder and Stoughton, 1981.

Lawal-Osula, U. (ed.) *Benin Native Authority: New Constitution of 1948.* Benin City: Two Brothers Press, 1949.

Liboro, Eddy. *NCNC or the AG: The Mid-West State Issue.* Warri: Kaigho Industrial Enterprises, 1961.

Mackintosh, J.P. *Nigerian Government and Politics.* London: Allen and Unwin, 1966.

Macridis, R.C. (ed.) *Political Parties: Contemporary Trends and Ideas.* New York: Harper and Row, 1967.

Magid, Alvin. *Man in the Middle: Leadership and Conflict in a Nigerian Society.* Manchester: University Press, 1976.

Mazrui, Ali A. *The African Condition: A Political Diagnosis.* London: Heinemann, 1980.

McEwen, F.S. *NCNC on the March: Being the Text of the National Secretary's Report to the 1960 Annual Convention of the Party at Lagos, 10 and 11 September, 1960.* Yaba: NCNC Bureau of Information and Publicity, 1960.

Melson, Robert and Wolpe, Howard (eds.) *Nigeria: Modernisation and the Politics of Communalism.* East Lansing: Michigan State University Press, 1971.

Morel, E.D. Nigeria: *Its Peoples and Its Problems.* London: Smith-Elder, 1911.

Murray-Brown, J. *Kenyatta.* London: Allen and Unwin, 1972.

Nee-Ankrah, S.W. *Whither Benin?* Ibadan: Union Press, 1951.

Neuman, Stephanie G.(ed.) *Small States and Segmented Societies.* New York: Praeger, 1976.

Numa, Yamu. *Why I Break Faith with the NCNC.* Ibadan: African Press for the Action Group Bureau of Information, 1955.

Obano, G.A. *Path to National Unity in Benin.* Ibadan: Ife-Olu Press, 1953.

Odiete, J.E. *Problems of Nigerian Minorities.* Lagos: n.d.

Okoh, D.E.E. *Men and Matters: The Struggles for the Creation of the New Mid-West Region.* Benin City: Mid-West Publishing Company, 1963.

Okpara, M.I. *Presidential Address at the NCNC Annual Convention, Kano, 21 February. 1964.* Enugu: Government Printer, 1964.

Okpu, Ugbana. *Ethnic Minority Problems in Nigerian Politics.* Uppsala: Almquist and Wiksell International, 1977.

Olorunsola, V.A. (ed.) *The Politics of Cultural Sub-Nationalism in Africa.* New York: Anchor Books, 1972.

Omoregie, S.O. *A Glance at Benin Politics.* Sapele: Central Press, 1952.

Otite, Onigu. *Autonomy and Dependence: The Urhobo Kingdom of Okpe in Modern Nigeria.* London: Hurst, 1973.

Palmer, Monte. *Dilemmas of Political Development*. Chicago: Peacock Publishers, 1973.

Parrinder, Geoffrey. *Religion in an African City*. London: Oxford University Press, 1953.

Perham, Margery. *Lugard: The Years of Authority, 1898-1945*. Vol.II. London: Collins, 1960.

Post, K.W.J. The *Nigerian Federal Election of 1959*. London: Oxford University Press for the Nigerian Institute of Social and Economic Research, 1963.

Post, K.W.J. and Jenkins, G.D. *The Price of Liberty: Personality and Politics in Colonial Nigeria*. Cambridge: University Press, 1973.

Post, K.W.J. and Vickers, M. *Structure and Conflict in Nigeria: 1960-66*. London: Heinemann, 1973.

Ronen, Dov. *The Quest for Self-Determination*. New Haven: Yale University Press, 1979.

Roth, H.L. *Great Benin: Its Customs, Arts and Horrors*. Halifax: 1903.

Rothchild, D.C. *Safeguarding Nigeria's Minorities*. African Reprint Series. Pittsburgh: Duquesne University Press, 1964.

Ryder, A.F.C. *Benin and the Europeans, 1485-1897*. Ibadan History Series. London: Longmans, 1969.

Sandbrook, Richard and Cohen, Robin. *The Development of an African Working Class*. London: Longmans, 1975.

Sklar, R.L. *Nigerian Political Parties*. Princeton: University Press, 1963.

Sklar, R.L. and Whittaker, C.S. *Nigerian Political Parties, and The Nigerian Political Class*. Two papers reproduced by special permission of the authors for the Peace Corps Training Programme, at Teachers College, Columbia University, 1963.

Smelser, Neil J. *Theory of Collective Behaviour*. New York: The Free Press, 1962.

Talbot, P.A. *Tribes of the Niger Delta*. London: The Sheldon Press, 1930.

— *The Peoples of Southern Nigeria*. Vol.I. London: Humphrey Milford, 1926.

Thomas, N.W. *Anthropological Report on the Edo-Speaking Peoples*. London: Harrison and Sons, 1910.

Tseayo, J.I. *Conflict and Incorporation in Nigeria: Integration of the Tiv*. Zaria: Gaskiya Corporation, 1975.

Ughulu, E.O. *A Short History of Esan*. Lagos: Ribway Printers, 1950.

Uwaifo, H.O. *Benin Community Intelligence Report on Benin Division: Being the Political History of Benin from 1936 to 1948*. Oshogbo: FMS Press, n.d.

— *My Past Public Performances in Benin*. Benin City: Aguebor Printers, 1955.

Van den Berghe, P.L. *The Ethnic Dimension.* New York: Elsevier Press, 1981.

Weber, Max. *The Theory of Social and Economic Organisation.* New York: MacMillan, 1947.

Whittaker, C.S. *The Politics of Tradition, Continuity and Change in Northern Nigeria.* Princeton: University Press, 1970.

Zolberg, Aristide. *One Party Government in the Ivory Coast.* Princeton: University Press, 1964.

— *Creating Political Order: The Party States of West Africa.* Chicago: Rand-McNally, 1966.

The Case for a Mid-West State. (Mimeo.) Warri: 1957.

Problems of Nigerian Minorities. Lagos: Pacific Printing Works, 1959.

Proceedings of the Summit Conference of Independent African States. Vol.II., Addis Ababa: 1963.

Planting the Vineyard: Six Months of Interim Administration in Mid-Western Nigeria. Benin City: MOI, 1964.

Mid-Western Nigeria at a Glance. Benin City: MOI, 1971.

ARTICLES AND CONFERENCE PAPERS*

Ajayi, J.F.A. "Nineteenth Century Origins of Nigerian Nationalism", *Journal of the Historical Society of Nigeria*, Vol.II, No.1 (December, 1961), pp. 196-211.

Ake, Claude, "Political Integration and Political Stability", *World Politics*, Vol. XIX, No.3 (April 1967), pp.486-499.

Akenzua, Edun. "Benin... 1897: A Bini's View", *Nigeria*, No.65, (June 1960).

Anene, J.C. "The Foundations of British Rule in Southern Nigeria, 1885-1891", *Journal of the Historical Society of Nigeria*, Vol.I, No.4 (December 1959), pp.253-262.

Armstrong, Robert G. "The Development of Kingdoms in Negro Africa", *Journal of the Historical Society of Nigeria*, Vol.II, No.1, December, 1961), pp.27-40.

Bierstedt, R. "The Sociology of Majorities", *American Sociological Review*, Vol.XIII (December 1948), pp.701-23.

Binder, Leonard. "National Integration and Political Development", *American Political Science Review*, Vol.LVII, (September 1964), pp. 622-63.

---

* Listing is alphabetical by author. Entries with no author are listed chronologically at the end of this section

Bradbury, R.E. "Chronological Problems in the Study of Benin History", *Journal of the Historical Society of Nigeria*, Vol.I, No.4 (December 1959), pp.263-87.

— "Ezomo's Ikegobo and the Benin Cult of the Hand", *Man*, Vol.LXI (August 1961), pp.129-32.

— "The Historical Uses of Comparative Ethnography with Special Reference to Benin and the Yoruba", in Jan Vansina *et al*, *The Historian in Tropical Africa*. London: Oxford University Press for the International African Institute, 1964.

— "The Kingdom of Benin", in D. Forde and P. Kaberry(eds.), *West African Kingdoms in the Nineteenth Century*. London: Oxford University Press for the International African Institute, 1967.

— "Patterns of Political Incorporation in West African Kingdoms", *Centre of West African Studies Seminar Series*, University of Birmingham (Fall 1967), mimeo.

— "Continuities and Dis-continuities in Pre-Colonial Benin Politics", in Michael Banton(ed.), *History and Social Anthropology*, ASA Monograph Series, No.7. London: Tavistock, 1968.

Brand, J.A. "The Mid-West State Movement in Nigerian Politics", *Political Studies*, Vol.XIII, No.3 (1965), pp.346-65.

Connor, Walker. "Nation-Building or Nation-Destroying?", *World Politics*, Vol.24 (April 1972), pp.318-42.

Davidson, Basil. "The Fact of African History", *Africa South*, Vol.II (1958), pp-44-49.

Deutsch, K.W. "Communication Theory and Political Integration", and "Transaction Flows as Indicators of Political Cohesion", in P.E. Jacob and J.V. Toscano(eds.), *The Integration of Political Communities*. Philadelphia: Lippincott, 1964.

Eisenstadt, S.N. "Breakdowns in Modernisation", *Economic Development and Cultural Change*, Vol.12 (July 1964), pp.245-67.

Enloe, C.H. "Beyond Modernisation: The Implications for Under-Developed Nations", *Journal of Developing Areas*, Vol.3, No.3(April 1969), pp. 313-18.

Feit, Edward. "Military Coups and Political Development", *World Politics*, Vol. 20, No.2 (January 1968), pp.174-89.

Gallwey, H. "Journeys in Benin", *Geographical Journal*, Vol.I (1893).

Glickman, Harvey. "Dialogues on the Theory of African Political Development", (Parts I and II), *Africa Report*, (May 1967), pp.38-39, and (June 1967), pp.31-32.

Granville, R.K. and Roth, H.L. "Notes on the Jekris, Sobos and Ijos of the Warri District of the Niger Coast Protectorate", *Journal of the Anthropological Institute*, Vol.XXVIII (1898), pp.104-26.

Hopkins. A.G. "Economic Aspects of Political Movements in Nigeria and the Gold Coast", *Journal of African History*, Vol.VII, No.I (1966), pp.133-152.

Hughes, Arnold. "The Nation-State in Black Africa", in Leonard Tivey (ed.), *The Nation-State: The Formation of Modern Politics*. Oxford: Martin Robertson, 1981.

Igbafe, P.A. "British Rule in Benin, 1897-1920: Direct or Indirect?", *Journal of the Historical Society of Nigeria*, Vol.III, No.4, (June 1967).

— "The Pre-Colonial Economic Basis of the Benin Kingdom", University of Ife, *History Seminar Series*, No.4 (1968-69), mimeo.

Ikime, Obaro. "The Anti-Tax Riots in Warri Province, 1927-28", *Journal of the Historical Society of Nigeria*, Vol.III, No.3 (December, 1966), pp.559-75.

Lloyd, P.C. "The Itsekiri", in R.E. Bradbury, *The Benin Kingdom*. London: International Affairs Institute,1957.

— "The Development of African Kingdoms", *Centre of West African Studies Seminar Series*, University of Birmingham, (Autumn 1966).

— "The Itsekiri in the Nineteenth Century: An Outline Social History", *Journal of African History*, Vol.IV, No.2 (1963), pp.207-32.

— "Tribalism in Warri", in the *Proceedings of the Fifth Annual Conference of the West African Institute of Social and Economic Research*, University College: Ibadan, 1956.

Mason, Philip. "Conference and Minorities Commission: I, Prospects for Permanence", *West Africa*, 22 November, 1958, p.1115.

— "Conference and Minorities Commission: II, Safeguards for Citizens", *West Africa*, 29 November, 1958, p.1135.

Melson, Robert. A Review of P.C.W. Gutkind and I. Wallerstein, The Political Economy of Contemporary Africa, London: 1977, in American Political Science Review, Vol.72 (September 1978), p.1104.

Miller, Norman. "The Political Survival of Traditional Leadership", *Journal of Modern African Studies*, Vol.6, No.2 (1968), pp.183-201.

Mittlebeeler, E.U. "Legal Controls over Local Government in the Western State of Nigeria", *The Quarterly Journal of Administration*, Vol.5, No.2 (January 1971).

Mortimer, Robert. "Politics and Greed", being a Review of H.L. Bretton's *Power and Politics in Africa*, Chicago: 1973, in *African Studies Review*, Vol.XVI, No.3 (December 1973), pp.460-62.

Newbury, Colin. "Benin and Itsekiri", A Review of *The Benin Kingdom*, by R.E. Bradbury, (London: 1957), in *West Africa*, 27 July, 1957, p.709.

Oloyo, M.O. "Afenmai Country in the Pre-Colonial Era: A Preliminary Survey of the Land, the People and their Traditions of Origin", University of Ife, *History Seminar Series*, No.8 (1968-69), mimeo.

Ross, George. "Party and Mass Organisation", in S. Farrow and D. Blackmer, *Communism in Italy and France*, Princeton: University Press, 1975.

Ryder, A.F.C. "Egharevba". A Review of *A Short History of Benin*, by Jacob Egharevba, (Ibadan: 1960), in *Journal of the Historical Society of Nigeria*, Vol.II, No.I (December 1961), p.286.

— "Reconsideration of the Ife-Benin Relationship", *Journal of African History*, Vol.V, No.I (1965), pp.25-38.

Salubi, A. "The Establishment of British Administration in the Urhobo Country", *Journal of the Historical Society of Nigeria*, Vol.I, No.3, December 1958), pp.184

Sartori, Giovanni. "The Typology of Party Systems: Proposals for Improvements", in E. Allardt and S. Rokkan(eds.) *Mass Politics*. New York: The Free Press, 1970.

Shaw, T.M. "From Dependence to Self-Reliance: Africa's Prospects for the Next Twenty Years", *International Journal*, Vol.XXXV, (Summer, 1980) pp . 821-44.

Shils, E.A. "Authoritarianism: Right and Left", in R. Christie and M. Jahoda (eds.) *Studies in the Scope and Method of the Authoritarian Personality*. Glencoe: The Free Press, 1954.

Weiner, Myron. "Political Integration and Political Development", *Annals of the American Academy of Political and Social Sciences*, Vol.358 (March 1965), pp.52-64.

Welch, J.W. "The Isoko Tribe", *Africa*, Vol.VII (1934), pp.160-73.

Williams, B.A. "The Mid-West and the New Region Issue", in his *Political Trends in Nigeria. 1960-64*. Ibadan: African Educational Press, n.d.

Wraith, R.E. "Local Government", in J.P. Mackintosh, *Nigerian Government and Politics*. London: 1966.

"Historic Debate in Lagos", *West Africa*, 6 April, 1957, p.319.

Nigeria's New Constitution", *West Africa*, 13 July, 1957, p 655.

"Awolowo and Azikiwe", *West Africa*, 17 August, 1957, p.801.

"Alhaji Abubakar's Team", *West Africa*, 7 September, 1957, p.862.

"Minorities Commission's First Stage", *West Africa*, 11 January, 1958, p.58.

"Labour Lawyers Join the Minorities", *West Africa*, 15 February, 1958, p.147.

"Western Nigeria and Minorities", *West Africa*, 30 August, 1958, p.818.

"Nigeria's Minorities: I. The Two Wests", *West Africa*, 30 August, 1958, p.819.

"The Golfing Minister", A Brief Biography of Chief Anthony Enahoro, *West Africa*, 20 September, 1958, p.893.

"The Minorities Mouse", *West Africa*, 20 September, 1958, p.891.

"Nigeria's Unfinished Business", *West Africa*, 27 September, 1958, pp.913-14.

"Constitution for Minorities", *West Africa*, 25 October, 1958, p.1002.

"The Unknown Giant", *West Africa*, 1 November, 1958, p.1031.

"The Conference Communique", *West Africa*, 1 November, 1958, p.1035.

"Straitjacket or Safeguard for Nigeria?", *West Africa*, 15 November, 1958, p.1085.

"Nigeria's Independence Constitution: II. The Structure of the Federation", *West Africa*, 22 November, 1958, p.1111.

"Notes on the Form of Bini Government", *Man*, Vol.IV, No.33 (1904).

"A Survey of the Development of Local Government in the African Territories Since 1947", Supplement to the *Journal of African Administration*, Vol.IV, No.4 (October 1952) .

African Conference: Being a Conference of Delegates from the Legislative Councils of the British African Colonies and Protectorates Held at Lancaster House, London, 29 September to 9 October, 1948. mimeo.

Principles and Methods of Colonial Administration. Collected papers from Symposium Conducted Jointly by the Colston Research Society and the University of Bristol, 1950. mimeo.

Summer Conference on Local Government in Africa. Held under the Auspices of Cambridge University Overseas Studies Committee, 28 August to 9 September, 1961, at King's College, Cambridge. mimeo.

GOVERNMENT PUBLICATIONS[*]

UNITED KINGDOM AND FEDERATION OF NIGERIA

Conference of Yoruba Chiefs, 1937: Records of Proceedings held held at Oyo 31 March and 1 April, 1937. Lagos: Government Printer, 1937. (UIA)

Conference of Yoruba Chiefs, 1938. Records of Proceedings Held at Ife, 16 and 17 March, 1938. Lagos: Government Printer, 1938. (UIA)

Conference at Yoruba Chiefs, 1939. Records of Proceedings Held at Ibadan, from 29 May to 1 June, 1939. Lagos: Government Printer, 1939. (UIA).

---

[*] Entries are listed in chronological order.

Conference of Chiefs of the Western Provinces of Nigeria: Record of Proceedings Held at Abeokuta from 14 to 16 May, 1940. Lagos: Government Printer, 1940. PX/El. (INA).

Conference of Chiefs of the Western Provinces of Nigeria: Record of Proceedings Held at Benin City, from 25 August to 1 September, 1942. Lagos: Government Printer, 1942. PX/El. (INA)

Proposals for Revision of the Constitution of Nigeria, 1945. Cmnd. 6599. Lagos: Government Printer, 1945.

Review of the Constitution: Regional Recommendations. Lagos: Government Printer, 1945.

Despatch from the Secretary of State For the Colonies to Governors of African Territories. London: HMSO, 1947.

Proceedings of the General Conference on Review of the Constitution. Lagos: Government Printer, 1950.

Report of the Drafting Committee of the Constitution. Lagos: Government Printer, 1950.

Report by the Conference on the Nigerian Constitution held in London July and August 1953. Cmnd. 8934. London: HMSO, 1953.

Nigeria: Report of the Fiscal Commissioner on the Financial Effects of the Proposed New Constitutional Arrangements. Cmnd. 9026. London: HMSO, 1953.

An Economic Survey of the Colonial Territories, 1951. Vol.III. London: HMSO, 1953.

Report by the Resumed Conference on the Nigerian Constitution Held in Lagos, January and February, 1954. Cmnd. 9059. London: HMSO, 1954.

Constitutional Progress in the Federation of Nigeria. No. R3172. November 1955.

Who's Who in Nigeria. Lagos: Nigerian Printing and Publishing Company, 1956.

Report by the Nigeria Constitutional Conference held in London, May and June, 1957. Cmnd. 207. London: HMSO, 1957.

Facts about the Federation of Nigeria. No. R3222. February, 1957.

Report of the Constituency Delimitation Commission, 1958. Lagos: Government Printer, 1958.

Nigeria: Report of the Commission Appointed to Enquire into the Fears of Minorities and the Means of Allaying them. Cmnd. 505. London: HMSO, 1958.

Report by the Ad-Hoc Meeting of the Nigeria Constitutional Conference. Lagos: Federal Government Printer, 1958.

Report by the Resumed Nigeria Constitutional Conference held in London. September and October, 1958. Cmnd. 569. London: HMSO, 1958.

Nigeria: Report of the Fiscal Commission. Cmnd. 481. London: HMSO, 1958.

Nigeria: Report of the Constituency Delimitation Commission, 1958. Lagos: Federal Government Printer, 1958.

Who's Who in the Federal House of Representatives. Lagos: Federal Information Service, 1958.

Guide to the Parliament of the Federation. Lagos: MOI, 1961.

Emergency Power Regulations, Federation of Nigeria Official Gazette, Supplement to No. 38, Vol. 49, (29 May, 1962).

Report of the Commission of Inquiry into the Affairs of Certain Statutory Corporations in Western Nigeria, Four Vols. Lagos: Federal Printing Offices, 1962)

Federation of Nigeria Official Gazette (Extraordinary), of 12 June, 1963. Vol. 50, No. 38.

Legislative Council of Nigeria Debates.

House of Representatives Debates.

Parliamentary Debates.

WESTERN REGION

Report of the Commission of Inquiry into the Disturbances at Burutu June 1947. Lagos: Government Printer, 1947. (UIA).

Local Government in the Western Provinces of Nigeria, 1939-49: A Factual Record of Political Developments During the Last Ten Years. Lagos: 1950.

Forest Department Policy for the Western Region, Nigeria. by the Ministry of Agriculture and Natural Resources, June 1952. Ibadan: Government Printer, 1952.

Report on the First Elections to the Western House of Assembly General Elections, 1951. Ibadan: Government Printer, 1952.

Who's Who in the Western House of Assembly. Lagos: Public Relations Department, 1952.

The Electoral Ladder. An Explanation of the Electoral System from the Village Level to the Western House of Assembly. Ibadan: Public Relations Department, 1953.

Top of the Ladder. An Explanation of Functions and Activities of Houses of Assembly and Chiefs. Ibadan: Public Relations Department, 1953.

Steps of the Ladder. A Practical Guide to Elections from the Village Level to the Western House of Assembly. Ibadan: Public Relations Department, 1953.

Self-Government for the Western Region. Sessional Paper No. 3 of 1955.

Development of the Western Region of Nigeria, 1955-60. Sessional paper No.4 of 1955.

Lloyd, R.D. *Report of a Commission of Inquiry into Disturbances at Oyo.* Ibadan: MOI, 1955.

Population Census of the Western Region of Nigeria, 1952. Lagos: Census Superintendent, 1956.

Report of the Commission of Inquiry into the Administration of the Ibadan District Council. Abingdon: 1956.

Report on the Holding of the 1956 Parliamentary Election to the Western House of Assembly, Nigeria. Ibadan: Government Printer, 1957.

Local Government Manual. Ibadan: 1957.

Iles, C.E. *Report of an Inquiry into the Affairs of the Asaba Urban District Council.* 1956.

Report on Local Government Elections in the Western Region of Nigeria, 1958. Ibadan: Government Printer, 1958.

Statement by the Hon. the Premier Chief Obafemi Awolowo on the Regional Civil Service. 1958.

West Regional Legal Notices. Legislation of the Western Region of Nigeria. Annual Volumes, 1951-1959. Ibadan: Government Printer.

Proposals for the Creation of a Minority Area for the Mid-West Area of the Western Region and the Establishment of a Mid-West Minority Council. Sessional paper No.14 (1960), Ibadan: Government Printer, 1960.

Report of the Commission of Inquiry into the Warri Division (Itsekiri Communal Lands) Trust. Western Nigeria Official Document No. 2 (1963). Ibadan: Government Printer, 1963.

Report of the Commission of Inquiry into the Sapele Urban District (Okpe Communal Land) Trust. Western Nigeria Official Document No.1 (1963). Ibadan: Government Printer, 1963.

Western Region Production Development Board. Annual Reports, 1954-62.

Western Region Marketing Board. Annual Reports, 1954-62.

Western Region Finance Corporation. Annual Reports and Accounts, 1955-62.

Debates: House of Assembly.

Debates: House of Chiefs.

OTHER REGIONS

The Hudson Report on Provincial Authorities. Kaduna: Government Printer, 1956).

Report of the Commission Appointed to Enquire into the Owegbe Cult. (Benin City: MOI, 1966).

Report of the Inquiry into the Assets of Public Officers in the Mid-Western State of Nigeria. 2 Vols. Benin City: MOI, 1969.

NIGERIAN NEWSPAPERS

The Benin Voice

Daily Express

Daily Times

The Edo Voice

The Mid-West Echo

The Mid-West Champion

Nigerian Star

Nigerian Tribune

Southern Nigeria Defender

Sunday Post

West African Pilot

Part II: Unpublished Materials*

1. *Nigerian National Archives, Ibadan*

(a) *Provincial and Constitutional Papers*

Papers on the Agreement Between the Oba and Council of Benin to the British Government re: the Obiariti Forest Reserve in Benin Province, 1921. Ben Prof l/BP/4222.

Papers on the Agreement Between the Oba and Council of Benin to the British Government Re: The Middle Ovia River (Timber) Reserve 1922. Ben Prof 1/4221 and 4223.

Report on Proposed Forest Reserves within Benin Division 1934. Ben Prof 6 BP/1/21.

Political Situation in Benin Division, 1939. Ben Prof BP/1472.

Papers on Sapele Land Case Between the Itsekiri and the Urhobo, 1942. Ben Prof 2/BP/2102.

Report of the First Meeting of the Benin Provincial Council, Held 11 November, 1946. Ben Prof BP/2328.

Official Correspondence: Warri Province. 1946. WP/85/Vol.I.

Report of the Second Meeting of the Benin Provincial Council Held at Agbor, on 8 January, 1947. BP/2328.

Report of An Ad Hoc Meeting of the Benin Provincial Council, Held at Ubiaja, on 6 December, 1947. BP/2328.

Report of the Benin Provincial Annual Conference,Held at Auchi, on 23 November, 1948. BP/2328.

Annual Reports on the Benin Province, 1939 to 1948. CSO/14617/Vol.XII. *Papers on the Reorganisation of Benin Native Administration, 1935-48.* BP/1088/1 to BP/1088/5.

Freedom Charter: Being the Proposed Constitution of the Commonwealth of Nigeria and the Cameroons, Adopted by the People's National Assembly (of the NCNC) at Kaduna, April, 1948. BP/2678/1.

Political and Constitutional Future of Nigeria, 1945-1948. Papers of the Colonial Administration. Ben Prof BP/3828/Vol.V.

Report of the Benin Provincial Annual Conference, Held at the Oba's Palace, Benin City, on 18 January, 1949. BP/2328.

Memorandum of the Etsako Union, 1949. Memo submitted to the Benin Provincial Conference on Constitutional Reform, 1949. BP/2671/1.

---

* Listed by Archive or Collection Source. Entries are listed chronologically. Any items remaining are listed alphabetically at the end of each section.

Memorandum of the Egbe Omo Oduduwa, 1949. Memo submitted to the Benin Provincial Conference on Constitutional Reform, Held at Benin City, July, 1949. BP/2671/1.

Grading of Chiefs, 1949. BP/2681.

Annual Report for Warri Province, 1942. WP/235/Vol.II.

Proceedings of the Benin Provincial Conference on Constitutional Reform Held at Benin City, July, 1949. BP/2678/1.

Provincial Conference on Constitutional Reform. 1949. **Correspondence Between Benin and Warri Provinces Political and Ethnic Group Organisations, and the Resident, Benin Province.** BP/2678/1.

Colonial Social Science Research Council, 1945-49. BP/2342.

Papers and Memos Submitted to the Benin Conference on Constitutional Reform, 1949. BP/2678/5.

Papers Relating to the Warri Provincial Conference on Constitutional Reform, 1948-50. WP/569/Vol.I.

Revenue Allocation Committee, 1950-51. BP/2678/2.

Report of the Benin Provincial Conference, Held at Ogwashi-Uku, 23 June, 1952. BP/2328/1.

Official Correspondence not to be Communicated to Private Persons, 1932-52. **Ben Prof** BP/742.

Standing Rules, Appointment and Establishment of Native Authorities, 1949-53. **Ben Prof** BP/684/1 and 2.

Papers on Revision of the Ten-Year Development Plan, 1949-53. BP/2726.
Papers Relating to the Tour of Local Government Councils by West Regional Governmental Dignitaries, 1953. BP/2452.

Ika Federal Council Minutes, 1951-53. BP/764/1.

Papers Relating to Local Government Instruments and their Implementation in the Mid-West Provinces, 1954. **Ben Prof** 2/BP/3186/Vols.III-XVIII.

Papers Relating to Native Authorities and Local Government Councils: Meetings and Programmes of Councils and Committees, 1954. BP/3192.

Papers Relating to Staffing Problems in Local Government Councils, 1954. **Ben Prof** 2/BP/3193.

Whiting Report on the Application of the West Region Local Government Law to Benin Division, 1954. BP/2676/10.

Political Activities of Government Servants, 1951-54. BP/2678/9.

Papers on District and Local Government Elections in Asaba Division, 1953-54. **Ben Prof** 2/BP/3092-3094.

Papers on Phased Elections to the Western House of Assembly, 1951-55. BP/2678/1O, 11, 13, B Vol.II, 14 and 15.

Papers on Results of Local Government Elections in Benin Province, Kukuruku, 1954-55. BP/2913/1.

Papers on Results of Local Government Elections in Benin Province, Benin, 1954-55. BP/2913/4.

Papers on Results of Local Government Elections in Benin Province, Agbor, 1954-55. BP/2913/5.

Papers Relating to the Proposed Western Ibo Province, 1950-55. Ben Prof 2/BP/3254.

Annual Report for Benin Division, 1956. BP/1659/1.

Papers Relating to Local Government Reform in Asaba, Benin and Ishan Divisions, 1954-55. See Ben Prof 2/BP/3116, 3119, 3124, 3125.

Papers Relating to Local Government Council and Committees: Minutes and Instructions Regarding Operation and Procedure, 1955. Ben Prof 2/BP/3246.

Memorandum by the West Regional Government Submitted to the Minorities Commission, 1957. Ibadan: 1957. (copy). CE/W3E.

Annual Confidential Reports, 1957-57. BP/1750

Papers Relating to Local Government Instructions for Benin Division, 1958. BP/3080.

Benin Progress Report, 1947-58. BP/2495.

Legislative Council Questions. Correspondence between the Secretary, Western Provinces, Ibadan, and the Resident, Benin Province, Benin City. BP/3267/Vol. II.

(b) *Political Party Papers*

Papers Relating to the Benin Youth Movement, 1937. BP/1358.

Ewu Political Papers, 1943. BP/2250.

Papers Relating to the Urhobo Progressive Union, 1937-48. BP/1431.

Papers Relating to the Reformed Benin Community, 1948. BP/2647.

Papers on the Aboriginal Society for Changing the National Misnomer (Kukuruku), 1942-49. BP/724.

Papers Relating to the Asaba Union, 1937-49. BP/1381.

Papers Relating to the Ijaw (Olodiama) Tribal Society, 1938-49. BP/1509.

Papers Relating to the Ekpoma Progressive Union, 1936-50. BP/1277.

Papers Relating to the Ibusa Youth Congress, 1950. BP/2756.

Papers Relating to the Semolika Progress Union, 1949-50. BP/2727.

Papers Relating to the Western Ibo Union, 1944-50. BP/1853.

Zikist Movement: Declaration to be an Unlawful Society, 1950. BP/2771.

Papers Relating to the Etsako Union, 1944-51. BP/2303.

Papers Relating to the Onitsha-Ugbo Patriotic Union, 1939-51. BP/1833.

Papers Relating to the Benin Neutral Party, 1951-52. BP/2885.

Papers Relating to the Ishan Progress Union, 1938-53. BP/1744

Papers Relating to the Iyayi Society, 1953. BP/3028.

Papers Relating to Activities of the Otu Edo Union, 1951-54. BP/1170/1 to BP/1170/5.

Papers Relating to the Position and Activities of the NPC in the Mid-West Provinces, 1955. Ben Prof 2/BP/4060.

Papers Relating to the Benin-Delta People's Party, 1953-55. BP/3022.

Papers Relating to the Position and Activities of the NCNC in the Mid-West Provinces, 1956. Ben Prof 2/BP/4061.

2. Institute of Race Relations, London

Proceedings of the Minorities Commission Sitting at Ibadan, 29 November-2 December, 1957.

Proceeding of the Minorities Commission Sitting at Benin City, 10-18 December, 1957.

Proceedings of the Minorities Commission Sitting at Warri, 20-23 December 1951.

Proceedings of the Minorities Commission Sitting at Lagos, 27 December. 1957 to 2 January, 1958; and 24-25 March, 1958.

3. Ighodaro Papers, Benin City.

Section A: *Papers Relating to 1957-58 Constitutional Conference and Minorities Commission.*

Minutes of the Third Plenary Session Held in the State Drawing Room, Lancaster House, London, 27 May, 1957. N.C. (57), 3. (mimeo.).

Minutes of the Ninth Plenary Session Held at Lancaster House, London, 4 June, 1957. N.C. (57), 9. (mimeo.).

Minutes of the Twelfth Plenary Session Held at Lancaster House, London, 7 June, 1957. N.C. 57 , 12. (mimeo.).

Memorandum Submitted to the Conference on the Nigerian Constitution Held in London, May, 1957, on Behalf of the Mid-West State Movement. (mimeo.).

Nigerian Constitutional Conference Proposals by the Action Group Delegation, 1957. (mimeo.).

Collected Memoranda Submitted to the 1957 Constitutional Conference by Various Different Groups from the Mid-West Provinces. (mimeo.).

Listing of Official Delegates and Observers to the 1957 London Conference on the Nigerian Constitution. (mimeo.).

Memorandum on the Nigerian Constitution Submitted to the Conference Meeting in London, May and June, 1957, by the Nigerian Union of Great Britain and Ireland. (mimeo.).

Minutes of the Twelfth Meeting of the 1958 Conference on the Nigerian Constitution, London. N.C. (58), 12. (mimeo.).

Minutes of the Twenty-Fifth Meeting of the 1958 Conference, London. N.C.(58), 25.

Minutes of the Thirty-First Meeting of the 1958 Conference. London. N.C. (58), 31.

Memorandum on the Review of the Nigerian Constitution, Submitted by the Zikist National Vanguard to the London Conference of September, 1958. (mimeo.)

Memorandum Submitted to the 1958 Constitutional Conference by the NCNC on Behalf of the Mid-West State Movement. N.C. (58), 65.

New States: Memorandum Submitted to the 1958 Conference by the Action Group Delegation. N.C. (58), 22. (mimeo.).

Reply from the Action Group Delegation to the Memorandum of the Nigerian Union of Great Britain and Ireland 1958. (mimeo.).

Proposals for the Provisions in the Constitution of a Procedure for Creating New Regions, 1958. (mimeo.).

Listing of Official Delegates and Observers to the 1958 London Conference on the Nigerian Constitution. (mimeo.).

Creation of a Yoruba Central State: Memorandum Submitted by the NCNC-Mobalaje Grand Alliance. (mimeo.).

Creation of New States: Memorandum by the Students National Front, University College, Ibadan, Nigeria. (mimeo.).

Joint Proposals by the NPC and NCNC and Action Group Delegations on the Creation of New States, (mimeo.).

Notes on Meetings of Commission with Nigerian Federal Leaders, November, 1957—April, 1958.

Notes on Meetings of Commission with East Region Nigerian Leaders, November, 1957—April, 1958.

Notes on Meetings of Commission With West Region Nigerian Leaders, November, 1957—April, 1958.

Notes on Meetings of Commission with North Region Nigerian Leaders, November, 1957—April, 1958.

Memoranda and Notes on Meetings of Commission with East and West Regional Governors, November, 1957—April, 1958.

Notes on Meetings of Commission with Colonial Officials in the Service of the North Regional Government, November, 1957—April. 1958.

Letters and Correspondence of Commission with Colonial Officers in Nigeria and at Whitehall, July—August, 1958.

Miscellaneous Interviews, Meeting Notes, Statements and Other Unclassified Commission Papers, November, 1957—August, 1958.

Memoranda and Notes on Meetings of the Commission with Religious Interest Groups, Together with Correspondence Between the Commission,and the Christian Council of Nigeria.

SECTION B: *Political Party Papers*.

Minutes of the Central Executive Committee of the Action Group Held at Glover Hall, Lagos, 26 May, 1951. (mimeo.).

Correspondence Between Benin Branch and Ibadan Secretariat of the Action Group Concerning Patronage Distribution in the Mid-West Provinces, 1953.

Papers and Correspondence Relating to Competition between the Otu Edo and the BTPA, March, 1953.

Report on the Benin Divisional Native Authority Audit Investigation, June. 1953.

Correspondence and Report of Benin Divisional Action Group Branch to the Action Group Secretariat, Ibadan, on Meeting with the Oba of Benin, September, 1953.

Papers and Correspondence Relating to the Inaugural of the BDPP, September, 1953.

Papers and Correspondence Relating to Complaints of the Otu Edo Concerning Alleged Sanctions Imposed by the Action Group Government at Ibadan, October, 1953.

Correspondence between Benin Branch and Ibadan Secretariat of the Action Group Concerning Patronage Distribution in the Mid-West Provinces, May, 1954.

Papers and Correspondence on Intra-Action Group Conflict in Benin Division, May, 1954.

Reports and Papers on Alleged Victimisation of Agbor Action Group Supporters, May, 1954.

Confusion in the Otu Edo. Benin City: Otu Edo Secretariat, 1955.

Papers and Correspondence on Intra-Otu Edo Conflict in Benin Division, March, 1955.

Report and Papers on the Otu Edo Break-away Branch, 1955.

Papers and Correspondence Commenting on the Conduct of the Local Government (Whiting) Enquiry, April, 1954.

Address of the Oba of Benin to the Benin Provisional Council, 12 September, 1955. (mimeo.).

Papers and Correspondence on Alleged Action Group Attempts to Control the Benin Divisional Judiciary, 1956.

Memorandum Submitted to the Alexander Commission on the Owegbe Inquiry, June, 1965. (mimeo.).

4. MISCELLANEOUS SOURCES.

Avbenake, J.C. "Rubber Development in the Mid-West: The Birth of West Enterprises Corporation Limited and Other Allied Bodies". (Typescript copy). Sapele n.d. (In possession of writer).

Azikiwe N. *The Anvil of National Unity.* Speech Delivered by Dr. Azikiwe at the Opening of the 1957 Constitutional Conference, held at Lancaster House, London, May 23, 1957. (mimeo.) (ADELP).

Brice-Smith, H.M. "A Plea for Ogboni". Being a Report from Ijebu Province. mss. Afr. 230(667), No.15. (OXCRC)

Butcher, H.L.M. "An Intelligence Report on Ekpoma Village Group of Ishan Division in Benin Province". mss. Afr. 544, No.5. (OXCRC).

Cohen, N. "Papers and Reports Relating to Activities in Asaba 1947 and Western Ijaw, 1952". mss .Afr. s.727. (OXCRC)

Fowler, W. *Report of the Drafting Committee on the Constitution. 1949.* mss. Afr. t.15. (OXCRC)

MacRae-Simpson, J. *Political Intelligence Report on Benin Division, April, 1936.* mss. Afr. r.526. (OXCRC)

Odiase, W.G. "Field Administration and Local Government in Mid-West Nigeria Considered as Aspects of Political Development". Unpublished *mss.* (Typescript copy). London: 1972. (In Writer's possession.)

Osadebay, Chief D.C. "We Built a Nation". Unpublished *mss.* (Typescript copy). London: 1972. (In possession of the Writer)

Osaghae, G. "The Struggle for the Mid-West State". Being an Unpublished Typescript and Notes. Benin City: n.d. (Copy in possession of the writer).

Resident's Address to the Benin Divisional Council, 19 April, 1948. In File No. BNA 7730/2 (BCA)

Address by Gaius Obaseki to the Benin Divisional Council, 23 April, 1948. In File No. BNA/730/2 (BCA)

Address by Governor MacPherson to the Benin Divisional Council, 25 May, 1948. In File No. BNA/730/2 (BCA)

Edo National Union Memorandum, 28 May, 1948. In File No. BNA/730/2. (BCA)

Benin Native Authority: New Constitution, 1948. In File No. BNA/730/2. (BCA)

Report of the 1951 Local Government Elections. In File. No. BNA/730/2, Appendix III. (BCA)

BDPP Enrolment Form. Benin City: 1953. (In possession of writer)

Guide for the BDPP. Benin City: 1953. (In possession of writer)

Instructions to Branch Executives of the BDPP. Benin City: 1953. (mimeo.) (In possession of the writer).

Report on Oba's Tour to Afenmai, 13-15 May, 1954. (mimeo.) (In possession of writer).

Inaugural Meeting of the Provisional (BNA) Council at Conference Hall, Benin City, 2 April, 1955. In File No. BNA/730/4. (BCA)

Minutes of the Provisional Council Meeting of 5 May, 1955. In File No. BNA/730/5 (BCA)

Minutes of the Benin Divisional Council Meeting, held 15-17 December, 1955. In File No. BDC 2/127 (BCA)

Motion of No Confidence in the Oba of Benin (1955). In File No. BNA, Vol. 120. (BCA)

Mid-West State Movement: Report of Tour of Benin and Delta Provinces 18-25 August, 1956. (mimeo.) (In possession of writer)

The Case for More States: Memorandum Submitted to the Minorities Commission by the Citizen's Committee on Independence. Publication No.2. Ibadan: 1957. mimeo. (UIA)

Nigerian Constitutional Conference, 1957: A Record of the Opening Ceremony held at Lancaster House, 23 May, 1957. (mimeo.) (ADELP)

Units of the Federation of Nigeria. Memorandum No.2, Submitted to the Nigerian Constitutional Conference, London, 1957, by the NCNC Delegation. mimeo. (ADELP)

Statement to be Made by Hon. Adegoke Adelabu Concerning Self-Government for the Western Region. Paper Submitted to the London Conference on the Nigerian Constitution, 1957. mimeo. (ADELP)

No Confidence Motion (in Oba) at Mass Meeting, Benin City, 13 June, 1958. (mimeo.) (In possession of writer)

Letter from Permanent Secretary, Ministry of Local Government, Ibadan, to Secretary, Otu Edo, Benin City, 22 August, 1958. (In possession of writer)

Minutes of the Meeting of the Central Executive Committee of the Mid-West State Movement, held 30 August, 1958, at Osana House, Benin City. (mimeo.) (In possession of writer)

An Address of the Honourable Chief Anthony Enahoro, Minister for Home and Mid-West Affairs, at the Inaugural Meeting of the Mid-West Advisory Council, Benin City, 11 October, 1958. (mimeo.) (IFEA)

NCNC: Mid-West Working Committee. Memo Circular dated 16 March, 1959. (In possession of writer).

14-Point Programme (Action Group). (mimeo.) circular dated 4 June, 1959. (In possession of writer)

A Welcome Address by Members of the Opposition, Etsako District Council, presented to the Commissioner for Mid-West Affairs, Hon. B.M. Uzorka, on his Maiden Visit to Etsako, 24 July, 1962. Benin City: 1962. (mimeo). (INA)

Minutes of Round-Table Conference of Mid-West Political Leaders held at the Oba's Palace, Benin City, 9 September, 1962. (mimeo.) (In possession of writer)

Mid-West Plebiscite: Directives to Campaign Leaders. An NCNC Circular, dated 2 July, 1963. (In possession of the writer)

Results of the Mid-West Referendum, 1963. (mimeo.) circular dated 18 July, 1963. (In possession of writer)

Proceedings of the Tribunal of Inquiry into Rebel Activities, 1967-68. (mimeo.) (IFEA)

5. *INTERVIEWS*

a) *Nigeria Interview Notebooks** (In possession of writer)

Int. I
Int. II
Int. III
Int. IV
Int. IVa
Int. V
Int. VI
Int. VII

b) *Listing of Additional Interviews Conducted in Nigeria between February and September, 1969.*

Akenzua II, *Oba* of Benin; Amadasun, V.I.; Avbenake, Chief J.C.; Edewor, James; Edukugho, Chief Reece; Eke, A.Y.; Eke, S.Y.; Ejaife, M.J.; Idahosa J.O.; Igbafe, P.A.; Ighodaro, Mr. Justice S.O.; Iyamu, Alfred; Lawal-Osula, Chief U.; Mowoe, Chief James; Obaseki, Judge Andrew; Okumagba, D.; Omo-Osagie, Chief H.; Omoregie, O.; Osaghae, G.; Osagie, S.O.; Otobo, James E.; Oviasu, G.I.; Oweh, Chief O.; Partridge, D.B.; Rerri, A.T.; Rewane, O.N.; Uwaifo, H.O.

c) *Listing of Non-Nigerian Respondents and Correspondents.*

Abernethy, Dr. David; Ansell, Dr. Kurt; Baker, The Rt. Hon. Sir George G.; Baker, Mr. Justice John A.; Beeley, J.H.; Brand, Dr. J.A.; Cruddas, J.C.; Lennox-Boyd, The Rt. Hon. Viscount Alan; Mason, Philip; Morgan, Dr. Wm.; Rankine, Sir John.

---

* From Interviews completed between May and September, 1972

INDEX